DISCARD

W9-BZC-629

This Book Comes With Lots of
FREE Online Resources

Nolo's award-winning website has a page dedicated just to this book. Here you can:

KEEP UP TO DATE. When there are important changes to the information in this book, we'll post updates.

GET DISCOUNTS ON NOLO PRODUCTS. Get discounts on hundreds of books, forms, and software.

READ BLOGS. Get the latest info from Nolo authors' blogs.

LISTEN TO PODCASTS. Listen to authors discuss timely issues on topics that interest you.

WATCH VIDEOS. Get a quick introduction to a legal topic with our short videos.

And that's not all.
Nolo.com contains thousands of articles on everyday legal and business issues, plus a plain-English law dictionary, all written by Nolo experts and available for free. You'll also find more useful **books, software, online apps, downloadable forms,** plus a **lawyer directory.**

NOLO
LAW for ALL

Get updates and more at
www.nolo.com/back-of-book/DELL.html

12th Edition

Every Landlord's Tax Deduction Guide

Stephen Fishman, J.D.

TWELFTH EDITION   JANUARY 2016

Editor   DIANA FITZPATRICK

Book Production   COLLEEN CAIN

Proofreading   ROBERT WELLS

Index   SONGBIRD INDEXING SERVICES

Printing   BANG PRINTING

ISSN: 1945-8770 (print)
ISSN: 2325-2960 (online)
ISBN: 978-1-4133-2239-2 (pbk)
ISBN: 978-1-4133-2240-8 (epub ebook)

This book covers only United States law, unless it specifically states otherwise.

Please note

We believe accurate, plain-English legal information should help you solve many of your own legal problems. But this text is not a substitute for personalized advice from a knowledgeable lawyer. If you want the help of a trained professional—and we'll always point out situations in which we think that's a good idea—consult an attorney licensed to practice in your state.

Acknowledgments

Many thanks to:

Diana Fitzpatrick and Janet Portman for their superb editing

Colleen Cain for book layout, and

Songbird Indexing Services for the useful index.

About the Author

Stephen Fishman is a San Francisco-based attorney and tax expert who has been writing about the law for over 20 years. He is the author of many do-it-yourself law books, including *Deduct It! Lower Your Small Business Taxes, Home Business Tax Deductions,* and *Working for Yourself: Law & Taxes for Independent Contractors, Freelancers & Consultants.* All of his books are published by Nolo.

He is often quoted on tax-related issues by newspapers across the country, including the *Chicago Tribune, San Francisco Chronicle,* and *Cleveland Plain Dealer.*

His website and blog are at Fishmanlawandtaxfiles.com.

Table of Contents

Your Tax Deduction Companion for Landlords 1

1 Tax Deduction Basics for Landlords 3

How Landlords Are Taxed 4

How Income Tax Deductions Work 8

How Property Ownership Affects Taxes 16

The IRS and the Landlord 31

2 Landlord Tax Classifications 37

The Landlord Tax Categories 38

Business Owner Versus Investor 39

Are You Profit Motivated? 46

Real Estate Dealers 57

3 Deducting Your Operating Expenses 65

Requirements for Deducting Operating Expenses 66

Operating Expenses That Are Not Deductible 73

4 Repairs..75

The New IRS Rules: Repairs Versus Improvements............................76

How to Deduct Repairs and Maintenance......................................107

Tips for Maximizing Your Repair Deductions...................................110

5 Depreciation Basics..115

Depreciation: The Landlord's Best Tax Break...................................117

Understanding the Basics..119

How to Depreciate Buildings..126

Depreciating Land Improvements...142

Deducting Personal Property.. 144

When You Sell Your Property..171

Tax Reporting and Record Keeping for Depreciation 180

6 Maximizing Your Depreciation Deductions............... 183

Determining the Value of Your Land and Buildings......................... 184

Segmented Depreciation 195

7 Interest.. 205

Interest Landlords Can (and Can't) Deduct..................................... 206

Mortgage Interest... 207

Other Interest Expenses..210

Points and Prepaid Interest..212

Interest on Construction Loans 213

Loans With Low or No Interest 214

Loans on Rental Property Used for Nonrental Purposes 215

Keeping Track of Borrowed Money...216

8 Start-Up Expenses 219

What Are Start-Up Expenses? 220

Determining Your Business Start Date... 222

Avoiding the Start-Up Rule's Bite 225

How to Deduct Start-Up Expenses 226

If Your Business Doesn't Last 15 Years 231

If Your Business Never Begins... 232

9 The Home Office Deduction 233

Qualifying for the Home Office Deduction...................................... 234

Calculating the Home Office Deduction 240

Simplified Home Office Deduction Method 248

IRS Reporting Requirements.. 250

Audit-Proofing Your Home Office Deduction 251

Deducting an Outside Office 252

10 Car and Local Transportation Expenses 255

Deductible Local Transportation Expenses..................................... 256

The Standard Mileage Rate..261

The Actual Expense Method 263

Other Local Transportation Expenses 273

Reporting Transportation Expenses on Your Tax Return 274

11 Travel Expenses...275

What Are Travel Expenses?...276

Deductible Travel Expenses... 281

How Much You Can Deduct... 283

Maximizing Your Travel Deductions 288

12 Hiring Help 291

Deducting Payments to Workers 292

Employees Versus Independent Contractors 294

Tax Rules When Hiring Independent Contractors 298

Tax Rules for Employees 306

Hiring Your Family 311

Hiring a Resident Manager 318

13 Casualty and Theft Losses 323

What Is a Casualty? 324

Calculating a Casualty Loss Deduction 326

Disaster Area Losses 332

Repair and Replacement Costs for Casualty Losses 332

Casualty Gains 333

Tax Reporting and Record Keeping for Casualty Losses 335

14 Additional Deductions 337

Dues and Subscriptions 338

Education Expenses 338

Gifts 341

Insurance for Your Rental Activity 342

Legal and Professional Services 344

Meals and Entertainment 345

Taxes 347

Unpaid Rent 351

15 Vacation Homes 353

The Vacation Home Tax Morass 354

Regular Rental Property 356

Tax-Free Vacation Home 357

Vacation Home Used as Rental Property 359

Vacation Home Used as Residence 363

Calculating Personal and Rental Use 367

Converting Your Home to a Rental Property 372

16 Deducting Rental Losses 373

What Are Rental Losses? 375

Overview of the Passive Loss Rules 376

The $25,000 Offset 380

The Real Estate Professional Exemption 386

Rental Activities Not Subject to PAL Real Property Rental Rules 406

Vacation Homes 408

Deducting Suspended Passive Losses 409

Tax Reporting for Passive Rental Losses 412

Strategies for Dealing With the Passive Loss Rules 413

At-Risk Rules 415

How to Deduct Rental Losses 418

17 Record Keeping and Accounting 423

What Records Do You Need? 424

A Simple Record-Keeping System 427

Accounting Methods 454

Tax Years 459

18 All About Schedule E 461

Who Must File Schedule E? 462

Filling Out Schedule E 464

19 The Net Investment Income Tax 475

How the NII Tax Works 476

Real Estate Professional Exemption From the NII Tax 480

Planning to Avoid the NII Tax 483

Index 485

Introduction

Your Tax Deduction Companion for Landlords

This is a book about income tax deductions for landlords—that is, people who own residential rental property. If you are one of the millions of Americans who owns a small number of residential rental units (one to ten), this book is for you. And even landlords who own dozens of residential rental properties will find lots of useful information in this book that can help them save money.

No landlord would pay more than necessary for utilities or other operating expenses for a rental property. But, every year millions of landlords pay more taxes on their rental income than they have to. Why? Because they fail to take advantage of all the tax deductions available to owners of residential rental property.

Rental real estate provides more tax benefits than almost any other investment. Often, these benefits make the difference between losing money and earning a profit on a rental property. But tax deductions are worthless if you don't take advantage of them. That's where this book comes in. It gives you all the information you need to maximize your deductions—and avoid common deduction mistakes. You can (and should) use this book all year long, to make April 15 as painless as possible.

To take advantage of the benefits tax deductions offer, you'll have to figure out which deductions you are entitled to take—and keep proper records documenting your expenses. You will also learn how to make the most of the deductions available to you as a landlord. For example, did you know that:

- Landlords can greatly increase the depreciation deductions they receive the first few years they own rental property by using segmented depreciation (Chapter 6).
- Careful planning can permit you to deduct in a single year the cost of improvements to rental property that you would otherwise have to deduct over 27.5 years (Chapter 5).
- You can rent out a vacation home tax free in some cases (Chapter 15).

- Although the IRS doesn't publicize it, landlords can qualify for the home office deduction (Chapter 9).
- Many small landlords can deduct up to $25,000 in rental property losses each year (Chapter 16).
- A special tax rule permits some landlords to deduct 100% of their rental property losses every year, no matter how great those losses are (Chapter 16).
- People who rent property to their family or friends could lose virtually all of their tax deductions (Chapter 15).

If you didn't know one or more of these facts, you could be paying far more in taxes than you need to.

Even if you work with an accountant or another tax professional, you need to learn about rental property tax deductions. No tax professional will ever know as much about your rental business as you do, and you can't expect a hired professional to search high and low for every deduction you might be able to take, especially during the busy tax preparation season. The information in this book will help you provide your tax professional with better records, ask better questions, obtain better advice, and, just as importantly, evaluate the advice you get from tax professionals, websites, and other sources.

If you do your taxes yourself (as more and more landlords are doing, especially with the help of tax preparation software), your need for knowledge is even greater. Not even the most sophisticated tax preparation program can decide which tax deductions you should take or tell you whether you've overlooked a valuable deduction. That's where this book comes in. We provide you with the practical advice and information you need so you can rest assured you are taking full advantage of the many deductions available to landlords.

Get Updates Online

When there are important changes to the information in this book, we'll post updates online, on a page dedicated to this book:

www.nolo.com/back-of-book/DELL.html

Tax Deduction Basics for Landlords

How Landlords Are Taxed 4

    Income Taxes on Rental Income 4

    Income Taxes on Profits When You Sell Your Property 5

    Social Security and Medicare Payroll Taxes 5

    Net Investment Income Tax 6

    Property Taxes 8

How Income Tax Deductions Work 8

    What Can You Deduct? 11

    How Your Tax Status Affects Your Deductions 14

    The Value of a Tax Deduction 14

How Property Ownership Affects Taxes 16

    Individual Ownership 17

    Ownership Through a Business Entity 24

    The Mini-Landlord: Renting Out a Room in Your Home 29

The IRS and the Landlord 31

    Automated Underreporter Program 31

    Six Tips for Avoiding an Audit 32

The tax code is full of deductions for landlords. Before you can start taking advantage of these deductions, however, you need a basic understanding of how landlords pay taxes and how tax deductions work. This chapter gives you all the information you need to get started, including:

- how the IRS taxes landlords
- how tax deductions work
- how forms of property ownership affect landlord taxes, and
- IRS audits—how they work and how to avoid them.

How Landlords Are Taxed

When you own residential rental property, you are required to pay the following taxes:

- income taxes on rental income and profits from property sales
- property taxes, and
- Social Security and Medicare taxes (for some landlords).

Let's look at each type of tax.

Income Taxes on Rental Income

You must pay federal income taxes on the net income (rent and other money minus expenses) you receive from your rental property each year. When you file your yearly tax return, you add your net rental income to your other income for the year, such as salary income from a job, interest on savings, and investment income.

This book covers rental property deductions for federal income taxes. However, 43 states also have income taxes. State income tax laws generally track federal tax law, but there are some exceptions. The states without income taxes are Alaska, Florida, Nevada, South Dakota, Texas, Washington, and Wyoming. For details on your state's income tax law, visit your state tax agency's website, or contact your local state tax office. You can find links to all 50 state tax agency websites at www.taxsites.com/state.html.

Income Taxes on Profits When You Sell Your Property

When you sell your property, any profit you earn is added to your income for the year and is subject to taxation. Profits from the sale of rental property owned for more than one year are taxed at capital gains rates. These rates are lower than income tax rates, except for taxpayers in the lowest tax brackets. (See Chapter 5 for an example of the tax effects of a rental property sale.)

However, you may be able to defer tax on your profits—perhaps indefinitely—by selling your property through a like-kind exchange (also called a Section 1031 exchange or tax-free exchange). This kind of exchange involves swapping your property for similar property owned by someone else. These property swaps are subject to complex tax rules that are beyond the scope of this book, since they have nothing to do with income tax deductions. For more information, see IRS Publication 544, *Sales and Other Dispositions of Assets.*

Social Security and Medicare Payroll Taxes

Everyone who works as an employee or who owns his or her own business must pay Social Security and Medicare payroll taxes (known as FICA. or Federal Insurance Contributions Act, taxes). Employees pay half of these taxes themselves and their employers pay the other half. Self-employed people must pay them all themselves. These are two separate taxes:

Social Security tax. The Social Security tax is a flat 12.4% tax on net self-employment income or employee wages up to an annual ceiling, which is adjusted for inflation each year. In 2015, the ceiling was $118,500.

Medicare payroll tax. Medicare payroll taxes, which are used to fund the Medicare system, underwent significant changes in 2013 as part of the implementation of Obamacare. In the past, the Medicare payroll tax consisted of a single 2.9% flat tax with no annual income ceiling. Starting in 2013, however, there are two Medicare tax rates: a 2.9% tax up to an annual ceiling—$200,000 for single taxpayers and $250,000 for married couples filing jointly. All income above the ceiling is taxed at a 3.8% rate. Thus, for example, a single taxpayer with $300,000 in net self-employment income would pay a 2.9% Medicare tax on the first

$200,000 of income and a 3.8% tax on the remaining $100,000. This 0.9% Medicare payroll tax increase applies to high-income employees as well as to the self-employed. Employees must pay a 2.35% Medicare tax on the portion of their wages over the $200,000/$250,000 thresholds (their one-half of 2.9% = 1.45% + plus the 0.9%).

For both the self-employed and employees, the combined Social Security and Medicare tax is 15.3%, up to the Social Security tax ceiling.

You may have to pay (and withhold) Social Security and Medicare taxes if you hire employees to work in your rental activity—for example, if you hire a resident manager. The employer's share of such taxes is a deductible expense. (See Chapter 12.)

The income you earn from your rental property is not subject to Social Security and Medicare payroll taxes. (I.R.C. § 1402(a)(1).) This is so even if your rental activities constitute a business for tax purposes. (See Chapter 2.) This is one of the great tax benefits of owning rental property. A person who owns a hot dog stand must pay the 15.3% self-employment tax on his or her annual profits, whereas a person who owns a rental house or other real estate need pay no self-employment taxes on his or her rental income.

There is one exception to this rule, which will not apply to many readers of this book: You must pay Social Security and Medicare taxes on rental income if you provide "substantial services" along with the rental. This exception would apply, for example, if you owned a boardinghouse, hotel, or motel and provided maid service, room service, or concierge services. The exception does not apply to services commonly provided for residential rentals, such as repairs, cleaning, maintenance, trash removal, elevators, security, or cable television.

In addition, if you qualify as a real estate dealer, you'll have to pay Social Security and Medicare taxes on your annual profits. (See Chapter 2.)

Net Investment Income Tax

Starting with the 2013 tax year, a new Net Investment Income tax went into effect. This 3.8% tax affects many higher-income landlords. For details, see Chapter 19.

Estimated Taxes for Landlords

If your rentals earn a profit and you expect to owe at least $1,000 in income tax on the profit, you may need to pay estimated taxes to the IRS to prepay your tax liability. However, if you work and have income tax withheld from your pay, you'll need to pay estimated tax only if your total withholding (and any tax credits) amounts to less than 90% of the total tax you expect to pay for the year. Thus, you can avoid paying any estimated tax at all by having your withholding increased. But, you'll be able to hold on to your money a bit longer if you pay estimated tax instead of having the money taken out of your paychecks every pay period.

If you pay estimated tax, the payments are due four times per year: April 15, June 15, September 15, and January 15. To avoid having to pay an underpayment penalty, your total withholding and estimated tax payments must equal the lesser of either (1) 90% of your tax liability for the current year, or (2) 100% of what you paid the previous year (or 110% if you're a high-income taxpayer—those with adjusted gross incomes of more than $150,000, or $75,000 for married couples filing separate returns).

The easiest way to calculate your quarterly estimated tax payments is to subtract your total expected income tax withholding for the current year from the total income tax you paid last year. The balance is the total amount of estimated tax you must pay this year. But, if you're a high-income taxpayer, add 10% to the total. Note, however, that if your income is higher this year than last, you'll owe extra tax to the IRS on April 15. To avoid this, you can increase your estimated tax payments or simply save the money you'll need to pay the taxes when you file your annual return.

You pay the money directly to the IRS in four equal installments, so divide the total by four. You can pay by mail, electronic withdrawal from your bank account, or by credit or debit card. For details, see the IRS estimated tax Web page at www.irs.gov/Businesses/Small-Businesses-&-Self-Employed/Estimated-Taxes.

Property Taxes

Property owners in all states pay property taxes imposed by cities, counties, and other local governments. They are a tax on the value of your rental property. Property taxes are not covered in this book.

How Income Tax Deductions Work

The tax law recognizes that you must spend money on your rental properties for such things as mortgage interest, repairs, maintenance, and many other expenses. The law allows you to subtract these expenses, plus an amount for the depreciation of your property, from your effective gross rental income (all the money actually earned from the property) to determine your "taxable income." You pay income tax only on your taxable income, if any. Expenses you can deduct from your income are called tax deductions or tax write-offs. These deductions are what this book is about.

Although some tax deduction calculations can get a bit complicated, the basic math is simple: The entire tax regimen for rental real estate can be reduced to the following simple equation:

	Effective Gross Rental Income
minus	Operating Expenses (including mortgage interest)
minus	Depreciation and Amortization Expenses
=	Taxable Income

(People who analyze real estate investments don't include mortgage interest as a real estate operating expense, but it is an operating expense for tax purposes.)

EXAMPLE: Karen owns a rental house. This year, her effective gross rental income (all the income she actually earned from the property) was $10,000. She doesn't pay tax on the entire $10,000 because she had the following expenses—$5,000 in mortgage interest, $1,000 for other operating expenses, and $2,000 for depreciation. She gets to deduct these as outlined in the above equation:

Effective Gross Rental Income	$ 10,000
Operating Expenses	– 6,000
Depreciation and Amortization	– 2,000
Taxable Income	$ 2,000

Karen only pays income tax on her $2,000 taxable income.

What Is Rental Income?

Your rental income consists primarily of the rent your tenants pay you each month. But it also includes:

Security deposits. If, when you receive a security deposit, you plan to use it for the tenant's final rent payment, you should include it in your income for the year you receive it. However, do not include a security deposit in your income when you receive it if you plan to return it to your tenant at the end of the lease term. But if you keep part or all of the security deposit during any year because your tenant does not live up to the terms of the lease, include the amount you keep in your income in that year.

Interest earned on security deposits is also rental income that should be included in your income the year it is earned, unless your state or local law requires landlords to credit such interest to tenants.

Tenant property or services. Property or services you receive from a tenant, instead of money, as rent, must be included in your rental income. For example, your tenant is a painter and offers to paint your rental property instead of paying rent for two months. If you accept the offer, include in your rental income the amount the tenant would have paid for two months' worth of rent.

What Is Rental Income? (cont'd)

Tenant payment of rental expenses. Any rental expenses paid for by a tenant are rental income—for example, payments a tenant makes to you for repairs, utilities, or other rental costs. These costs are then deductible by you as rental expenses.

Lease cancellation payments. If a tenant pays you to agree to cancel a lease, the amount you receive is rent that must be included in your rental income in the year you receive it.

Leases with option to buy. A lease with an option to buy occurs if the rental agreement gives your tenant the right to buy your rental property. The payments you receive under such an agreement are generally rental income.

Advance rent payments. Advance rent is any amount you receive before the period that it covers. Include advance rent in your rental income in the year you receive it regardless of the period covered. For example, to get you to agree to a one-year lease, a tenant with poor credit pays you six months' rent in advance in December. You must include the entire amount as rental income the year it was received.

Fees. Fees or other charges tenants pay are also rental income. These include, for example:

- fees you charge tenants for paying rent late
- garage or other parking fees
- fees you charge tenants for use of storage facilities, and
- laundry income from washers and dryers you provide for tenants' use.

Of course, real property ordinarily increases in value each year, often substantially. Your rental property appreciation is not rental income until you sell or otherwise dispose of your property. Any profit you earn on the sale or other disposition is taxable income.

Many landlords have so many deductions that they end up with a net loss when they subtract all their deductions from their effective gross rental income. In that situation, they owe no tax at all on their rental income. This is especially common in the early years of owning rental property, when you haven't had time to raise the rents much. Indeed, it is common for landlords to have a loss for tax purposes even if they take in more in rental income than they pay in expenses each month.

Having a tax loss on your rental property is not necessarily a bad thing. You may be able to deduct it from other income you earn during the year, such as salary income from a job or income from other investments. However, there are significant restrictions on a landlord's ability to deduct rental losses from nonrental income. Many small landlords can avoid them, but not all. These restrictions—known as the passive loss rules and at-risk rules—are covered in detail in Chapter 16.

What Can You Deduct?

All tax deductions are a matter of legislative grace, which means that you can take a deduction only if it is specifically allowed by one or more provisions of the tax law. You usually do not have to indicate on your tax return which tax law provision gives you the right to take a particular deduction. If you are audited by the IRS, however, you'll have to provide a legal basis for every deduction you take. If the IRS concludes that your deduction wasn't justified, it will deny the deduction and charge you back taxes and penalties.

Landlords can deduct three broad categories of rental expenses:

- start-up expenses
- operating expenses, and
- capital expenses.

This section provides an introduction to each of these categories (they are covered in greater detail in later chapters).

CAUTION
Keep track of your rental expenses. You can deduct only those expenses that you actually incur. You need to keep records of these expenses to know for sure how much you actually spent and prove to the IRS that you really spent the money you deducted on your tax return, in case you are audited. Accounting and bookkeeping are discussed in detail in Chapter 17.

Tax Credits for Landlords

Tax credits are not the same as tax deductions—they are even better. A tax credit is subtracted from your tax liability after you calculate your taxes. For example, a $1,000 tax credit will reduce your taxes for the year by $1,000. There are many different types of federal income tax credits, but only two can be used by owners of residential rental property:

- the rehabilitation tax credit, available to owners of historic property, and
- the low-income housing tax credit.

There are no federal income tax credits for the cost of eliminating lead paint, asbestos, or mold contamination. However, your state may offer tax credits or other tax incentives for such environmental remediation.

Historic property. The rehabilitation tax credit can be used only by owners of residential rental property that is listed on the National Register of Historic Places or located in a Registered Historical District and determined to be "significant" to that district. Moreover, the Secretary of the Interior must certify to the Secretary of the Treasury that the project meets their standards and is a "Certified Rehabilitation." The property owner obtains this certification by filing an application with the National Park Service.

Obviously, not many rental properties are registered historic sites. But, if you own a property that qualifies, you can receive a tax credit equal to 20% of the amount you spend to rehabilitate your historic building, up to certain limits. You can nominate your building for historic status, if you think it qualifies, by contacting your state historical officer. The following websites provide detailed information on the rehabilitation tax credit:

- National Trust for Historic Preservation: www.nationaltrust.org, and
- National Park Service Heritage Preservation: www.nps.gov/tps/tax-incentives.htm.

Low-income housing. Congress enacted the low-income housing tax credit to encourage new construction and rehabilitation of existing rental housing for low-income households. The IRS and state tax credit allocation agencies jointly administer the low-income housing tax credit, which is used mostly by large real estate developers to build new low-income housing projects. For more information, contact your state tax credit allocation agency. You can find a list at www.novoco.com/low_income_housing/lihtc/state_agencies.php. Useful information can also be obtained from the National Housing & Rehabilitation Association website at www.housingonline.com.

Start-Up Expenses

The first money you will have to shell out will be for your rental activity's start-up expenses. These include most of the costs of getting your rental business up and running, like license fees, advertising costs, attorney and accounting fees, travel expenses, market research, and office supplies expenses. Start-up expenses do not include the cost of buying rental property. If your rental activity qualifies as a business, up to $5,000 of start-up expenses may be deducted for the year in which they're incurred. The remainder, if any, must be deducted in equal installments over the first 180 months you're in business—a process called amortization. (See Chapter 8 for a detailed discussion of deducting start-up expenses.)

Operating Expenses

Operating expenses are the ongoing, day-to-day costs a landlord incurs to operate a rental property. They include such things as mortgage interest, utilities, salaries, supplies, travel expenses, car expenses, and repairs and maintenance. These expenses (unlike start-up expenses) are currently deductible—that is, you can deduct them all in the same year when you pay them. (See Chapter 3.)

Capital Expenses

Capital assets are things you buy for your rental activity that have a useful life of more than one year. A landlord's main capital asset is the building or buildings he or she rents out. However, capital assets also include such things as equipment, vehicles, furniture, and appliances. These costs, called capital expenses, are considered to be part of your investment in your rental activity, not day-to-day operating expenses.

The cost of your capital assets must be deducted a little at a time over several years—a process called depreciation. Residential rental buildings are depreciated over 27.5 years. Capital assets other than real estate are depreciated over a much shorter period—for example, vehicles and furniture are depreciated over five years. The cost of land is not deductible—you must wait until land is sold to recover the cost. (See Chapter 5 for more on this topic.)

How Your Tax Status Affects Your Deductions

Owning rental property can be a business for tax purposes, an investment, or, in some cases, a not-for-profit activity. Landlords whose rental activities qualify as a business are entitled to all the tax deductions discussed in this book. However, those whose rentals are an investment lose certain useful deductions, such as the home office deduction. Tax deductions are extremely limited for landlords who, in the eyes of the IRS, are operating a not-for-profit activity.

Your tax status is determined by how much time and effort you put into your rental activity, and whether you earn profits each year or act like you want to. Most landlords who manage their property themselves qualify as for-profit businesses. (See Chapter 2 for more on determining your tax status.)

The Value of a Tax Deduction

Most taxpayers, even sophisticated businesspeople, don't fully appreciate just how they save with tax deductions. Only part of any deduction will end up back in your pocket as money saved. Because a deduction represents income on which you don't have to pay tax, the value of any deduction is the amount of tax you would have had to pay on that income had you not deducted it. So a deduction of $1,000 won't save you $1,000—it will save you whatever you would otherwise have had to pay as tax on that $1,000 of income.

To determine how much income tax a deduction will save you, you must first figure out your income tax bracket. The United States has a progressive income tax system for individual taxpayers with six different tax rates (called tax brackets), ranging from 10% of taxable income to 39.6% (see the chart below). The higher your income, the higher your tax rate will be.

You move from one bracket to the next only when your taxable income exceeds the bracket amount. For example, if you are a single taxpayer, you pay 10% income tax on all your taxable income up to $9,225. If your taxable income exceeds $9,225, the next tax rate (15%) applies to all your income over that amount—but the 10% rate still applies to the first $9,225. If your income exceeds the 15% bracket amount, the next tax rate

(25%) applies to the excess amount, and so on until the top bracket of 39.6% is reached.

The tax bracket in which the last dollar you earn for the year falls is called your marginal tax bracket. For example, if you have $75,000 in taxable income, your marginal tax bracket is 25%. To determine how much federal income tax a deduction will save you, multiply the amount of the deduction by your marginal tax bracket. For example, if your marginal tax bracket is 25%, you will save 25¢ in federal income taxes for every dollar you are able to claim as a deductible business expense (25% × $1 = 25¢).

The following table lists the 2015 federal income tax brackets for single and married individual taxpayers.

2015 Federal Personal Income Tax Brackets		
Tax Bracket	Income If Single	Income If Married Filing Jointly
10%	Up to $9,225	Up to $18,450
15%	$9,226 to $37,450	$18,451 to $74,900
25%	$37,451 to $90,750	$74,901 to $151,200
28%	$90,751 to $189,300	$151,201 to $230,450
33%	$189,301 to $411,500	$230,451 to $411,500
35%	$411,501 to $413,200	$411,501 to $464,850
39.6%	All over $413,200	All over $464,850

Taxpayers who are subject to the Net Investment Income (NII) tax must add 3.8% to these tax rates. This applies only to taxpayers (1) whose adjusted gross income exceeds $200,000 if single, or $250,000 if married filing jointly, and (2) who have net investment income, which includes income and gains from rentals. Ordinarily, only taxpayers in the 33% and higher tax brackets are subject to this tax. See Chapter 19 for details about the NII tax.

You can also deduct your rental activity expenses from any state income tax you must pay. The average state income tax rate is about 6%, although seven states (Alaska, Florida, Nevada, South Dakota, Texas, Washington, and Wyoming) don't have an income tax. You can find a list of all state income tax rates at www.taxadmin.org.

When you add up your savings in federal and state income taxes, you can see the true value of a tax deduction. For example, if you're in the 25% federal income tax bracket, a deduction can be worth 25% (in federal income taxes) plus 6% (in state income taxes). That adds up to a whopping 31% savings. (If you itemize your personal deductions, your actual tax savings from a business deduction is a bit less because it reduces your state income tax and therefore reduces the federal income tax savings from this itemized deduction.) If you buy a $1,000 computer for your rental activity and you deduct the expense, you save about $310 in income taxes. In effect, the government is paying for almost one-third of your rental expenses. This is why it's so important to know all the deductions you are entitled to take and to take advantage of every one.

You should get into the habit of thinking about your rental expenses in terms of after-tax dollars—what the item really costs you after you deduct the cost from your income taxes.

CAUTION

Don't buy things just to get a tax deduction. Although tax deductions can be worth a lot, it doesn't make sense to buy something you don't need just to get a deduction. After all, you still have to pay for the item, and the tax deduction you get in return will cover only a portion of the cost. If you buy a $500 lawn mower to use for your rental properties, you'll be able to deduct less than half the cost. That means you're still out over $300—money you've spent for something you may not have needed. On the other hand, if you really do need a new lawn mower, the deduction you're entitled to is like found money— and it may help you buy a better lawn mower than you could otherwise afford.

How Property Ownership Affects Taxes

How you own your residential rental property affects the tax returns you must file each year. The main ownership options for a small landlord are:
- sole proprietorship
- general partnership
- limited partnership

- limited liability company (LLC)
- corporation
- tenancy in common, or
- joint tenancy.

These can be sorted into two broad categories: individual ownership and ownership through a business entity. If you don't know how you hold title to the rental property you already own, look at your property deed.

Individual Ownership

Most small landlords (owners of from one to ten residential rental units) own their property as individuals—either alone, or with one or more co-owners. Indeed, a government study found that individuals owned approximately 83% of the 15.7 million rental housing properties with fewer than 50 units. (Department of Housing and Urban Development and Department of Commerce, U.S. Census Bureau, *Residential Finance Survey*: 2001 (Washington, DC: 2005).)

One Property Owner

The simplest way to own rental property is for a single individual to own it in his or her own name. When you do this you are a sole proprietor for tax purposes. Any rental income you earn is added to your other income, such as salary from a job, interest income, or investment income. Losses you incur can be deducted from your other income, subject to the restrictions discussed in Chapter 16. You report your rental income and losses on IRS Schedule E and attach it to your individual tax return. (See Chapter 18 for a detailed discussion of Schedule E.)

Things are a bit more complex if you acquired the property while married and you live in one of the nine community property states: Arizona, California, Idaho, Louisiana, Nevada, New Mexico, Texas, Washington, and Wisconsin. Although the rental is held in your name alone, unless you and your spouse agree otherwise, it will be jointly owned community property under your state's marital property laws. However, for tax purposes, you may still treat the rental activity as a sole proprietorship with only one spouse listed as owner on Schedule E. (See "Spouses who live in community property states," below.)

Co-Owners Not Married to Each Other

It's not uncommon for two or more relatives, friends, or colleagues to own rental property together. If you acquire the property with one or more co-owners, you don't necessarily have to form a separate business entity like a partnership, limited liability company, or corporation to own and operate it. Instead, for tax purposes, each owner can in essence be treated like a sole proprietor. This can be accomplished where co-owners take title to the property together as tenants in common or, more rarely, joint tenants. (See "Co-Ownership by Spouses," below, for the difference between the two.) Each co-owner owns an undivided interest in the entire property. In the case of a tenancy in common, the interests can be equal or divided in unequal amounts; whatever the owners agree upon. The ownership interest of each owner should be listed on the property deed.

> EXAMPLE: Al and Alice, brother and sister, buy a rental house together, taking title as tenants in common. They decide that because Al put more money down on the property, he should own a 60% interest and Alice 40%. This means that Al is legally entitled to 60% of the income the property generates and is supposed to pay 60% of the expenses. Alice gets the remaining 40%.

Although they own rental property together, each cotenant is treated like a sole proprietor for tax purposes. Each cotenant reports their share of the income and deductions from the rental property on their own tax return, filing Schedule E. Each owner's share is based on his or her ownership interest—for example, Alice in the example above lists her 40% share of the income and deductions from the co-owned rental house on her Schedule E and pays tax on that amount. Al lists the other 60% on his own Schedule E.

If one cotenant pays more than his or her proportionate share of the expenses, the overpayment is treated as a loan to the other cotenants and may not be deducted. The cotenant who overpays is legally entitled to be reimbursed by the other cotenants. (T.C. Memo 1995-562.)

EXAMPLE: Alice from the example above pays 80% of the annual expenses for the rental house this year, instead of the 40% she should pay based on her ownership interest. She may not deduct her overpayment, which amounts to $10,000. Instead, it is treated as a loan to her cotenant Al. Alice is entitled to be repaid the $10,000 by Al. If he doesn't pay, she can sue him to collect. If he does pay, he can deduct the amount as a rental expense.

Are cotenants partners? The type of cotenancy described above may seem like a partnership, but it's really not. Unlike in a partnership, a cotenant cannot act or contract on behalf of the other cotenants without their authorization. Moreover, one cotenant is not liable for any debts incurred by another cotenant without his or her consent. Each tenant in common may lease, mortgage, sell, or otherwise transfer all or part of his or her interest without obtaining consent from the other cotenants, or even telling them about it. This power to transfer property also applies upon the death of a tenant in common. It's often desirable, but not required, that the co-owners enter into a written cotenancy agreement.

Not being in a partnership can save time and expense. Filing a partnership tax return and dealing with complex partnership tax laws is not easy. If you are a partnership, here is what you're supposed to do:

- complete and file Form 1065, *Return of Partnership Income*, reporting all the partnership's income, deductions, gains, and losses
- complete a Schedule K-1 for each partner showing his or her share of the partnership's income or loss
- transfer the Schedule K-1 information onto a Schedule E, *Supplemental Income or Loss*, for each partner
- complete a Schedule SE for each partner, listing his or her share of partnership income as self-employment income, and
- transfer the data from the individual schedules onto the joint Form 1040.

Obviously, this requires a lot of time and money—tax pros can charge $1,000 or more to prepare partnership returns.

Co-owners who provide services to tenants. IRS regulations provide that tenants in common or joint tenants do not become partners in a partnership as long as all they do is own rental property together and merely maintain, repair, and rent it. (IRS Reg. § 1.761-1(a), IRS Reg. § 301.7701(a)(2).) See also IRS Publication 541, *Partnerships:* "co-ownership of property maintained and rented or leased is not a partnership unless the co-owners provide services to the tenants."

However, the tax situation changes if co-owners of a rental property provide significant services to their tenants. In this event, the IRS will consider them partners in a partnership for tax purposes.

Significant services do not include furnishing heat and light, cleaning of public areas, normal repairs, trash collection, or similar services. Instead, they are services that primarily benefit the tenants personally, such as maid service, linen changing, food service, or concierge services. (IRS Reg. § 301.7701-1(b); Rev. Rul. 75-374.) Providing occasional cleaning or concierge services would probably not constitute significant services. Would providing tenants with an Internet connection or cable TV constitute significant services? It's unclear.

If co-owners are deemed to be partners in a partnership, the partnership must file a partnership tax return (unless they are married and elect qualified joint venture status—see "Co-Ownership by Spouses," below). The individual or partnership members are each given a Schedule K-1 by their partnership reporting their individual shares of annual income or loss from the rental activity. The individuals then list this amount in Part II of Schedule E, on page 2. This doesn't increase or decrease the owners' deductions but it does result in a more complex tax return.

Co-Ownership by Spouses

Spouses who own rental property together typically take title as joint tenants—rather than tenants in common. Joint tenants are treated exactly the same as tenants in common for tax purposes, but there are significant nontax differences. Joint tenants must own the property 50-50. In addition, joint tenancy always includes "the right of survivorship." When one joint tenant dies, his or her share automatically goes to the survivor. This is not the case with tenants in common, who can leave their share of the co-owned property to anyone they want. Unmarried people can also be joint tenants, but this isn't commonly done.

If a married couple that jointly owes rental property files a joint income tax return, as most do, they are treated as a single taxpayer by the IRS. The spouses' shares of the income and deductions from the rental property are combined on their single joint tax return. The couple reports their income and deductions from the jointly owned property on a single Schedule E they file with their joint return.

Are co-owner spouses partners in a partnership? Like other co-owners of rental property, spouses who are landlords of property they own together are ordinarily not considered partners in a partnership as long as all they do is maintain, repair, and rent their property. However, spouses who provide significant services to their tenants will be viewed as partners in a partnership by the IRS. (See "Co-owners who provide services to tenants," above.) This means they would have to file a partnership tax return—unless they can elect joint venture status.

Electing qualified joint venture status to file Schedule C. To avoid having to file a partnership tax return, spouses who provide significant services to their tenants can elect to be taxed as a "qualified joint venture." When this is done, both spouses are treated as sole proprietors of a Schedule C business for tax purposes. They each file an IRS Schedule C, *Profit or Loss From Business,* with their joint return.

This election is available only where the spouses own the rental property as individuals in their own names. It may not be made when the activity is held in the name of a state law business entity such as a partnership or LLC.

To qualify for qualified joint venture status, the spouses must share all their rental income, losses, deductions, and credits according to their ownership interest in the property. If, as is usually the case, each spouse owns 50% of the property, they equally split their rental income or loss on their Schedules C.

In addition, the spouses must:
- be the only owners of the activity
- file a joint return
- both elect not to be treated as a partnership, and
- both materially participate in the business.

Material participation is determined by the same rules as those used to determine whether real estate owners qualify as real estate professionals for purposes of the passive activity loss (PAL) rules. This means that each spouse must be involved with their business's day-to-day operations on a regular, continuous, and substantial basis. Working more than 500 hours in the business during the year meets this requirement. So does working over 100 hours if no one else worked more, or doing substantially all the work for the activity. (See "Material Participation Test" in Chapter 16 for a detailed discussion.)

In addition, the IRS says that married couples cannot make a qualified joint venture election if the business is owned and operated through a state law entity—this includes a partnership, limited liability company, limited liability partnership, or corporation. Thus, you cannot make this election if you've formed an LLC or corporation to own and run the business.

If you qualify, you and your spouse elect this status simply by filing a joint IRS Form 1040 with the required Schedule C. Once you elect this status, it cannot be revoked without IRS approval.

Electing qualified joint venture status to file Schedule E. The instructions to Schedule E provide that spouses whose rental activity constitutes a business for reasons other than providing their tenants with services may also elect qualified joint venture status. The same requirements discussed above must be satisfied. In this event, the co-owner spouses file one Schedule E to report their income and expenses from the rental property. However, each spouse must report his or her interest as separate properties on Schedule E. There is a special box to check on Schedule E to elect qualified joint venture status. (See Chapter 18 for a detailed discussion of Schedule E.)

It's not entirely clear when this election is necessary. The IRS regulations discussed above make clear that it is not necessary if the spouses merely maintain, repair, and rent out their property—this activity is not a partnership for tax purposes. There must be something more that makes the activity a partnership business—something other than providing services. What this is remains unclear. But, spouses who want to ensure that their rental activity is viewed as a business by the IRS may wish to make this election if they meet the requirements. It costs nothing. The spouses will have to split their rental income and expenses between them for each rental property when they file their sole Schedule E.

Spouses who live in community property states. There are some special rules for co-owner spouses who live in community property states. There are nine such states: Arizona, California, Idaho, Louisiana, Nevada, New Mexico, Texas, Washington, and Wisconsin.

If you live in one of these states, you and your spouse will automatically be co-owners of any rental property you acquire while you're married, unless you agree otherwise. Like married people in noncommunity property states, spouses in community property states ordinarily take title to their real property as joint tenants. However, they may take title as tenants in common instead, if they wish; or just one spouse may be named on the deed as owner.

The IRS says that spouses in community property states may treat their rental activity either as a sole proprietorship (technically, a "disregarded entity") or a partnership. Either one is fine. If sole proprietorship status is selected, they would file one Schedule E and would not have to allocate their rental income and expenses between themselves. All they need do to elect this status is file their one Schedule E. They do not need to elect qualified joint venture status to avoid having to file a partnership return. (Rev. Proc. 2002-69 (10/9/2002).)

What Happens If a Husband and Wife File the Wrong Type of Return?

What happens if a husband and wife who co-own a rental should file a partnership return but fail to do so? Basically, nothing. In theory, the IRS can impose a penalty. But this never happens. Over 30 years ago, the IRS decided it was impossible to actively enforce the partnership filing rules for husband-and-wife businesses. Instead, it issued a revenue procedure waiving penalties for small businesses that "historically had not filed partnership returns." The waiver did not "eliminate the filing requirement for partnerships … ; it merely provide[d] that a penalty for failure to file will not be assessed." (Rev. Proc. 81-11.)

Ownership Through a Business Entity

Instead of owning your rental property in your own name, you can form a business entity to own it, and own all or part of the entity.

> **EXAMPLE:** Vicki and Victor, a married couple, own a small apartment building. Instead of taking title in their own names as joint tenants, they form a limited liability company (LLC). The LLC owns the building and they, in turn, own the LLC.

The tax deductions available from rental property are the same whether you own it in your own name or through a business entity.

RESOURCE

This section provides only the briefest possible introduction to business entities. To learn more, refer to *LLC or Corporation? How to Choose the Right Form for Your Business*, by Anthony Mancuso (Nolo).

Types of Entities

There are several different business entities that can own rental property:

Partnerships. A partnership is a form of shared ownership and management of a business. The partners contribute money, property, or services to the partnership; in return, they receive a share of the profits it earns, if any. The partners jointly manage the partnership business. Although many partners enter into written partnership agreements, no agreement is required to form a partnership. A partnership can hold title to real estate and other property.

Limited partnerships. A limited partnership is a special type of partnership that can only be created by filing limited partnership documents with your state government. It consists of one or more general partners who manage the partnership and any number of limited partners who are passive investors—they contribute money and share in the partnership's income (or losses) but do not actively manage the partnership business. Limited partnerships are especially popular for real estate projects that are owned by multiple investors.

Corporations. A corporation can only be created by filing incorporation documents with your state government. A corporation is a legal entity distinct from its owners, who are called shareholders. It can hold title to property, sue and be sued, have bank accounts, borrow money, hire employees, and perform other business functions. For tax purposes, there are two types of corporations: S corporations (also called small business corporations) and C corporations (also called regular corporations). The most important difference between the two types of corporations is how they are taxed. An S corporation pays no taxes itself—instead, its income or loss is passed on to its owners, who must pay personal income taxes on their share of the corporation's profits. A C corporation is a separate taxpaying entity that pays taxes on its profits. C corporations are rarely used to own rental property.

Limited liability companies. The limited liability company (LLC) is like a sole proprietorship or partnership in that its owners (called members) jointly own and manage the business and share in the profits. However, an LLC is also like a corporation because its owners must file papers with the state to create the LLC and it exists as a separate legal entity.

Tax Treatment of Business Entities

Partnerships, limited partnerships, LLCs, and S corporations are all pass-through entities. A pass-through entity does not pay any taxes itself. Instead, the business's profits or losses are passed through to its owners, who include them on their own personal tax returns (IRS Form 1040). When a profit is passed through to the owner, the owner must add that money to any income from other sources, and pay tax on the total amount. If a loss is passed through to the owner, he or she can deduct it from other income, subject to the restrictions on deducting rental losses discussed in Chapter 16. Because pass-through taxation permits property owners to deduct losses from their personal taxes, it is considered the best form of taxation for real estate ownership.

Although pass-through entities don't pay taxes, their income and expenses must still be reported to the IRS as follows:

Partnerships and limited partnerships. These must file an annual tax form with the IRS (Form 1065, *U.S. Return of Partnership Income*). Form 1065 is used to report partnership revenues, expenses, gains, and losses. The partnership must also provide each partner with an IRS Schedule K-1, *Partner's Share of Income, Deductions, Credits, etc.*, listing the partner's share of partnership income and expenses (copies of these schedules must also be attached to IRS Form 1065). The partners must then file IRS Schedule E, *Supplemental Income and Loss*, with their individual income tax returns, showing the income or losses from all the partnerships in which they own an interest. Partners complete the second page of Schedule E, not the first page, which individuals use to report their income and deductions from rental property. (See Chapter 18.)

S corporations. These entities must file information returns with the IRS on Form 1120-S, *U.S. Income Tax Return for an S Corporation*, showing how much the business earned or lost and each shareholder's portion of the corporate income or loss. (An information return is a return filed by an entity that doesn't pay any taxes itself. Its purpose is to show the IRS how much tax the entity's owners owe.) Like partners in a partnership, the shareholders must complete the second page of Schedule E, showing their shares of the corporation's income or losses, and file it with their individual tax returns.

LLCs. LLCs with only one member are ordinarily treated like a sole proprietorship for tax purposes. The member reports profits, losses, and deductions from rental activities on Schedule E. An LLC with two or more members is treated like a partnership for tax purposes, except in the unusual situation where the owners choose to have it treated like a C or S corporation. However, an LLC owned by just one person is treated as a "disregarded entity" for tax purposes. This means that the single LLC owner is treated the same as a sole proprietor.

Landlords who own their properties through business entities don't use individual Schedule Es to report their rental income or losses. Instead, the partnership, limited partnership, LLC, or S corporation files IRS Form 8825, *Rental Real Estate Income and Expenses of a Partnership or an S Corporation,* to report the income and deductions from the property owned by the entity. This form is very similar to Schedule E.

Why Form a Business Entity?

The primary reason small landlords form business entities to own their property has nothing to with taxes. Rather, they use business entities to attempt to avoid personal liability for debts and lawsuits arising from rental property ownership.

> **TIP**
>
> **Forming a business entity may help show your rental activity is a business.** Another reason to form a business entity that may be more important now than it was in the past is to help establish that the rental activity is a business for tax purposes, not an investment activity. Qualifying as a business provides a landlord with many benefits. (See "Business Owner Versus Investor" in Chapter 2.) Moreover, real estate professionals whose rental activities qualify as a business can completely avoid the 3.8% Net Investment Income tax that went into effect in 2013. (See Chapter 19.)

When you own rental property in your own name, alone or with co-owners, you are personally liable for all the debts arising from the property. This means that a creditor—a person or company to whom you owe money for items you use in your rental activity—can go after all your assets, both business and personal. This may include, for example, your personal bank accounts, your car, and even your house. Similarly, a personal creditor—a person or company to whom you owe money for personal items—can go after your rental property. The main creditor that rental property owners worry about is the bank or some other financial institution from which they have borrowed money to purchase their property. If they default on their loan, they could be personally liable for the debt. (However, this isn't always the case. It depends on the nature of your loan and how your state law deals with real estate foreclosures.)

If you own property in your own name, you'll also be personally liable for rental-related lawsuits—for example, if someone slips and falls at your rental property and sues for damages.

In theory, limited partnerships, LLCs, and corporations provide their owners with limited liability from debts and lawsuits. (Only the limited partners in a limited partnership have limited liability. General partners are personally liable for partnership debts and lawsuits.) Limited liability means that you are not personally liable for the debts incurred by your business entity, or for lawsuits arising from its ownership of rental property. Thus, your personal assets are not at risk; at most, you'll lose your investment in the business entity (which, of course, is often substantial).

In real life, however, limited liability is often hard to come by, even when you form a business entity. Lenders may require small landlords who form business entities to personally guarantee any loans their entities obtain to purchase property. This means the landlord will be personally liable if there is a default on the loan. In addition, you'll always be personally liable if someone is injured on your property due to your personal negligence. For example, if someone slips and falls on your property, they can sue you personally by claiming your own negligence caused or contributed to the accident. This is so even though your property is owned by a business entity, not you personally. You can far more effectively protect yourself from such lawsuits by obtaining liability insurance for your rental property. The cost is a deductible rental expense. (See Chapter 14.)

However, if you're dead set on owning your rental property through a business entity, the entity of choice is the LLC. It provides the same degree of limited liability as a corporation, while also giving its owners pass-through taxation—the most advantageous tax treatment for real property. As a result, LLCs have become very popular among real property owners in recent years.

Out of an abundance of caution (or paranoia), some landlords set up a separate LLC for each rental property they own. However, this can be expensive, especially in states that make LLCs pay minimum annual taxes or fees, no matter how much money they earn. For example, LLCs in California must pay $800 per year. Thus, if you set up five California LLCs to own five buildings, you'd have to pay $4,000 in fees every year—even if your rental activates incurred losses. Again, you'd probably be better off spending the money on rental property insurance.

RESOURCE

For detailed guidance about LLCs, refer to *Form Your Own Limited Liability Company,* by Anthony Mancuso (Nolo).

The Mini-Landlord: Renting Out a Room in Your Home

If you rent out a room in your home, the tax deductions and other tax rules discussed in this book apply to you in the same way as they do for landlords who rent out entire properties. There is one big difference however: You must divide certain expenses between the part of the property you rent out and the part you live in, just as though you actually had two separate pieces of property.

You can fully deduct (or, where applicable, depreciate) any expenses *just for the room you rent*—for example, repairing a window in the room, installing carpet or drapes, painting the room, or providing your tenant with furniture (such as a bed). In addition, if you pay extra homeowners' insurance premiums because you're renting out a room, the full cost is a deductible operating expense. If you install a second phone line just for your tenant's use, the full cost is deductible as a rental expense. However, you cannot deduct any part of the cost of the first phone line even if your tenant has unlimited use of it.

Expenses for your entire home must be divided between the part you rent and the part you live in. This includes your payments for:

- mortgage interest
- repairs for your entire home—for example, repairing the roof or furnace, or painting the entire home
- improvements for your entire home—for example, replacing the roof
- homeowners' insurance
- utilities such as electricity, gas, and heating oil
- housecleaning or gardening services for your whole home
- trash removal
- snow removal costs
- security system costs, and
- condominium association fees.

You can also deduct depreciation on the part of your home you rent.

You can use any reasonable method for dividing these expenses. It may be reasonable to divide the cost of some items (for example, water) based on the number of people using them. However, the two most common methods for dividing an expense are either based on the number of rooms in your home or based on the square footage of your home.

> **EXAMPLE 1:** Jane rents a room in her house to a college student. The room is 10 × 20 feet, or 200 square feet. Her entire house has 1,200 square feet of floor space. Thus, one-sixth, or 16.67% of her home is rented out. She can deduct as a rental expense one-sixth of any expense that must be divided between rental use and personal use.

> **EXAMPLE 2:** Instead of using the square footage of her house, Jane figures that her home has five rooms of about equal size, and she is renting out one of them. She determines that one-fifth, or 20%, of her home is being rented. She deducts 20% of her expenses that must be divided between rental and personal use.

As the examples show, you can often get a larger deduction by using the room method instead of the square footage of your home. This is discussed in greater detail in the chapter on the home office deduction (Chapter 9).

Let's see how much Jane can deduct for her bedroom rental.

Expense	Deduction Percentage	Deductible Amount
Mortgage Interest—$12,000	20%	$ 2,400
Painting entire home exterior—$2,000	20%	400
Utilities—$1,200	20%	240
Trash removal—$500	20%	100
Painting rental bedroom—$400	100%	400
Total		$ 3,540

Jane also gets to depreciate 20% of the cost of her home over 27.5 years. Her home cost $200,000 so she depreciates $40,000. The first year she deducts 3.485% of this amount for a $1,394 deduction.

The IRS and the Landlord

Are small landlords a target for the IRS? No one knows for sure, but the answer appears to be no. An analysis of over 1,200 tax returns conducted by a professor of statistics in the mid-1990s could find no correlation between filing Schedule E (the tax form used to report rental income and losses) and an increased risk of an audit. (See *How to Beat the IRS at Its Own Game*, by Amir D. Aczel (BasicBooks, 1996).)

The IRS does not release any statistics on how many owners of residential real property are audited. However, it does provide statistics for the audit rate for all Schedule E filers (which includes many activities other than real estate rentals), plus farmers who file Schedule F. In 2011, 1% of all Schedule E and Schedule F filers were audited.

Automated Underreporter Program

In addition to audits, the IRS conducts an Automated Underreporter program. Under this program, IRS computers collect information on rent received and mortgage interest paid by landlords from the Schedule Es they file. The IRS tries to match this information to what third parties—primarily banks and other financial institutions and rental management companies—report on Forms 1099-MISC and 1098. When mismatches arise between amounts on tax returns and Forms 1099-MISC or 1098, the IRS may send a notice asking the landlord to explain the discrepancies or pay additional taxes.

Unfortunately for the IRS, this program is not terribly effective because most of the rent residential landlords receive is not reported to the IRS on Form 1099-MISC. Residential renters are not required to report to the IRS the rent they pay to their landlords. The only time the IRS receives a 1099-MISC for a rental payment is when an individual taxpayer receives rent of $600 or more through a rental agent, such as a rental management company. In this event, the agent is required to file a Form 1099-MISC with the IRS reporting the amount of rent paid to the individual landlord. Less than one-third of landlords who own fewer than 50 rental units use management companies, so the IRS computers usually have no 1099-MISC to match against the amount of rent listed on landlords' Schedule Es. For tax year 2001, for example, the IRS received Forms 1099-MISC reporting rent received for about 327,000 landlords. By comparison, there were about 8.2 million taxpayers who reported rent on their tax returns for whom the IRS did not receive a corresponding Form 1099-MISC from a third party reporting the rent.

Information reporting for mortgage payments by landlords is much better than it is for rent. But even here, the underreporter program is hampered because financial institutions are not required to include on Form 1098 the address of the property for which they are reporting mortgage interest. This makes it difficult for the IRS to determine if the interest is for a property used for rental or personal purposes.

Six Tips for Avoiding an Audit

Here are six things you can do to minimize your chances of getting audited.

Tip #1: Be Neat, Thorough, and Exact

If you file by mail (as you should) and submit a tax return that looks professional, this will help you avoid unwanted attention from the IRS. Your return shouldn't contain erasures or be difficult to read. Your math should be correct. Avoid round numbers on your return (like $100 or $5,000). This looks like you're making up the numbers instead of taking them from accurate records. You should include, and completely fill out, all necessary forms and schedules. Moreover, your state tax return should be consistent with your federal return. If you do your own taxes, using a tax preparation computer program will help you produce an accurate return that looks professional.

Tip #2: Mail Your Return by Registered Mail

Mail your tax return by registered or certified mail, return receipt requested. In case the IRS loses or misplaces your return, your receipt will prove that you submitted it. The IRS also accepts returns from a few private delivery services, including Federal Express and United Parcel Service. Contact these companies for details on which of their service options qualify and how to get proof of timely filing.

Tip #3: Don't File Early

Unless you're owed a substantial refund, you shouldn't file your taxes early. The IRS generally has three years after April 15 to decide whether to audit your return. Filing early just gives the IRS more time to think about whether you should be audited. You can reduce your audit chances even more by getting an automatic extension to file until October 15. (However, partnerships and S corporations may receive an automatic extension only until September 15 (five months, instead of six).) Note, however, that filing an extension does not extend the date by which you have to pay any taxes due for the prior year—these must be paid by April 15.

Tip #4: Don't File Electronically

The IRS would like all taxpayers to file their returns electronically—that is, by email. There is a good reason for this: It saves the agency substantial time and money. Every year, the IRS must hire thousands of temp workers to enter the numbers from millions of paper returns into its computer system. This is expensive, so the IRS only has about 40% of the data on paper returns transcribed. The paper returns are then sent to a warehouse where they are kept for six years and then destroyed. The IRS makes its audit decisions based on this transcribed data. By filing electronically, you give the IRS easy electronic access to 100% of the data on your return instead of just 40%. Moreover, if you file electronically, you cannot add written explanations of any deductions the IRS might question (see Tip #5). No one can say for sure whether filing a paper return lessens your chance of an audit, but why make life easier for the IRS if you don't have to?

New IRS rules that went into effect in 2011 require professional tax preparers to file their clients' returns electronically unless the client elects to opt out of electronic filing. To opt out, you have to file a special form with your paper tax return. Ask your tax preparer about this.

Tip #5: Explain Items the IRS Will Question

If your return contains an item that the IRS may question or that could increase the likelihood of an audit, include an explanation and documentation to prove everything is on the up and up. For example, if your return contains a substantial casualty loss deduction, explain the circumstances. This won't necessarily avoid an audit, but it may reduce your chances. Here's why: If the IRS computer determines that your return is a good candidate for an audit, an IRS classifier screens it to see whether it really warrants an audit. If your explanation looks reasonable, the screener may decide you shouldn't be audited after all.

Such explanations ("disclosures" in tax parlance) can be made on plain white paper and attached to your return, or you can use special IRS forms. IRS Form 8275, *Disclosure Statement*, can be used to explain or disclose any information that there isn't room to include on your other tax forms. Another IRS form, Form 8275-R, *Regulation Disclosure Statement*, must be used to disclose tax positions that are contrary to IRS regulations or other rules. You shouldn't file Form 8275-R without professional help.

Over Half of All Landlords Misreport Rental Activities

A recent report by the General Accounting Office concluded that 53% of all individual taxpayers with rental real estate misreport their rental real estate activities, resulting in the loss to the government of $12.4 billion of income taxes each year. The biggest problem is that many landlords either understate the rent they receive or overstate their deductible expenses, or do both. The reason for this is clear: very little third-party information reporting is required for payments to or from residential landlords. The IRS generally knows how much money independent contractors earn each year because most payments to them must be reported by the payer to the IRS on Form 1099-MISC (see Chapter 12). In contrast, most residential landlords never have their rental income reported to the IRS on Form 1099-MISC (see "Automated Underreporter Program" above).

Tip #6: Report All Your Rental Income

You should always report all the income you receive. The IRS has a pretty good idea how much money rental properties ordinarily bring in. If the income you list on your Schedule E looks disproportionately low for the size, location, or value of your rental property, your return may be tagged for an audit.

Landlord Tax Classifications

The Landlord Tax Categories..38

Business Owner Versus Investor 39

    Are You a Business Owner or an Investor?...39

    The Importance of Good Records..43

    Tax Consequences..44

Are You Profit Motivated? 46

    What Is a Not-for-Profit Activity?..47

    Tax Consequences of Not-for-Profit Rentals 49

    How to Show Your Profit Motive..50

Real Estate Dealers..57

    What Is a Real Estate Dealer?..57

    Determining If You Are a Dealer 58

    Tax Consequences of Being a Dealer..61

This chapter explains how to determine your tax status—that is, how to classify your rental activities for tax purposes. This is not a topic that most residential landlords give much thought to. However, your tax status is extremely important because it will determine whether (and to what extent) you can deduct your rental expenses. Your tax status also significantly affects your taxes when you sell your property.

The Landlord Tax Categories

A landlord can fall into any one of the following four tax categories:

- a business owner
- a real estate investor
- a dealer in real estate, or
- a person who owns rental property as a not-for-profit activity.

The vast majority of residential landlords are either business owners or investors—although this doesn't necessarily mean that you'll fall into one of these two categories. Ultimately, your behavior and motive for owning rental property will determine your tax status.

Initially, it's up to you to decide which category your rental activities fall into for tax purposes. However, if the IRS audits you, it can review your tax classification. If the IRS decides that you misclassified your rental activities, you could have to pay back taxes, interest, and penalties.

You can determine your status by answering the following questions:

- Do you work regularly and continuously at your rental activity?
- Is earning a profit the primary reason you own rental property?
- Do you make your money primarily by buying and selling real estate?

Let's take a look at each of these questions—this will help you figure out which category you fall into. The tax consequences of the different classifications are also explained.

Business Owner Versus Investor

The crucial tax question for most landlords is whether they qualify as business owners or investors. This distinction has important tax consequences. If, like most landlords, you are a business owner, you get certain valuable tax deductions that investors can't use (including the home office and start-up expenses deductions, and Section 179 expensing). It is important, therefore, to understand the difference between these two categories and know where you belong.

CAUTION
Do you continually lose money on your rentals? If you do, the IRS may claim you're engaged in a not-for-profit activity, with disastrous tax consequences. See "Are You Profit Motivated?" below, for detailed guidance on how to show the IRS that you want to earn a profit from your rental property.

Are You a Business Owner or an Investor?

What's the difference between an investor and a business owner? It's not their motivation—they both want to earn a profit. The difference is that business owners earn their profits by actively running a business, either themselves or with the help of others they hire, such as managers. Investors are passive—they put their money in someone else's business and hope their investment will increase in value due to the other person's efforts. Or, they buy an item like land or gold, and then sit and wait for it to increase in value.

Owning rental property qualifies as a business if you do it to earn a profit and work at it regularly, systematically, and continuously. (*Alvary v. United States*, 302 F.2d 790 (2d Cir. 1962).)

> **EXAMPLE:** Edwin Curphey, a dermatologist, owned six rental properties in Hawaii. He converted a bedroom in his home into an office for his real estate activities. Curphey personally managed his rentals, which included seeking new tenants, supplying furnishings, and cleaning and otherwise preparing the units for new tenants. The court held that these activities were sufficiently systematic and continuous to place him in the business of real estate rental. (*Curphey v. Comm'r.*, 73 T.C. 766 (1980).)

However, you don't have to do all the work yourself: You can hire a manager to help you and still qualify as a business as long as the manager or other person you hire works regularly, systematically, and continuously.

> **EXAMPLE:** Gilford, her two sisters, and other relatives jointly owned eight apartment buildings in Manhattan. They hired a real estate agent to manage the properties and pay each family member his or her share of the net income. Gilford was found to be in business even though she spent little or no time managing the buildings. The court reasoned that the ownership and management of the buildings was a business because it required considerable time and effort by the real estate agent over several years. Because the agent acted for Gilford and was ultimately under her control, Gilford was in business through her agent. (*Gilford v. Comm'r.*, 201 F.2d 735 (2d Cir. 1953).)

Moreover, it's not necessary that your property actually be rented out for you to be in business. It's sufficient that you offer it for rent to the public at a fair market rental. The fact that you have had trouble finding a renter doesn't mean you're not in business.

> **EXAMPLE:** Mr. Jephson purchased a 26-room brownstone on Riverside Drive in Manhattan. He offered it for rent through a real estate agency, improved the heating system, and had a caretaker who was in charge of keeping it clean, making general repairs, and showing it to prospective renters. The owner, Mr. Jephson, received rental offers, but deemed none to be satisfactory. As a result, the house remained unoccupied for nine years. Nevertheless, his real estate activity qualified as a business for tax purposes. (*Jephson v. Comm'r*, 37 B.T.A. 1117 (1938).)

How Many Units Must You Own to Be in Business?

There is no specific number of rental properties or rental units you must own for your rental activity to qualify as a business. In one case, a married couple was found to be engaged in business even though all they owned was a 25% time-share interest in two condominium units. And, the actual work of renting out the units and keeping them in repair was performed by a management company that acted as their agent. (*Murtaugh v. Comm'r.*, T.C. Memo 1997-319.) Indeed, the general rule followed by the courts is that rental of a single property constitutes a business. (*Balsamo v. Comm'r.*, T.C. Memo 1987-477.)

Moreover, the IRS has itself recently stated that "rental of a single property may require regular and continuous involvement such that the rental activity is a trade or business." (Preamble to IRS Reg. § 1.1411, TD 9644, https://federalregister.gov/a/2013-28410.)

However, the IRS and courts have also said that renting of a single unit (or more) doesn't always constitute a business—it all depends on the facts and circumstances, including the number of properties rented, the day-to-day involvement of the owner or its agent, and the type of rental—for example, a short-term versus long-term lease.

How Many Hours Must You Work to Be in Business?

Neither the IRS nor the courts have established a minimum number of hours you (or your agent) must work in your rental activity for it to qualify as a business. However, IRS regulations that went into effect in 2014 establish a safe harbor rule for when a rental activity conducted by a real estate professional is a business for purposes of the Net Investment Income (NII) tax: So long as a real estate professional devotes a minimum of 501 hours per year to the rental activity, it will automatically qualify as a business and the rental income will not be subject to the NII tax. Alternatively, if a real estate pro has participated in rental real estate activities for more than 500 hours per year in five of the last ten tax years, the rental activity will qualify as a business. (IRS Reg. § 1.1411-4(g)(7).) (See Chapter 19 for a detailed discussion of the NII tax.)

This regulation applies only to real estate professionals who own rental properties—people who work over half the time in the real estate field. (In Chapter 16, see "The Real Estate Professional Exemption.") Most small landlords do not qualify as real estate professionals, thus the regulation doesn't directly apply to them. However, it does establish the general principle that, as far as the IRS is concerned, anyone who works at least 500 hours a year at a rental activity is engaged in a business for tax purposes. That's less than ten hours per week. If you work at least this much in your rental activity, you should point to this regulation if an IRS auditor claims you're not in business.

And keep in mind that 501 hours per year is a safe harbor rule, not a minimum number. It's quite possible to work less than 501 hours per year and still have your rental activity qualify a business. Clearly, a landlord with only one rental unit would likely not work over 500 hours per year. Yet the IRS and courts have both said that ownership of a single rental property can qualify as a business.

When Rentals Are Not a Business

If you own only one or a few units and spend minimal time dealing with them, you could have trouble showing that your management activities (or those of an agent) are sufficiently continuous, systematic, and regular to be a business. Ironically, this is more likely where you have good stable tenants who cause few problems and make little demand on your time.

EXAMPLE: Edgar Grier inherited a house from his mother that she had rented out for many years to the same tenant. This same tenant continued to occupy the property until Grier sold it 14 years later. Over the years, Grier managed the property himself or with the help of an agent. Little management work was required, but Grier did take care of such details as replacing the furnace. The IRS and court found that the house was an investment, not a business for Grier. The court noted that this was the only rental property Grier had ever owned and concluded that his landlord activities were too minimal to rise to the level of a business. (*Grier v. United States,* 120 F.Supp. 395 (D. Conn. 1954).)

Other cases where landlords have been found to be investors are those involving triple net leases of commercial properties where the tenant is required to manage the property and pay all taxes, insurance, and other expenses. The landlord does nothing but deposit the rent checks. (*Neill v. Comm'r.,* 46 B.T.A. 197.) Triple net leases are not usually used for residential rental properties. However, if you have an arrangement with a tenant that requires the tenant, not you, to take care of the property the IRS could conclude you're not in business. Courts have also held that landlords were not in business where they rented out their property only to their children or friends (*Vandeyacht v. Comm'r,* T.C. Memo. 1994-148; *Rivera v. Comm'r.,* T.C. Summary Opinion 2004-81.)

Also, if your rental property is vacant all or most of the time, the IRS could decide that you are an investor, because you wouldn't need to spend much time dealing with the property. The IRS might also take the position that vacant properties involve a not-for-profit activity.

Finally, people who purchase interests in business entities that own real estate, but aren't actively involved in management of the entities, are also investors for tax purposes. These include the limited partners in limited partnerships that own real estate, and people who own shares in corporations and REITs (real estate investment trusts).

If none of these exceptions apply, your rental activity will likely qualify as a business for tax purposes if you offer your property for rent to the general public at a fair market rent.

The Importance of Good Records

If you want to make sure you qualify as a business owner, it is important that you keep track of the landlord tasks you perform and the time you spend performing these tasks. Your records don't have to be fancy—notes on a calendar will do. (See Chapter 17.) But keep track of the dates and time you spend on tasks such as taking care of repairs, dealing with tenant complaints, showing the property, negotiating leases, and so forth. This will show that you were actively engaged in the business of being a landlord. Good record keeping will not only help establish you are in business, but can also help you avoid restrictive rules on deducting losses from real estate. (See Chapter 16.) In addition, whenever you pay $600 or more to an independent contractor during the year to perform services for your rental business, be sure to file all required IRS Form 1099-MISCs. (See Chapter 12.)

Tax Consequences

At first glance, there may not seem to be much difference, taxwise, between landlords who are business owners and those who are investors. They both file the same tax form to report their income and expenses—Schedule E. And, they don't need to indicate on their tax returns whether their rental activities are businesses or investments. In addition, neither one has to pay self-employment taxes on any rental income. (See Chapter 12.)

Investors and business owners are also entitled to many of the same deductions. People who own businesses are entitled to deduct their ordinary and necessary expenses. (I.R.C. § 162.) Investors are entitled to deduct any ordinary and necessary expenses they incur in connection with producing or collecting income, or managing, conserving, or maintaining property they hold to produce income—for example, a real estate rental. (I.R.C. § 212.)

Thus, both business owners and investors may deduct:
- repair costs (see Chapter 4)
- depreciation (see Chapter 5)
- interest (see Chapter 7)
- taxes (see Chapter 14)
- car and local travel expenses (see Chapter 10)
- long distance travel expenses (see Chapter 11)
- meal and entertainment expenses (see Chapter 14)
- the costs of hiring workers (see Chapter 12)
- casualty losses (see Chapter 13)
- payments for professional services (see Chapter 3), and
- other operating expenses, such as advertising and insurance (see Chapter 3).

And the requirements to qualify for these deductions are the same for business owners and investors.

The similarities end there, however. Taxwise, business owners are much better off than investors because they are entitled to take certain valuable deductions that investors can't take. These business-only deductions include:

- **Net Investment Income tax.** Rental income earned by a taxpayer who qualifies as a real estate professional for tax purposes will not be subject to the 3.8% Net Investment Income tax if the rental activity qualifies as a business. If the activity is an investment, the rental income will be subject to the tax even though the landlord is a real estate professional.

- **Home office deduction.** Investors can't take a home office deduction. This important deduction is available only for businesses conducted from home. (See Chapter 9.)

- **Section 179 expensing.** Investors cannot take advantage of Section 179, the tax code provision that allows businesspeople to deduct a substantial amount in purchases of long-term personal property in a single year. (See Chapter 5.)

- **Seminar or convention deductions.** Investors cannot deduct their expenses for attending conventions, seminars, or similar events. Thus, for example, the cost of attending a real estate investment seminar is not deductible for investors. Businesspeople can qualify for such deductions. (See Chapter 11.)

- **Start-up expense deduction.** Up to $5,000 of the costs you incur to start your rental business may be deducted in the first year your business is in operation. Any amount over the limit must be deducted in equal installments over the first 180 months you're in business. (See Chapter 8 for more on deducting start-up costs.) You get no deduction at all for expenses incurred in starting up an investment activity.

- **Real estate losses.** If an investor loses money when he or she sells real estate, the loss is a capital loss. Investors can deduct only $3,000 in capital losses each year from their ordinary income— that is, income not derived from capital assets like real estate, stocks, bonds, and other investments. Business owners get much better tax treatment when it comes to losses. Any gains they earn when they sell real estate used in their business and held for more than one year are taxed at capital gains rates—usually lower than the normal income tax rates. But, if a business owner sells business real property at a loss, the loss is deductible in full from all of the owner's income, not just income from capital assets. (I.R.C. § 1231.) Thus, when it comes to buying and selling real estate, business owners have the best of both worlds—their gains are taxed as capital gains, but their losses are treated as ordinary losses. (See Chapter 16 for more on real estate losses.)

Because of these valuable deductions, it is better to qualify as a business owner than an investor. Be careful, however, when you decide which deductions you are entitled to take. If you decide you are a business and take some business-only deductions, the IRS could audit your return and conclude that you are an investor instead. Not only would you be denied the business-only deductions in the future, you would also have to pay back taxes and interest on any business-only deductions you took.

> **EXAMPLE:** Byron Anderson, a nurse-anesthetist, owned an 80-acre farm that he rented to a tenant farmer. He used a room in his home as a home office from which he conducted his landlord activities. He claimed a home office deduction for the room. The IRS audited Anderson and denied the deduction because it claimed his rental activities were an investment, not a business. The tax court agreed with the IRS, and Anderson lost the deduction. (*Anderson v. Comm'r.*, T.C. Memo 1982-576.)

Are You Profit Motivated?

It goes without saying that the primary reason most people own residential rental property is to earn a profit—that is, to make more money than they spend on the activity. But this isn't always the case. If your primary motivation for owning a rental is something other than earning a profit, your rental activity must be classified as a not-for-profit activity. This is a classification to be avoided whenever possible—it is a tax disaster.

> **SKIP AHEAD**
>
> **If you earn a profit from your rental activities every year (or at least most years), you can skip this section.** If you're earning a profit, you'll have no trouble showing the IRS that you are profit motivated. Indeed, under those circumstances, it's highly unlikely that the profit issue would even be brought up in an audit.

What Is a Not-for-Profit Activity?

A not-for-profit activity is something you do primarily for a reason other than earning money—for example, for recreational or charitable purposes. Activities like artwork, coin and stamp collecting, and writing typically qualify as not-for-profit activities for tax purposes. Horse and dog breeding are also frequently found to be not-for-profit activities by the IRS.

Owning rental real estate, on the other hand, is not usually a not-for-profit activity. However, there are three common situations where owning rental property could be a not-for-profit activity:

- you rent out a vacation home you or your family also use
- you rent property to others at below-market rates, or
- you allow your rental property to sit vacant for a substantial time.

Vacation Homes

If you consistently lose money on a vacation home or second home that you rent out part of the year and also live in part of the time, there's a good chance the IRS will view your home ownership as a not-for-profit activity. To overcome this, you would have to be able to show that you made real efforts to earn a profit.

> **EXAMPLE:** Mr. and Mrs. Hilliard, both full-time physicians, purchased a rental condominium for $106,000 in beautiful Lake Tahoe. Unfortunately, their investment didn't turn out to be so beautiful—they consistently spent more on mortgage payments, maintenance, interest, taxes, and depreciation than they took in in rental income. They averaged only $711 in rental income per year over a five-year period, while their expenses averaged over $19,000. Both the IRS and tax court found that the Hilliards' vacation rental was a not-for-profit activity. (*Hilliard v. Comm'r.*, 70 T.C. Memo 898.)

Renting to Relatives

Renting out property at below-market rates (or for nothing) to relatives, friends, or others can be a red flag for the IRS and courts, indicating that you lack a profit motive.

> EXAMPLE: Eugene Walet, a successful businessman, purchased a house in New Orleans and allowed his ex-wife and their son to live in it rent-free for seven years. Walet's ex-wife had health problems and didn't work, so Walet never expected to be able to collect rent from her. Both the IRS and tax court found that Walet had purchased and maintained the house for the personal motive of helping his ex-wife and son and not to earn a profit, either from rent or appreciation. Therefore, the activity had to be classified as a not-for-profit activity for tax purposes. As a result, Walet could not deduct depreciation and repair expenses for the house. (*Walet v. Comm'r.,* 31 T.C. 461.)

CAUTION

Vacation homes used as residences and below-market rentals are subject to special tax rules. Even if you have a profit motive, you could be subject to special tax rules if you or your family use the property more than 15 days a year, or an amount equal to more than 10% of the time it's rented out. The same goes for the time you rent the property at below-market rates. These rules have much the same effect as the not-for-profit rules—you'll only be able to deduct your rental expenses against your rental income. (See Chapter 15.)

Vacant Rental Property

Allowing your rental property to stand vacant for a substantial time can also lead the IRS to conclude you lack a profit motive unless there is a good reason you've been unable to find a tenant.

> EXAMPLE: Gertrude Gorod lived in the upper unit of a duplex near Boston and attempted to rent out the lower unit. Although she continually advertised the unit for rent in newspapers and at supermarkets, she was unable to find a suitable renter and the unit remained vacant for ten years. The IRS audited her and found that her rental was a not-for-profit activity.

Gorod objected, claiming that she wanted to rent out the unit and earn money from it, but was unable to do so because her duplex was located in a high-crime, run-down area. The tax court agreed and found that Gorod had a profit motive in keeping the vacant rental. (*Gorod v. Comm'r.*, 42 T.C. Memo 1569.)

However, Gorod was audited by the IRS again three years later. Her rental unit was still vacant, and the IRS again found that she lacked a profit motive. Gorod appealed again, but this time she lost. The tax court noted that by this time, the unit had been vacant for over 13 years and Gorod had allowed the space to become uninhabitable and had it boarded up. Thus, the court concluded that Gorod no longer had a profit motive. (*Gorod v. Comm'r.*, 49 T.C. Memo 526.)

Tax Consequences of Not-for-Profit Rentals

If your rental activity is deemed a not-for-profit activity by the IRS, your deductions will be severely limited. Namely, you will be able to deduct only your expenses from whatever income your rental activity generates. If you have no income, you get no deductions. And you can't carry over any deductions to use in future years when you earn income—you lose them forever.

> **EXAMPLE:** Charles, a Chicago resident, inherits a small house in Ann Arbor, Michigan. The house is old and vacant, and Charles doesn't want to go to the time and trouble of fixing it up and renting it out. Instead, he allows his unemployed brother-in-law to live in the house rent-free. He spends $2,000 on taxes for the house each year. If his rental activity is classified as not-for-profit, his $2,000 in expenses may be deducted only from any income he earns from the not-for-profit activity. Because he earned no money from the house during the year, he can't deduct any of his expenses this year and he can't carry over the deduction to any future years.

Even if you have income, if your activity is considered not-for-profit, you must deduct your expenses in a way that is less advantageous (and more complicated) than regular landlord deductions. With a not-for-profit activity, you must deduct your expenses as a miscellaneous itemized deduction on IRS Schedule A (the form that you file with your Form 1040 to claim itemized deductions). This means that you must itemize your deductions instead of taking the standard deduction. You can do this only if your total deductions are greater than the standard deduction. (In 2015, the standard deduction was $6,300 for single people and married people filing separately, and $12,600 for married people filing jointly.)

If you itemize your deductions, your not-for-profit activity expenses can be used to offset your not-for-profit activity income, but only to the extent that all of your expenses plus your other miscellaneous itemized deductions exceed 2% of your adjusted gross income (your total income minus business expenses and a few other expenses).

> **EXAMPLE:** In 2015, Charles decides to rent his Ann Arbor house for one weekend to football fans visiting town for the Michigan–Ohio State game (he kicks his brother-in-law out for that weekend). He earns $300 in rent, has no other income from the property for the year, and has a total of $2,000 in expenses from the property for the year. If this rental is a not-for-profit activity, his deductions for the year would be limited to a maximum of $300—he could not deduct the remaining $1,700 in expenses he had. Moreover, he would have to deduct the $300 as an itemized deduction. To do this, his total personal deductions for the year would have to exceed $6,300 (the standard deduction amount for single people) and his expenses plus his other miscellaneous itemized deductions would have to exceed 2% of his adjusted gross income (AGI) for the year. In contrast, if the rental was profit motivated, Charles could deduct the entire $2,000 as a rental expense on his Schedule E. The amount could be deducted from any income he earned that year, subject to the passive loss rules covered in Chapter 16.

How to Show Your Profit Motive

It's usually not difficult to show that your primary motive for owning real estate is to earn a profit. You can do this by actually earning a profit from your rental activities or acting like you want to earn a profit.

Three-of-Five Test

If you earn a profit from your rentals in three out of five consecutive years, the IRS must presume that you have a profit motive. Any legitimate profit no matter how small qualifies; you don't have to earn a particular amount or percentage. If you meet the three-of-five test, the IRS can still claim that your activity is a not-for-profit activity, but it will have to prove that you don't have a profit motive. In practice, the IRS usually doesn't attack ventures that pass the profit test unless the numbers have clearly been manipulated to meet the standard.

The presumption that you are engaged in a for-profit activity applies to your third profitable year and extends to all later years within the five-year period beginning with your first profitable year.

> EXAMPLE: Tom purchased a fixer-upper duplex in 2010 and rented out both units. Because Tom had to make extensive repairs to the property, the rent he collected was less than his expenses for the first two years. However, he managed to earn a profit in the next three years so he passed the three-of-five profit test.
>
> | Year | Losses | Profits |
> |------|--------|---------|
> | 2010 | $5,000 | |
> | 2011 | $2,000 | |
> | 2012 | | $2,000 |
> | 2013 | | $4,000 |
> | 2014 | | $5,000 |
>
> If the IRS audits Tom's taxes for 2014, it must presume that he was engaged in a for-profit activity during that year. Tom earned a profit during three out of the five consecutive years ending with 2014, so the presumption that Tom is not engaged in a not-for-profit activity extends to 2017, five years after his first profitable year.

The IRS doesn't have to wait for five years after you become a landlord to decide whether it is a for-profit or not-for-profit activity. It can audit you and classify your venture as a business or not-for-profit activity at any time. However, you can give yourself some breathing room by filing IRS Form 5213, which requires the IRS to postpone its determination until you've been engaged in the activity for at least five years. Although this may sound like a good idea, filing the election only alerts the IRS to the fact that you might be a good candidate to audit on the not-for-profit activity issue after five years. It also adds two years to the statute of limitations—the period in which the IRS can audit you and assess a tax deficiency. For this reason, almost no one ever files Form 5213.

Behavior Test

It is not necessary that you actually earn a profit for your rental activities to be viewed as profit motivated. Even if you consistently lose money, your rental activity is profit motivated if you entered into the activity primarily to earn profits—not to get tax deductions, help your relatives, have a place to vacation, or for some other reason not involving profit. Many people who want to earn profits from real estate rentals have negative cash flows—that is, they spend more on their rental property than they get back in rent. Indeed, IRS statistics show that of the 8.6 million tax returns filed by landlords in one recent year, more than 4.5 million showed a loss. However, these landlords expect to eventually earn a profit either from an appreciation in the value of the real estate, an increase in rent, a decrease in expenses, or some combination of these.

How does the IRS figure out whether you really want to earn a profit? IRS auditors can't read your mind to establish your motives, and they certainly aren't going to take your word for it. Instead, the IRS looks at the following "objective" factors to determine whether you are behaving like a person who wants to earn a profit. You don't have to satisfy all of these factors to pass the test. The first three listed below (acting like a business, expertise, and time and effort expended) are the most important. Studies show that taxpayers who meet these three factors are always found to be profit motivated, regardless of how they do on the rest of the criteria.

- **How the activity is carried on.** Among other things, acting like a business means you keep good books and other records and carry on your rental activities in a professional manner.
- **Your expertise.** People who are trying to make money usually have some knowledge and skill in the field of their endeavor.

- **The time and effort you spend.** People who want to make profits work regularly and continuously. You don't have to work full time, but you must work regularly.
- **Your track record.** Having a track record of success in other businesses—whether or not they are related to your landlord activities—helps show that you are trying to make money in your most recent venture.
- **Your history of income and losses.** Even if you can't satisfy the profit test described above, earning a profit in at least some years helps show that you have a profit motive.
- **Your profits.** Earning a substantial profit, even after years of losses, can help show that you are trying to make a go of it. On the other hand, earning only small or occasional yearly profits when you have years of large losses and/or a large investment in the activity tends to show that you aren't in it for the money.
- **Appreciation.** Your profit includes money you make through the appreciation (increase in value) of your business assets. For a land-lord, this primarily includes the increase in value of the rental properties that are owned. Even if you don't make any profit from your day-to-day rental operations, you can still show a profit motive if you stand to earn substantial profits when you sell your real estate.
- **Your personal wealth.** The IRS figures that you probably have a profit motive if you don't have substantial income from other sources. After all, you'll need to earn money from your venture to survive. On the other hand, the IRS may be suspicious if you have substantial income from other sources (particularly if the losses from your real estate venture generate substantial tax deductions).
- **Elements of fun or recreation.** You'll have a harder time convincing the IRS that you're profit motivated if your rental activity involves fun or recreation. For example, a person who owns a rental unit at a resort and spends substantial time vacationing there, will have a hard time claiming he is profit motivated (assuming no profits are earned on the rental).

Analysis of a Time-Share: For Profit or Not-for-Profit?

Douglas and Gina Rundlett owned 11 time-share units that they rented out for one week each during the year. Over a four-year period, they lost $217,705 and earned only $40,995 from the activity. The IRS denied their substantial deductions for travel and other expenses because it claimed activity was not profit-motivated. The Rundletts appealed to the tax court, which examined each of the nine factors discussed above and found as follows:

How the activity was carried on. The court held that this factor did not favor the Rundletts because they didn't act in a particularly businesslike manner. The court was particularly swayed by the fact that they did not have an up-to-date business plan; nor did they prepare any profit or loss statements, balance sheets, or financial break-even analyses for the activity.

Expertise. This did not favor the Rundletts because they never studied the business of renting time-share units or consulted with experts.

Time spent. This indicated a lack of a profit motive because the Rundletts spent no more than 100 hours per year working at the rental activity.

Track record in other businesses. This was neutral because there was no evidence that the Rundletts carried on any successful businesses similar to the time-share activity.

History of income and losses from rental activity. This was neutral even though the Rundletts lost $123,955 during the relevant time period. The court found that these two years were during the activity's start-up phase and losses are common during this time.

Amount of occasional profits, if any. The Rundletts never earned any profits from the activity. Thus, there were no occasional profits: another factor showing it was not profit-motivated.

Appreciation. This was neutral because there was no evidence about it one way or another.

Personal wealth. The Rundletts earned income in excess of $170,000 a year from their regular jobs, and they deducted over $62,000 per year on their joint returns due to their time-share activity losses. This indicated they were more interested in obtaining deductions than earning a profit from the activity.

> ## Analysis of a Time-Share: For Profit or Not-for-Profit? (cont'd)
>
> **Fun or recreation.** The court held that this was neutral because Ms. Rundlett spent time reserving and renting the time-share unit—an activity that could not be classified as pleasurable or recreational.
>
> The tax court concluded that five of the nine factors favored not-for-profit status for the Rundletts' rental activity, while four were neutral. It therefore found that the activity was not-for-profit. As a result, the Rundletts lost all their rental deductions and owed the IRS over $29,000 in back taxes and interest. (*Rundlett v. Comm'r.*, T.C. Memo 2011-229 (2011).)

How to Pass the Behavior Test

If you continually lose money on your rentals, particularly if you rent them out at below-market rates or keep them vacant, you should take steps to ensure that the IRS will not claim that you lack a profit motive in the event you're audited.

- **Keep good business records.** Keeping good records of your expenses and income from your activity is the single most important thing you can do to show that you want to earn a profit. Lack of records shows that you don't really care whether you make money or not. You don't need an elaborate set of books; a simple record of your expenses and income will usually suffice. (See Chapter 17 for a detailed discussion of record keeping.)
- **Keep a separate checking account.** Open up a separate checking account for your rental activity. This will help you keep your personal and rental expenses separate—another factor that shows you want to make money.
- **Keep track of the time you spend.** It is not necessary that you work full time at being a landlord in order to have a profit motive. However, the more time you spend at being a landlord, the more it will look like you want to earn a profit. Keep track of your time. This will also be necessary if you want to avoid application of the restrictive rules on deducting real estate losses (see Chapter 16).

What If You Make a Bad Investment?

What if you went into rental property ownership to make money, but your investment turned out badly? Fortunately, the IRS recognizes that owning rental property can end up being a bad investment, but still be profit motivated. IRS regulations provide that a taxpayer may be deemed to be profit motivated, even if his or her property is not currently productive and "there is no likelihood that the property will be sold at a profit or will otherwise be productive of income; and even though the property is held merely to minimize a loss." (IRS Reg. § 1.212-1(b).) Thus, you can be profit motivated even if your rental property doesn't produce any current income. For example, an owner of a vacant rental might want to earn a profit, but be prevented from doing so by a bad rental market or other circumstances beyond his or her control.

- **Make efforts to rent your property.** Letting a property stand vacant without making any efforts to find a renter tends to show you don't care about earning a profit. If your property is vacant, try to find renters by advertising and listing it with rental services. Keep records of your efforts.
- **Establish your expertise.** If you lack a solid background in owning and managing rental property, make up for it by attending educational seminars and other programs—for example, educational events sponsored by your local apartment owners' association.
- **Show you expect your property to appreciate in value.** Real estate appreciation is often the pot of gold at the end of the landlord rainbow. The fact that you expect your property to substantially increase in value in the future is strong evidence you want to earn a profit, even if you are incurring losses right now. You can show the IRS that you expect your property to appreciate in value because (1) you've owned similar properties that have gone up in value, (2) similar properties in the area have appreciated, and (3) the property has, in fact, gone up in value since you bought it.

- **Prepare a business plan showing how much money you expect to earn or lose over the next several years.** This is a projection of how much money your rental activity will bring in, your expenses, and how much profit you expect to make (or losses you'll incur). The forecast should cover at least the next five or ten years. It should show you earning a profit sometime in the future (although it doesn't have to be within five years). This profit can result from anticipated increases in your rents, decreases in expenses, appreciation in the value of your property, or some combination of all three. You can prepare such projections yourself (special software is available for this purpose), or you can have an accountant or real estate professional create one for you.

Real Estate Dealers

Some people who own rental real estate are not primarily interested in earning money from collecting rents or the long-term appreciation of their property. Instead, they try to earn profits from buying and selling real estate. The IRS calls these people real estate dealers. They have a special tax status, which is generally not advantageous.

What Is a Real Estate Dealer?

A real estate dealer is someone who is in the business of owning property primarily for the purpose of reselling it. A dealer buys property and resells it, usually at a price higher than the purchase price, and normally after only a short holding period.

A real estate dealer resembles a merchant or retailer of goods, except that his or her product is real estate. For example, a merchant in the business of selling computers typically purchases numerous computers each year—not for his own use or to rent out to users—but to resell as quickly as possible to customers at a profit. Likewise, a real estate dealer buys real property to resell at a profit to customers. A real estate dealer's holdings are inventory for sale to customers, the same as any merchant's inventory.

Real estate dealers typically include (but are not limited to):
- real estate speculators who buy and sell many properties each year
- subdividers who buy large tracts of vacant land, divide them into smaller lots, and then resell the lots piecemeal
- real estate developers and home builders who construct new houses and resell them soon after completion, and
- people in the business of converting apartment buildings into condominiums for resale.

Determining If You Are a Dealer

An owner of residential rental property can be classified as a dealer. The IRS and courts look at the following factors to determine if a person holds property as a dealer. The first three factors are the most important.

Dealer Versus Nondealer Status: Number of Sales	
Dealer	**Nondealer**
26 lots sold over 5 years (*Harris v. Comm'r.*, 47 T.C. Memo 760 (1983))	8 lots sold over 9 years (*Rice v. Comm'r.* T.C. Memo 2009-142 (2009)).
39 sales over 7 years (*Norris v. Comm'r.*, T.C. Memo 1986-151)	22 sales over 3 years (*Byram v. Comm'r.*, 705 F.2d 1418 (9th Cir. 1983))
71 properties sold in 3 years (*Sottong v. Comm'r.*, 25 T.C. Memo 1366 (1966))	28 lots sold over 3 years (*Brodnax v. Comm'r.*, 29 T.C. Memo 733 (1970))
244 sales over 32 years (*Biedenharn Realty Co. v. United States*, 526 F.2d 409 (5th Cir. 1976))	45 sales over 7 years (*Williams v. Comm'r.*, 53 AFTR2d 84-844)

The Number and Frequency of Sales

Numerous and continuous sales over an extended time period are the hallmark of a real estate dealer. Indeed, this factor alone is often enough to make a person a property dealer. On the other hand, someone who sells property infrequently is less likely to be a dealer, particularly if a sale is due to changed circumstances or results from an unsolicited offer.

There is no set number of sales required to make a person a dealer. As the above chart shows, courts have been inconsistent in deciding how many sales make you a dealer. However, if you only sell one or two properties in a year, it's not likely you'll be classified as a dealer, and it's possible you could sell substantially more and still avoid dealer status.

Intent for Buying Property

A real estate dealer buys properties with the intent of making money from reselling them. A person who buys property to earn income and/or benefit from long-term appreciation is not a dealer. However, the fact that you buy a rental property with the idea that you will eventually resell it does not automatically make you a real estate dealer. A dealer is a person who is in the business of buying and selling properties. Buying a single, or even a few, properties to resell does not mean you are in the resale business.

Some real estate purchasers attempt to establish their intent to hold the property as an investment by adding a clause to that effect in their purchase agreement. Such a clause is unlikely to be much of help in establishing you are not a dealer; on the other hand, it can't hurt. Keep in mind that your intent can change—for example, you could purchase a rental property for quick resale and then change your mind and decide to hold onto it long-term for the rental income.

Extent of Improvements

Dealers often improve the property they own to increase its value for purposes of resale. Flipping is the practice of buying a run-down property, fixing it up, and then quickly reselling it at a profit. A person who frequently flips property would likely be a dealer.

Other Factors That Point to Dealership

The IRS uses additional factors when deciding whether a person's activities amount to those of a real estate dealer. They include:

Sales efforts. Dealers make extensive efforts to resell their properties—for example, they hire real estate brokers, list their property for sale, engage in advertising, and may have their own sales office and sales staff. A person who engages in extensive marketing efforts is more likely to be considered a dealer than one who takes a passive sales approach.

How the property is acquired. Dealers go out and buy properties themselves. A person who acquires real property through an inheritance or gift is not likely to be viewed as a dealer.

Holding period. Like any merchant, real estate dealers want to sell their inventory as quickly as possible. People who hold onto real property for a long time before selling it are much less likely to be considered dealers than those who hold their properties for a short time.

Income generated by sales. A person is more likely to be viewed as a dealer if the income generated from selling real estate constitutes a substantial amount of the total income he or she earns.

Continuous effort. Dealers work continuously throughout the year to sell their properties and spend substantial time at their business. A person whose sales transactions are only intermittent is not likely to be a dealer.

Facilities. Real estate dealers often have outside offices or other facilities to help them conduct their frequent real estate sales. They are often licensed real estate brokers and associated with real estate sales companies. However, not all licensed brokers are dealers; this is just one factor that is considered.

A landlord who owns rental property primarily to earn income from rents and/or long-term appreciation is not a dealer. This is so even though a landlord ultimately sells his or her property. This includes the great majority of landlords.

EXAMPLE: Randolph Rouse purchased about 40 rental houses in a Washington, DC, suburb and owned them for over two years, during which time he earned income from the rents. When he first purchased the homes, rentals were in great demand in the area and he had no trouble finding good tenants. However, these conditions began to change and it became more and more difficult to obtain desirable tenants. Some of Rouse's rental houses stood vacant for several months at a time and in some instances the rent had to be reduced. Whenever Rouse was unable to rent a house within a reasonable time, he would offer it for sale. Prospective purchasers were often referred to him by real estate agents who had seen his For Rent sign on vacant houses. He ended up selling all his houses over a four-year period, and didn't purchase any other rental houses. The court held that he was not a real estate dealer because he purchased the houses to earn rental income, not to profit from resales. (*Rouse v. Comm'r.*, 36 T.C. 70.)

Even if you are a real estate dealer, you can still own nondealer property (also called investment property). Whether you are a dealer is determined on a property-by-property basis. You can own some property for sale as a dealer, and other property as a long-term investment.

EXAMPLE: Peter Miller, a real estate broker, purchased an apartment building and sold it two years later for a substantial profit. At the same time, he worked as a dealer in real estate: He was involved in several real estate sales businesses, including subdividing land for resale and home building. Nevertheless, the tax court found that the apartment building was not dealer property. Miller owned the apartment building primarily to earn rental income, not for resale. (*Miller v. Comm'r.*, 20 B.T.A. 230.)

However, the mere fact that you rent a property does not by itself make it investment property. Many dealers rent out property they have up for sale, but earning income from rentals is not the primary reason they own the property. Their rental income is simply icing on the cake— the cake itself consists of the profits they earn from their sales.

If you are a real estate dealer who also owns investment property, be sure to keep the two types of property separate. Keep separate records for your investment property. If possible, establish a separate business entity for your dealer activities and purchase your investment property as an individual in your own name, not through your business.

Tax Consequences of Being a Dealer

Being classified as a dealer is usually not advantageous taxwise, particularly where real property is sold for a substantial gain. On the other hand, it can be advantageous when property is sold at a loss. For these reasons, there have been many legal disputes over whether a real estate seller should be classified as a dealer.

Real estate dealer classification has the following important tax consequences:

- **Ordinary income or loss treatment.** Gains and losses from sales of real property by a dealer are subject to ordinary income tax rates. In contrast, gains realized by a nondealer are usually taxed at capital gains rates, which are lower. However, dealers are better off if real estate proves to be a money-losing proposition, because a dealer is typically permitted to deduct the full amount of a loss, while an investor's deductions for losses may be strictly limited.

- **No depreciation.** Real estate dealers may not take a deduction for depreciation of their property.

- **No tax-free exchanges.** Taxpayers who are not real estate dealers may take advantage of a special provision of the tax law that allows them to exchange their property for other similar property without having to pay any income tax. Real estate dealers cannot use tax-free exchanges.

- **No installment sales.** Real estate dealers are also barred from using installment sales. This is where the purchase price for real estate is paid over several years, with the taxes due being paid by the seller over the same period as the payments are made, instead of in one lump sum in the year of sale.

- **Self-employment tax due.** Since they sell real estate as a business, real estate dealers must pay self-employment taxes on their profits. Real estate investors and businesspeople who are not dealers do not have to pay such taxes. (See Chapter 12.)

- **Medicare taxes.** Starting in 2013, a 3.8% Net Investment Income tax is imposed on high-income taxpayers' net investment income, including income from rentals (except for those owned by real estate professionals), interest, dividends, royalties, and annuities. High-income taxpayers are those with adjusted gross income over $200,000 for singles and $250,000 for married taxpayers filing jointly. Real estate dealers are not subject to this tax on rental income they earn from property they hold for sale as a dealer. However, they have to pay 3.8% Medicare payroll tax on their net self-employment income above the same levels.

- **Schedule C must be filed.** Real estate dealers who are sole proprietors file IRS Schedule C, *Profit or Loss From Business*, to report their income and expenses from real estate sales. However, they file Schedule E to report their income and expenses from real estate they own as an investment or for speculation.

Deducting Your Operating Expenses

Requirements for Deducting Operating Expenses 66

    Ordinary and Necessary 66

    Current Expense 68

    Business-Related 69

    Reasonable in Amount 72

Operating Expenses That Are Not Deductible 73

This chapter covers the basic rules for deducting operating expenses you incur from your residential rental activities. These are the bread and butter expenses virtually every landlord has for things like repairs, management fees, and advertising.

Requirements for Deducting Operating Expenses

There are so many different kinds of operating expenses that the tax code couldn't possibly list them all. Instead, the code gives you the definition of an operating expense, and it's up to you to make sure the expenditures you deduct meet the requirements. If they do, they will qualify as deductible operating expenses. To qualify, the expense must be:

- ordinary and necessary
- current
- directly related to your rental activity, and
- reasonable in amount. (I.R.C. § 162.)

Ordinary and Necessary

The first requirement is that the expense must be ordinary and necessary. This means that the expense is common, "helpful and appropriate" for your activity. (*Welch v. Helvering*, 290 U.S. 111 (1933).) The expense doesn't have to be indispensable to be necessary; it need only help your rental activity in some way—even if it's minor. A one-time expenditure can be ordinary and necessary.

It's usually fairly easy to figure out whether an expense passes the ordinary and necessary test. Many of the most common types of landlord operating expenses are listed on IRS Schedule E, including:

- advertising your rental units in newspapers or on the Internet
- auto and travel expenses incurred by you or your staff
- cleaning and maintenance
- commissions you pay to rental brokers, if you use them
- insurance, such as property and commercial general liability insurance, and part of your automobile insurance if you use your car for rental activities

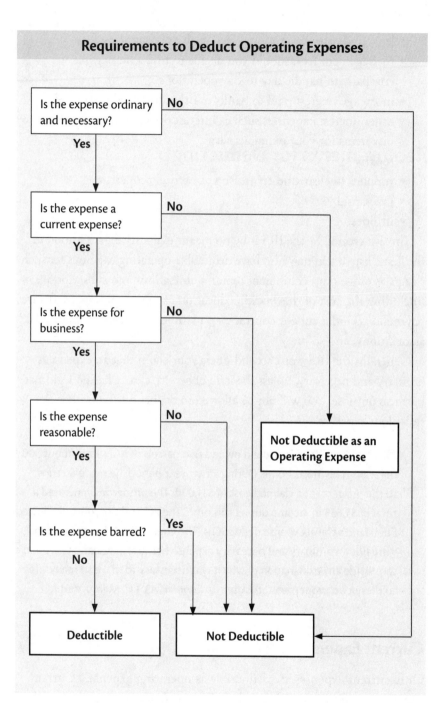

- legal and other professional fees, such as accounting fees
- management fees, should you decide to hire a management company to handle day-to-day operations
- mortgage interest paid to banks or other financial institutions
- other interest expenses, such as interest on a credit card you use to buy items for your rental activity
- repairs
- supplies to clean and refurbish your rental property
- taxes, and
- utilities.

This list created by the IRS is by no means exhaustive. In addition to the items listed, you may also have deductible operating expenses for such things as office rent, equipment rental, publications and subscriptions (including the cost of this book!), education expenses, postage, software, payments to independent contractors, membership fees for landlord associations, and so on.

Generally, the IRS won't second-guess your claim that an expense is ordinary and necessary, unless the item or service clearly has no legitimate business purpose. You will not be allowed to deduct off-the-wall or clearly ridiculous expenses.

> **EXAMPLE:** Rayford Strickland owned two parcels of real estate about 500 miles from his Texas home. During a two-year period, he made 80 trips to the property at a claimed cost of $11,000. The properties generated a total of $1,653 in income during this time. The IRS and tax court disallowed Strickland's travel expense deductions. The court found that the 80 trips were not an ordinary and necessary expense because Strickland was unable to provide any explanation of why it was necessary to make so many trips to these two properties. (*Strickland v. Comm'r*, 43 T.C. Memo 1061.)

Current Expense

Only current expenses are deductible as operating expenses. Current expenses are for items that will benefit your rental activity for less than one year. These are the costs of keeping your rental venture going on a day-to-day basis, including money you spend on items or services that get used up, wear out, or become obsolete in less than one year. A good example of a current expense is the monthly fee a landlord pays to a gardener to perform landscaping work on a rental property. Each monthly fee benefits the landlord's rental activity for less than one year, so it is a current expense.

You deduct operating expenses in the year in which they're incurred—this helps your bottom line. Not everything you buy for your rental activity qualifies as a current expense. Anything you purchase that will benefit your rental activity for more than one year is a capital, not a current, expense. For example, if a landlord purchases a lawn mower to use for his rental properties, the purchase would be a capital expense (not a current expense) because the lawn mower will benefit the rental activity for more than one year. In contrast to current expenses, capital expenses may only be deducted a little at a time over many years. This process is known as depreciation.

Repairs to real property are current expenses that may be deducted in a single year. For example, the cost of buying a replacement part for a water heater in a rental unit is a repair that can be currently deducted. However, improvements to real property that extend the property's useful life or make it more valuable must be depreciated. Thus, the cost of purchasing a brand-new water heater for a rental unit would be a capital expense that would have to be depreciated over several years. It is sometimes difficult to tell the difference between a deductible repair and depreciable improvement. This important issue is covered in detail in Chapter 5.

Business-Related

An expenditure must be *directly related to your rental activity* to be deductible as an operating expense. This means that you cannot deduct personal expenses. For example, the cost of a personal computer is a deductible operating expense only if you use the computer for your rental activities; it is not deductible if you use it to pay personal bills or play computer games.

Allocating Business and Personal Use

If you buy something for both personal and landlord use, you can deduct only the business portion of the expense. You must figure out how much of the time you used the item for landlord purposes and how much for personal purposes. You then allocate the total cost between the two purposes, and deduct only the landlord portion of the cost.

> EXAMPLE: Sam rents a personal computer for $100 per month. He uses it five hours a week for his rental activities and 15 hours for personal use. Therefore, he uses it 25% of the time for landlord purposes and 75% for personal reasons. He may deduct only 25% of the cost of the computer, or $25 per month, as an operating expense.

The same allocation rule applies when you rent out part of a house that you live in.

> EXAMPLE: Sheila owns a three-bedroom house that she uses as her residence. She rents out one of the bedrooms, which represents 15% of the total house. Her tenant pays her $300 per month rent and Sheila pays for the utilities for the whole house. Sheila may deduct 15% of the cost of utilities and maintenance for the whole house as a landlord operating expense. She could deduct 100% of the cost of any expense incurred just for the rented bedroom—for example, the cost of repainting the bedroom.

Special allocation rules apply when you rent out your entire residence, or a vacation or second home. These are discussed in detail in Chapter 15.

Stricter Rules for Certain Expenses

Many expenses have both a personal and a business component, which can make it difficult to tell if an expense is business related. For example, what if a landlord drives to the hardware store and buys one item for his rental property and another for his personal residence? Should he be allowed to deduct all, part, or none of the cost of driving to the hardware store?

The IRS has created rules and regulations for some operating expenses that commonly involve a crossover of personal and business use. Some of these rules lay out guidelines to help you figure out when an expense is and isn't deductible. Others impose record-keeping and other requirements to prevent abuses by dishonest taxpayers. Much of the complexity in determining whether an expense is deductible as a business operating expense involves understanding and applying these special rules and regulations.

The expenses that present the most common problems (and are, therefore, subject to the most comprehensive IRS rules and regulations) include:

- home office expenses (see Chapter 9)
- meals and entertainment (see Chapter 14)
- travel (see Chapter 11)
- car and truck expenses (see Chapter 10)
- business gifts (see Chapter 14)
- bad debts (see Chapter 14)
- employee benefits (see Chapter 12)
- interest payments (see Chapter 7)
- casualty losses (see Chapter 13)
- taxes (see Chapter 14), and
- education expenses (see Chapter 14).

Landlord's Personal Labor Not Deductible

A landlord may never deduct the value of his or her own time and personal labor working on rental activities. For example, a landlord who spends 50 hours repainting an apartment building gets no deduction for the value of his time. He may only deduct the cost of the paint, brushes, and other materials he uses. This rule prevents the kind of abuse the IRS fears would happen if personal labor were deductible.

Landlords may deduct labor costs only when they hire other people to do the work and pay them for it. The labor can be performed by an employee or independent contractor (nonemployee), or even a member of the landlord's family. (See Chapter 12.)

However, this doesn't mean landlords should never do any work on their rental properties themselves. Although your personal labor is not deductible, you'll still save money by doing the work yourself because only a part of the money you deduct for labor costs ends up as a tax savings. (See Chapter 12.)

Reasonable in Amount

Subject to some important exceptions, there is no limit on how much you can deduct, as long as the amount is reasonable and you don't deduct more than you spend. As a rule of thumb, an expense is reasonable unless there are more economical and practical ways to achieve the same result. If the IRS finds that your deductions are unreasonably large, it will disallow them or at least disallow the portion it finds unreasonable.

Certain areas are hot buttons for the IRS—especially entertainment, travel, and meal expenses. The IRS won't allow any lavish expenses here, and you will have to follow strict rules requiring you to fully document these deductions (see Chapters 11 and 14). The reasonableness issue also comes up when a business pays excessive salaries to employees to obtain a large tax deduction. For example, a landlord might hire his 14-year-old son to do yard work for his rental units and pay him $50 an hour— clearly an excessive wage for this type of work.

For a few types of operating expenses, the IRS limits how much you can deduct. These include:

- the home office deduction, which is limited to the profit from your business (although you can carry over and deduct any excess amount in future years) (see Chapter 9)
- business meals and entertainment, which are only 50% deductible (see Chapter 14)
- travel expenses, which are limited depending on the length of your trip and the time you spend on business while away (see Chapter 11), and
- business gifts, which are subject to a $25 maximum deduction per individual per year (see Chapter 14).

Operating Expenses That Are Not Deductible

Even though they might be ordinary and necessary, some types of operating expenses are not deductible under any circumstances. In some cases, this is because Congress has declared that it would be morally wrong or otherwise contrary to sound public policy to allow people to deduct these costs. In other cases, Congress simply doesn't want to allow the deduction. These nondeductible expenses include:

- fines and penalties paid to the government for violation of any law— for example, tax penalties, parking tickets, or fines for violating city housing codes (I.R.C. § 162(f))
- illegal bribes or kickbacks to private parties or government officials (I.R.C. § 162(c))
- lobbying expenses or political contributions; however, a landlord may deduct up to $2,000 per year in expenses to influence local legislation (state, county, or city), not including the expense of hiring a professional lobbyist (such lobbyist expenses are not deductible)
- real estate examination or licensing fees, or other professional examination fees (see Chapter 8)
- charitable donations by any business other than a C corporation (these donations are deductible only as personal expenses; see Chapter 14)
- country club, social club, or athletic club dues
- federal income taxes you pay on your rental income (see Chapter 14), and
- certain interest payments (see Chapter 7).

4

Repairs

The New IRS Rules: Repairs Versus Improvements 76

    Three New Safe Harbors 78

    Safe Harbor for Small Taxpayers (SHST) 79

    Routine Maintenance Safe Harbor 83

    De Minimis Safe Harbor 88

    Repair Versus Improvement Analysis Under the Regulations 89

    Defining the "Unit of Property" (UOP) 89

    What Is an Improvement? 93

    Other Issues Under the Repair Regulations 101

    How New IRS Regulations Affect Prior Years 105

How to Deduct Repairs and Maintenance 107

    Making Tenants Pay for Repairs 108

    Repairs Paid for or Performed by Tenants 109

Tips for Maximizing Your Repair Deductions 110

    Patch, Mend, and Make Do—Don't Replace 110

    Properly Document Repairs 111

    Do Preventive Maintenance 112

    Delay Big Repair Expenses 113

Repair expenses are among the most valuable deductions landlords have. However, many landlords are surprised to discover that some of the changes they make to their property are not repairs at all; instead, they are improvements that must be deducted much more slowly than repairs. This chapter shows you how to tell the difference between a repair and an improvement, and how to deduct as quickly as possible the expenses you incur to maintain your property.

The New IRS Rules: Repairs Versus Improvements

Provided they are ordinary, necessary, and reasonable in amount, repairs to your rental property are operating expenses that are fully deductible in the year in which they are incurred. However, not all upkeep constitutes a repair for tax purposes. Some changes landlords make to their rental property are capital improvements. Unlike repairs, improvements cannot be deducted in a single year. Instead, their cost must be depreciated over several years. Improvements to residential rental property must be depreciated over an especially long period—27.5 years.

You don't need to understand depreciation to learn about deducting repairs. All you need to know is that you are usually better off taxwise if you can characterize an expense as a repair instead of an improvement. If it's a repair, you can deduct the whole cost in a single year instead of having to deduct a little at a time over many years. In simple terms, when it comes to taxes, repairs are good and improvements are bad.

Unfortunately, telling the difference between a repair and an improvement isn't always easy. Indeed, for decades this issue has resulted in bitter disputes between landlords and the IRS. In an effort to clarify matters, the IRS issued a 222-page set of final regulations in 2013. These regulations lay out complicated rules for determining what constitutes a currently deductible repair versus a capital improvement that must be depreciated over several years.

The regulations took full effect on January 1, 2014 and are supposed to be followed starting then and for all subsequent years. Moreover, as explained below, larger landlords had to apply them to expenses for repairs and improvements to rental property owned before 2014 as well. The regulations are contained in Internal Revenue Bulletin 2013-43 (available at www.irs.gov/irb/2013-43_IRB/ar05.html).

Eight years in the making, the new regulations cover all types of tangible business and investment property—both real and personal property—but they are particularly significant for owners of rental buildings. Indeed, as far as landlords are concerned, the new regulations represent the most significant change in the tax laws since 1986 when the passive loss rules (covered in Chapter 16) took effect. All in all, the regulations are a mixed bag for landlords, containing both good and bad elements. On the good side, they include three new safe harbors that will permit many landlords—particularly those with small holdings— to currently deduct all or most of their expenses, whether they are classified as repairs or improvements.

But, in cases where the safe harbors can't be used, the regulations will likely make it more difficult to classify fix-ups and other building expenses as currently deductible repairs. This is bad news if you're a landlord because, when it comes to taxes, repairs are far more valuable than improvements.

On the other hand, the new regulations give landlords a new deduction: Landlords can elect to take an immediate deductible loss when building components are replaced instead of having to continue to depreciate the old components over many years. This will greatly speed up the process of deducting old building components that are replaced when they wear out, become obsolete, or are damaged.

CAUTION
You may need help from a tax pro. As the following discussion shows, the IRS regulations are extremely complex. You may wish to seek the help of a tax pro to analyze how they affect you. This is particularly wise if you have owned or made substantial repairs or improvements to your rental property in the past ten to 15 years.

Three New Safe Harbors

Usually, landlords would prefer to currently deduct an expense as a repair in a single year rather than depreciate the cost a little at a time over several years (residential buildings and improvements thereto must be depreciated over 27.5 years). The new IRS repair regulations contain three new safe harbors that landlords may use to currently deduct building-related expenses:

- a safe harbor for small taxpayers
- the routine maintenance safe harbor, and
- the de minimis safe harbor.

If an expense comes within any safe harbor, and it is an ordinary and necessary expense, you may automatically treat the item as a currently deductible expense without having to go through the complexities of the regular repair versus improvement regulations.

You always have the option of using the regular repair regulations if you wish. But the safe harbors are designed to make your life easier and simpler, and often enable you to deduct expenses that otherwise would have to be depreciated under the more complicated regular rules. Thus, you usually will want to take advantage of them if you can. It's possible for an expense to fall within more than one safe harbor although you only need to come within one of the three.

To determine whether an expense qualifies for a current deduction under the IRS's repair regulations, you can use a two-step approach:

- First, determine whether the expense qualifies as a current deduction under one of three new safe harbor tests.
- Second, if none of the safe harbors apply, determine whether the expense is a deductible repair or improvement under the regular repair versus improvement rules laid out in the final IRS repair regulations.

When you are figuring out if an expense falls within a safe harbor, you should analyze it under the safe harbors in the order presented below.

Safe Harbor for Small Taxpayers (SHST)

The safe harbor for small taxpayers (SHST) is the single most important safe harbor for smaller landlords; IRS Reg. § 1.263(a)-3h. If you qualify to use it, you may currently deduct on Schedule E all your annual expenses for repairs, maintenance, improvements, and other costs for a rental building. If so, you won't need to worry about any of the other safe harbors or the regular repair versus improvement regulations. However, there are significant restrictions on which landlords may use this safe harbor. In addition, to take advantage of this safe harbor, landlords need to keep careful track of all their annual expenses for repairs, maintenance, improvements, and similar items—something they should be doing anyway.

Rental Business Size Limitations

As the name implies, the SHST is intended to be used by landlords with relatively small rental businesses. Thus, there are strict limits on the value of buildings that may qualify under the safe harbor and on the annual amounts landlords can spend and earn. You cannot use this safe harbor in any year any of these limits are exceeded. But, so long as you come within these limits, you may use the SHST for any number of rental buildings or units—you are not limited to just one.

$1 million building value limit. The SHST may be used only for buildings—including condos and co-ops—with an unadjusted basis of $1 million or less. Thus, it can't be used for many larger apartment buildings or other more expensive rental buildings. "Unadjusted basis" usually means a building's original cost (also called its cost basis), not including the cost of the land. See Chapter 5 for a detailed discussion of how to determine a building's basis. To determine a building's unadjusted basis, you don't subtract the annual amounts you deduct for depreciation. But you add the value of any improvements you make to the building while you own it and that you are depreciating along with the rest of the building.

> **EXAMPLE:** Suzy owns an apartment building with an unadjusted basis of $900,000. In 2015, she installs a new roof at a cost of $110,000. Her building's basis is now over $1 million and does not qualify for the SHST.

Segmented Depreciation Can Help You Qualify for SHST

To come within the $1 million SHST limit, you can reduce a rental building's unadjusted basis by using segmented depreciation. As discussed in Chapter 6, building owners ordinarily include the value of land improvements and personal property inside their buildings in the building's basis. However, by using segmented depreciation (also called cost segregation), you can separately depreciate land improvements (like driveways and landscaping) and personal property in rental units such as appliances. This will reduce the basis of the building and can make the difference in a building qualifying for the SHST.

EXAMPLE: Sonia owns a five-unit apartment building that cost $1.2 million. This is $200,000 over the SHST limit. However, she determines that the land improvements cost $100,000 and the personal property in the units cost another $100,000. She depreciates the land improvements and personal property separately, over 15 and five years respectively. This leaves the apartment building itself with an unadjusted basis of $1 million, allowing her to use the SHST.

Additionally, the money you spend on repairs, maintenance, and improvements for such separate land improvements and personal property is not counted toward the $10,000 annual SHST limit discussed below.

EXAMPLE: Assume that one year Sonia spends $5,000 to repave the parking lot of her apartment building and another $10,000 on maintenance and improvements for the building itself. She need not include the $5,000 when determining whether her building qualifies for the SHST because the parking lot is a land improvement she is depreciating separately from the building. As a result, her total expenses for the year are $10,000—within the SHST annual limit.

If you own more than one rental unit or building, the $1 million limit is applied to each separately. Thus, for example, a landlord with ten rental buildings each with an unadjusted basis of less than $1 million can use the SHST for each of them. If the taxpayer is leasing the building, the unadjusted basis of the leasehold interest is equal to the total amount of (undiscounted) rent paid or expected to be paid over the entire lease term, including expected renewals.

Annual expense limit. A landlord may use the SHST only if the total amount paid during the year for repairs, maintenance, improvements, and similar expenses for a building does not exceed the lesser of $10,000 or 2% of the unadjusted basis of the building.

> EXAMPLE: Sam owns a rental home with a $100,000 unadjusted basis (that is, it cost $100,000). He may use the SHST only in those years where the total amount he spends on the building is $2,000 or less (2% x 100,000 = $2,000).

The 2% of the adjusted basis rule means that a building with basis greater than $500,000, but not more than $1,000,000, will still have the $10,000 annual limit.

The limit is applied on a per-building basis—for example, if you own three rental homes, you apply the limit to each home separately. Thus, you may be able to use the SHST for some, but not others.

> EXAMPLE: Randy owns two rental homes, both with an unadjusted basis of $200,000. He may spend a maximum of $4,000 on each and qualify for the SHST. During the year he spends $3,000 on house A and $6,000 on house B. He may use the SHST for house A, but not house B.

When computing the amount you spend for purposes of the SHST annual limit, you count everything you spent during the year, including amounts that may come within the routine maintenance and de minimis safe harbors discussed below. If you can't use the SHST because the limit is exceeded, you may still use these other safe harbors.

> EXAMPLE: Stu owns a rental building with an unadjusted basis of $500,000. His annual SHST limit is $10,000. During 2015, Stu spends the following amounts on his rental building: $2,000 for new appliances that come within the de minimis safe harbor, $6,000 for a new furnace, and $4,000 on various maintenance items that come within the routine maintenance safe harbor. Stu doesn't qualify for the SHST because he spent $12,000 on his building. But he may still deduct $6,000 by using the de minimis and routine maintenance safe harbors.

Annual Income limit. Finally, to qualify for the SHST a landlord must have average annual gross receipts of no more than $10 million during the three preceding tax years. Gross receipts include income from sales (unreduced by cost of goods), services, and investments. This poses no problem for smaller landlords.

Claiming the SHST

The small taxpayer safe harbor must be claimed anew each year by filing an election with your timely filed tax return, which is due by October 15 (if you obtain an extension of time to file). Thus, you can use the SHST for amounts paid during 2015 by filing the election with your 2015 tax return, which must be filed no later than October 15, 2016 (if you obtain an extension; September 15 for returns filed by most multi-member LLCs, corporations, and partnerships).

> EXAMPLE: Sam owns a single family home that he rents out. It has a $100,000 unadjusted basis (that is, it cost $100,000). During 2015, he paid $200 to a plumber to fix a leak, repaired a window for $400, and replaced the home's water heater for $1,200. Sam qualifies for the small taxpayer safe harbor because the $1,800 he spent on repairs, improvements, and maintenance during 2014 is less than 2% of his building's unadjusted basis (2% x $100,0000 = $2,000). By filing an election to use the SHST, Sam may currently deduct the entire $1,800 on his 2015 IRS Schedule E. This is so whether or not any of these expenses, such as the water heater replacement, might constitute an improvement under the regular repair rules discussed below—those complex rules need not be applied where the SHST is used.

You can claim the SHST for some years and refrain from doing so for other years—it's entirely up to you. The SHST is also claimed on a building-by-building basis. Thus, if you own more than one rental building, you can claim the SHST for some rental buildings and not use it for others.

There is no IRS form for this election. However, it is a very simple document you can easily create yourself and attach to your return. You can use the following format:

Section 1.263(a)-3(h) Safe Harbor Election for Small Taxpayers

Taxpayer's name:
Taxpayer's address:
Taxpayer's identification number:

The taxpayer is hereby making the safe harbor election for small taxpayers under Section 1.263(a)-3(h) for the following building property:
_____[*describe*]_____.

If the rental property covered by the SHST is owned by a partnership, limited liability company, or S corporation, the election must be made by the business entity, not by the individual partners, LLC members, or corporate shareholders.

Once this annual election is made, it may not be revoked for the year it covers.

Routine Maintenance Safe Harbor

The second potentially useful safe harbor for landlords is the routine maintenance safe harbor. (IRS Reg. § 1.263(a)-3(i).) Expenses that qualify as routine maintenance under this provision are deductible in a single year. Unlike with the safe harbor for small taxpayers, there are no annual dollar limits with this safe harbor. Any landlord can use it, no matter the cost of the building involved, the amount of the landlord's income, or the amount spent on the maintenance. However, there are some significant limits on when rental building owners may use this safe harbor.

What Is "Routine Maintenance"?

Routine maintenance consists of recurring work a building owner does to keep an entire building, or each system in a building, in ordinarily efficient operating condition. Under the IRS's regulations, a building includes the building structure as a whole and nine separate systems (see "Defining the 'Unit of Property'" below).

Routine maintenance includes two activities:
- inspection, cleaning, and testing of the building structure and/or each building system, and
- replacement of damaged or worn parts with comparable and commercially available replacement parts.

The first activity—inspection, cleaning, and testing of buildings and building systems—is typically currently deductible in any event as an ordinary and necessary business expense. The ability to currently deduct replacement parts for the building structure and each of the nine separate building systems is the particularly helpful part of this safe harbor.

EXAMPLE: Howard buys an apartment building that contains an HVAC system that requires maintenance by an outside contractor every four years. This includes disassembly, cleaning, inspection, repair, replacement, reassembly, and testing of the HVAC system and many of its component parts. If inspection or testing discloses a problem with any component, the part is repaired, or if necessary, replaced with a comparable and commercially available replacement part. This expense—no matter how much—qualifies for the routine maintenance safe harbor and is currently deductible by Howard. No muss, no fuss, just deduct the entire amount.

However, there are two big limitations on routine maintenance: the ten-year rule and the no betterments rule.

Ten-Year Rule

Routine maintenance can be performed and deducted under the safe harbor any time during the property's useful life, including after it has been fully depreciated. However, building maintenance qualifies for the routine maintenance safe harbor only if, when you placed the building or building system into service, you reasonably expected to perform such maintenance more than once every ten years.

EXAMPLE: Sue owns a duplex she rents out. She reasonably expects to have to replace the low-cost carpet in the building at least once every five years. Because Sue expects to perform this replacement at least twice within ten years, she may deduct the cost of carpet replacement under the routine maintenance safe harbor. Note that Sue could also deduct this expense under safe harbor for small taxpayers (SHST) if she qualified to use it. The advantage of the SHST is that there is no twice-every-ten-years requirement.

In determining whether you can reasonably expect to have to perform the maintenance more than once every ten years, you are supposed take into consideration factors such as the recurring nature of the activity, industry practice, manufacturers' recommendations, and your own experience with similar or identical property.

A nonexclusive list of examples of maintenance for rental properties routinely performed more than once every ten years likely includes such items as:

- inspecting, cleaning, and repairing HVAC units
- clearing and replacing rain gutters
- inspecting and replacing sprinklers
- smoke detector inspection and replacement
- lighting inspection and replacement
- paint touch-up
- chimney inspection and cleaning
- furnace inspection, cleaning, and repair, and
- inspecting and replacing washing machine hoses.

The more-than-once-every-ten-year requirement would seem to eliminate use of the routine maintenance safe harbor for building components that typically don't need such frequent maintenance— for example, roofs, windows, and wooden or tile flooring. However, repairs to such components may be currently deductible under the regular IRS repair regulations discussed below. For example, the regulations provide that installation of a new waterproof membrane (top layer) on a building's roof to eliminate leaks through an original (worn) membrane is a deductible repair.

Although not strictly required by the IRS, you may wish to create a written long-term maintenance plan for your rental property, showing when major maintenance needs to be performed on each building system. You don't need to file the plan with your return. Just keep it in your tax files in the event of an IRS audit (or to show your tax pro who prepares your return).

What if you reasonably expected you'd have to do certain maintenance more than once every ten years, but it turns out it was not required? This is not necessarily a problem. The IRS says that you'll still qualify for the safe harbor if you can show that, when you placed the property in service, you reasonably expected you'd have to perform the maintenance more than once in ten years. However, your actual maintenance experience with similar property will be considered in determining whether your expectation was reasonable.

The IRS provides an example of an owner of an office building who reasonably expected that it would have to do detailed testing, monitoring, and preventive maintenance on its HVAC system every four years. The owner does in fact have such maintenance performed four years after the system was placed in service, but does not have such maintenance done again until seven years later—11 years after the placed-in-service date. Even so, the owner may use the routine maintenance safe harbor.

No Betterments or Restorations

The routine maintenance safe harbor is intended for expenses property owners incur to keep their property in ordinarily efficient operating condition. Moreover, the maintenance must be attributable to the taxpayer's use of the property, not that of a previous owner. Thus, the safe harbor does not apply to scheduled maintenance performed shortly after purchasing a building.

In addition, this safe harbor is not supposed to be used to currently deduct major remodeling or restoration projects. It specifically does not apply to expenses for betterments or restorations of buildings or other business property in a state of disrepair. Thus, for example, you can't use the routine maintenance safe harbor to currently deduct the cost of a building remodel or replacing an entire roof. You also can't use the routine maintenance safe harbor for property on which you've taken a casualty loss or made a partial disposition election (see "Deducting Costs for Replacing Building Components" in Chapter 5 for a detailed discussion).

One example the IRS provides in its regulations is that of a cattle rancher who allows his irrigation system canals to fall into such a state of disrepair that they no longer function. The expenses the rancher incurs to drain the canals and do extensive cleaning, repairing, reconditioning, and replacement of parts do not fall within the safe harbor.

Counts Against Small Taxpayer Safe Harbor Limit

Any expense you deduct under the routine maintenance safe harbor is counted toward your annual limit under the small taxpayer safe harbor. For example, if your annual SHST limit is $5,000 and you deduct $4,000 for maintenance under the routine maintenance safe harbor, you'll only be able to deduct an additional $1,000 under the small taxpayer safe harbor.

No amount is deductible under the small taxpayer safe harbor if the annual limit is exceeded. Thus, for example, if your annual SHST limit is $5,000 and you deduct $6,000 under the routine maintenance safe harbor, you won't be entitled to any deduction under the small taxpayer safe harbor. But you can still use the routine maintenance safe harbor.

Applies to Personal Property

The routine maintenance safe harbor may be used for maintenance for personal property—that is, property other than buildings and building components. In this event, the safe harbor applies only if, when you placed the property into service, you reasonably expected to have to perform the maintenance more than once during the property's class life—that is, during the recovery period prescribed by the IRS under the MACRS Alternative Depreciation System (ADS). The ADS class lives for most types of property used by landlords are shown in the following chart:

Asset	ADS Class Life
Office furniture, fixtures, and equipment (includes furniture and fixtures that are not a structural component of a building—for example, refrigerators, stoves, countertops, carpets, kitchen cabinets)	10 years
Computers and peripherals	5 years
Automobiles	5 years
Construction equipment	6 years

Thus, for example, maintenance for a computer would come within the routine maintenance safe harbor only if the taxpayer reasonably expected to have to perform such maintenance at least twice during the first five years after the asset was placed into service.

> EXAMPLE: Landlord Bob purchases a sit-down lawnmower with a five-year class life. Unfortunately, the mower turns out to be a lemon. During the first five years he owns it, he has to have its engine replaced twice. This expense was not something he could have reasonably expected to incur when he brought the mower. Thus, the expense does not qualify as currently deductible under the routine maintenance safe harbor.

Adopting the Routine Maintenance Safe Harbor

Unlike the safe harbor for small taxpayers discussed above, the routine maintenance safe harbor is not elective—that is, it is not claimed each year by filing an optional election with your tax return. Rather, the routine maintenance safe harbor is a method of accounting you adopt. Moreover, after you adopt it, you must use it every year. You adopt the routine maintenance safe harbor by currently deducting expenses that come within it on your books and on your tax return. If you don't want to use this safe harbor, don't adopt it for 2015 or a future year. Its use is completely voluntary.

De Minimis Safe Harbor

The third safe harbor is the de minimis safe harbor (IRS Reg. § 1.263(a)-1(f)). Landlords may use this safe harbor to currently deduct any low-cost personal property items used in their rental business, regardless of whether or not the item would constitute a repair or an improvement under the regular repair regulations. For most landlords, the maximum amount that can be deducted under this safe harbor is $500 per item. Like the SHST, this safe harbor is claimed by filing an election with your annual tax return. You must also adopt an accounting policy requiring such treatment.

EXAMPLE: Landlord Bill owns a five-unit apartment building. During 2015, he purchases new electric stoves for each unit at a cost of $500 apiece. He may deduct the entire $2,500 cost using the de minimis safe harbor by filing an election with his 2015 tax return.

As with the routine maintenance safe harbor, all expenses you deduct using the de minimis safe harbor must be counted toward the annual limit for using the safe harbor for small taxpayers (the lesser of 2% of the rental's cost or $10,000). For example, if your annual SHST limit is $2,000, and you deduct $2,500 using the de minimis safe harbor, you may not use the SHST that year. But if you deducted only $1,000 using the de minimis safe harbor, you could deduct an additional $1,000 using the SHST.

See Chapter 5 for a detailed analysis of the de minimis safe harbor.

Repair Versus Improvement Analysis Under the Regulations

If you are unable to take advantage of any of the safe harbors described above, you must determine whether the expense involved is for an improvement or a repair. The cost of improvements must be depreciated over several years, while repair costs may be currently deducted in a single year. You must apply the new complex IRS repair regulations to make this determination. To do so, you must:

- determine the unit of property involved, and
- decide whether the expense involved resulted in an improvement or repair to such property.

Defining the "Unit of Property" (UOP)

You will need to determine what property is involved in order to decide if you have an improvement or repair. The IRS calls this the "unit of property" ("UOP"). How the UOP is defined is crucial. The larger the UOP, the more likely work done on a component will be considered a repair as opposed to an improvement. For example, if the UOP for an apartment building is defined as the entire building structure, you could claim that replacing the fire escapes in the building is a repair because it isn't that significant in scope or cost when compared to the whole building. On the other hand, if the UOP consists of the fire protection system alone, replacing fire escapes would likely be considered an improvement.

Until now, there have been no guidelines from either the IRS or courts as to what constitutes the UOP for a building. This was great for building owners who could claim that the entire building was the UOP. Thus, building owners could claim repair deductions for installing new roofs, replacing heating and air conditioning systems, and making major interior structural changes because these projects could be considered relatively minor when compared to the building and its structural components as a whole.

This is no longer possible. Under the new regulations, buildings must be divided up into as many as nine different UOPs, which makes it much harder to classify work as repair work.

UOP #1: The Building Structure

Under the new IRS regulations, the building structure is a single UOP. A building structure consists of a building and its structural components (other than those components designated as building systems listed below). (IRS Reg. § 1.263(a)-3(e)(2)(ii).) The structural components include a building's walls, partitions, floors, and ceilings, as well as any permanent coverings for them such as paneling or tiling; windows and doors; the roof, and other components relating to the operation or maintenance of the building.

Thus, if a landlord improves a rental building's structural component—for example, by replacing the entire roof—the expense is treated as an improvement to the single UOP consisting of the building. On the other hand, a repair to a structural component—such as replacing a few roof shingles—may be currently deducted.

If you own an apartment complex consisting of more than one separate building, each building must be its own UOP. (See "What Is an Improvement?" below for more on the difference between a repair and an improvement.)

UOPs #2–#9: Building Systems

The following eight building systems are also considered separate UOPs under the new IRS rules. The rules must be separately applied to each such system.

1. **Heating, ventilation, and air conditioning ("HVAC") systems.** This includes motors, compressors, boilers, furnaces, chillers, pipes, ducts, and radiators.

2. **Plumbing systems.** This includes pipes, drains, valves, sinks, bathtubs, toilets, water and sanitary sewer collection equipment, and site utility equipment used to distribute water and waste.

3. **Electrical systems.** This includes wiring, outlets, junction boxes, lighting fixtures and connectors, and site utility equipment used to distribute electricity.

4. **Escalators.**

5. **Elevators.**

6. **Fire-protection and alarm systems.** This includes sensing devices, computer controls, sprinkler heads, sprinkler mains, associated piping or plumbing, pumps, visual and audible alarms, alarm control panels, heat and smoke detectors, fire escapes, fire doors, emergency exit lighting and signage, and firefighting equipment, such as extinguishers and hoses.

7. **Security systems.** This includes window and door locks, security cameras, recorders, monitors, motion detectors, security lighting, alarm systems, entry and access systems, related junction boxes, associated wiring, and conduits.

8. **Gas distribution system.** This includes pipes and equipment used to distribute gas to and from the property line and between buildings.

Any work to any of the above building systems that improves that system must be depreciated under the new IRS rules.

EXAMPLE: Landlord Bob owns a four-unit apartment building. This year, he performs major work on the HVAC system to make it operate more efficiently and cheaply. Under the old rules, Bob could claim that the UOP was the entire building structure and that the HVAC work was a repair because it was relatively minor compared to the entire building. Under the new rules, the HVAC system is a separate UOP. This means that the HVAC work must be compared with the HVAC system alone, not the whole building. This makes the expense much more significant and likely to constitute an improvement.

Condominiums

If you own a condominium, the individual unit you own and the structural components are the UOP. Therefore, any improvements you make in your unit to any portion of the eight building systems defined above must be depreciated.

Improvements to Unit of Property

An improvement to a unit of property is not ordinarily considered a separate UOP. Instead, it becomes part of the UOP that is improved. For example, an addition to a building is not a separate UOP. The UOP remains the entire building, including the addition. This is so even though the improvement is separately depreciated starting in the year it is made. (IRS Reg. § 1.263(a)-3(e)(4).) However, as explained below, if the addition or improvement is not depreciated using the same depreciation period and method as the building, it is considered a separate unit of property.

UOP for Separately Depreciated Property Components

As covered in detail in Chapter 6, it is possible to separately depreciate building components that are not part of the building structure itself. These include personal property items such as appliances in rental buildings and land improvements such as parking lots and landscaping. This property is depreciated over a much shorter period than a building structure. When you do this, either at the time you put the property in service or later, each separately depreciated property component is treated as a separate unit of property for depreciation purposes. (IRS Reg. § 1.263(a)-3(e)(5)(ii).)

EXAMPLE: In Year One, the ABC LLC bought and placed in service an apartment building that included a paved parking lot. It depreciates the entire property as residential real property over 27.5 years. In Year Three, ABC completes a cost segregation study under which it properly determines that the parking lot qualifies as a land improvement that may be depreciated over 15 years. ABC changes its method of accounting to use a 15-year depreciation period and accelerated depreciation (the 150% declining balance method) for the parking lot. Beginning in Year Three, ABC must treat the parking lot as a UOP separate from the apartment building.

UOP for Personal Property

In the case of personal property—that is, property other than buildings—the unit of property consists of all components that are functionally interdependent. Personal property components are functionally interdependent if placing in service of one component is dependent on the placing in service of the other component. (IRS Reg. § 1.263(a)-3(e)(3)(i).)

EXAMPLE 1: Landlord Bob purchases a new refrigerator, stove, and dishwasher for his single-family residence rental. Each appliance is its own UOP because placing one into service does not depend on the other. For example, the stove can be placed into service regardless of whether the refrigerator and dishwasher are available for use in the home.

EXAMPLE 2: The refrigerator Bob purchased includes a cooling mechanism, light, and ice-cube maker. Each of these components are functionally interdependent on each other and thus make up the single UOP consisting of the refrigerator.

What Is an Improvement?

The new regulations define what constitutes an improvement to a unit of property. The rules don't break new ground, but they codify existing case law and IRS rulings in a systematic way. Under the regulations, a UOP is improved whenever it undergoes a **B**etterment, **A**daptation, or **R**estoration (or, B-A-R).

The regulations provide few concrete "bright line" tests for determining if something is an improvement. Rather, all the facts and circumstances must be considered, including the purpose and nature of the work performed and its effect on the UOP. Repairs usually cost less than improvements, but under the IRS regulations quite large expenditures can qualify as repairs. It all depends on the extent and nature of the change to the UOP involved.

Repair Versus Improvement Checklist

To determine whether an expense is a currently deductible repair or an improvement that must be depreciated over many years, you must ask the following three questions. If the answer to all three is "no," the expense is a repair. If the answer to any question is "yes," the expense is an improvement.

1. Does the expense add to the value of the UOP (betterment)?
   Yes _____ No _____
2. Does the expense adapt the UOP to a new or different use (adaptation)? Yes _____ No _____
3. Does the expense substantially prolong the useful life of the UOP (restoration)? Yes _____ No _____

If the need for the expense was caused by a particular event—for example, a storm—you must compare the UOP's condition immediately before the event to after the work is done to make your determination. On the other hand, if you're doing normal wear and tear work to a UOP, you must compare the item's condition after the last time normal wear and tear work was done (whether maintenance or an improvement) to its condition after the new work is done. If you've never had any wear and tear work done on the UOP, use its condition when placed in service as your point of comparison.

Maintenance Versus Repairs

Maintenance is not the same thing as repairs. Maintenance is undertaken to prevent something from breaking down. A repair is done after a breakdown has occurred. For example, the cost of oiling the circulator pump in a hot water heater is maintenance; the cost of fixing an unlubricated pump that has failed is a repair. There is no practical tax difference between maintenance and repairs—they are both currently deductible operating expenses. However, because IRS Schedule E requires that you separately list what you spent for each category, you must keep track of these expenditures separately.

CAUTION

Repairs made before property is placed in service are not deductible. You are allowed to deduct the cost of repairs to a rental building only if they are made after it is placed in service in your rental activity—that is, after you have offered it for rent to the public. The cost of repairs you make before a building is in service must be added to its tax basis (cost) and depreciated along with the rest of the building. (IRS Reg. § 1.263(a)-2(d)(1).)

For example, if you purchase a building and, before offering it for rent, you pay to repaint the interior or exterior, patch holes in the walls, or refinish the wood floors, you must add the cost to the basis of the building and depreciate it. However, if you incur these same expenses after the building is placed in service, you can currently deduct them.

The only exception to this rule is where the repairs qualify as start-up expenses for a brand-new rental business. This is a limited deduction of up to $5,000 you may take for getting a new rental business up and going. It normally doesn't apply if you already have an ongoing rental business and purchase a new building. (See Chapter 8 for a detailed discussion of business start-up expenses.)

Betterments

An expenditure is for a betterment if it:

- ameliorates a "material condition or defect" in the UOP that existed before it was acquired
- is for a "material addition" to the UOP—for example, physically enlarges, expands, or extends it, or adds a new component
- is for a material increase in the capacity of the UOP, such as additional cubic or linear space, or
- is reasonably expected to materially increase the productivity, efficiency, strength, or quality of the UOP or its output (the productivity and output factors don't usually apply to buildings). (IRS Reg. § 1.263(a)-3(j)(1).)

It's important to understand that only "material" changes to the UOP are betterments that must be depreciated. A material change is one that is significant or important. For example, adding a new bathroom to a rental home would be a material change to the UOP (the building structure). However, punching a hole in a kitchen wall to open up the space between the kitchen and dining room would likely not be viewed as material.

Moreover, there is no betterment if you replace part of a UOP with an improved, but comparable, part because the old part wasn't available. For example, the IRS says there would be no betterment if a building owner replaced the entire wood shingle roof of a building with comparable asphalt shingles because wood shingles were unavailable.

Fixing preexisting material conditions. Fixing a material defect or condition that existed before you acquired the UOP is a betterment. It makes no difference whether or not you were aware of the material defect before you purchased the property. Fixing conditions that occur after you acquire a UOP is not a betterment, but may be a restoration.

Betterment	Repair
Remediation of contaminated soil caused by leakage from underground gas storage tanks that were in place before landowner purchased the property (IRS Reg. § 1.263(a)-3(j)(3), Ex. 1.)	Replacing asbestos insulation in an old building that was constructed when dangers of asbestos were unknown and that began to deteriorate after building was purchased (IRS Reg. § 1.263(a)-3(j)(3), Ex. 2.)

Building refreshes. Work you periodically do to refresh a rental is not a betterment and need not be depreciated if the refresh consists of cosmetic and layout changes and general repairs and maintenance to keep the unit in ordinarily efficient condition. For example, the cost of painting an apartment or refinishing the floors after a tenant moves out need not be depreciated. However, any substantial remodeling you perform during a refresh must be depreciated. Also, any refresh you pay for before a building you purchase is available to rent must be depreciated (unless it constitutes a start-up expense incurred before your rental business began; see Chapter 8).

Betterment	Repair
Extensive building remodel including replacing large parts of exterior walls with windows, rebuilding interior and exterior facades, replacing vinyl floors with ceramic flooring, replacing ceiling tiles with acoustical tiles, and removing and rebuilding walls to move rooms (IRS Reg. § 1.263(a)-3(j)(3), Ex. 8.)	Cosmetic and layout changes to retail store building, including flooring repairs, moving one wall, patching holes in walls, repainting, replacing damaged ceiling tiles, cleaning and repairing wood flooring, and power washing building exterior (IRS Reg. § 1.263(a)-3(j)(3), Ex. 6.)

Material increases in capacity, efficiency, quality of UOP. The regulations provide no percentages as to what constitutes a material increase in capacity, efficiency, or quality of a UOP. However, various examples included in the regulations indicate that a 25% or less increase would likely be viewed as not material and therefore not a betterment.

Betterment	Repair
Reinforcing the columns and girders supporting a building's second floor to permit storage of supplies with a gross weight 50% greater than the previous load-carrying capacity of the storage area (IRS Reg. § 1.263(a)-3(j)(3), Ex. 14.)	Replacement of worn rubber roof membrane (top layer) with comparable new membrane after water seepage and leaks began—change merely restored roof to its condition when placed in service (IRS Reg. § 1.263(a)-3(j)(3), Ex. 13.)
Paying an insulation contractor to apply new insulation throughout a building, including the attic, walls, and crawl spaces, resulting in a 50% reduction in the building's annual energy and power costs (IRS Reg. § 1.263(a)-3(j)(3), Ex. 21.)	Replacing two of ten roof-mounted HVAC units that are many years old with new units that are 10% more efficient (IRS Reg. § 1.263(a)-3(j)(3), Ex. 20.)
Adding a stairway and mezzanine to a building to increase the structure's usable square footage (IRS Reg. § 1.263(a)-3(j)(3), Ex. 19.)	Removing a building interior's drop-ceiling to fully expose windows on building's first floor and repainting the original ceiling (IRS Reg. § 1.263(a)-3(j)(3), Ex. 18.)

Restorations

An expenditure is for a restoration if you:

- replace a major component or a substantial structural part of a UOP
- rebuild the UOP to like-new condition after it has fallen into disrepair
- replace a component of a UOP and deduct a loss for that component (other than a casualty loss)

- replace a component of a UOP and realize gain or loss by selling or exchanging the component
- restore damage to a UOP caused by a casualty event and make a basis adjustment to the UOP (see Chapter 13), or
- rebuild a UOP to like-new condition after the end of its IRS class life. (IRS Reg. § 1.263(a)-3(k).)

Replacing major component or structural part. Replacing a major component or a substantial structural part of a UOP is a restoration that must be depreciated. A major component is a part or combination of parts that perform a discrete and critical function in the UOP—for example, the furnaces contained in a building's HVAC system, the sprinklers in a building's fire protection system, or the wiring in a building's electrical system. A substantial structural part of a UOP is a combination of parts that comprise a large portion of the UOP's physical structure—for example, a building's roof, floors, windows, or walls.

The replacement of a *significant portion* of a major component of the building structure as a whole, or any of the eight building systems, is also a restoration (Reg. § 1.263(a)-3(k)(6)(ii)(A).) The IRS repair regulations provide no precise numerical guidelines as to how much is a "significant portion." However, numerous examples in the regulations indicate that replacing no more than 30% or so of a major component of a UOP is a deductible repair, while replacing more than this amount is usually a restoration.

Fixing UOPs in disrepair. Once you allow a unit of property to fall into disrepair—that is, it no longer performs its intended function—amounts you spend to get it working again are improvements.

> EXAMPLE: A taxpayer allows a building he uses for storage to fall into disrepair—that is, it could no longer be used because it was structurally unsound. He pays a contractor to shore up the walls and replace the siding. This expense constitutes a restoration that must be depreciated. (IRS Reg. § 1.263(a)-3(k)(7), Ex. 6.)

A disrepair restoration must be depreciated even if the expense would have qualified for the routine maintenance safe harbor if the UOP was not in a state of disrepair. The routine maintenance safe harbor cannot be used for UOPs in a state of disrepair.

Restoration	Repair
Replacing 200 of 300 exterior building windows (IRS Reg. § 1.263(a)-3(k)(7), Ex. 26.)	Replacing 100 of 300 windows (IRS Reg. § 1.263(a)-3(k)(7), Ex. 25.)
Replacing entire leaking roof that caused structural damage to building (IRS Reg. § 1.263(a)-3(k)(7), Ex. 14.)	Replacing only the waterproof membrane portion of roof to solve leakage problem—membrane not a significant portion the roof (IRS Reg. § 1.263(a)-3(k)(7), Ex. 15.)
Replacing the sole chiller unit in a building's HVAC system (IRS Reg. § 1.263(a)-3(k)(7), Ex. 17.)	Replacing one of three furnaces in a building's HVAC system (IRS Reg. § 1.263(a)-3(k)(7), Ex. 16.)
Replacing old wood flooring with new wood flooring in all of a building's public areas, amounting to 40% of building's square footage (IRS Reg. § 1.263(a)-3(k)(7), Ex. 29.)	Replacing wood flooring only in building lobby, amounting to less than 10% of building's square footage (IRS Reg. § 1.263(a)-3(k)(7), Ex. 28.)
Replacing all wiring in building's electrical system (IRS Reg. § 1.263(a)-3(k)(7), Ex. 20.)	Replacing 30% of wiring in building's electrical system (IRS Reg. § 1.263(a)-3(k)(7), Ex. 21.)
Replacing plumbing fixtures in all of building's restrooms, including all the toilets and sinks (IRS Reg. § 1.263(a)-3(k)(7), Ex. 22.)	Replacing eight of the total of 20 sinks located in the a building's restrooms (IRS Reg. § 1.263(a)-3(k)(7), Ex. 23.)

Rebuild to like-new condition after class life ends. The IRS has established class lives for all types of business assets. For example, the class life for residential rental property is 40 years, while the class life for furniture and fixtures that are not a structural component of a building—such as refrigerators, stoves, countertops, carpets, kitchen cabinets—is ten years. If you rebuild an asset to like-new condition after its class life ends, you must treat the cost as a restoration and depreciate it. You can find a list of the class lives for all kinds of assets in IRS Publication 946, *How to Depreciate Property* (look for the ADS depreciation chart in Appendix B).

Replace component for which loss taken. The IRS has issued proposed regulations that permit a building owner to elect to recognize a loss when a building structural component such as a roof is replaced, or not make the election and continue to depreciate the replaced component (see Chapter 5). If you elect to take a loss on a replaced component, you must treat the cost of the new component as a restoration and depreciate it.

> EXAMPLE: The owner of a building containing four elevators replaces one of the elevators. If the owner doesn't elect to recognize a loss on the retirement of the old elevator, he may treat the cost of the new elevator as a repair. But, if he does recognize a loss on the old elevator, he must depreciate the new one. (IRS Reg. § 1.263(a)-3(k)(7), Exs. 30, 31.)

Adaptations

You must also depreciate amounts you spend to adapt a UOP to a new or different use. A use is "new or different" if it is not consistent with your "intended ordinary use" of the UOP when you originally placed it into service. (IRS Reg. § 1.263(a)-3(l).) Adaptations aren't terribly common in the context of residential rentals. Examples would include converting an office or factory building to an apartment building, or converting a regular rental building to a bed and breakfast.

Other Issues Under the Repair Regulations

Additional significant issues arising under the regulations include the following.

Repairs Combined With Improvements

Repairs and maintenance are often conducted at the same time as improvements. The IRS repair regulations provide that a taxpayer must depreciate all the direct costs of an improvement, and all the indirect costs that directly benefit from, or are incurred due to, an improvement. Repairs and maintenance are never included within the direct costs of an improvement. But they will constitute indirect costs that must be depreciated if they directly benefit from, or were incurred because of, an improvement. To put it another way, expenses for repairs made at the same time as an improvement to a UOP do not have to be depreciated if (1) they do not directly benefit from the improvement, and (2) they were not incurred because of it. (IRS Reg. § 1.263(a)-3(g)(1)(i).)

> EXAMPLE: The owner of a hotel building pays to replace all the bathtubs, toilets, and sinks in the guest rooms. This expense constituted an improvement—the restoration of a major component of the building's plumbing system. Installation of these new plumbing system components also made it necessary to repair, repaint, and retile the bathroom walls and floors in the guest rooms. The building owner must treat these costs as improvements because they directly benefited from, and were incurred by reason of, the improvement to the building. (IRS Reg. § 1.263(a)-3(k)(7), Ex. 24.)

> EXAMPLE: The owner of a tractor replaces the engine—an improvement that must be depreciated. At the same time, he has a broken taillight repaired. The amount paid to repair the broken taillight is a deductible repair, even though it was incurred at the same time as the engine improvement. The taillight repair did not directly benefit from, nor was it incurred because of, the replacement of the engine. (IRS Reg. § 1.263(a)-3(k)(7), Ex. 11.)

Plan of Rehabilitation Doctrine Eliminated

The new regulations eliminate the plan of rehabilitation doctrine. This was a judge-created rule that often trapped building owners into treating repairs as improvements. Under this rule, repairs that were part of an overall plan of rehabilitation or modernization to property had to be depreciated as improvements—even though the work, standing alone, would be currently deductible. As a result, you had to depreciate any routine repair work that was performed at the same time as other major improvements. Under the new regulations, it makes no difference if repairs are made as part of an overall plan of improvement.

To be on the safe side, if you hire a contractor or repairperson to perform both improvements and repairs on a building, ask to be billed separately for each category of work. That is, have the contractor submit one (or more) invoices for the improvements and another for the repairs. If both kinds of work are covered in a single bill, you must separate the charges for repairs from those for improvements and deduct them accordingly.

> EXAMPLE: Jessica owns a two-unit rental. She hires a plumber to install a new bathtub and toilet in one unit and to fix a leak in the plumbing of another unit. The cost of the tub and toilet replacement is an improvement, whereas fixing the leak is a repair. She should have the contractor submit separate invoices for each.

Removal Costs

The basic rule is that the cost of removing a unit of property or a component of a UOP must be depreciated if done as part of an improvement, but may be currently deducted if done as part of a repair.

> EXAMPLE 1: The owner of a building with a leaky roof pays to have the roof shingles replaced with comparable new shingles. The expense is a repair, not an improvement. Thus, the cost of removing the old shingles may be currently deducted as part of the repair. (IRS Reg. § 1.263(a)-3(g)(2)(ii), Ex 3.)

> EXAMPLE 2: A building owner pays to have the original columns and girders on the building's first floor removed and replaced with new substantially stronger girders and columns. The expense is a building improvement. Thus, the cost of removing the girders and columns must be depreciated. (IRS Reg. § 1.263(a)-3(g)(2)(ii), Ex 1.)

However, the IRS regulations give property owners the option of deducting the adjusted basis of building components that are replaced and disposed of. In this event, the removal costs need not be depreciated, even if they were removed as part of an improvement. But the cost of the new components must be depreciated. (See Chapter 5 for a detailed discussion.)

> EXAMPLE: A building owner replaces and disposes of the building's old roof shingles. The owner elects to treat the disposal of these components as a partial disposition of the building and deducts their adjusted basis as a loss. The removal costs need not be depreciated. But, because a loss was taken on the old shingles, the cost of the new shingles must be depreciated as an improvement. (IRS Reg. § 1.263(a)-3(g)(2)(ii), Ex 4.)

Note that the cost of demolishing a building must always be depreciated. (IRC § 280B.) For a building other than a certified historic structure, a modification of a building is not a demolition if: (1) 75% or more of the existing external walls of the building are retained in place as internal or external walls, and (2) 75% or more of the existing internal structural framework of the building is retained in place. (Rev. Rul. 95-27, 1995-1 CB 704.)

Work Done to Comply With Government Regulations

As far as the IRS is concerned, the fact that you made changes to a rental property to comply with government regulations, such as bringing the building up to building health codes, is irrelevant. The normal repair rules apply.

> EXAMPLE: To comply with new building code earthquake standards, a building owner pays for the installation of new expansion bolts to anchor the building's wooden frame to its cement foundation. This expense was an improvement because it materially increased the building's strength. The fact the change was made to comply with the building code is irrelevant. (IRS Reg. § 1.263(a)-3(j)(3), Ex. 11.)

Two Tax Breaks Unaffected by New Regulations

There are two special tax breaks that permit building owners to take special deductions for changes to make a building more accessible to the disabled or that increase its energy efficiency. These are not affected by the new IRS regulations. For a detailed discussion, see "Tax Break for Accessibility Changes" and "Energy Efficient Deduction" in Chapter 14.

How New IRS Regulations Affect Prior Years

The IRS repair regulations took effect on January 1, 2014. Starting on that date, you had to apply the new regulations to all improvements and repairs you made to long-term property used in your rental activity. If your rental activity began during 2014 or later, that's the end of the story and you need not read the rest of this section.

For others who owned rental real estate before 2014, it was more complicated. Initially, the IRS required all landlords to apply the repair regulations retroactively—that is, to years before 2014. This involved reviewing depreciation, repair, and improvements records for 2013 and earlier years to see whether depreciation practices followed in prior years jibed with the new regulations. If not, landlords had to depreciate amounts previously deducted and recognize taxable income based on the difference in treatment. On other hand, they may have also been able to currently deduct some amounts previously depreciated and take an immediate deduction for the difference. All landlords were supposed to file IRS Form 3115, *Application for Change in Accounting Method*, along with schedules supporting any adjustments no later than the due date for their 2014 tax return (plus extensions).

However, in response to widespread complaints about the expense and difficulties involved in filing IRS Form 3115 and applying the IRS repair regulations to years before 2014, the IRS issued new regulations in mid-February 2014 (Revenue Procedure 2015-20). These new regulations provided smaller landlords with optional relief from the requirement that they apply the IRS repair regulations retroactively to years before 2014. This relief was available for all landlords with (1) assets under $10 million (as of the first day of the tax year) or (2) less than $10 million in annual gross receipts for each distinct business they own. Obviously, the vast majority of landlords qualified to use Revenue Procedure 2015-20.

To choose this option, landlords simply had to file their 2014 returns as normal and begin applying the repair regulations as of January 1, 2014. They did not need to go back to years before 2014 and make any changes in how they classified expenses as repairs or improvements or make any changes in their depreciation deductions. And they did not have to file the complex Form 3115, *Application for Change in Accounting Method*. There was no requirement that landlords include any statement in their returns that they were adopting Revenue Procedure 2015-20. Thus, if you filed your 2014 return without Form 3115, you may have adopted this option without even being aware of it.

Large landlords with assets or receipts over $10 million who are not eligible for the relief provided by Revenue Procedure 2015-20 had to apply the repair regulations retroactively and file IRS Form 3115, *Application for Change in Accounting Method*, with their 2014 tax returns. For calendar year taxpayers, these were due by October 15, 2015 for individuals and single-member LLCs, and September 15, 2015 for multi-member LLCs, partnerships, and corporations. If you were required to file this form with your 2014 tax return and failed to so, you should consult a tax professional.

For more details on this complex topic, visit the IRS Tangible Property Regulations—Frequently Asked Questions Web page at www.irs.gov/Businesses/Small-Businesses-&-Self-Employed/Tangible-Property-Final-Regulations#Whenandhowdoyouchange.

Downside to Using New Revenue Procedure 2015-20

The relief provided by Revenue Procedure 2015-20 saved smaller landlords the time and money involved in retroactively applying the repair regulations and filing Form 3115 with their 2014 returns. However, it had a downside as well. Smaller landlords were often conservative about classifying past building expenses as improvements instead of repairs before 2014. Thus, many likely had pre-2014 expenses that they had been mistakenly depreciating for many years. Applying the regulations retroactively would have enabled them to take an immediate deduction in 2014 for these items. This could have resulted in a substantial tax savings in 2014, even a tax refund. The value of such favorable adjustments on past years' taxes could have far outweighed the time and expense involved in examining old depreciation schedules and completing Form 3115.

Downside to Using New Revenue Procedure 2015-20 (continued)

Also, one of the most significant changes brought about by the new repair regulations was a new rule allowing building owners to take an immediate loss when a building structural component such as a roof or HVAC system was replaced. This was done by making a partial disposition election on the tax return and then deducting the adjusted basis (cost minus depreciation taken) of the component. Such losses have never been allowed before. Applying the repair regulations retroactively gave landlords the option of making partial disposition elections for building components replaced in years before 2014. This could have resulted in a substantial tax deduction. Unfortunately, if you didn't file Form 3115 with your 2014 return, you lost forever the ability to make such partial disposition election for years before 2014.

How to Deduct Repairs and Maintenance

Repairs and maintenance expenses are operating expenses that you deduct on IRS Schedule E (see Chapter 18). The schedule helpfully includes separate lines for each type of expense.

You need to keep track of what you spend on repairs and maintenance throughout the year and list the total in Schedule E when you do your taxes for the year. The cost includes what you spend on materials, parts, and labor. If you do the work yourself, you don't get a deduction for the value of your own labor.

EXAMPLE: One of Kim's tenants complains that the fan in his bathroom is making a funny noise. Kim hires Andy, a handyman, to repair the fan. Andy finds that the fan just needs to be cleaned. He does so, and charges Kim $50, which she pays. Kim may add the $50 to the expenses she lists in her Schedule E for the year.

If instead of hiring Andy, Kim cleans the fan herself, the value of her labor does not count as a deductible maintenance. Kim spent nothing for materials or parts, so she gets no deduction for repairing the fan herself.

Making Tenants Pay for Repairs

It's common for landlords to require their tenants to pay for repairs when they cause damage. Typically, this is done after the tenant moves out, and the landlord deducts the cost of the repair from the tenant's security deposit. Landlords may charge tenants for any repairs necessary to restore a rental unit to its condition at the beginning of the tenancy. This includes the cost of repairing damage to rental property caused by tenants and restoring property that has been subjected to unreasonable wear and tear. Landlords may not, however, use the tenant's security deposit to cover the costs of ordinary wear and tear.

Moreover, you may not use a tenant's deposit to repair damage the tenant did not cause—for example, you can't deduct the cost of repairing a broken window caused by a windstorm. Nor may you use a deposit to pay for improvements to a rental unit—for example, replacing a wooden kitchen counter with a granite counter.

A security deposit does not constitute taxable income for a landlord. But, where a landlord keeps all or part of a security deposit because the tenant has caused damage to the rental unit, that amount is taxable income. When the landlord fixes the damage, the amount spent on the repair is a deductible expense that will offset the landlord's additional income.

> EXAMPLE: Ed owns a three-unit apartment building. After one of his tenants moves out, he discovers a broken window in the unit. He hires a repairman to fix the window at a cost of $100 and deducts the amount from the tenant's $1,000 security deposit. He refunds the remaining $900 to the tenant. The $100 Ed kept is rental income he must report on his Schedule E for the year. But the $100 he spent to fix the window is an expense he can deduct that year. This offsets the $100 he kept, so he ends up paying no tax on the amount.

If you deduct money from a tenant's deposit for damage and don't fix it, you'll have no expense deduction to offset the increased rental income. Of course, no decent landlord would do this. This is one case where the tax law encourages landlords to act honestly.

Ordinary Wear and Tear: Landlord's Responsibility	Damage or Excessive Filth: Tenant's Responsibility
Curtains faded by the sun	Cigarette burns in curtains or carpets
Water-stained linoleum by shower	Broken tiles in bathroom
Dents in the wall where a door handle bumped it	Door off its hinges
A few small tack or nail holes in wall	Lots of picture holes or gouges in walls that require patching as well as repainting
Worn gaskets on refrigerator doors	Broken refrigerator shelf
Faded paint on bedroom wall	Water damage on wall from hanging plants
Toilet flushes inadequately because mineral deposits have clogged the jets	Toilet won't flush properly because it's stopped up with a diaper

Repairs Paid for or Performed by Tenants

What happens if a tenant pays for a repair? For example, your tenant hires a handyman to fix a broken bathroom fan and pays him $50. If you reimburse the tenant or allow him to deduct the amount from the next month's rent, the repair is treated like any other repair for tax purposes: You get to currently deduct the full amount.

However, if a tenant takes it upon him- or herself to pay for a repair without your prior knowledge and consent, you have no legal obligation to reimburse him or her. The same goes for improvements the tenant pays for without your approval. If you don't reimburse the tenant, you'll get no tax deduction, but you'll get a free repair or improvement. You'll also own the repaired item or improvement. This is the result of an age-old doctrine of property law called the law of fixtures: Whatever a tenant attaches to a landlord's property, as an alteration or an improvement, becomes the landlord's property unless there is an agreement to the contrary. You need not pay any tax on the value of a repair or improvement the tenant makes without your approval.

The rules are exactly the same if a tenant performs a repair, instead of hiring someone else to do it. You can deduct the amount of any reimbursement you give the tenant, whether in cash or a rent reduction. But you have no legal obligation to pay for any repairs a tenant performs without your prior approval.

Tips for Maximizing Your Repair Deductions

Here are some simple tips that will help you maximize your repair deductions.

Patch, Mend, and Make Do—Don't Replace

There is no law that says that if something in your rental property is broken it has to be replaced. A replacement is almost always an improvement—not a repair—for tax deduction purposes. You'll obtain the best tax results if you patch, mend, or fix things that are broken, instead of replacing them. For example:

- if the roof is leaking or damaged, repair or replace only the damaged shingles; don't replace the whole roof
- if a tenant damages the carpet in the bedroom of a two-bedroom apartment, replace the carpet in the bedroom only, not the carpet in the entire apartment, and
- if the dryer in your laundry room stops working, have a repairperson fix it; don't buy a new dryer.

You'll be able to deduct the entire cost of such repairs in a single year, rather than depreciating them over many years. Moreover, repairs are usually much cheaper than replacements.

Of course, sometimes an item is so old or worn out, it makes more economic sense to replace it than repair it. Tenants like shiny new things and sometimes it pays to keep your tenants happy. Also, you should factor into the repair-or-replace equation the fact that you may be able to charge more rent for a unit with new appliances, carpets, or other things than one with old mended appliances or other amenities.

Also, if you qualify for the safe harbor for small taxpayers discussed above, you can make any improvements you want during the year and still deduct them in a single year—but the total cost of all your improvements, repairs, and maintenance must not exceed the limit for the safe harbor.

> CAUTION
>
> **Be careful with upgrades—they are improvements.** When you fix something that is broken you should use the same quality materials and parts it contained originally. Your goal is to restore the item to the condition it was in before it stopped working, not to make it better. Upgrades are usually improvements, not repairs. In one case, a landlord who replaced wooden roof shingles with better composition shingles was found to have made an improvement.

Properly Document Repairs

Good documentation is the key to winning any argument with the IRS. Here are some tips for properly documenting your repairs:

- Repairs to rental property usually happen after a tenant complains. Document the complaint by writing a note—this can be on your calendar, appointment book, or on an invoice a repairperson gives you. This will help show that something was broken and you had it fixed—which is what a repair is. (For a sample written request for repair form, see *Every Landlord's Legal Guide*, by Marcia Stewart, Ralph Warner, and Janet Portman (Nolo).)
- Get an invoice for every repair. Make sure it describes the work in a way that is consistent with a repair, not an improvement. Good words to use include repair, fix, patch, mend, redo, recondition, and restore. An invoice should not include any words that indicate

an improvement—for example: improvement, replacement, remodel, renovation, addition, construction, rehab, upgrade, or new. Of course, your invoice will not, by itself, establish whether something is a repair or an improvement—the facts must be consistent with what the invoice says.

- Make sure your repairs are classified as such in all your books and accounting records. This problem can easily crop up if you have a bookkeeper or accountant do your books—they may list a repair as a capital improvement. If an IRS auditor sees this, it will be curtains for your repair deduction.

- If you're doing an extensive repair, take before-and-after photographs to show the extent of the work and that the property has not been made substantially more valuable.

Do Preventive Maintenance

Maintenance means taking steps to prevent your property from breaking down or deteriorating. Preventive maintenance costs are always currently deductible operating expenses. A great way to avoid the repair versus improvement hassle—and to keep your tenants happy—is to keep your rental property well maintained. This will prevent it from breaking or wearing out quickly, thereby avoiding the need for replacements. Examples of preventive maintenance include periodically changing the filters on your heating and air conditioning system, and installing zinc control strips on a wood shake or shingle roof to keep fungus and algae away. Such maintenance may qualify for the routine maintenance safe harbor discussed above. But, even if it doesn't, it will usually be currently deductible.

Delay Big Repair Expenses

Under the new IRS regulations, expenses that would normally be considered currently deductible repairs must be depreciated along with the rest of the building if they are incurred before the building is placed in service—that is, before it is offered for rent to the public (except in cases where the repairs qualify as start-up expenses for a new rental business; see Chapter 8).

For this reason, you'll get larger repair deductions if you spend as little money as possible refreshing a building immediately after you buy it. Instead, do as much of this work as possible after the building is offered for rent. Of course, you should do whatever work is necessary to make the property rentable and habitable.

Depreciation Basics

Depreciation: The Landlord's Best Tax Break 117

Understanding the Basics 119

What Property Can Be Depreciated? 119

How Depreciation Works 122

Taking Separate Deductions 124

How to Depreciate Buildings 126

What Is a Building? 126

When a Building Is Placed in Service 126

Determining a Building's Basis 127

The Depreciation Period 134

How Much You Depreciate Each Year 135

Depreciating Additions and Improvements 137

Depreciating Land Improvements 142

Changes to Land 142

Structures Other Than Buildings 143

Depreciation Methods 143

Deducting Personal Property 144

What Is Personal Property? 145

How to Deduct or Depreciate Personal Property 147

De Minimis Safe Harbor 148

Materials and Supplies Deduction 153

Bonus Depreciation 155

Regular Depreciation 158

When Is Personal Property Placed in Service? 159

Determining the Basis of Personal Property 159

Depreciation Period 161

First-Year Depreciation 162

Depreciation Methods 164

Listed Property 166

Section 179 Expensing 168

When You Sell Your Property 171

Adjusted Basis 172

Effect of Adjusted Basis When You Sell 173

Like-Kind Exchanges: Deferring Taxes on Rental Property 175

The Home Sale Exclusion—
Avoiding Taxes When You Sell Your Rental 178

Tax Reporting and Record Keeping for Depreciation 180

O f all the chapters in this book, this one should give you the most pleasure to read. Admittedly, depreciation is a rather dry, technical subject. But depreciation means money in a landlord's pocket. So, whenever you hear the word "depreciation," think "money."

This chapter covers the basics of depreciation. It shows you why depreciation is such a great deal for landlords, and how to calculate and take the deduction. It also explains Section 179 expensing, an alternative to depreciation that landlords can use for certain personal property.

Depreciation: The Landlord's Best Tax Break

The largest expense landlords have is the purchase price for the rental property they own. However, unlike the interest you pay on a loan to buy the property or other operating expenses related to the property, you can't deduct the cost of the rental property in the year in which you pay for it. Because real estate lasts for more than one year, you must deduct its cost over a much longer time period through a process called depreciation.

The basic idea behind depreciation is simple: Real estate and other long-term property may last longer than a year, but not forever. Little by little, year by year, buildings and other types of long-term property wear out, decay, become unusable or obsolete, or get used up. The annual decline in the value of such property is a cost of doing business or engaging in an investment activity. Depreciation is an annual tax deduction that business owners and investors take to reflect this annual cost.

The reason depreciation is such a valuable deduction for landlords is that you get it year after year (27.5 years for residential real property) without having to pay anything beyond your original investment in the property. Moreover, rental real property owners are entitled to depreciation even if their property goes up in value over time (as it usually does).

> EXAMPLE: George buys a rental condominium with a depreciable value of $100,000. He is entitled to an annual depreciation deduction of $3,636 for the next 27.5 years (excluding the first and last years, which will be somewhat less). All George has to do to obtain these annual deductions

is continue to own the condo as a rental property, file a tax return every year, and do some simple bookkeeping. He need not spend an additional penny on his property. And he is entitled to depreciation even though his condominium increases in value every year. What a deal!

It's true that if you sell your property you'll likely have to pay a 25% tax on the total amount of depreciation deductions you took over the years. (See "Effect of Adjusted Basis When You Sell," below.) However, in the meantime your annual taxes have been lowered by these annual deductions. In effect, depreciation allows you to defer payment of tax on your rental income from the years in which it was earned to the year it is sold. And, there will be an additional tax savings if your regular income tax rate when you sell is more than the 25% rate you'll have to pay on your depreciation deductions. Moreover, if you never sell the property you'll never have to pay the 25% tax—this is one reason many veteran landlords hold onto their property for years and years.

Depreciation is a complicated subject. The IRS publication describing it is over 100 pages long (IRS Publication 946, *How to Depreciate Property*). Many landlords simply have their accountants handle their depreciation and never bother to learn much about it. However, it's worth your time and trouble to understand it in some detail. This will enable you to:

- make sure your accountant determines your depreciation deductions properly—depreciation is not as cut and dried as you might think, and the way your accountant figures your depreciation may not be the best way
- figure your depreciation deduction yourself if you choose to prepare your own tax returns, and
- make better-informed decisions on whether to invest in a particular rental property, since you fully understand the tax benefits you can obtain.

Depreciation is one of the largest deductions a landlord has. It can be the difference between earning an annual profit or losing money each year on a rental property. That's why it's so important that you understand it and take full advantage of it.

CAUTION

Depreciation is not optional. Unlike all the other tax deductions discussed in this book, depreciation is not optional. You *must* take a depreciation deduction if you qualify for it. If you fail to take it, the IRS will treat you as if you had taken it. This means that when you sell your property, its basis (value for tax purposes) will be reduced by the amount of depreciation you failed to claim. As a result, you'll have a larger profit from the sale that you'll have to pay taxes on.

If you have unclaimed depreciation, you should act to claim it this year. To claim such depreciation, you must make what is known as an I.R.C. § 481(a) adjustment. You can deduct the entire amount in a single year by filing IRS Form 3115 to request a change in accounting method. This type of change ordinarily is granted automatically by the IRS (see Rev. Proc. 2004-11) and you don't need to file any amended tax returns. Unfortunately, IRS Form 3115 is an extremely complex form. You'll likely need help from a tax professional to complete it properly.

Understanding the Basics

The fundamentals of depreciation are not difficult to grasp. Gaining familiarity with these basic concepts will help you understand the later sections in this chapter that describe in detail how to depreciate real and personal property.

What Property Can Be Depreciated?

You may depreciate property that:
- lasts for more than one year
- wears out or gets used up over time
- you own for more than one year, and
- you use in your rental activity (or some other business or income-producing activity). (I.R.C. § 167.)

Let's look at these requirements in some detail.

Long-Term Property

You can depreciate only property that lasts longer than one year—for example, buildings, tangible personal property like stoves and refrigerators, office or construction equipment, cars, and other vehicles. In tax parlance, such long-term property is called a capital asset because it is part of your capital investment in your rental business or investment activity.

Inventory—property a business holds for sale to others—is not a capital asset and may not be depreciated. Instead, this cost is deducted as it is sold. Inventory includes real property held for sale by real estate dealers. Thus, real estate dealers may not take depreciation deductions for the property they buy and sell—one reason why you should avoid being classed as a dealer whenever possible. (See Chapter 2.)

Items you buy that are for, or related to, your rental activity that are not long-term property (such as the food you eat when traveling for your rental activity, fertilizer you use for your rental property landscaping, and chlorine you buy to clean an apartment complex swimming pool) can usually be fully deducted in the year in which you purchase them as operating expenses. (See Chapter 3.)

Property That Wears Out or Gets Used Up

You can depreciate only property that wears out, decays, gets used up, or becomes obsolete over time. Thus, for example, you can't depreciate stocks, bonds, or other securities. These assets never wear out. And you can't depreciate collectibles that appreciate in value over time—for example, antiques, coins, or artwork.

Land—that is, the ground a building rests on and the surrounding area—cannot be depreciated because, for all practical purposes, it lasts forever. (If the land you own permanently disappears due to flooding, earthquake, or some other catastrophe, you'll have a deductible casualty loss; see Chapter 13.) When you determine your depreciation deduction for a rental building or other structure, you cannot include the value of the land it rests on in its value for tax purposes. Only the cost of the building itself can be depreciated.

Unlike land, buildings and structures on land don't last forever and, therefore, can be depreciated. Indeed, all or most of your depreciation deduction will come from the value of your rental buildings. You can depreciate any type of structure you use for your rental activity—apartment buildings, houses, duplexes, condominiums, mobile homes, swimming pools, parking lots, parking garages, tennis courts, clubhouses, and other facilities for your tenants. You can also depreciate structures that you own and use for your rental activity even though they are not used by your tenants—for example, a building you use as your rental office, or a storage shed where you keep maintenance equipment. The cost of landscaping for rental property can also be depreciated.

You can also depreciate tangible *personal* property that lasts for more than one year. This includes property inside a rental unit, such as stoves, refrigerators, furniture, and carpets. Other personal property that you use in connection with your rental activity can also be depreciated, even if it is not located on your rental property—for example, a computer, cell phone, lawn mower, or automobile you use to conduct your rental activity.

You get no annual tax deductions for capital assets that can't be depreciated. This is one reason why depreciable assets like rental properties are better investments, taxwise, than nondepreciable assets like stocks, antiques, or art.

Property You Own for More Than One Year

You can only depreciate property that you own. You can't depreciate property that you lease for your rental activity (such as office space). In addition, you must own the property for at least one year to depreciate it. You get no depreciation for property you buy and sell, or otherwise dispose of, in the same year.

It makes no difference if you own the property free and clear or if you borrow money to buy it. If you hold title to the property, you get the depreciation—even if you have little or no equity in the property. The amount of your depreciation is determined by the cost of the property; how much you borrowed to purchase it is irrelevant.

Property You Use in Your Rental Activity

You may only depreciate property that you use in your rental business or investment activity (or some other business or investment activity you conduct). You may not depreciate property you use solely for personal purposes. This means you get no depreciation for your personal residence. If you convert a rental property to personal use, you must stop taking the depreciation for the property.

If you use property for both rental and personal uses, you may depreciate only a part of its value, based on the percentage of the property used for rental purposes.

> **EXAMPLE:** Jennifer owns a duplex. She lives in one unit and rents the other. Because she uses 50% of the duplex for rental purposes, she may depreciate only 50% of its value.

How Depreciation Works

At its core, depreciation is simple: You figure out how much the property is worth for tax purposes (the property's basis), how long the IRS says you must depreciate it for (its recovery period), and then you deduct a certain percentage of its basis each year during its recovery period. The devil is in the details:

- When does depreciation begin (and end)? This depends on when rental property is placed in service.
- How do you determine how much your property is worth for depreciation purposes? You'll have to understand the concept of basis and how to calculate it.
- How long do you have to depreciate your property? The answer lies in knowing which recovery period applies.
- How much of your property's value do you get to deduct each year? This depends on which depreciation method you use and which depreciation convention applies.

All of these topics are explained below.

When Depreciation Begins and Ends

You don't necessarily begin to depreciate property when you buy it. Rather, depreciation begins when property is "placed in service." Property is considered placed in service in a rental activity when it is ready and available to rent. This can occur at the same time that you buy the property, or later (see "How to Depreciate Buildings," below).

You stop depreciating property either when you have fully recovered its value or when you retire it from service, whichever occurs first.

Property is retired from service when you stop using it for your rental activity, sell it, destroy it, or otherwise dispose of it.

> EXAMPLE: Wilma purchased a rental house that she placed in service by advertising it as available for rent in January of 2002. She rented the property to various tenants over the next 13 years. She sold it on April 15, 2015. She gets no more depreciation as of the date of the sale—April 15, 2015. Had she not sold the property, she would have continued to depreciate the property over its 27.5-year depreciation period.

Determining Your Property's Basis

Depreciation allows you to deduct your total investment in a long-term asset that you buy for your rental activity. You take this deduction over the property's depreciation period, as determined by the IRS. In tax lingo, your investment is called your basis or tax basis. Basis is a word you'll hear over and over again when the subject of depreciation comes up. Don't let it confuse you; it just means the amount of your total investment in the property for tax purposes.

Usually, your basis is the cost of the property, plus expenses of the sale such as real estate transfer taxes and other fees. Land cannot be depreciated, so it must be deducted from the cost of real property to determine its basis for depreciation.

> EXAMPLE: Jean buys a rental house that cost $100,000, not including the value of the land. The $100,000 cost is her basis in the property. She uses this amount to determine her annual depreciation deduction.

Your Recovery Period

The depreciation period (also called the recovery period) is the time over which you must take your depreciation deductions for an asset. The tax code has assigned depreciation periods to all types of business assets. These periods are somewhat arbitrary. However, property that can be expected to last a long time generally has a longer recovery period than property that has a short life. Thus, software has a three-year period, while the period for commercial real property is 39 years.

Real property placed into service after 1986 is depreciated under the Modified Accelerated Cost Recovery System (MACRS). Under this system, the depreciation period for residential real property placed in service after 1986 is 27.5 years. Prior to 1987, different depreciation methods with different depreciation periods were in effect.

The periods are the same whether the property being depreciated is old or new. When you buy property, you start a new depreciation period beginning with year one, even if the prior owner previously depreciated the property for several years or fully depreciated it. If you buy an old building that has changed hands many times over the years, it may have been fully depreciated several times. This makes no difference to you— your depreciation period starts when you purchase the property and lasts for 27.5 years.

Calculating Your Deduction Amount

Your depreciation deduction is a set percentage of the basis of your property each year. The amount of the percentage depends on the depreciation method you use. All real property must be depreciated using the straight-line method. Under this method, you deduct an equal amount each year over the depreciation period (see "How to Depreciate Buildings," below, for more on how to calculate your depreciation deduction). Personal property can be deducted using accelerated depreciation, which provides larger depreciation deductions in the early years than the straight-line method (see "Deducting Personal Property," below, for more on depreciating personal property).

The amount of your first-year deduction is prorated depending upon which month you place your property into service. Special depreciation rules called conventions govern how much you can depreciate the first year.

Taking Separate Deductions

Typically, landlords don't have a single depreciation deduction. Instead, they have many separate depreciation deductions over time.

Rental Property Placed in Service

When a rental property is first placed in service, the landlord gets to depreciate its value. This includes the value of:

- the building and building components
- land improvements, such as landscaping and fences, and
- personal property items that are inside the building, but that are not physically part of it—for example, refrigerators, stoves, dishwashers, and carpeting.

These items can all be depreciated together. However, you have the option of separately depreciating personal property inside a rental property and certain land improvements. This is more complicated, but yields a larger total deduction during the first years that you own the property. Such segmented depreciation is described in detail in Chapter 6.

Later Additions and Improvements

Landlords typically make additions and improvements to their rental property after it has been placed into service—that is, after it has been made available for rent. These may consist of:

- improvements to the building itself, or building components—for example, replacing iron pipes with copper
- land improvements, such as planting new trees or shrubbery, and
- adding new personal property to the rental building—for example, placing a new refrigerator in a rental unit.

You depreciate these additions and improvements separately from the original rental property.

Personal Property Used by the Landlord

Landlords usually have some personal property that they use in connection with their rental activity—computers and office furniture, for example. This property is for the landlord's use, not the tenant's. The landlord separately depreciates this property as it is placed into service each year.

How to Depreciate Buildings

By far, the largest portion of your depreciation deductions will consist of the building or buildings you use in your rental activities. The good news is that the rules for depreciating buildings are relatively simple. The bad news is that they require that buildings be depreciated over a long time using the slowest method possible, which reduces your annual deductions.

What Is a Building?

Buildings are made up of various structural components that are assembled together, including walls, floors, ceilings, windows, doors, plumbing fixtures (such as sinks and bathtubs), pipes, ducts, bathroom fixtures, stairs, fire escapes, electrical wiring, lighting fixtures, chimneys, air conditioning and heating systems, and other parts that form the structure. These structural components are all part of the building for depreciation purposes.

The land on which a building sits is not depreciable—it's not part of the building for depreciation purposes.

Buildings that are rented out for people to live in are called residential real property. Buildings that people do not live in are called nonresidential real property.

When a Building Is Placed in Service

Depreciation begins when property is placed in service, that is, when it's ready and available for use in your rental activity. A building doesn't have to be occupied by tenants to be depreciated. Rather, a building is considered placed in service in a rental activity when it is ready and available to rent. This can occur at the same time that you buy the property, or later.

> EXAMPLE 1: On April 6, Jan purchased a house to use as residential rental property. She made extensive repairs to the house during May and June. By July 5, she had it ready to rent and placed an ad in the local paper. She

rented it in August with the rental date beginning September 1. The house is considered placed in service in July because it was ready and available for rent on that date. Jan can begin to depreciate the house in July.

EXAMPLE 2: On February 1, Jan buys a house that is already being used as a rental and is currently occupied by a tenant. She continues renting out the unit to the tenant. She can begin to depreciate the house on February 1 because she placed it in service on that date.

EXAMPLE 3: Jan moved from her home in July. During August and September, she made several repairs to the house. On October 1, she listed the property for rent with a real estate company and rented it on December 1. The property is considered placed in service on October 1.

TIP
Keep documentation showing the date your property was placed in service. For example, keep copies of any rental ads or other rental listings you place to rent a newly acquired vacant property.

Determining a Building's Basis

How much you can depreciate each year depends, first and foremost, on how much your property is worth for tax purposes—its basis. The larger your basis, the larger your depreciation deductions will be.

Cost Basis

If, like most landlords, you've purchased your rental property, your starting point for determining the property's basis is what you paid for it. Logically enough, this is called its cost basis. Your cost basis is the purchase price, plus certain other expenses, less the cost of your land.

Purchase price. You use the full purchase price as your starting point, regardless of how you pay for the property—with cash or a loan. If you buy property and take over an existing mortgage, you use the amount you pay for the property, plus the amount that still must be paid on the mortgage.

EXAMPLE: Jan buys a building for $60,000 cash and assumes a mortgage of $240,000 on it. The starting point for determining her basis is $300,000.

Facilitative costs. Facilitative costs are amounts you spend in the process of investigating or otherwise pursuing the purchase of a rental property. These include most of the transaction costs involved in purchasing real property. These costs must be added to the building's basis and depreciated. (IRS Reg. § 1.263(a)-2(f).)

The following costs are "inherently facilitative" and must always be included in the building's depreciable basis:

- bidding costs, application fees, and similar expenses
- costs to appraise or otherwise determine the property's value
- architectural, engineering, environmental, geological, or inspection services for the property—for example, termite inspection fees
- expenses for preparing or reviewing the property's acquisition documents, such as bids, offers, sales agreements, or purchase contracts
- costs to negotiate the purchase terms or structure, including tax advice
- expenses for evaluating and examining the property's title—for example, abstract fees and attorneys' fees
- costs to obtain regulatory approval or secure permits
- property conveyance costs, including sales and transfer taxes and title registration costs—for example, recording fees and title insurance fees
- finders' fees and brokers' commissions, including amounts contingent on successful closing of the purchase (broker's commissions are ordinarily paid by the seller, but include any in your basis if paid by you, the buyer), and
- the cost of services provided by a qualified intermediary in a like-kind exchange.

Many of these costs will be listed on the closing statement you receive after escrow closes. However, they may not all be listed there, so be sure to check your records to see if you've made any other payments that should be added to your property's basis.

Costs incurred before putting building into service. Expenses incurred before the building is placed in service—that is, before it is offered for rent to the public—must also be added to the building's basis and depreciated. These include costs for installing utility services and any building refresh you perform.

The cost of any repairs or improvements you make to the building before it's offered for rent must be added to its basis. For example, if you purchase a building and, before offering it for rent, pay to repaint the walls or refinish the floors, you must add that cost to the basis of the building and depreciate it. However, if you incur this expense after the building is placed in service, you can currently deduct it. The only exception to this rule is where repairs qualify as start-up expenses for a brand new rental business. This is a limited deduction of up to $5,000 you may take for getting a new rental business up and going. It normally doesn't apply if you already have an ongoing rental business and purchase a new building. It applies only to repairs, not improvements. (See Chapter 8 for a detailed discussion of business start-up expenses.)

Real estate taxes. If you buy a building and agree to pay real estate taxes on it that were owed by the seller and the seller did not reimburse you, the taxes you pay are treated as part of your basis in the property. You cannot deduct them as taxes paid.

If you reimburse the seller for real estate taxes the seller paid for you, you can usually deduct that amount. Do not include that amount in your basis in the property.

Other costs. You must also add to your property's basis any amounts the seller owes that you agree to pay, such as back taxes or interest, recording or mortgage fees, charges for improvements or repairs, and sales commissions.

The cost of your land. Ordinarily, when you purchase a building with a structure or structures on it, you pay a single lump sum to the seller that includes both the cost of the building (along with its contents) and the land on which it sits. Because you can't depreciate land, you must deduct the value of the land from the purchase price to figure the basis for depreciation of the building.

EXAMPLE: Leslie buys a rental house for $200,000. She determines that the land is worth $50,000. She must deduct the value of the land ($50,000) from the purchase price ($200,000) to determine her basis ($150,000).

Costs Not Included in Your Property's Basis

The following costs need not be added to your property's basis:

- **Investigatory expenses.** Investigatory expenses generally are those you incur to determine whether to buy real property or which property to buy. These costs, often called "whether or which" expenses, may be currently deducted if they are not one of the "inherently facilitative" expenses listed above. For example, if you hire a consultant to help you find the best location to buy an apartment building, the cost is a "whether or which" investigatory expense that is currently deductible. But you would have to add to the basis the cost of hiring an appraiser to value the properties the consultant recommends (appraisal fees are on the "inherently facilitative" list").
- **Fire insurance.** Fire insurance premiums are operating expenses deducted as paid (see Chapter 3).
- **Loan expenses.** Not included in your rental property's basis are charges connected with getting or refinancing a loan, such as points (discount points, loan origination fees), mortgage insurance premiums, loan assumption fees, credit report costs, and fees for an appraisal required by a lender. (See Chapter 7 for how to deduct these costs.)
- **Amounts left in escrow for future payments.** Do not include in your basis amounts placed in escrow for the future payment of items, such as taxes and insurance.
- **De minimis safe harbor.** You don't have to include expenses that are currently deductible under the de minimis safe harbor or as materials and supplies. For most landlords, these are personal property items that cost $500 or less. (See "De Minimis Safe Harbor," and "Materials and Supplies Deduction" below.)

There are several ways to determine how much your land is worth. Obviously, the less it's worth, the more depreciation you will have to deduct. Land valuation is the single most important factor within your control affecting the amount of your depreciation deductions. This topic is covered in detail in Chapter 6.

Condos Have Land Too

Some people think that condominium owners own only the airspace inside their condo unit, and don't own any land. This is not true. When you buy a condo, you receive title to the airspace inside your unit, and you also get an undivided part interest in the land the condominium building occupies and other common areas. For example, if a condominium building contains ten units, each unit owner could own an undivided one-tenth interest in all the land. However, the interests don't have to be equal. The size of your undivided interest in the land should be listed on your deed. You need to calculate the land value to determine a rental condo's basis.

EXAMPLE: Ondine purchases a rental house for $200,000. She figures her starting basis in the property as follows:

Purchase price		$ 200,000
Other expenses		
Real estate taxes	$1,200	
Transfer taxes	2,000	
Title insurance	250	
Recording fees	50	
Total other		3,500
Cost of land:		(40,000)
Basis ($200,000 + $3,500) – $40,000		$ 163,500

When Cost Is Not the Basis

You cannot use cost as a basis for property that you received:

- in an exchange for other property
- as a gift, or
- as an inheritance.

The basis of property you inherit is usually the property's fair market value at the time the owner died. Thus, if you hold on to your rental property until death, your heirs will be able to resell it and pay little or no tax—the ultimate tax loophole.

> EXAMPLE: Victoria inherits an apartment building from her late Uncle Ralph. The property's fair market value (excluding the land) is $300,000 at the time of her uncle's death. This is Victoria's basis. She sells the property for $310,000. Her total taxable profit on the sale is only $10,000 (her profit is the sales price minus the property's tax basis).

The basis of rental property you receive as a gift is its adjusted basis in the hands of the gift giver when the gift was made. (The adjusted basis is generally the property's original basis, minus depreciation deductions, plus the cost of improvements.)

> EXAMPLE: Victoria's Uncle Ralph gave her his apartment building before he died. Ralph purchased the building in 1990 and his adjusted basis in the property at the time he gave it to her was $150,000. This is Victoria's basis.

For more information about determining basis other than cost basis, see IRS Publication 551, *Basis of Assets*.

Property Converted to Rental Use

When you change property you held for personal use to rental use (for example, you rent your former home), your basis is the *lesser* of the following values on the date of the change:

- the property's fair market value, or
- your adjusted basis.

Your adjusted basis is calculated as described in "Cost Basis," above. Fair market value is the price at which the property would change hands between a buyer and a seller, neither under undue pressure to buy or sell, and both having reasonable knowledge of all the relevant facts. Sales of similar property in the area are helpful in figuring out the fair market value of the property. You may also elect to have the property's value appraised as of the date of its conversion to rental property.

Ordinarily, your adjusted basis will be lower than the fair market value because residential real estate usually appreciates in value each year.

> **EXAMPLE:** Several years ago, John built his home for $140,000 on a lot that cost $14,000. Before changing the property to rental use last year, he added $28,000 of permanent improvements. Because land is not depreciable, John only includes the cost of the house and improvements when figuring his adjusted basis for depreciation—$168,000 ($140,000 + $28,000). The house has a fair market value of $250,000. John must use his adjusted basis of $168,000 as the basis for depreciation on the house because it is less than the fair market value on the date of the conversion to rental use.

Because of this rule, if your personal residence has lost value since you bought it, turning it into a rental home won't allow you to deduct the loss when you eventually sell it. Only the drop in value *after* the conversion is deductible.

> **EXAMPLE:** Jessica purchased a home in Chicago for $250,000; $50,000 of the total cost was for the land. She lived in the home for seven years and then moved to Houston. Because of the poor real estate market, Jessica decided to rent her house instead of sell it. The home's adjusted basis when she moved out was $200,000. However, due to the decline in real estate values, its fair market value was only $175,000—a loss of $25,000. Jessica must use the $175,000 fair market value as the basis for depreciation on the house because it is less than its adjusted basis on the date of conversion to rental use. If she sells the house instead for $175,000, she has no deductible loss.

Mixed-Use Property

If you use a building for both rental and personal purposes, you must reduce your depreciable basis by the proportion of the property you use personally.

EXAMPLE: Mary owns a triplex whose cost, excluding the cost of the land, was $300,000. She rents two of the units and lives in the other one. All of the units are the same size. She must reduce her depreciable basis by one-third—that is, her basis is $200,000. If the units were different sizes, she would determine their value by counting the number of rooms or by comparing their square footage (see Chapter 9).

Buildings You Construct Yourself

If you construct a rental building yourself, your basis is the cost of construction. The cost includes the cost of materials, equipment, and labor. However, you may not add the cost of your own labor to the property's basis. Add the interest you pay during the construction period, but deduct interest you pay before and after construction as an operating expense. (See Chapter 3.)

Property Acquired in an Exchange

A like-kind exchange is where you swap your property for similar property owned by someone else. If the two properties have the same value, the basis of your old property becomes the basis of the new property received in the exchange. The new property's basis is called a substitute basis because the basis of the old property is substituted for the basis of the new property. This is one of the most complex areas of real estate taxation and is beyond the scope of this book. For more information, see IRS Publication 544, *Sales and Other Dispositions of Assets*, and IRS Inst. 8824, Instructions for Form 8824, *Like-Kind Exchanges*.

The Depreciation Period

The depreciation period for residential real property is 27.5 years. The period for nonresidential real property is 39 years. Either way, it takes a long time to collect all of your depreciation deductions. Indeed, the great majority of landlords sell their rental property before they fully depreciate it. The recovery periods for personal property—office furniture and computers, for example—are much shorter, usually five or seven years.

If a building is used for both commercial and residential purposes, the 27.5-year period applies only if 80% or more of the gross rental income for the tax year is from the dwelling units. How much space the dwelling units take up in the building is irrelevant; all that counts is how much money you earn from them. Thus, you could have to use the 39-year period for nonresidential property even if a majority of the space in the building is used for dwelling units.

> EXAMPLE 1: Bill owns a two-story building that consists of a storefront on the first floor and four apartments on the second floor. He receives $1,000 rent per month from the store and $4,000 per month from the four apartments. He may use the 27.5-year depreciation period because 80% of his total rental income from the property comes from the apartments ($4,000 is 80% of $5,000).

> EXAMPLE 2: Bill raises the rent on the store to $1,500 per month, while leaving the rents on the apartments the same. Now, less than 80% of his total rental income comes from the apartments ($4,000 of $5,500 is only 73%). Thus, he must use the 39-year depreciation period, which gives him a much smaller depreciation deduction each year.

If you live in any part of the building, the gross rental income includes the fair rental value of the part you occupy. In a boon to landlords with home offices, the IRS has held that the 27.5-year depreciation period for residential buildings (instead of the 39-year period for commercial buildings) may be used to depreciate such offices so long as the 80% rule is met. (ILM 200526002 (May 9, 2005).)

How Much You Depreciate Each Year

To depreciate buildings, use the straight-line method, which is the simplest—though the slowest—depreciation method. Deduct an equal amount of the property's basis each year, except for the first and last years. Thus, you deduct approximately $1/27$ of the basis of residential real property each year.

You can continue to claim a deduction for depreciation on property used in your rental activity even if it is temporarily idle (not in use). For example, if you must make repairs after a tenant moves out, you still depreciate the rental property during the time it is not available for rent.

You do not get a full year's worth of depreciation for the first year your property is placed in service. Instead, your first-year deduction depends on what month of the year you placed the property into service—the later in the year, the less depreciation you get. No matter what day of the month you place your residential real property into service, you treat it as being placed in service at the midpoint of that month. You then get an extra one-half month of depreciation the year you sell your property. This rule is called the mid-month convention.

The IRS has a table in Publication 956, *How to Depreciate Property*, showing how much depreciation you are entitled to for each year you own residential real property (expressed as a percentage of the property's starting basis). The table takes into account the mid-month convention. Except for the first and last years, you depreciate 3.636% of your property's basis each year (give or take 0.001%). If you use the IRS tables to figure your depreciation for the first year, you must continue to use them for the remainder of the asset's recovery period unless you deduct a casualty loss, in which case you must stop using them.

Using the IRS tables is not mandatory. You can figure your depreciation yourself—this requires some serious math. If you use tax preparation software, it will calculate your depreciation deduction for you. If you don't use the tables, you'll usually end up with a slightly different amount than when using the tables—but not enough to matter. Even if you don't use the IRS tables, they are still a helpful guide if you ever want to know how much depreciation you'll be able to deduct for a property each year.

> **EXAMPLE:** Jim purchased a single-family rental house and placed it in service in June. His basis in the house is $160,000. Using the table, he finds that the percentage for property placed in service in June of Year 1 is 1.970%. His depreciation deduction for that year is $3,152 ($160,000 × 0.01970 = $3,152). The following year, the applicable depreciation percentage is 3.636%. Thus, his depreciation deduction for that year is $5,817.60 ($160,000 × 0.03636 = $5,817.60).

If you sell your property, figure your depreciation for the year of sale by multiplying a full year of depreciation by the number of months you owned the property, and then divide by 12. Treat the month of the sale as one-half of one month, no matter what day of the month you actually sold the property.

> EXAMPLE: Jim sells his rental house in the fifth year after he placed it in service. Title passes to the buyer on July 2. A full year of depreciation for Jim's property is worth $3,636. To figure his depreciation for the year of sale, he multiplies this amount by 6.5 (January through June, plus one-half of July = 6.5). He then divides the total by 12. The result is $1,969.50 in depreciation for the year (($3,636 × 6.5) ÷ 12 = $1,969.50).

Depreciating Additions and Improvements

Additions and improvements to a building must also be depreciated. However, you'll do this separately from the original building itself.

What Is a Building Improvement?

A building addition or improvement is a change you make to the structures on your land, or to structural components of the building, that makes it much better than it was before (a "betterment"), restores it to operating condition after it has fallen into disrepair (a "restoration"), or adapts it to a new use (an "adaptation").
For example, you:
- add a new bathroom or bedroom
- replace the roof
- put in new cabinets
- put up a fence
- install a new plumbing or wiring system, or
- install new kitchen appliances.

Changes that are not a betterment, restoration, or adaptation are repairs, not improvements. These include:
- painting a bedroom
- patching the roof, or
- mending a hole in a worn carpet.

Unlike improvements, the cost of repairs is a landlord operating expense that can be fully deducted in one year. Obviously, you're much better off taxwise if you can characterize a change as a repair, rather than an improvement. The differences between repairs and improvements are discussed in detail in Chapter 4.

Special Assessments for Improvements

If your rental is in a condominium complex that is governed by a homeowners' association, you may be required to pay special assessments to cover building improvements. Such assessments are depreciated in the same way as any building improvement described above. Special assessments are not the same as the monthly homeowners' association fees condo owners must pay to cover the condo's operating expenses. These monthly fees are currently deductible each year as an operating expense.

EXAMPLE: Ida owns a one-bedroom condominium in a 20-story high-rise that she rents out. The condominium homeowners' association requires every owner to pay a special $2,000 assessment for a major upgrade of the building's aging plumbing system. This is a building improvement that Ida must depreciate over 27.5 years. Ida also pays $2,400 each year in homeowners' association fees. She may deduct that entire amount as an operating expense.

Depreciating Building Improvements

Treat depreciable additions or improvements that you make to any property as separate property items for depreciation purposes.

When depreciation begins. Depreciation of an addition or improvement to a building begins when the improvement is placed in service—that is, when it is ready for use in your rental property.

Basis for depreciation. Depreciate the amount that an addition or improvement actually costs you, including any amount you borrowed to make the addition or improvement. This includes all direct costs, such as material and labor, but not your own labor. It also includes all expenses related to the addition or improvement. For example, if you had an architect draw up plans for remodeling your property, the architect's fee is a part of the cost; or, if you had your lot surveyed to put up a fence, the cost of the survey is a part of the cost of the fence.

Depreciation method and recovery period. If the improvement is to the building structure or structural components, depreciate it over 27.5 years, using the same method used for the original building as described above.

> EXAMPLE: Mona buys a rental house in 2000. In 2015, her old tenant moves out and she hires a contractor to remodel the house, adding a new kitchen and bathroom, and installing new floors. The cost of this building improvement was $10,000. The work was completed on June 1, 2015, and she immediately placed the house into service as a rental unit by offering it for rent. She depreciates the $10,000 over 27.5 years. The beginning date for her first year of depreciation is June 2015. She gets $197 in depreciation for this improvement the first year and $367 each year thereafter. She claims this amount in addition to the depreciation she has already been receiving on the house since she placed it in service in 2000.

You must keep separate accounts for depreciable additions or improvements made after you place your rental property in service.

You add the cost of depreciable additions and improvements to the adjusted basis of your property, which will reduce your tax liability when you sell the property.

Deducting Costs for Replaced Building Components—New IRS Rules

If you replace the old roof on your rental building with a new roof, you separately depreciate the cost of the new roof. But what about the old roof? Do you get to deduct its cost? Until recently, the answer was no. You had to go on depreciating building components you replaced along with the rest of the original structure. This meant that, in effect, you could end up depreciating two or more roofs at the same time! However, new IRS regulations that went into effect in 2014 change this rule. (IRS Reg. § 1.168(i)-8.)

The regulations apply when a building owner disposes of a structural component (or a portion of a component, no matter how small)—for example: roofs, HVAC units, and windows. The building owner has two options: (1) continuing to depreciate the cost of the replaced component, or (2) deduct the unrecovered cost of such component. (IRS Reg. § 1.168(i)-8.)

The building owner needs to do nothing to select option 1. The component continues to be depreciated along with the rest of the building.

Option 2 is chosen by making a "partial disposition election" on the owner's tax return. In this event, the adjusted basis (original basis minus depreciation taken) of the retired component is deducted that tax year. In addition, the building owner must depreciate the cost of the replacement component, even if it might have otherwise been currently deductible as a repair under the IRS's repair regulations. This election must be made on a timely filed return including extensions in the taxable year in which the disposition occurs. No formal election statement is required. The taxpayer simply reports the loss on the disposed portion of the asset on his or her return.

> **EXAMPLE:** Alice has owned an apartment building for ten years. She replaces the roof, which is a structural component. Alice may not recognize a loss and must continue to depreciate the retired old roof unless she elects to treat the roof retirement as a partial disposition of the building. If she decides not to make this election, she separately depreciates the cost of the new roof and continues to include the cost of the old roof in the amount she depreciates for the building as a whole. If she does make the election, depreciation on the old roof ceases at the time of its retirement. Alice recognizes a loss upon the retirement equal to the remaining undepreciated basis of the roof.

When such an election is made, it is necessary to allocate a portion of the original cost (depreciable basis) of the whole building to the replaced component. For example, the cost of the replaced roof in Alice's building would have to be determined since depreciation was not separately claimed on the original roof. Any reasonable method may be used to determine the adjusted basis of the old replaced component at the time of its replacement, including:

- recreate the actual cost with invoices or other cost records
- if the replaced asset is a restoration, discounting the cost of the replacement asset to its placed-in-service year cost using the Producer Price Index for Finished Goods, and its successor, the Producer Price Index for Final Demand (may not be used for betterments or adaptations)
- a pro rata allocation based on the replacement cost of the disposed-of component
- a study (that is, a cost segregation study) allocating the cost of the building's individual components, or
- any other reasonable method.

> EXAMPLE: Alice elects to use the Producer Price Index for Finished Goods (PPIFG) method to determine the basis of the old roof, which was placed in service ten years ago. She spent $10,000 to replace the roof this year. The PPIFG has risen by 24.7% over the last ten years, so the old roof's placed-in-service-year cost is valued at $7,530. Over ten years, Alice took a total of $3,115 in depreciation deductions for the roof, leaving her with a $4,415 adjusted basis she may deduct in full.

There are some exceptions to the rule that a building owner is not required to recognize a loss (or gain) on a disposition of a building component. The regulations make such recognition mandatory if the disposition is the result of casualty event, sale of a portion of an asset, like-kind exchange, or involuntary conversion.

Late Partial Asset Dispositions

If you decide not to do a partial asset disposition, you treat the new work as a repair and currently deduct the cost (if it qualifies under the IRS regulations). If you do a partial asset disposition, you must depreciate the new work, even if it would otherwise qualify as a repair. What happens if you elect not to do a partial asset disposition, deduct the new work as a repair, and the IRS later decides such work should have been treated as an improvement and depreciated? In this event, the IRS takes some pity on you. You have the option of doing a late partial asset disposition and deducting the adjusted basis of the replaced component.

Depreciating Land Improvements

Land cannot be depreciated because it lasts virtually forever. However, certain improvements you make to your land can be depreciated. There are two types of land improvements:

- changes to the land itself, and
- changes or additions to permanent structures on the land other than buildings and building components.

Changes to Land

Changes to the land include grading, clearing, excavations, and landscaping. The IRS says that such changes are depreciable only if they are "directly associated" with a building, rather than "inextricably associated" with the land itself. (Rev. Rul. 65-265.) Translated into English, this means that these land improvements are depreciable if they are intended for use with a specific building. Changes that permanently improve the land itself are not depreciable.

The rationale is that work directly associated with a building will cease to be useful when the building is demolished; thus, it has a determinable useful life. But work inextricably associated with land is not depreciable because we don't know whether it will cease to be useful. The cost of such work is added to the basis of the land. Thus, landscaping is depreciable if it will have to be replaced when the building is replaced.

EXAMPLE 1: Milt plants some new bushes and trees right next to his rental triplex. If he replaced the building, he'd have to destroy these bushes and trees. They have a determinable useful life so he may depreciate them.

EXAMPLE 2: Milt also plants trees and bushes around the outer boundary of his lot. These trees and bushes would not have to be replaced if the building was demolished. Thus, they can't be depreciated and Milt must instead add their cost to the basis of his land.

Similarly, preliminary land clearing and grading to get land ready for construction is not depreciable. However, excavating, grading, and dirt removal costs necessary for the proper setting of a specific building can be depreciated because this work will have to be redone when the building is replaced.

Structures Other Than Buildings

Permanent structures other than buildings include fences, outdoor lighting, swimming pools, driveways, paved parking areas and other pavements, walkways, sprinkler systems, and drainage facilities.

In contrast to changes to land, depreciation of permanent structures other than buildings is straightforward—they are depreciated over 15 years as described below. You don't have to worry about the "directly associated" or "inextricably associated" test because man-made structures, unlike changes to land itself, have a determinable useful life—that is, none of them can last forever.

Depreciation Methods

Land improvements can always be depreciated using regular depreciation. Regular depreciation for land improvements is done over 15 years, using the 150% declining balance method. This way, you get your depreciation deductions more quickly than you would for a building or building improvement, which you must depreciate over 27.5 years. Other than the fact that the 150% declining balance method and 15-year depreciation period must be used, regular depreciation for land improvements works the same as for personal property. See the discussion of regular depreciation for personal property below.

Bonus Depreciation for Land Improvements?

For the past several years, building owners have had the option of using bonus depreciation to depreciate land improvements much more quickly than by using regular depreciation. Under the 50% bonus depreciation provision that was in effect in 2014, 50% of the cost of land improvements could be deducted in a single year. Although bonus depreciation expired at the end of 2014, it is expected to be extended by Congress at least through 2015. See "Bonus Depreciation" below.

The depreciable basis of a land improvement is its cost, including labor and installation charges. If you depreciate a new improvement, you'll have no problem determining the cost—just look at your bills and use the total you paid for it.

If you wish to depreciate an existing improvement—for example, a driveway in a rental property you have purchased—you can determine the cost by using construction cost guides such as the *National Repair & Remodeling Estimator* (Craftsman Book Company, available as a download at www.craftsman-book.com). You can also obtain cost estimates from experts such as garden supply companies, landscape architects, and local builders and contractors. You don't need to obtain a precise formal written cost estimate prepared by the expert—which the expert will probably charge you for. You can simply obtain a ballpark estimate from the expert over the phone—be sure to write it down, date it, and keep it in your records. (See Chapter 6 for a detailed discussion of how to determine the tax basis of land improvements.)

Deducting Personal Property

Obviously, all landlords own real property—that is, land and buildings and other permanent structures on the land. But they own personal property as well—for example, computers, maintenance equipment, and appliances in rental units. Thus, you need to understand how to deduct personal property. There are several different ways you may be able to deduct the cost of long-term personal property:

- de minimis safe harbor deduction
- the materials and supplies deduction
- bonus depreciation (if extended to 2015)
- regular depreciation, or
- Section 179 expensing (available only for rental business property not contained in rental units).

What Is Personal Property?

For tax purposes, personal property is any tangible property other than:
- land and land improvements
- buildings and other inherently permanent structures, such as swimming pools and parking lots, and
- structural components of buildings and other permanent structures. (IRS Reg. § 1.48-1(e)(2); *Whiteco Industries, Inc. v. Comm'r.*, 65 T.C. 664.)

Often, you'll be able to deduct all or most of the cost of personal property used in your rental business in a single year by using the de minimis safe harbor, materials and supplies deduction, or Section 179 deduction. However, if you can't use any of these methods, you must depreciate the cost of personal property. For example, a $750 washing machine inside a rental unit would have to be depreciated because it is not deductible under these other methods. Fortunately, personal property is depreciated over a much shorter time period than real property—usually five or seven years. Moreover, you may be able to use bonus depreciation to write off 50% of the cost of the property the first year you use it in your rental business. This means you'll get your full depreciation deduction much more quickly. It is to a landlord's advantage to be able to classify as much rental property as possible as personal property, rather than real property.

A landlord's personal property falls into one of two broad categories:
- personal property contained in a rental building or individual apartment, or
- other personal property used in a rental activity.

Personal Property Inside Rental Buildings

Anything inside your rental building that is not a structural component of the building is personal property. Often it is easy to tell whether or not an item is a structural component of a rental building—for example, refrigerators and other kitchen appliances are not structural components, while load-bearing walls obviously are. Other examples of items inside rental buildings that are not structural components include:

- carpeting that is tacked down (but not glued down)
- drapes and blinds
- furniture (only depreciable if you own it)
- personal signs
- movable and removable partitions
- laundry equipment in a laundry room
- weights and other exercise equipment in an exercise room
- pool tables, ping-pong tables, televisions, and other recreational equipment in a recreation room, and
- office furniture and equipment located in a manager's office.

In many cases, however, it can be very difficult to determine whether property is a structural component—for example, is tile flooring a structural component? The IRS says that it is if it is cemented, mudded, or otherwise permanently affixed to the floor. There have been many disputes with the IRS on what constitutes a structural component, resulting in many court decisions, often disagreeing with each other. Refer to Chapter 6 for a detailed discussion of the tests used to determine if property is a structural component of a rental building.

Personal Property Not Inside Rental Buildings

Landlords typically own various items of long-term property that they use in connection with their rental activities, but the items are not actually inside their rental buildings—for example, lawn mowers and other landscaping and maintenance equipment, computers, cell phones, fax machines, office furniture, and automobiles.

As long as this property is not a structural component of a building or other permanent structure, it is personal property for depreciation purposes. For example, a lawn mower is personal property even if it is kept inside a building or other permanent structure such as a storage shed—a lawn mower is obviously not a building component. On the other hand, carpeting in your rental office will not be personal property if it is glued to the floor—such carpeting is a building component, and is considered part of the building for depreciation purposes. See Chapter 6 for detailed guidance on when property is a building component.

How to Deduct or Depreciate Personal Property

There can be differences in how you deduct personal property, depending on how and when you acquire it.

Personal Property Included in Purchase

When you buy a rental property, you pay one lump sum that covers both the structure and the personal property it contains. When you initially place the property into service, you can simply depreciate the entire property as a whole (as outlined in "How to Depreciate Buildings," above). The IRS requires no separate allocation for, or depreciation of, the personal property in the building. This saves you the time and trouble of having to figure out the basis of each item of personal property the building contains, and keeping separate depreciation records for them.

However, you have the option of depreciating personal property within a rental building separately from the building itself. Such segmented depreciation is often advantageous taxwise, because it will give you larger deductions in the first few years you own the property. Segmented depreciation is discussed in detail in Chapter 6.

Personal Property Improvements

You must separately depreciate or deduct personal property that you add to a building after you place it into service—for example, if you install a new stove or refrigerator in a rental property you've already made available for rent, you'll depreciate it separately from the other appliances already in the unit. Your depreciation begins the year you place the item in service.

Other Personal Property

Depreciate or deduct personal property not contained in your rental property, such as computers and office furniture, as you buy it. Depreciate or deduct each item separately.

De Minimis Safe Harbor

The IRS repair regulations that went into effect in 2014 created a new de minimis safe harbor deduction ("de minimis" is Latin for minor or inconsequential). (IRS Reg. § 1.263(a)-1(f).) Most landlords may use the de minimis safe harbor to currently deduct the cost of personal property items that cost up to $500 apiece. This can result in a substantial deduction.

The de minimis safe harbor is particularly helpful for landlords because they can use it to currently deduct the cost of personal property such as appliances purchased for rental units. The cost of such personal property can't be deducted in one year using I.R.C. Section 179 because Section 179 doesn't apply to personal property in residential rental units (see "Section 179 Expensing" below). Thus, until now landlords have had to depreciate the cost of such personal property over several years.

What Can be Deducted

If you elect to use the de minimis safe harbor, you must use it to deduct all expenses for the following types of property whose cost is within your de minimis limit ($500 for most landlords as described below). The de minimis safe harbor can't be used to deduct the cost of land or inventory (items held for sale to customers).

Tangible personal property. The de minimis safe harbor is most often used to deduct the cost of tangible personal property items (units of property) you use in your rental business. Such property can be in a rental building or elsewhere, such as your office.

> EXAMPLE: John owns five rental homes. He purchases new refrigerators for each at a cost of $500 apiece. Ordinarily, he would have to depreciate the cost of each refrigerator over five years. He can't use Section 179 to deduct the cost in one year. However, by using the de minimis safe harbor, he can deduct the entire $2,500 expense in a single year provided that the requirements to use the safe harbor are satisfied.

Components of Property. Components acquired to maintain or repair a unit of tangible property—that is, spare parts—are also deducted under the de minimis safe harbor if within the de minimis limit ($500 for most landlords). This category does not include components that are acquired as part of a unit of property—for example, the original engine in an automobile.

> EXAMPLE: Landlord Larry pays $400 for new window panes to replace broken panes in an apartment building he owns. The panes are replacement parts used in a repair and the cost to acquire and deliver them is deducted as a de minimis expense. The cost of installing the panes is deductible as a repair.

This deduction is available only for components used to repair or maintain property. Components used to improve property do not qualify for the de minimis safe harbor. Instead, they must depreciated as part of the cost of the improvement. (IRS Reg. § 1.263(a)-3(c)(2).) This means that you should keep track of the ultimate use of such items.

> EXAMPLE: Landlord Barbara purchases lumber (a component) to use as part of an improvement to her rental building. Its cost may not be deducted under the de minimis safe harbor. It must be depreciated as an improvement (along with other related improvement costs).

Property with an economic useful life of 12 months or less. Any item with an economic useful life of 12 months or less must be deducted under the de minimis safe harbor if the cost is within the de minimis limit ($500 for most landlords). The economic useful life of a UOP is the period it may reasonably be expected to be useful to the taxpayer—which may be shorter than its depreciation period.

> EXAMPLE: Landlord Jill spends $500 for cut flowers to place in the lobby of her rental buildings during the holiday season. The flowers have a useful life of less than 12 months and may be deducted under de minimis safe harbor.

Maximum De Minimis Amount

The maximum amount you can deduct under the de minimis safe harbor depends on whether your rental business has an "applicable financial statement" for the year. This includes a certified financial statement prepared by a CPA. It also includes a financial statement (other than a tax return) your business files with the SEC or other state or federal agency (not including the IRS)—for example, a Form 10-K or an Annual Statement to Shareholders. Only larger corporations or businesses that are publicly traded usually file such statements.

Certified financial statements by CPAs usually cost at least several thousand dollars, and few smaller landlords (or other small businesses) have them. If, like most smaller landlords, you don't have such a financial statement, you may use the de minimis safe harbor only for property whose cost does not exceed $500 per invoice, or $500 per item as substantiated by the invoice. If the cost exceeds $500 per invoice (or item), no part of the cost may be deducted by using the de minimis safe harbor. If you have an applicable financial statement, then you may increase the per item or per invoice amount up to $5,000. The $500/$5,000 are maximum limits, you can use a smaller limit if you wish, or even have different limits for different types of property.

> EXAMPLE: Landlord Abe has no applicable financial statement. Abe purchases ten trash compactors for his rental units at $250 each for a total cost of $2,500 as indicated by the invoice. Abe has accounting procedures in place at the beginning of the year to expense amounts paid for property costing less than $500, and Abe treats the amounts paid for the compactors as an expense on his books and records. The amounts paid for the compactors meet the requirements for the de minimis safe harbor. Abe may currently deduct the entire amount as an ordinary and necessary business expense.

Since the $500 de minimis limit is based on the cost of an item as shown on the invoice, you might be tempted to artificially break an item down into separate costs on the invoice, each of which is less than the limit. However, the IRS does not allow this. You cannot break into separate components property that you would normally buy as a single unit.

> **EXAMPLE:** Landlord Jill purchases a desk for her rental office for $1,000. She instructs the office supply store to separately bill her $150 for each of four desk drawers and $400 for the remainder of the desk. Since an office desk is normally purchased along with its drawers as a single unit, the IRS adds the cost of each component to determine that the actual cost is $1,000. Thus, the desk does not qualify for the de minimis safe harbor.

In determining whether the cost of an item exceeds the $500 (or $5,000) threshold, you must include all additional costs included on the same invoice with the property—for example, delivery and installation fees. If the additional costs on a single invoice apply to several items, you must divide the costs among them in a reasonable way. IRS regulations give you three options: (1) equal division for each item, (2) specific identification (for example, if the installation costs apply only to one item), or (3) weighted average based on the property's relative cost.

> **EXAMPLE:** Alexander pays $1,200 for three dishwashers for his rental units. They cost $400 each, and he also paid a single $150 fee for installation. He can treat the installation cost as $50 per dishwasher ($150 ÷ 3). This results in a total price of $450 for each dishwasher. Since this is less than the $500 de minimis limit, he can currently deduct the entire $1,350 cost using the de minimis safe harbor.

When you make this election, it applies to all expenses you incur that qualify for the de minimis safe harbor. You cannot pick and choose which items you want to include. You must also include items that would otherwise be deductible as materials and supplies.

Qualifying for the Safe Harbor

To qualify for the de minimis expensing safe harbor, a taxpayer must:
- establish before the first day of the tax year (January 1 for calendar year taxpayers) an accounting procedure requiring it to expense amounts paid for property either (1) costing less than a certain dollar amount, and/or (2) with an economic useful life of 12 months or less, and
- actually treat such amounts as currently deductible expenses on its books and records.

If you have an "applicable financial statement" and wish to qualify to use the $5,000 de minimis limit, your accounting procedure must be in writing and signed before January 1 of the tax year. If you don't have such a statement and qualify only for the $500 limit, you do not need to put your procedure in writing (although you may do so). But—whether or not in writing—it should still be in place before January 1 of the tax year. Here is an example of such a written procedure for a taxpayer without an applicable financial statement:

De Minimis Safe Harbor Procedure

Effective January 1, 2014, XYZ hereby adopts the following policy regarding certain expenditures: Amounts paid to acquire or produce tangible personal property will be expensed, and not capitalized, in the year of purchase if: (1) the property costs less than $500, or (2) the property has a useful life of 12 months or less.

You need not attach your de minimis policy to your tax return. Just keep it in your accounting files. During the year you must follow your policy and actually treat all expenses that fall under the de minimis safe harbor as a currently deductible expense in your books and records.

Claiming the De Minimis Safe Harbor

To take advantage of the de minimis safe harbor, you must file an election with your tax return each year, using the following format:

Section 1.263(a)-1(f) De Minimis Safe Harbor Election

Taxpayer's name:
Taxpayer's address:
Taxpayer's identification number:

The taxpayer is hereby making the de minimis safe harbor election under Section 1.263(a)-1(f).

You can use the de minimis safe harbor for amounts paid during 2015 and file the election with your 2015 tax return. It must be filed no later than October 15, 2016, if you obtain an extension of time to file. This election is irrevocable for the year it covers.

Materials and Supplies Deduction

IRS regulations that went into effect in 2014 established a new deduction for materials and supplies. "Materials and supplies" are tangible property used or consumed in your rental business operations that fall within any of the following categories:

- any item of tangible personal property (unit of property) that cost $200 or less
- any item of personal property with an economic useful life of 12 months or less, and
- components acquired to maintain or repair a unit of tangible property—that is, spare parts.

The cost of such items may be deducted in the year the item is used or consumed in your rental business—which may be later than the year purchased. To use this deduction, you are supposed to keep records of when such items are used or consumed in your business—something few small landlords do in practice. For this reason, this deduction will be useless for most landlords. Fortunately, they can use the de minimis safe harbor discussed above instead to deduct materials and supplies.

Incidental Materials and Supplies

"Incidental" materials and supplies are personal property items that are carried on hand and for which no record of consumption is kept or for which beginning and ending inventories are not taken. (IRS Reg. § 1.162-3(a)(2).) They must be small in both an operational and financial sense. In other words, these are inexpensive items not worth keeping track of. Costs of incidental materials and supplies are deductible in the year they are paid for, not when the items are used or consumed in your rental business.

EXAMPLE: Landlord John purchases one dozen lightbulbs he plans to use as replacements for the bulbs in his rental units. The cost was minimal and he does not keep an inventory of each bulb. These are incidental compared to his business and deductible in the year he paid for them.

Interaction With De Minimis Safe Harbor

If you elect to use the de minimis safe harbor discussed above, you must apply it to amounts paid for all materials and supplies that meet the requirements for deduction under the safe harbor. (IRS Reg. § 1.263(a)-1(f)(3)(ii).) Thus, if you use the de minimis safe harbor, you can largely ignore the materials and supplies deduction. This is to your advantage since the de minimis safe harbor has a $500 limit for most landlords, as opposed to the $200 materials and supplies limit. Moreover, the de minimis safe harbor permits you to deduct the cost of items the year they are purchased, instead of when they are actually used or consumed in your rental business.

One exception where the materials and supplies deduction could prove useful, even where a de minimis safe harbor election is made, is for components used to repair property. If the components cost more than $500 the de minimis safe harbor can't be used. But the materials and supplies deduction can be used, no matter how much the components cost. The deduction may be taken in the year when the components are actually used in the course of a repair or maintenance.

EXAMPLE: Landlord Phil purchases $1,000 worth of roofing shingles he keeps on hand to repair the roof of his apartment building as it deteriorates over time. He can't deduct the cost using the de minimis safe harbor because his deduction limit under the safe harbor is $500. However, he can deduct them as materials and supplies the year or years he uses them to repair the roof. The cost of installing the shingles is deductible as a repair.

Bonus Depreciation

Since 2008, businesses have had the option of using bonus depreciation for qualifying personal property. By using bonus depreciation, a business owner can deduct a substantial percentage of a long-term asset's cost the first year it is placed in service—for 2012 through 2014, the amount was 50%. Fifty-percent bonus depreciation expired at the end of 2014. Unless Congress acts to extend it (as it has done several times before), it won't be available for 2015 or later years. As this book went to press Congress had not enacted an extension, though it was working on it. It was expected that bonus depreciation would be extended through 2015. Due to legislative gridlock, this extension may not be enacted by Congress until late 2015 or early 2016 (in which event, it will be made retroactive). You can keep up-to-date by visiting the update Web page for this book (see the Introduction for the link).

The rest of this section covers the rules that will apply if 50% bonus depreciation is extended to 2015.

During 2014, the percentage of property's basis (cost) you could deduct the first year was 50%. If bonus depreciation is extended to 2015, the bonus amount will likely be 50% as well. That means you can deduct 50% of the cost of the asset in the first year, with the remaining cost deducted over several years using regular depreciation and/or Section 179 expensing.

Bonus depreciation may not be used for real property—thus it may not be used for buildings and building improvements (see above). This means landlords may not use it for their greatest expense—the cost of their rental property. However, landlords may use bonus depreciation when they purchase new personal property and place it in service for their rental activity during the years listed above. This includes appliances, carpeting, and blinds purchased for rental units; and office furniture, computers, and other equipment used in landlord offices. It is also available for new depreciable land improvements such as swimming pools and driveways.

Bonus depreciation doesn't take the place of regular depreciation. Instead, you get it in addition to regular depreciation. Moreover, bonus depreciation is optional—you don't have to take it if you don't want to. If you don't want to take it, you must inform the IRS as described below. But if you want to get the largest depreciation deduction you can, you'll want to take advantage of the bonus.

> **EXAMPLE:** Barry owns a ten-unit apartment building. He spends $50,000 to put in a new parking lot and extensive new landscaping. He can't deduct this expense using Section 179 because it is an improvement to real property. However, he can deduct it using 50% bonus depreciation, which may be used for any property with a useful life of less than 20 years. For tax purposes, the landscaping has a useful life of 15 years. Barry may claim a $25,000 bonus depreciation deduction for the landscaping and deduct the remaining $25,000 using regular depreciation over 15 years. Without bonus depreciation, he'd have to deduct the $50,000 over 15 years using regular depreciation.

Property That Qualifies for Bonus Depreciation

Property qualifies for bonus depreciation only if the property:
- is new, and
- has a useful life of 20 years or less (this includes most types of property other than real property—see below).

Also, if the property is listed property, you must use it over 50% of the time for business (listed property consists of automobiles and certain other personal property—see "Listed Property" below).

Bonus depreciation is available only for property that is purchased and placed in service. Property is "placed in service" when it's ready and available for use in your rental business. As long as it is available for use, you don't have to actually use the property for business during the year to take depreciation.

Because bonus depreciation is available only for new property, you won't be able to use it for personal property items and/or land improvements when you purchase an existing (that is, used) rental building and its contents during that year. This is so even if you use segmented depreciation. (See Chapter 6.) However, new personal property or land improvements purchased and placed in service during the applicable time period for a building you already own does qualify for the bonus. Additionally, if you utilize segmented depreciation, bonus depreciation may be available where you construct a new rental building or remodel an existing building. (See Chapter 6.)

Bonus Depreciation Applies Class-Wide

If you use bonus depreciation, you must use it for all assets that fall within the same class. You may not pick and choose the assets you want to apply it to within a class. For example, if you buy a new refrigerator for your rental property and take bonus depreciation, you must take bonus depreciation for any other property you buy that year within the same class. Refrigerators are five-year property, so you must take bonus depreciation that year for any other five-year property—for example, computers and office equipment. (See below for a list of the various classes of property.)

Calculating the Bonus Amount

You use bonus depreciation to figure out your depreciation deduction for the first year that you own an asset. You figure the deduction by multiplying the depreciable basis of the asset by the applicable bonus percentage, which is expected to be 50% for 2015. (See "Determining the Basis of Personal Property," below, for how to figure an asset's depreciable basis.) The remaining 50% cost of the property is deducted over several years using regular depreciation.

> EXAMPLE: Assume that Barry spends $1,000 to purchase a washer and dryer for his apartment building laundry room and places them into service during 2015. He may deduct 50% of the cost using bonus depreciation in 2015, and deduct the remaining $500 using regular depreciation. His bonus depreciation deduction is $500. His regular depreciation is $100 (20% × $500). Thus, his total deduction is $600. (This example assumes 50% bonus depreciation was extended through 2015.)

If you take the Section 179 deduction (which is usually advisable if you qualify for it), you combine it with 50% bonus depreciation and regular depreciation, in that order. This can give you an enormous deduction. However, Section 179 ordinarily cannot be used for personal property contained in rental buildings. (See "Section 179 Expensing," below.)

Opting Out of the Bonus

If, as expected, 50% bonus depreciation is extended through 2015, it will be applied automatically to all taxpayers who qualify for it. However, the deduction is always optional. You need not take it if you don't want to. You can elect not to take the deduction by attaching a note to your tax return. It may be advantageous to do this if you expect your income to go up substantially in future years, placing you in a higher tax bracket.

CAUTION

When you opt out, you do so for the entire class of assets. It's very important to understand that if you opt out of the bonus, you must do so for the entire class of assets, not just one asset within a class. This is the same rule that applies when you decide to take the bonus.

Regular Depreciation

If personal property doesn't qualify for bonus depreciation (assuming it's extended through 2015), or you elect not to use it, you'll have to use regular depreciation. This process is much the same as for depreciating buildings, except it is done over a much shorter time period. Also, you can use accelerated depreciation which allows you to get larger deductions in the first few years you own an asset. To depreciate personal property, you must have the following information:

- when the property was placed in service
- its depreciable basis
- the depreciation period
- which first-year convention applies
- the depreciation method, and
- whether the property is listed property.

When Is Personal Property Placed in Service?

Depreciation begins when property is placed in service. Personal property inside or attached to a building is placed in service when it's installed in the building and is available and ready for rental use.

> **EXAMPLE:** On November 22, Jack purchased a dishwasher for his vacant rental property. The appliance was delivered, installed, and ready for use on December 7. However, he did not rent out the apartment until February of the following year. The dishwasher was placed in service on December 7, even though it was not actually used by his tenant until February.

Personal property you use yourself for your rental activity is placed in service when it is available for your use.

> **EXAMPLE:** Stan purchases a new computer to help him with the bookkeeping for his many rental properties. The computer is placed in service when Stan sets it up in his office for his use.

Keep copies of sales receipts showing when personal property was delivered.

Determining the Basis of Personal Property

Usually, your basis in personal property is whatever you paid for it. Its cost includes not only the purchase price, but also sales tax, delivery charges, installation, and testing fees, if any. You may depreciate the entire cost, no matter how you paid for the property—in cash, on a credit card, or with a bank loan.

> **EXAMPLE:** Victor buys a new refrigerator and stove for a duplex he's been renting for several years. The purchase price for the items was $900, plus $100 sales tax, and $100 for delivery and installation. Victor puts the entire amount on his credit card, except for the delivery charge, which he pays in cash. His basis in the items is $1,100.

There are certain situations, however, when you can't use the cost basis method for personal property.

Property Converted to Rental Use

If you convert property you have been using personally to use in your rental activity, your starting basis is equal to the property's fair market value when you start using it for rental purposes.

> **EXAMPLE:** Jeff wants to add some furniture to a vacant apartment he's trying to rent. Rather than buying new furniture, he moves in some old furniture from his personal residence, including a sofa, dinette set, and bed. The fair market value of these items when Jeff places them in his rental is $400. This is his starting basis when he begins to depreciate the property.

You determine your property's fair market value by figuring out how much someone would be willing to pay for it. If the property is new, or fairly new, you can use the cost to replace it. If the property is older, you'll need to figure out the value based on the new price minus an amount for the wear and tear the property has undergone. Look at classified ads and listings for similar property on eBay, or call people who buy and sell the type of property involved. If you think the property is extremely valuable, get an appraisal from an expert. Keep records of how you calculated the property's value.

Most personal property that you convert to rental use probably won't be worth much. You can't claim inflated values for old property just to maximize your depreciation deductions.

Property Bought With a Trade-In

If you buy property with a trade-in, your starting basis is equal to the adjusted basis in the trade-in property, plus any cash you pay for the new property.

> **EXAMPLE:** Phil owns a pickup truck he uses exclusively for his rental business. He trades in the truck for a new model, for which he pays $10,000. His old truck's adjusted basis was $3,000. His starting basis in the new truck is $13,000. This is so even though the new truck's list price was only $10,000.

Inherited and Gifted Personal Property

The starting basis of inherited personal property is its fair market value on the day the owner died. Your starting basis in gifted property is its fair market value at the time of the gift.

Mixed-Use Property

You may take a depreciation deduction for personal property you use both for your rental activity and personal purposes. Reduce your depreciable basis in the property by the percentage of your personal use. This will, of course, reduce the amount you can depreciate.

> EXAMPLE: Miranda owns an $800 lawn mower that she uses 75% of the time for her rental business and 25% of the time to mow her own lawn. Her depreciable basis in the mower is reduced by 25%, so her basis is $600 instead of $800 (75% × $800 = $600). Miranda can depreciate $600 over the asset's depreciation period.

You can take a depreciation deduction even if you use an asset only 1% of the time for business. (However, special rules apply if you use cars and other types of listed property less than 50% of the time for business— see "Listed Property," below.)

If you use property for both business and personal purposes, you must keep a diary or log listing the dates, times, and reasons the property was used in order to distinguish business from personal use. (See Chapter 17.)

Depreciation Period

Virtually all of the personal property you use in your rental activity will have a five- or seven-year depreciation period. The depreciation periods for most types of personal property used by landlords are listed below. These periods are also called recovery classes; all property that comes within a period is said to belong to that class. For example, computers have a five-year depreciation period and thus fall within the five-year class, along with automobiles and office equipment.

Type of Property	Depreciation Period
Computer software (Software included in the price of a computer is depreciated as part of the computer, unless you're billed separately for the software; other software is separately depreciated.)	3 years
Computers and their peripheral equipment Office machinery, such as typewriters, calculators, and copiers Automobiles Light trucks (actual weight less than 13,000 pounds) Appliances, such as stoves, refrigerators, dishwashers, washing machines, clothes dryers, and window air conditioners Carpets Furniture used in rental property Drapes and blinds	5 years
Office furniture and equipment, such as desks and files Cell phones, riding lawn mowers, snow blasters Any property that does not have a class life and that has not been designated by law as being in any other class	7 years
Shrubbery Permanent fences Sidewalks Driveways Paved parking areas Landscaping Sewer and drainage facilities Swimming pools	15 years

First-Year Depreciation

The IRS has established certain rules (called conventions) that govern how many months of depreciation you can take for the first year that you own an asset. The conventions for personal property are different than those for real property.

Half-Year Convention

The basic rule is that, no matter when you buy personal property, you treat it as being placed in service on July 1—the midpoint of the year. This means that you can take half a year of depreciation for the first year that you own personal property you use for your rental activity.

> EXAMPLE: Sam owns a small apartment building. In January, he purchases a new carpet for one of his rentals. In March, he buys a new stove for another rental unit. In December, he installs a new dishwasher in the same unit. Sam treats all these items as having been placed in service on July 1.

Mid-Quarter Convention

You are not allowed to use the half-year convention if more than 40% of the long-term personal property you buy during the year is placed in service during the last three months of the year. The 40% figure is determined by adding together the basis of all the depreciable property you bought during the year and comparing that to the basis of all of the property you bought during the fourth quarter.

If you exceed the 40% ceiling, you must use the mid-quarter convention. Group all of the property that you purchased during the year by quarter (depending on when you bought it) and treat it as if you had placed it in service at the midpoint of that quarter. (A quarter is a three-month period. The first quarter is January through March; the second quarter is April through June; the third quarter is July through September; and the fourth quarter is October through December.)

> EXAMPLE: Sam buys a $750 stove in January, an $800 refrigerator in October, and a $600 carpet in December. The basis for all three items he bought during the year is $1,500. He paid $1,000 of this amount during the fourth quarter, so more than 40% of his purchases were made in the fourth quarter of the year. Sam must use the mid-quarter convention. He must treat the stove he bought as being placed in service on February 15—the midpoint of the first quarter. The refrigerator and carpet must be treated as being placed in service on November 15—the midpoint of the fourth quarter. As a result, Sam gets very little depreciation that year for the refrigerator and carpet.

It's usually best to avoid having to use the mid-quarter convention, which means you'll want to buy more than 60% of your total depreciable personal property for your rental activity before September 30 of the year.

Depreciation Methods

Personal property is usually depreciated using the Modified Accelerated Cost Recovery System, or MACRS. (A slightly different system, called the Alternative Depreciation System or ADS, applies to certain property—see "Depreciating Listed Property," below.) You can ordinarily use three different methods to calculate personal property depreciation under MACRS: straight-line depreciation or one of two accelerated depreciation methods. Once you choose your method, you're stuck with it for the entire life of the asset.

In addition, you must use the same method for all property of the same class that you purchase during the year. For example, if you use the straight-line method to depreciate a computer, you must use that method to depreciate any other property in the same class as computers. Computers fall within the five-year class, so you must use the straight-line method for all other five-year property you buy during the year, such as office equipment.

Straight-Line Method

You can use the straight-line method to depreciate any type of depreciable property. (This is the method that you must use to depreciate real property.) Under the straight-line method, you deduct an equal amount each year over the useful life of an asset. If the midyear convention applies (as it often does), you deduct only a half-year's worth of depreciation in the first year. You make up for this by taking an extra one-half year of depreciation at the end. Most people don't choose this method for personal property, however, because you can deduct items faster using one of the accelerated depreciation methods described below.

Accelerated Depreciation Methods

Most people use accelerated depreciation to depreciate personal property. As the name implies, this method provides faster depreciation than the straight-line method. It does not increase your total depreciation deduction, but it permits you to take larger deductions in the first few years after you buy an asset. You make up for this by taking smaller deductions in later years.

The fastest and most commonly used form of accelerated depreciation is the double declining balance method. This is a confusing name, but all it means is that you get double the deduction that you would get for the first full year under the straight-line method. You then get less in later years. However, in later years, you may switch to the straight-line method (which will give you a larger deduction than using accelerated depreciation). This is built into the IRS depreciation tables. You may use this method to depreciate virtually all of the tangible personal property you buy for your rental activity. However, accelerated depreciation may not be used for real property.

> EXAMPLE: Sally decides to use the double declining balance method to depreciate the printer-fax-copier machine she buys for her rental business. Her annual depreciation deductions for the $1,000 cost basis are as follows:
>
> | | | |
> |---|---|---|
> | 2015 | $ | 200 |
> | 2016 | | 320 |
> | 2017 | | 192 |
> | 2018 | | 115 |
> | 2019 | | 115 |
> | 2020 | | 58 |
> | Total | | $ 1,000 |

An alternative to the double declining method is the 150% declining balance method. This method gives you one-and-one-half times the deduction in the first year that you would otherwise get using the straight-line method. The 150% method may be used for three-, five-, seven-, ten-, 15-, and 20-year personal property.

Using accelerated depreciation is not necessarily a good idea if you expect your income to go up in future years. There are also some restrictions on when you can use accelerated depreciation. For example, you can't use it for cars, computers, and certain other property that you use for your rental activity less than 50% of the time (see "Listed Property," below).

Depreciation Tables

You can figure out the amount of your yearly depreciation deduction using depreciation tables prepared by the IRS. These tables factor in the depreciation convention and method. They are all available in IRS Publication 946, *How to Depreciate Property*. There are also many online depreciation calculators you may use.

Listed Property

Fearing that taxpayers might claim depreciation for listed property but actually use it for personal reasons, the IRS imposes special rules on certain personal property that can easily be used for personal as well as business or investment purposes. These items, called listed property, include:

- cars and certain other vehicles
- motorcycles, boats, and airplanes
- computers, and
- any other property generally used for entertainment, recreation, or amusement—for example, televisions, cameras, stereos, and camcorders.

To prevent this kind of behavior, the IRS requires you to document your use of listed property. You can satisfy this requirement by keeping a logbook showing when and how the property is used. (See Chapter 17 for more on record keeping.)

These rules apply only to listed property that you use yourself in your rental activity—for example, a computer you use to do your rental bookkeeping. They do not apply to personal property contained in a rental unit—for example, a television you place in a rental unit for a tenant's use.

Exception for Cell Phones

Since 1989, cell phones have been treated as listed property by the IRS. This caused record-keeping headaches for the legions of businesspeople who purchased cell phones and used them for both business and personal calls. However, all this has changed. Starting in 2010, cell phones and similar personal communications devices are no longer considered listed property. Thus, the strict record-keeping requirements for listed property no longer apply to these devices. You can also use accelerated depreciation for cell phones, even if you use them less than 50% of the time for business. In addition, the fair market value of a cell phone provided to an employee for business purposes need not be included in the employee's gross income for tax purposes, as long as the cell phone is given to the employee for noncompensatory reasons (meaning primarily business reasons).

Exception for Computers

You generally have to document your use of listed property even if you use it 100% for business. However, there is an exception to this rule for computers: If you use a computer or computer peripheral (such as a printer) only for business and keep it at your office, you need not comply with the record-keeping requirement. This includes computers that you keep at your home office, as long as the office qualifies for the home office deduction. (See Chapter 9.)

This exception does not apply to items other than computers and computer peripheral equipment—for example, it doesn't apply to calculators, copiers, fax machines, or typewriters.

Depreciating Listed Property

If you use listed property for your rental activity more than 50% of the time, you may deduct its cost just like any other long-term personal property under the normal depreciation rules. However, if you use listed property 50% or less of the time for your rental activity, you must use the straight-line method—the slowest method of depreciation. And, the property doesn't qualify for the 50% bonus depreciation. You also can't use the normal depreciation periods allowed under the MACRS depreciation system. Instead, you must use the depreciation periods provided for by the Alternative Depreciation System (ADS for short). These are generally longer than the ordinary MACRS periods. However, you may still depreciate cars, trucks, and computers over five years. The main ADS depreciation periods for listed property are provided in the following chart.

ADS Depreciation Periods	
Property	**Depreciation Period**
Cars and light trucks	5 years
Computers and peripheral equipment	5 years
Communication equipment	10 years
Personal property with no class life	12 years

If you start out using accelerated depreciation and in a later year your business use drops to 50% or less, you have to switch to the straight-line method and ADS period for that year and subsequent years. In addition, you are subject to depreciation recapture for the prior years—that is, you must calculate how much more depreciation you got in the prior years by using accelerated depreciation and count that amount as ordinary taxable income for the current year. This will, of course, increase your tax bill for the year.

Section 179 Expensing

Section 179 of the tax code is one of the greatest tax boons available for owners of most types of small businesses. Under Section 179, business owners can deduct the entire cost of long-term personal property that they use in their business, rather than having to depreciate the cost over several years. This is called first-year expensing or Section 179 expensing. Unfortunately, because of restrictions on how it may be used, Section 179 has relatively little importance for most landlords.

What Property Can Be Deducted

A business can use Section 179 to deduct tangible, long-term personal property. However, Section 179 specifically excludes personal property used in residential rental property. This means that landlords can't use Section 179 to deduct the cost of items they purchase for use inside rental units—for example, kitchen appliances, carpets, drapes, or blinds. The only exception is for property in hotels, motels, or vacation homes where the guests stay less than 30 days (see Chapter 15 for a discussion of vacation homes).

In addition, you can't use Section 179 to deduct the cost of:

- land
- land improvements, including swimming pools, paved parking areas, and fences
- permanent structures attached to land, including buildings and their structural components, fences, swimming pools, or paved parking areas
- inventory
- intangible property such as patents, copyrights, and trademarks
- property used outside the United States, or
- air conditioning and heating units.

So, what can a landlord use Section 179 for? Only for personal property not contained in your rental property, such as computers, office equipment, and office furniture you use in your office or other place of business. You can also use it for cars and other vehicles and to deduct the cost of software for your rental business that you placed in service before 2015.

CAUTION
Make sure your rental activities qualify as a business before you use Section 179. Section 179 can only be used if your rental activities qualify as a business for tax purposes. You can't use it if your rental activity is an investment, not a business. Thus, make sure you're a business before you even think about using Section 179. This topic is covered in detail in Chapter 2.

Other Restrictions

Section 179 expensing may be used only for used or new property that you purchase for cash during that year (cash includes amounts you borrow). It may not be used for leased property or property you inherit or are given. Nor may it be used for property you buy from a relative, or from a corporation or other organization you control.

If you use property both for business and personal purposes, you may deduct it under Section 179 only if you use it for business purposes more than half of the time. Reduce the amount of your deduction by the percentage of personal use. You'll need to keep records showing your business use of such property. If you use an item for business less than half the time, you must depreciate it.

Deduction Limit

There is a limit on the total amount of business property expenses you can deduct each year using Section 179. This limit has varied over the past few years. During 2010 through 2014, the limit was $500,000. Starting January 1, 2015, the limit went down to $25,000. However, as this book went to press, it was expected that Congress would act to extend the $500,000 limit through 2015. Due to legislative gridlock, this extension may not be enacted by Congress until late 2015 or even early 2016 (in which event, it will be made retroactive). You can keep up-to-date by visiting the update Web page for this book (see the Introduction for the link).

This dollar limit applies to all your businesses together, not to each business you own and run. You do not have to claim the full amount. It's up to you to decide how much of the cost of property you want to deduct. But you don't lose out on the remainder; you can depreciate any cost you do not deduct under Section 179.

If you purchase more than one item of Section 179 property during the year, you can divide the deduction among all the items in any way, as long as the total deduction is not more than the Section 179 limit. It's usually best to apply Section 179 to property that has the longest useful life and therefore the longest depreciation period. This reduces the total time you have to wait to get your deductions.

Because Section 179 is intended to help smaller businesses, there is also a limit on the total amount of Section 179 property you can purchase each year. You must reduce your Section 179 deduction by one dollar for every dollar your annual purchases exceed the applicable limit. For 2014, the limit was $2 million, and this will likely be the limit for 2015 if Congress extends the $500,000 Section 179 limit for 2015 as is expected.

Income Limit on Section 179 Deduction

Here's yet another big limitation: You can't use Section 179 to deduct more in one year than the total of your profit from all of your businesses and your salary (if you have one). If you're married and file a joint tax return, you can include your spouse's salary and business income in this total as well. You can't count investment income—for example, interest you earn on your savings.

You can't use Section 179 to reduce your taxable income below zero. But you can carry to the next tax year any amount you cannot use as a Section 179 deduction and possibly deduct it then.

> **EXAMPLE:** In 2015, Amelia earned a $5,000 profit from her rental house and $10,000 from a part-time job. She spent $17,000 for computer and office equipment. She can use Section 179 to deduct $15,000 (her total profit and salary for the year) and she can deduct the remaining $2,000 the following year.

Minimum Period of Business Use

When you deduct an asset under Section 179, you must continue to use it for business at least 50% of the time for as many years as it would have been depreciated. For example, if you use Section 179 for a computer, you must use it for business at least 50% of the time for five years, because computers have a five-year depreciation period.

If you don't meet these rules, you'll have to report as income part of the deduction you took under Section 179 in the prior year. This is called recapture.

When You Sell Your Property

When you sell your property, you'll have to pay tax on any gain (profit) you earn ("realize," in tax lingo), unless you do a like-kind exchange. If you lose money, you'll be able to deduct the loss, subject to important limitations covered in Chapter 16. Whether you have a gain or loss depends on your adjusted basis in the property.

Adjusted Basis

Your basis in property is not fixed. It changes over time to reflect the true amount of your investment. This new basis is called the adjusted basis because it reflects adjustments from your starting basis. Increases in basis are good because they'll reduce any taxable profit when you sell your property. Decreases in basis are bad because they have the opposite effect.

Reductions in Basis

Each year, you must subtract from the property's basis the amount of depreciation allowed for the property—this is true regardless of whether you actually claimed any depreciation on your tax return. If you hold on to your property for the full recovery period—27.5 years for residential rental property—your adjusted basis will be reduced to zero, and there will be nothing left to depreciate.

Your starting basis in property must also be reduced by any items that represent a return of your cost. These include:

- the amount of any insurance or other payment you receive as the result of a casualty or theft loss
- any deductible casualty loss not covered by insurance (see Chapter 13), and
- any amount you receive for granting an easement.

Your basis is also reduced if you took the wrong amount of depreciation on your tax return. If you claimed too little depreciation, you must decrease the basis by the amount you should have taken. If you took too much depreciation, you must decrease your basis by the amount you should have deducted, plus the part of the excess you deducted that actually lowered your tax liability for any year.

Increases in Basis

You must increase the basis of any property by:

- the cost of any additions or improvements
- amounts spent to restore property after it is damaged or lost due to theft, fire, flood, storm, or other casualty (see Chapter 13)
- the cost of extending utility service lines to the property, and

- legal fees relating to the property, such as the cost of defending and perfecting title.

In addition, assessments for items that tend to increase the value of your property, such as streets and sidewalks, must be added to its basis. For example, if your city installs curbing on the street in front of your rental house, and assesses you for the cost, you must add the assessment to the basis of your property.

Effect of Adjusted Basis When You Sell

When you sell your rental property, your gain or loss for tax purposes is determined by subtracting its adjusted basis on the date of sale from the sales price (plus sales expenses, such as real estate commissions). Thus, reductions in basis can increase your tax liability when you sell your property because they will increase your gain. Increases in basis will reduce your gain and therefore your tax liability.

EXAMPLE: Viola bought a small apartment building in January 2010 and sold it for $300,000 in December 2015. Her starting basis was $200,000. The following chart shows her adjusted basis for each year.

Year	Depreciation Deduction	Increases in Basis	Adjusted Basis (increases – reductions)
Original Cost			$ 200,000
2010	$ 6,970	None	193,030
2011	7,272	None	185,758
2012	7,272	None	178,486
2013	7,272	None	171,214
2014	7,272	None	163,942
2015	6,969	$13,027 for new roof	170,000
Total depreciation	$ 43,027		

Viola calculates her taxable gain on the property by subtracting her adjusted basis from the sales price: $300,000 – $170,000 = $130,000.

As you can see, when you sell your property, you effectively give back the depreciation deductions you took on it. Since they reduce your adjusted basis, they increase your taxable gain. Thus, Viola's taxable gain was increased by the $43,027 in depreciation deductions she took. The amount of your gain attributable to the depreciation deductions you took in prior years is taxed at a single 25% rate (however, if your top tax rate is below 25%, the lower rate applies). Viola, for example, would have to pay a 25% tax on the $43,027 in depreciation deductions she received. The remaining gain on the sale is taxed at capital gains rates for 2014. The gain must also be added to Viola's net investment income and her adjusted gross income. This could make her subject to the 3.8% Net Investment Income tax (see Chapter 19).

		Tax Rate	Tax
Sales price	$300,000		
Adjusted basis	170,000		
Total gain (sales price – adjusted basis)	$130,000		
	$130,000		
Gain due to prior depreciation	– 43,027	x 25% =	$10,757
Remaining capital gain (total gain – depreciation)	$ 86,973	x 15% =	13,046
Total Tax			$23,803

You can't avoid this result by failing to take depreciation deductions each year. The IRS will treat you as if you had taken the depreciation and reduce your adjusted basis accordingly. Thus, you'll end up paying tax on depreciation deductions you never claimed. A true tax disaster!

Capital Gains Rates

2015 Income If Married Filing Jointly	Long-Term Capital Gains Tax Rates
$74,900 or less	0
$74,901 to $464,850	15%
All over $464,850	20%

2015 Income If Single	Long-Term Capital Gains Tax Rates
$37,450 or less	0
$37,451 to $413,200	15%
All over $413,200	20%

In addition, taxpayers subject to the Net Investment Income tax have to pay an additional 3.8% tax on some or all of their gains. This tax applies to single taxpayers with an adjusted gross income over $200,000, and married couples filing jointly who have an AGI over $250,000. Depending on their income, such taxpayers will pay an 18.8% or 23.8% tax on their gains. (See Chapter 19.)

Like-Kind Exchanges: Deferring Taxes on Rental Property

In a like-kind exchange (also called a Section 1031 exchange), you can defer paying taxes upon the sale of property by swapping your property for similar property owned by someone else. The property you receive in a like-kind exchange is treated as if it were a continuation of the property you gave up. The result is that you postpone the recognition (taxation) of gain by shifting the basis of old property to the new property. So you defer paying taxes on any profit you would have received and own new property instead. Such deferral applies not only to regular capital gains taxes, but to the new 3.8% Net Investment Income tax as well.

! CAUTION
Like-kind exchanges are one of the most complex areas of taxation.
There are many rules that are strictly enforced by the IRS. These exchanges should
be done only with professional assistance.

> **EXAMPLE:** Eve exchanges a rental house with an adjusted basis of $250,000
> for other real estate held for investment. The fair market value of both
> properties is $500,000. The basis of Eve's new property is the same as the
> basis of the old ($250,000). No gain is recognized on the transaction.

You may only exchange property for other similar property, called
like-kind property by the IRS. Like-kind properties have the same
nature or character, even if they differ in grade or quality. All real estate
owned for investment or business use in the United States is considered
to be like kind with all other such real estate in the United States, no
matter the type or location. For example, an apartment building in New
York is like kind to an office building in California.

If you keep exchanging your property for property worth at least as
much as yours, you'll never recognize any gain on which you must pay
tax. However, sooner or later you'll probably want to sell the replacement
property for cash, not exchange it for another property. When this occurs,
the original deferred gain, plus any additional gain realized since the
purchase of the replacement property, is subject to tax. For this reason, a
like-kind exchange is tax deferred, not tax free.

> **EXAMPLE 1:** Assume that five years after the exchange described in the
> above example, Eve sells her rental house for $800,000 cash. Now she has
> to pay tax—and quite a lot at that—because she has a $550,000 long-term
> capital gain. Her gain is $550,000 because her basis in the property is only
> $250,000 (the basis of the property she exchanged for the building five years
> earlier). The $800,000 sales price minus the $250,000 basis = $550,000 gain.

However, if you convert the last property you exchange into your
personal residence, you can permanently exclude up to $500,000 of your
gain from its sale. You must own the property for at least five years and
live in it for at least two years to qualify for this exclusion.

EXAMPLE 2: Assume that Eve rents out her house for all of 2010, 2011, and 2012. On April 15, 2013, she moves into the house and uses it as her personal residence. She can sell the property any time after April 14, 2015 (after five years of ownership and living there for two years), and pay no tax at all on up to $500,000 of her gain because she is a married taxpayer filing jointly (the exclusion is only $250,000 for single taxpayers).

In practice, it's rarely the case that two people want to swap their properties with each other. Instead, one of the property owners usually wants cash for his or her property, not a swap. This transaction can still be structured as a like-kind exchange. This is often done with the help of a third party called a qualified intermediary or QI, in the business of facilitating like-kind exchanges.

EXAMPLE: Abe owns a rental triplex he bought for $400,000 and is now worth $500,000. He wants to exchange it for other property instead of selling it and having to pay tax on his $100,000 profit. He puts his property up for sale and in the meantime contacts Carl, a qualified intermediary. Carl locates a small apartment building worth $500,000 that Abe likes. Bob, the owner of the building, however, has no interest in exchanging it for other property. Carl and Abe enter into an exchange agreement. Carl purchases Bob's building for $500,000 cash that he borrows and then exchanges it for Abe's triplex. Carl receives a fee for facilitating the exchange and sells Abe's triplex to repay the funds he borrowed to buy Bob's property. With Carl's help, Abe has exchanged his triplex for Bob's building, even though Bob didn't want to do an exchange.

There are strict time limits on such delayed exchanges, which can be more complicated than the above example, involving as many as four parties. You must identify the replacement property for your property within 45 days of its sale. And your replacement property purchase must be completed within 180 days of the initial sale. Because of these time limits, it's a good idea to have a replacement property lined up before you sell your property. Professional exchange companies (also called accommodators or facilitators) can help you find replacement property and handle the transaction for you. You can find listings for such companies through the website of the Federation of Exchange Accommodators at www.1031.org.

For more information on real property exchanges, see IRS Publication 544, *Sales and Other Dispositions of Assets*, and IRS Inst. 8824, *Instructions for Form 8824, Like-Kind Exchanges*. Also, refer to *The Real Estate Investor's Tax Guide*, by Vernon Hoven (Dearborn).

The Home Sale Exclusion— Avoiding Taxes When You Sell Your Rental

You may be familiar with the home sale exclusion, which allows individuals who sell their principal home to exclude from their taxable income up to $250,000 of the gain from the sale, or up to $500,000 if the sellers are a married couple who file a joint return. (The exclusion applies not only to regular income tax, but to the 3.8% Net Investment Income tax as well; see Chapter 19.) What you may not know, however, is that this valuable exclusion can be used for rental property too. To qualify for the $250,000/$500,000 home sale exclusion you (or your spouse or former spouse) must own and occupy a home as your principal residence for at least two of the five years before you sell it. This means that the home may not be a rental property during those two years. However, you don't have to be living in the house at the time you sell it. Your two years of ownership and use may occur anytime during the five years before the date of the sale. This means, for example, that you can move out of the house for up to three years and still qualify for the exclusion. (I.R.C. § 121(a).) This rule has a very practical application: It means you may rent out your home for up to three years prior to the sale and still qualify for the exclusion. Be sure to keep track of this time period and sell the house before it runs out.

> EXAMPLE: Connie purchases a one-bedroom condo on January 1, 2010 and lives in it for two full years. She then moves to another state to take a new job. Rather than sell the condo, she elects to rent it out. If she sells the condo by January 1, 2016, she'll qualify for the $250,000 home sale exclusion because she owned and used the condo as her principal home for two years during the five-year period before the sale. If she waits even one more day to sell, she will get no exclusion at all.

However, starting in 2009, the tax law limits the $250,000/$500,000 exclusion for taxpayers who initially use their home as a rental, vacation home, or for any other use than as a principal residence (a "nonqualifying use" in IRS-speak). The amount of gain eligible for the applicable exclusion is reduced pro rata based on how many years after 2008 the home was used other than as the taxpayer's principal residence. The effect is to reduce the exclusion for landlords who convert a rental home into their personal residence.

> **EXAMPLE:** Timmy, a single taxpayer, buys a home on January 1, 2010 for $500,000 and rents it out for the next two years. On January 1, 2012, he evicts his tenants and moves into the house, making it his personal residence on that date. Timmy sells the property for $750,000 on January 1, 2015. Timmy owned the house for five years and had a $250,000 gain on the sale. Is his entire gain eligible for the $250,000 exclusion, thereby wiping out his entire gain for tax purposes? Unfortunately for Timmy, the answer is no. Because Timmy used the home as a rental for two years before he converted it into his principal residence, 40% of his total use of the property during the five years he owned it constitutes a nonqualifying use (two years is 40% of five years). Thus, the amount of his $250,000 gain eligible for the exclusion must be reduced by 40%, or $100,000. Timmy must pay income tax on this amount (at long-term capital gains rates). The remaining $150,000 of his gain is eligible for the exclusion and is tax free.

This reduction in the $250,000/$500,000 exclusion can only occur if the home was used as a rental or other nonqualifying use before it became the taxpayer's principal residence. Rental or other uses of the home after it was used as the principal residence do not constitute a nonqualified use and thus do not reduce the exclusion. This is why Connie's rental of her condo in the first example above, after she lived in it, does not reduce her $250,000 exclusion.

This rule applies only to nonqualifying uses occurring during 2009 and later. Uses before 2009 are not counted and do not reduce the amount of gain eligible for the applicable exclusion.

RESOURCE

For more information on the home sale exclusion, refer to IRS Publication 523, *Selling Your Home.*

Tax Reporting and Record Keeping for Depreciation

You must report depreciation on IRS Form 4562, *Depreciation and Amortization (Including Information on Listed Property).* Carry over the amount of your depreciation to your Schedule E and subtract it from your gross rental income along with your other rental expenses.

TIP

Use a tax software program for Form 4562. Form 4562 is one of the most complex and confusing IRS forms. If you want to complete it yourself, do yourself a favor and use a tax preparation program.

You need to keep accurate records for each asset you depreciate showing:

- a description of the asset
- when and how you purchased the property
- the date it was placed in service
- its original cost
- the percentage of time you use it for business
- the amount of depreciation you took for the asset in prior years, if any
- the asset's depreciable basis
- the depreciation method used
- the length of the depreciation period, and
- the amount of depreciation you deducted for the year.

If you use tax preparation software, it should create a worksheet containing this information. Be sure to check these carefully and save them. You can also use an accounting program such as *QuickBooks* to keep track of your depreciating assets. (Simple checkbook programs like *Quicken* are not designed to track depreciation.) You may also use a spreadsheet program to create your own depreciation worksheet. Spreadsheet templates are available for this purpose. Of course, you can also do the job by hand.

The instructions to IRS Form 4562 contain a blank worksheet you can use.

An example of a filled-out worksheet is shown below.

Depreciation Worksheet

Description of Property	Date Placed in Service	Cost or Other Basis	Business/ Investment Use Percentage	Section 179 Deduction and Special Allowance
House 666 First St.	2/10/05	$200,000	100%	0
New roof 123 Main St.	4/10/03	$10,000	100%	0

continued below

continued from above

Depreciation In Prior Years	Basis for Depreciation	Method/ Convention	Recovery Period	Rate or Table Percentage	Depreciation Deduction
0	$200,000	SL/MM	27.5	3.182%	$6,364
$258	$10,000	SL/MM	27.5	3.636%	$364

Be sure to keep all the documents you have showing the cost of your depreciable assets. This includes:

- your real property purchase agreement
- the settlement statement and closing statement you receive from the escrow company when your property purchase is completed
- canceled checks and receipts for all the expenses you paid for the purchase
- receipts and canceled checks for all improvements you make to the property
- property tax bills, and
- evidence for the improvement ratio (see Chapter 6).

If you use segmented depreciation (see Chapter 6), you need evidence of the personal property that was included with your purchase and its age—this includes carpeting, stove, refrigerator, dishwasher, drapes and other window coverings, washers, and dryers. You can include this information in your purchase agreement or a separate statement signed by the seller.

Maximizing Your Depreciation Deductions

Determining the Value of Your Land and Buildings 184

    There Is No One Way to Determine Land and Building Values.................... 186

    Figuring Your Improvement Ratio.. 187

    Property Tax Bill 188

    Replacement Cost 189

    Buyer–Seller Valuation.. 193

    Comparable Land Sales 194

Segmented Depreciation 195

    Identifying Your Personal Property.. 197

    Determining Fair Market Value of Personal Property.................................... 200

    Steps to Calculate Segmented Depreciation 201

This chapter shows you two important ways to maximize your depreciation deductions. First, you'll learn how to best determine the value of your rental buildings and nondepreciable land. Next, you'll see how you can use segmented depreciation to greatly increase the depreciation deductions you get each year during the first few years you own rental property.

Do You Really Need a Larger Depreciation Deduction?

Using the methods described in this chapter to increase your depreciation deductions will be a pointless exercise if you can't make use of the deductions. This will be the case if more deductions will only increase your real estate losses and the passive activity loss rules prevent you from currently deducting any more losses than you already are deducting (or deducting any losses at all). If you're uncertain about whether you can make use of more rental activity deductions, carefully read Chapter 16. If you can't benefit from more deductions, don't bother using segmented depreciation.

Determining the Value of Your Land and Buildings

As discussed in Chapter 5, you can't depreciate land because it lasts forever. However, when you buy a rental property, you usually pay one lump sum that covers the cost of both the land and buildings it contains. To determine the depreciable value of the buildings (their basis), you must allocate the purchase price between the land and buildings and other depreciable property.

How you do this allocation is the single most important factor that will determine how much depreciation you may deduct each year and in total. The more your land is worth, the less your basis in the property and the less depreciation you will receive.

EXAMPLE: Miranda owns a duplex that cost $200,000. If the land is worth $50,000, she'll have a $150,000 depreciable basis for the building. If the land is worth $20,000, her basis in the building will be $180,000. The chart below illustrates the difference in the depreciation deductions she'll receive assuming the property was placed in service in January. She receives over $1,000 more in depreciation each year with the lower land valuation.

Year	Depreciation: $150,000 basis ($50,000 land value)	Depreciation: $180,000 basis ($20,000 land value)
1	$5,228	$6,264
2–27	$5,454	$6,555
28	$2,955	$3,546

It's up to you (or your accountant or tax preparer) to decide how much your land and buildings are worth in the first year you depreciate your property. You don't need to provide your allocation or explain how you arrived at it on the forms you file with the IRS to claim depreciation—you simply list your property's depreciable basis. However, the IRS can review your determination if you're audited. In that event, you'll need to explain how you arrived at your basis.

If the IRS determines that your valuation is too low, you'll have to pay back some of the depreciation you received, along with interest and, in some cases, tax penalties. (See "Tax Penalties for Unreasonable Valuations," below.)

Most people don't give their land valuation much thought; they simply use a standard formula or their property tax bill to determine its value. But, as explained below, there are other ways to value your land and buildings that may yield much better results.

Tax Penalties for Unreasonable Valuations

The IRS may impose tax penalties if it determines that you overstated the value of your buildings and other depreciable property—and correspondingly, understated the value of your land. The penalty is equal to 20% of the amount of tax you underpaid. However, the penalty may be imposed only if you overstated the value of your depreciable property by at least 200% over the correct amount and the overstatement resulted in an underpayment of tax of at least $5,000. Few small landlords ever overstate the value of their property by this much. Moreover, even if you do over-state your values by this amount, the IRS must waive the penalty if you had a "reasonable basis" for your valuation and acted in good faith. (I.R.C. § 6662.) The fact that your property valuations must be wildly inflated before you'll be subject to tax penalties gives you an idea of how much leeway you have in deciding what depreciable rental property is worth.

There Is No One Way to Determine Land and Building Values

The IRS gives landlords virtually no guidance on how to go about calculating the value of their land and buildings for depreciation purposes. Its regulations simply provide that "In the case of the acquisition ... of a combination of depreciable and nondepreciable property for a lump sum, as for example, buildings and land, the basis for depreciation cannot exceed an amount which bears the same proportion to the lump sum as the value of the depreciable property at the time of acquisition bears to the value of the entire property at that time." (IRS Reg. § 1.167(a)-5.)

In other words, the basis of the nondepreciable land and the depreciable buildings and other improvements must be allocated in proportion to their relative values. But how do you arrive at these relative values? There is no single method to determine how much any property is worth, and the IRS does not require you to use any particular method. Different methods can yield very different results. The methods you may employ include using:

- your property tax bill
- the replacement cost of your building and improvements
- buyer–seller valuations, or
- comparable land sales.

You can try all these methods and use the best result, or average the various results you obtain. Remember, your valuation doesn't have to be precise, it just has to be a reasonable ballpark figure.

Figuring Your Improvement Ratio

The easy way to determine how much of the value of the property you can depreciate is to figure your property's improvement ratio (also called the land-to-building ratio or land-to-improvement ratio). This is the amount the improvements (buildings) are worth compared to the value of the total property, expressed as a percentage. This is a mathematical way to show the relative values of the land and improvements, as the IRS regulation requires.

For example, if you determine that the correct improvement ratio for your property is 80%, you multiply the total cost of the property by this amount to determine your depreciable basis. If your total cost (purchase price + certain depreciable expenses of the sale) is $100,000, the amount you can depreciate is $80,000 ($100,000 × 80% = $80,000). The other $20,000 is the value of the land, which may not be depreciated.

Improvement ratios vary from 85% to 40% or less depending on the location of the property. Obviously, land values vary widely—for example, land in Manhattan or San Francisco is worth much more than the same amount of land in Kansas City or Portland. Thus, an apartment building in San Francisco may have a 40% improvement ratio, while the same structure in Portland would have an 80% ratio.

It's important to understand that there's no such thing as a precise improvement ratio for a property. This is because land value is not a fact, like the size of a lot; rather, it's based on someone's opinion or calculations based on certain assumptions. Different opinions or assumptions can lead to different ratios. You want your improvement ratio to be as high as possible, but not so high that the IRS will likely conclude it's unreasonable if you're audited.

Don't Use a Standard Improvement Ratio

Many accountants and tax preparers use a standard ratio for every property—for example, 75% or 80%. They don't bother to look at any evidence of the property's value, such as the county tax assessor's valuation or lender's appraisal. Don't use this method—it leaves much to be desired. If the IRS audits you and questions the ratio, you'll have no evidence to back it up.

Property Tax Bill

Most landlords determine their improvement ratios by using their property tax bill. The bill usually provides a valuation of the land and buildings together, and a value for each alone, or for just the buildings alone. The ratio is determined by dividing the assessed improvement value by the total assessed value of the property (assessed improvement value ÷ total assessed value = improvement ratio).

If you don't have a copy of your tax bill handy, you may be able to find the assessor's valuation at its website. The following websites provide links to local tax assessor websites in the various states:

- Property assessment databases: www.propertyassessmentdirectory. com, and
- Tax assessor database: www.pulawski.net.

Often, the values listed on your property tax bill do not reflect the true market value of your property. This is not important, however, for purposes of determining your improvement ratio.

EXAMPLE: Suzy buys a rental duplex with a total basis of $200,000 (purchase price + depreciable sale expenses). The property tax bill lists the property's total value at $160,000, and provides that the improvements are worth $110,000 and the land $50,000. According to the county tax assessor, therefore, the property has a 69% improvement ratio. ($110,000 ÷ $160,000 = 69%.) Using this percentage, her depreciable basis is $138,000. (69% × $200,000 = $138,000.) She may use this amount to determine her depreciation each year.

This is a very easy and simple way to calculate the value of your land and buildings. It is what most people do, and the IRS will almost never object if you use this method. However, improvement ratios determined from a property tax assessment often do not reflect reality. County tax assessors aren't greatly concerned about arriving at an accurate break- down of the relative values of your land and improvements. This is because it has no effect on your property tax bill—your tax is based on the total assessed value of your property. Often, county assessors apply a standard percentage to all property in the area—for example, 70%. Or, they may use sales data from previous years that is out of date.

As a general rule, tax assessor improvement ratios are on the low side. You can usually do better using a different means to determine your basis.

You Don't Have to Use the Assessor's Valuation

Many people believe they have to use their county tax assessor's valuations to calculate their basis. This is not the case. There is nothing in the tax law or IRS regulations that requires you to use a county tax assessor valuation or hire an appraiser to do a valuation. Indeed, in at least one case, the tax court found that the improvement ratio derived from the county assessor's valuation should not be used, declaring that there was no evidence that "the assessor's allocations of value between land and building comport with reality." (*Meiers v. Comm'r.*, T.C. Memo 1982-5.) This is a good case to point out to any IRS auditor who says you have to use your county tax assessor's valuation.

Replacement Cost

Another way to determine your improvement ratio is to use the replace- ment cost of your building and other improvements. The replacement cost is the cost to build a brand-new structure that is identical with the structure currently on your land.

EXAMPLE: Steven Meiers purchased two condominiums in 1977. His property tax bill gave an improvement ratio of 55%—that is, the land was worth 45% of the purchase price and the building 55%. Meiers didn't think this was good enough. He investigated the replacement costs for his buildings, and determined that a fair improvement ratio was 80%. This, of course, gave him a much higher depreciable basis. Meiers was audited by the IRS, which insisted that he should use the tax assessor's ratio. Meiers appealed to the tax court and won. The court found that Meiers's 80% ratio was reasonable and should be used. How did Meiers calculate his ratio? He used the replacement cost of the buildings. (*Meiers v. Comm'r.*, T.C. Memo 1982-5.)

There are several ways to determine replacement cost:
- appraisal
- your own calculations
- expert opinion, or
- construction records.

Appraisal

If you borrowed money from a bank or other lender to acquire the property, the lender almost certainly required an appraisal before approving your loan. You should make sure to obtain and keep a copy of the appraisal. It should contain the appraiser's estimate of how much it would cost to replace the structure and how much the land is worth. This may be in the section of the appraisal report called cost approach. The appraiser provides an estimate of how much it would cost to replace the structure with an identical new structure, and then reduces this amount with an allowance for depreciation, depending on the age of the building. The appraiser also gives an estimate of the cost of replacing improvements other than the building—for example, walkways. These are added together to come up with the total replacement cost—often called indicated value by cost approach. The IRS will probably accept the appraiser's valuation, unless it's clearly unreasonable.

You calculate your improvement ratio by dividing the amount of the appraiser's replacement cost by the appraised value of the entire property (structures and land). In other words, appraiser's replacement cost of building and land improvements ÷ appraised value of entire property = improvement ratio.

EXAMPLE: Recall Miranda from the first example, who bought a rental duplex for $200,000. Her lender's appraisal provides that the value of the entire property is $210,000. The cost method section says that the replacement cost of the duplex and other property improvements is $150,000. This gives Miranda an improvement ratio of 71% ($150,000 ÷ $210,000 = 71%). This is better than the 69% improvement ratio the county assessor's valuation provided.

Calculating Replacement Value Yourself

Appraisers are not infallible. An appraisal is just one person's opinion as to how much a property is worth. Appraisals of the same property by different appraisers can and do differ. Your lender's appraisal of the replacement cost may have been poorly done or been too conservative. Like county tax assessors, lenders' appraisers are more concerned with the total value of the property than the relative values of the land and structures, so they may not have given the replacement cost calculation all the time and attention you would like.

If you think this is the case, you can hire an appraiser to do a new valuation of your property. An appraisal for a single-family residence costs about $375 to $400. Appraising an income property of two or more units costs at least $800 to $1,000. Your appraisal will carry the most weight with the IRS if it's done by a well-qualified appraiser. Well-qualified real estate appraisers ordinarily belong to the Appraisal Institute and use the initials MAI (Member of the Appraisal Institute). You can find a directory of MAI appraisers at www.appraisalinstitute.org.

If you want to pay for an appraisal, go ahead. However, you don't have to hire an expensive appraiser to determine your property's replacement cost. You can do it yourself. This is what Steven Meiers in the above example did. This will require that you spend a little time and effort, but will enable you to cheaply double-check the replacement cost determined by the lender's appraiser.

Figuring out the replacement cost for a building might sound hard, but it really isn't. The Marshall and Swift Valuation Service has a website that will calculate the replacement cost of a building for you (www.swiftestimator.com). All you have to do is plug in detailed information about the structure—its size, building materials, age, location, and so forth. It is very inexpensive to use—just a few dollars per estimate.

If you don't want to use a website, you can calculate your building's replacement cost by using one of the many readily available publications that provide estimates of how much it costs to build any type of structure. These include:

- The *National Building Cost Manual* (Craftsman Book Company; www.craftsman-book.com)
- The *National Building Cost Estimator* (Craftsman Book Company), and
- *Walker's Building Estimator's Reference Book* (Frank R. Walker Co., www.frankrwalker.com).

You should be able to find one or more of these in your public library. Make sure to use the current edition. These books are updated each year.

> **EXAMPLE:** Miranda wants to figure the replacement value of her duplex herself. She refers to the *National Building Cost Manual* in her local library. It tells her that the cost to build a four-unit building like hers of average quality is $60 per square foot. Her building contains 3,000 square feet, resulting in a $180,000 replacement cost. However, the $180,000 amount represents the cost to build a brand new building. Miranda's building is five years old. The *National Building Cost Manual* tells Miranda that a building like hers has approximately a 55-year useful life and will be worth 88% of its original cost after five years. 88% of $180,000 equals $158,400. This is the true approximate value of Miranda's building. This amount gives her an improvement ratio of 79% ($158,400 ÷ $200,000 = 79%). This is better than the 75% improvement ratio she obtained using the appraiser's valuation. She decides to use this improvement ratio to calculate her depreciation. She takes care to keep all the documentation showing how she calculated her duplex's replacement value, including making copies of the relevant pages from the *National Building Cost Manual*.

Expert Opinion

Another, perhaps easier, way to figure out a building's replacement cost yourself is to ask your insurance company. They insure buildings, so they need to know accurately how much they are worth. Ask your insurance agent when you purchase the insurance for your property. Local builders can also tell you how much it would cost to rebuild a structure like yours. Ideally, you should have the insurance agent or builder write down the estimate on his or her letterhead, and date and sign it. Be sure to keep it in your records.

Construction Records

Alternatively, if you built the building yourself, or bought it from a seller who built it, you may have ready access to construction documentation showing exactly how much it cost to build the structure. This will make it easy to figure the replacement value—use the original cost less a reduction for depreciation that you can calculate using the references listed above.

Buyer–Seller Valuation

When you buy real estate, you usually pay one lump sum for everything on the property. However, you and the seller could agree on how much the land and buildings are worth and list the values in your purchase agreement.

> **EXAMPLE:** Charles Nicholson had the following language added to the escrow instructions for commercial property he purchased in Northern California: "80% of the real estate value is attributed to the building and 20% to land." Unfortunately for Nicholson, the IRS didn't agree with this allocation and neither did the tax court. The court found that there wasn't a shred of evidence that the building was worth 80% of the property's purchase price. Instead, it concluded that a 10% improvement ratio was proper. (*Nicholson v. Comm'r.*, T.C. Memo 1993-183.)

As the *Nicholson* case shows, any allocation you and the seller agree on probably isn't worth much. Sellers ordinarily don't care about the cost allocation between the land and building—they're only concerned with the total purchase price. Thus, they are likely to agree to any allocation the buyer wants. This makes such allocations inherently suspect in the eyes of the IRS and courts.

However, this doesn't mean that it's necessarily a bad idea to allocate the purchase price between the land and buildings in your purchase agreement. It costs nothing to do so and the allocation could impress an IRS auditor who doesn't know what he or she is doing (more than a few fall into this category). Make sure, though, that your allocation is not unreasonable, or the IRS will likely ignore it.

Comparable Land Sales

An entirely different way to determine your depreciable basis is to estimate the value of your land alone by seeing what comparable unimproved real estate in the area sells for. To do this, you look at the selling prices of a number of vacant lots, calculate their average per-square-foot cost, and apply it to your land. Be warned, however, that this approach often leads to inflated land values.

> EXAMPLE: Miranda's rental duplex has a 10,000-square-foot lot. She looks at three similar vacant lots in the area that sold in the past two years. Their total square footage was 25,000, and the total sales price for the lots was $150,000. This results in an average per-square-foot cost of $6. By applying this average cost to her property, Miranda determines that her land is worth $60,000 ($6 × 10,000 square feet = $60,000). This is, by far, the worst result Miranda achieved with any of the methods she used. Even using the assessed valuation, her land was worth only $50,000.

You can look for comparable lots offered for sale in the area in the multiple listing service, or check the county recorder's office. However, it may be hard to find any comparable unimproved land if your property is in a highly urban area. Also, you need to make sure to compare the prices only of unimproved lots—that is, lots that don't have underground utilities, sidewalks, or grading. Improvements such as these increase land values, so you'll get an inflated result.

Segmented Depreciation

When you purchase a rental property—whether a house, duplex, apartment building, or condominium—you pay a single lump sum to the owner, but you are actually purchasing more than one asset. Rental property consists of:

- the land the building sits on, as well as any other surrounding land included with the purchase
- improvements that have been made to the land, such as landscaping
- the building itself, and
- personal property items inside the building that are not building components—for example, refrigerators, stoves, dishwashers, and carpeting.

Most landlords depreciate all these items together (excluding the land, which is not depreciable), using the 27.5-year recovery period for buildings and the straight-line depreciation method—which is how buildings must be depreciated (see Chapter 5).

However, you have the option of depreciating each asset separately. (*Hospital Corporation of America*, 109 T.C. 21 (1997).) This depreciation method is more complicated, and will require more record keeping, but it will result in a larger total depreciation deduction each year during the first several years you own the property. This is because personal property and land improvements have much shorter depreciation periods than residential real property and can be depreciated using accelerated depreciation. Your total depreciation deduction won't be any different, but you'll get it much more quickly.

However, you'll get no benefit from segmented depreciation if you can't deduct your real estate losses because of the passive loss rules. You'll just add on to your suspended passive losses that you can't use. (See Chapter 16.)

Moreover, the benefits gained from segmented depreciation may be minimal or nonexistent if you don't plan to keep the rental building very long before selling. This is because of depreciation recapture. When you sell your rental building, you'll have to recapture the depreciation you've previously taken on the personal property it contains and pay tax on it. To the extent of gain on the sale, the depreciation claimed on personal property is recaptured as ordinary income at tax rates up to 39.6%. In contrast, the gain attributable to depreciation of real property is taxed at a maximum rate of 25%.

The longer you wait before you sell, the less impact the depreciation recapture taxes will have because you've had many years to make use of the additional tax savings that accrued from using segmented depreciation. Moreover, you may not be in the 39.6% rate bracket at the time you make the sale.

The technical name for this type of depreciation is cost segregation. For convenience, we'll refer to it as segmented depreciation.

The IRS has created a highly detailed guide to segmented depreciation for its auditors. It's designed primarily for high-value real property, but still contains a valuable overview of the topic. You can access the guide, *Cost Segregation Audit Techniques Guide,* for free on the IRS website at www.irs.gov (search under "cost segregation").

Segmented Depreciation—Better Late Than Never (Sometimes)

If you've already purchased a property and started depreciating it as a single entity over 27.5 years, it might not be too late to use segmented depreciation. You can do an analysis now and currently deduct the increased depreciation deductions that you could have taken if you had used segmented depreciation from the time you acquired the property. This type of catch-up depreciation can amount to a large cash windfall.

The difference between what was deducted and what could have been deducted is known as an I.R.C. § 481(a) adjustment. You can deduct the entire difference in a single year by filing IRS Form 3115 to request a change in accounting method. This type of change is ordinarily granted automatically by the IRS (see Rev. Proc. 2004-11) and you don't need to file any amended tax returns. Unfortunately, IRS Form 3115 is an extremely complex form. You'll likely need help from a tax professional to complete it properly.

Cost Segregation Study
You may wish to hire an engineer to conduct a cost segregation study to determine how to classify and value your property's various components. A study by a qualified construction engineer may be viewed as more reliable by the IRS. Indeed, the IRS's cost segregation audit guide provides that "a preparer's credentials and level of expertise may have a bearing on the overall accuracy and quality of a study. In general, a study by a construction engineer is more reliable than one conducted by someone with no engineering or construction background."

The new IRS regulations that went into effect in 2014 make these studies more valuable than ever. (See Chapter 4 for a detailed discussion of these regulations.) The regulations divide buildings into up to nine separate units of property that a building owner may have to separately identify and value when building components are retired or replaced. A cost segregation study that values these units and components will prove useful for the life of the building.

The engineer should inspect the property and, wherever possible, use construction-based documents such as blueprints and specifications to determine the value of the building components. When estimates are required, they should be based on costing data from contractors or reliable published sources. The engineer should prepare a detailed written report that you can show to the IRS if you are audited and it questions your valuations. Such a study can be expensive—typically $10,000 to $25,000— but the cost is a tax deductible business expense. Whether paying for such a study makes sense for you depends on how much your rental property is worth. The speedier depreciation you'll obtain may justify the expense if your property is worth $750,000 or more. |

Identifying Your Personal Property

Experts estimate that anywhere from 20% to 35% of the property in apartments and other residential properties is personal property that can be depreciated much more quickly than the building itself. It is to your advantage to identify as many of these items of personal property inside and outside your rental building as you can. This way, you can depreciate them separately from your building and land improvements using accelerated depreciation and shorter recovery periods. Each component that is reclassified as personal property must be treated as an individual unit of property for depreciation purposes. See Chapter 4, "Defining the 'Unit of Property.'"

Any tangible property inside, or attached to, your rental building, that is not a structural component, is personal property for depreciation purposes. IRS regulations define structural components as:

- "all parts of a building," and
- "all other components relating to the operation or maintenance of a building." (IRS Reg. § 1.48-1(e)(2).)

Ordinarily, a building is planned, designed, and constructed with the expectation that the structural components will remain in place indefinitely. They are usually integrated with the building during the construction phase and are permanent parts of the building. They are not installed merely to meet the peculiar needs of a tenant. As a general rule, they are for the operation or maintenance of a building and "cannot be removed or relocated without doing at least temporary damage to the building itself." (*Metro Nat'l. Corp. v. Comm'r.*, T.C. Memo 1987-38.)

The tax court developed six questions designed to determine whether a particular asset qualifies as personal property:

1. Can the property be moved and has it been moved? A "Yes" indicates the item is personal property.
2. Is the property designed or constructed to remain permanently in place? A "Yes" indicates the property is a building component.
3. Are there circumstances that show that the property may or will have to be moved? A "Yes" indicates the item is personal property.
4. Is the property readily movable? A "Yes" indicates the item is personal property.
5. How much damage will the property sustain when it is removed? The less damage, the more likely the property is personal property.
6. How is the property affixed to land? The more permanently affixed, the more likely the property is a building component. (*Whiteco Industries, Inc. v. Comm'r.*, 65 T.C. 664, 672-673 (1975).)

The following tables list common types of assets inside rental buildings that are structural components and personal property.

Personal Property
Kitchen appliances, such as stoves, refrigerators, dishwashers, microwaves, and trash compactors (IRS Reg. § 1.48-1(c))
Removable partitions (Senate Report 95-163; *Metro Nat'l. Corp. v. Comm'r.*, T.C. Memo 1987-38)
Carpeting that is tacked down, not glued to the floor (Senate Report 95-163)
Tile flooring applied with adhesives designed to ease its removal—not cemented, mudded, or otherwise permanently affixed to the building floor (Senate Report 95-163)
Clothes washers and dryers (*Mandler v. Comm'r.*, 65 T.C. 586)
Furniture owned by the landlord (Rev. Rul. 81-133)
Ornamental fixtures (Senate Report 95-163)
Drapes, curtains, and window blinds (IRS Reg. § 1.48-1(c))
False balconies (Senate Report 95-163)
Awnings and canopies (PLR 7102269400A)
Fire extinguishers (Rev. Rul. 67-417)
Portable space heaters (Rev. Rul. 70-103)
Lighting to illuminate the exterior of a building, but not lighting for parking areas (Senate Report 95-163)
Decorative lighting, such as chandeliers and décor wall lights (*Morrison, Inc. v. Comm'r.*, T.C. Memo 1986)
Plants inside a building (*Texas Instruments, Inc. v. Comm'r.*, T.C. Memo 1992-306)
Advertising signs (*Whiteco Industries, Inc. v. Comm'r.*, 65 T.C. 664, 672-673 (1975))
Portable window air conditioners (*Film N' Photos v. Comm'r.*, 37 T.C. Memo 709)
Movable storage sheds (PLR 7102269400A)

Building Components
Walls and nonmovable partitions and permanent coverings for them, such as paneling (IRS Reg. § 1.48-1(e)(2))
Floors and permanent coverings for them, such as tiling that has been cemented or glued to the floor (IRS Reg. § 1.48-1(e)(2))
Ceilings, including suspended ceilings (IRS Reg. § 1.48-1(e)(2); *Boddie-Noelle Enters. v. United States*, 96-2 USTC ⁋ 50,627 (Fed. Cl. 1996))
Windows and doors (IRS Reg. § 1.48-1(e)(2))
All components of a central air conditioning or heating system, including motors, compressors, pipes, and ducts (whether in, on, or adjacent to the building) (IRS Reg. § 1.48-1(e)(2))
Plumbing and plumbing fixtures, such as sinks and bathtubs (IRS Reg. § 1.48-1(e)(2))
Electric wiring and lighting fixtures (IRS Reg. § 1.48-1(e)(2))
Chimneys and fireplaces (IRS Reg. § 1.48-1(e)(2))
Stairways and elevators (IRS Reg. § 1.48-1(e)(2))
Sprinkler systems (IRS Reg. § 1.48-1(e)(2))
Fire escapes (IRS Reg. § 1.48-1(e)(2))

Determining Fair Market Value of Personal Property

The tax basis of personal property you purchase as part of a rental property is its fair market value. If the property is new, or fairly new, you can use the cost to replace it. The new prices for any type of personal property can easily be researched on the Internet, or using publications such as the Sears catalog.

If the property is older, you'll need to figure out the value based on the new price minus an amount for the wear and tear the property has undergone. Look at classified ads and listings for similar property on eBay, or call people who buy and sell the type of property involved. If you think the property is extremely valuable, get an appraisal from an expert. Keep records of how you calculated the property's value.

If you don't want to spend a huge amount of time calculating fair market values, you can limit your segmented depreciation to big-ticket items, such as kitchen appliances and carpets. But, the more personal property you separately depreciate, the faster you'll get your deductions for the property.

Steps to Calculate Segmented Depreciation

You must calculate segmented depreciation in the proper order, or you'll get less than you should. Here are the steps:

Step 1: Determine the cost of your property as a whole—this is the purchase price plus certain other expenses (see Chapter 5).

Step 2: Determine the fair market value of the personal property included with the purchase and deduct it from your total cost. (See "Determining the Value of Your Land and Buildings," above.) We'll call this amount (cost minus personal property) your preliminary basis.

Step 3: Determine your improvement ratio (see "Determining the Value of Your Land and Buildings," above) and multiply it by your preliminary basis. This amount is the basis in your building and land improvements together.

Step 4: Determine the value of the depreciable land improvements on your property and deduct it from your basis. The remainder is the depreciable basis of your building alone. How to value land improvements is covered in Chapter 5. This can take some time and effort. If you want, you can skip this step and include the land improvements with your building for depreciation purposes. However, be aware that when you do this, it will take you over twice as long to fully depreciate your land improvements.

Step 5: Create three different depreciation schedules: one each for your personal property, land improvements, and building. (You don't need a schedule for land improvements if you don't separately depreciate them.)

EXAMPLE: Jack purchases a small rental house in January. He determines his depreciation deductions as follows:

1. He figures the total cost of the house—he paid $150,000 for the house, plus the following amounts:

Escrow fee	$ 375
Document preparation fee	150
Notary fee	30
Recording fee	145
Survey fee	50
Title insurance	900
Total	$ 1,650

    This gives Jack a total cost for the property of $151,650.

2. Jack determines the fair market value of the personal property included with the house. This consists of:

Wall-to-wall carpet (new)	$ 4,830
Stove (10 years old)	100
Refrigerator (5 years old)	200
Dishwasher (new)	707
Venetian blinds (3 years old)	500
Total	$ 6,337

    Jack deducts this amount from his total cost to determine his preliminary basis ($151,650 − $6,337 = $145,313).

3. Jack determines his improvement ratio to be 80%, based on the replacement cost of the house. He multiplies this by his preliminary basis to determine the basis for his building and improvements together (80% × $145,313 = $116,250). This is the value of his house and improvements, not counting the land they occupy.

4. Jack determines the cost of the land improvements on his property:

Landscaping	$ 1,000
Fence	2,000
Driveway	1,200
Walkway	800
Total	$ 5,000

Jack deducts the value of the land improvements from the basis for the house and improvements he calculated in Step 3 ($116,250 – $5,000 = $111,250). This is the depreciable basis for the house alone.

5. Jack creates separate depreciation schedules for the personal property, land improvements, and house.

Year	House ($111,250 basis; 27.5-year recovery period; straight-line method; property placed in service in January)	Land improvements ($5,000 basis; 15-year recovery period; 150% declining balance method)	Personal property ($6,337 basis; 5-year recovery period; 200% declining balance method)	Total
1	$3,877	$250	$1,267	$5,394
2	4,045	475	2,028	6,548
3	4,045	428	1,217	5,690
4	4,045	385	730	5,160
5	4,045	347	730	5,122
6	4,045	312	365	4,722
7–15	4,045	295		4,340
16	4,045	148		4,193
17–27	4,045			4,045
28	2,192			2,192

In contrast, if Jack simply depreciated the house, improvements, and personal property together, his depreciation schedule would look like this:

80% improvement ratio × $151,650 cost = $121,320 basis

Year	Depreciation
1	$4,186
2–27	$4,411
28	$2,390

As you can see, for the first six years Jack owns the house, he gets substantially larger depreciation deductions by using segmented depreciation.

Interest

Interest Landlords Can (and Can't) Deduct 206

Mortgage Interest 207

    Interest, Not Principal, Is Deductible 208

    Expenses to Obtain a Mortgage 209

    Private Mortgage Insurance 209

    Mortgage Refinancing 209

    Mixed-Use Properties 210

Other Interest Expenses 210

    Credit Cards and Loans 210

    Car Loans 211

    Home Offices 211

    Home Equity Loans 211

Points and Prepaid Interest 212

Interest on Construction Loans 213

Loans With Low or No Interest 214

Loans on Rental Property Used for Nonrental Purposes 215

Keeping Track of Borrowed Money 216

    30-Day Rule 217

    Allocation Rules 217

nterest is often a landlord's single biggest expense. This chapter explains when and how it can be deducted.

Interest Landlords Can (and Can't) Deduct

As a general rule, you may deduct interest on money you borrow for a business or investment activity, including being a landlord. A landlord's most common deductible interest payments are:

- mortgage interest payments to banks and other financial institutions on loans used to acquire rental property
- mortgage interest payments to financial institutions on loans used to improve rental property
- interest on credit cards for goods or services used in a rental activity, and
- personal loans for any item used in a rental activity.

The limitations on when and how these interest payments may be deducted are explained in more detail below.

> **CAUTION**
>
> **No deduction for money kept in the bank.** You get no rental deduction for interest you pay on loan proceeds that you keep in the bank. Your rental interest deduction begins only when you spend the money on your rental activity. Money kept in the bank is considered an investment—at best you might be able to deduct the interest you pay on the money as investment interest.

Certain types of interest can't be deducted under any circumstances:

Interest on money you don't owe. You may only deduct interest for money you legally owe. If you are liable for part of a debt, you can deduct only your share of the total interest paid or accrued.

> EXAMPLE: Sandra and her daughter, Sally, purchase a rental house together. Both their names are on the deed, but only Sally's name is on the mortgage. Because Sandra is not legally liable for the mortgage, she cannot deduct any interest she pays on it; only Sally gets this deduction.

Interest paid with funds borrowed from original lender. You cannot deduct interest you pay with funds borrowed from the original lender through a second loan, an advance, or any other arrangement similar to a loan. You can deduct the interest expense once you start making payments on the new loan. When you make a payment on the new loan, you first apply the payment to interest and then to the principal.

> EXAMPLE: Phil obtains a $20,000 high-interest, short-term loan from the Acme Finance Company to pay for repairs to get his aged rental building up to code and avoid a condemnation. Phil is personally liable for the loan. He falls behind in his loan payments. To avoid having Acme take his bank accounts or personal property, he obtains a second loan from Acme for $5,000, secured by his own house. He uses the second loan to pay $5,000 in overdue payments on his original loan from Acme. The $5,000 payment, which is almost all for interest charges, is not a deductible interest payment. Six months later, Phil pays back the $5,000 loan with interest. He can deduct the interest he pays on this loan.

Interest on income tax. Interest charged on income tax assessed on your individual income tax return is not deductible even though the tax due is related to income from your rental activity.

Mortgage Interest

Landlords typically borrow money from banks or other financial institutions to purchase their rental properties. The ability to borrow so much to purchase real estate is one of its great attractions as an investment. The more leverage you have, the more money you can make for each dollar invested. (Leverage means using borrowed funds to increase your total purchasing power.)

You can deduct the mortgage interest you pay for a rental property each year as it is paid. You list the deduction on Schedule E, on the line labeled "Mortgage interest paid to banks, etc."

Interest, Not Principal, Is Deductible

You only deduct the interest you pay on a loan to purchase or improve a rental property. You may not deduct payments of principal—that is, your repayments of the amount you borrowed. The principal is ordinarily added to the basis of your property and depreciated over 27.5 years. (See Chapter 5.)

> **EXAMPLE:** Ken takes out a $10,000 second mortgage on his rental house to remodel the kitchen. This is a home improvement loan. The $10,000 loan amount is not deductible. Instead, it is added to Ken's basis in the home and depreciated over 27.5 years.

In contrast, if you borrow money and use it to repair your rental property, you may deduct the principal amount of the loan in the year in which it is incurred as an operating expense. You deduct the interest as it is paid each year. (See Chapter 4 for a detailed discussion of the difference between a repair and an improvement.)

> **EXAMPLE:** Ken later takes out a $10,000 third mortgage on his rental home to repair the roof. This expense is a repair, not an improvement. The $10,000 principal amount of the loan is deductible in full in the year Ken takes out the loan. He deducts the interest on the loan as he pays it each year.

It's easy to keep track of how much of your loan payments are for interest and how much for principal. If you paid $600 or more of mortgage interest (including certain points) during the year on any one mortgage, you will receive an IRS Form 1098 from the lender listing how much you paid in interest during the year.

Depending on the length of the loan, your first few years' payments will be mostly for interest, not principal. However, as a loan becomes "seasoned" (gets older) more and more of the loan payments are for repayment of principal, not interest, and are therefore not deductible. When your loan is paid off, you'll get no more interest deductions. This is something to keep in mind when you figure the value of your tax deduction for a rental property.

Expenses to Obtain a Mortgage

You can't deduct as interest any expenses you pay to obtain a mortgage on your rental property. Instead, such expenses are deducted in equal annual amounts over the period of the loan. These expenses include:
- points (see "Points and Prepaid Interest" below)
- private mortgage insurance (see below)
- loan assumption fees
- costs of a credit report
- fees for an appraisal and/or inspection required by a lender
- mortgage commissions and fees.

Private Mortgage Insurance

Private mortgage insurance (PMI) is a special insurance policy that protects the lender if the borrower defaults on the loan. A landlord can deduct any PMI premiums he or she pays on rental property as they are paid each year. You list the deduction on Line 9 of Schedule E—write "PMI" on the dotted line.

Mortgage Refinancing

One way to use real estate to get cash is to do a "cash-out refinancing"—obtain a new loan to pay off your old loan, plus borrow more money to end up with cash in your pocket. However, you may not deduct the interest on the cash-out portion of the loan unless you use the money to do real estate improvements (or to pay for certain medical or education expenses).

> **EXAMPLE:** Tim owes $100,000 on his rental duplex, which has a fair market value of $200,000. He obtains a new $150,000 loan on the property. He pays off the original $100,000 loan and puts the other $50,000 in his pocket to use for a vacation, new car, and other personal purposes. He may only deduct two-thirds of the interest he pays on the new loan because the other third was a cash-out that he used for personal purposes. However, if Tim used the $50,000 to pay for new improvements to his duplex, he could deduct all of the interest.

Mixed-Use Properties

If you live in a multiunit building and rent out the other units, you claim the home mortgage deduction for the portion you live in and deduct the remainder as a landlord expense on your Schedule E. If you receive one bill, you should prorate the rental portion based on square footage.

> EXAMPLE: Samantha owns a duplex and lives in one unit and rents out the other. She has a $100,000 home loan on the entire property, for which she paid $6,000 in interest this year. Both units are the same size, so Samantha deducts 50% of her interest payment as a personal itemized deduction on her Schedule A, and the other 50% as a landlord expense on her Schedule E.

Other Interest Expenses

Landlords aren't just limited to deducting interest on mortgages. Other interest is also deductible.

Credit Cards and Loans

If you use your credit card or take out a loan to purchase goods or services for your rental activity, you can deduct the interest you pay to the credit card company or lender, even if you have to depreciate the principal amount of the purchase. This is considered trade or business interest because the borrowed money is used to help carry on your business. A typical example is interest on a credit card (or bank loan) used to purchase supplies for your rental activity.

Business interest is fully deductible in the year in which it is paid (or incurred in the case of accrual basis taxpayers; see Chapter 17).

> EXAMPLE: Andre uses his credit card to purchase and install a $900 dishwasher in a rental duplex he owns. The credit card interest he pays on the $900 is deductible as it is paid. However, the $900 cost of the dishwasher must be depreciated over five years. (See Chapter 5.)

It's a very good idea to use a separate credit card to buy things for your rental activity. If you use a credit card to buy rental-related items and personal items, you'll have to figure out how much of the monthly credit card interest you pay is for the rental items and how much for the personal items—often, a math nightmare.

Car Loans

If you use your car for your rental activity, you can deduct the interest that you pay on your car loan as an interest expense. You can take this deduction whether you deduct your car expenses using the actual expense method or the standard mileage rate, because the standard mileage rate was not intended to encompass interest on a car loan. The amount you can deduct depends on how much you use the car for business—for example, if you use it 25% of the time for your rental business, you may deduct 25% of your car loan interest payments. (See Chapter 10.)

Home Offices

If you take the home office deduction, you can deduct the home office percentage of your home mortgage interest as a business expense, instead of an itemized personal deduction. (See Chapter 9 for more on the home office deduction.)

Home Equity Loans

In some cases, it could be advantageous taxwise to use a home equity loan for landlord purposes. A home equity loan is a loan for which you use your main home or second home as collateral. Interest on home equity loans of less than $100,000 is deductible as an itemized personal deduction. This is so regardless of how the money is spent—for example, you could spend the money on your rental activities and still deduct the interest as a personal deduction.

This could be favorable for a landlord because these loans are not subject to the passive activity rules discussed in Chapter 16. Thus, you can deduct the interest regardless of whether the passive loss rules prevent you from deducting your other rental expenses.

Points and Prepaid Interest

If you are a cash basis taxpayer (the vast majority of small landlords are—see Chapter 17), you may not deduct interest that you prepay in a single year. Instead, you must allocate the interest over the tax years to which it applies and deduct it in those years.

The most common type of prepaid interest is points. The term points is often used to describe some of the charges paid by a borrower when the borrower takes out a loan or a mortgage. A point is equal to 1% of the loan amount—for example, one point on a $100,000 loan is $1,000. These charges are also called loan origination fees, maximum loan charges, loan discounts, or premium charges. If any of these charges (points) are solely for the use of money, they are interest for tax purposes. Because points are prepaid interest, you cannot deduct the full amount in the year paid. (However, there is an exception for points paid on your home mortgage— see IRS Publication 936, *Home Mortgage Interest Deduction*, for details.) Instead, you must allocate the interest payment portion over the term of the loan and only deduct for payments allocated for that tax year.

You deduct points in equal amounts over the life of the loan. You divide the points by the number of payments over the term of the loan and deduct points for the year according to the number of payments made in that year. This process is called amortization. If the loan ends prematurely, due to a payoff or refinancing, for example, then the remaining points are deducted in that year.

> **EXAMPLE:** Assume that you take out a 20-year loan in January to purchase a rental house. You pay $3,000 in points to obtain the mortgage. A 20-year loan has 240 payments (20 years × 12 months = 240); $3,000 ÷ 240 = $12.50. Thus, you deduct $12.50 for each month you pay off your loan. If you pay the loan for a full year, you get a $150 deduction for that year. If you sell the house after five years, you deduct the remaining $2,250 that year.

Some real estate loans are structured with balloon payments: The monthly loan payments are based on a relatively lengthy time period, which keeps the payments lower, but the entire loan must be paid off at an earlier date. In this event, you can amortize any loan points over the earlier time period.

> **EXAMPLE:** Vic obtained a $200,000 mortgage to buy a small apartment building. He pays three points for the loan ($6,000). His monthly payments are based on a 20-year term. However, he must pay off the entire loan with a balloon payment at the end of 60 months. He can deduct his points over 60 months instead of 240 months (20 years). This enables him to deduct $100 per month, instead of $25.

The first year you deduct points, you must list the amount in the amortization section of IRS Form 4562, *Depreciation and Amortization*. You then add the amount to your other mortgage interest deductions you list on IRS Schedule E (see Chapter 18).

Interest on Construction Loans

If you borrow money to construct a rental property, you may currently deduct as an operating expense the interest you pay before construction begins and after it ends. However, you may not deduct the interest you pay during the construction period. Instead, this cost must be added to the basis of your property and depreciated over 27.5 years. (See Chapter 5.) (I.R.C. § 263A(f)(1).)

The construction period for real property begins when physical construction starts. Physical construction includes:

- clearing, grading, or excavating land
- demolishing or gutting an existing building
- construction of infrastructure such as sidewalks, sewers, cables, and wiring
- structural, mechanical, or electrical work on a building, and
- landscaping.

The construction period ends when all production activities reasonably expected to be done are completed and the property is placed in service—that is, made available for rent.

Activities such as planning and design, preparing architectural blueprints, or obtaining building permits do not constitute physical construction. Thus, interest paid while these activities are going on, but before physical construction is done, can be currently deducted as an operating expense.

> **EXAMPLE:** Jennifer obtains a $100,000 loan to construct a rental house. She gets the loan on January 15 and starts paying interest on February 1. Because of problems in obtaining final approval for a building permit, physical construction of the house does not begin until June 1. Jennifer may deduct the interest she paid during February through May. She cannot, however, deduct the interest she pays while the house is being constructed from May through October. Instead, she must add it to the tax basis of the house and depreciate it over 27.5 years. The interest Jennifer pays after the house is completed and offered for rent she can currently deduct as she pays it each year.

Loans With Low or No Interest

One way a person who sells real property and finances all or part of the sale him- or herself can save on taxes is to charge little or no interest on the amount the buyer borrows. To make up for the low or no interest, the seller increases the property's purchase price. This is advantageous for the seller because interest payments are taxed at ordinary income tax rates, while the gain on the sale of real property owned for more than one year is taxed at lower capital gains rates (usually 20%).

> **EXAMPLE:** Joe owns a rental house with a fair market value of $100,000. He sells the property to Jean. Jean pays $120,000. She puts down $20,000 and Joe finances the remainder himself, charging Jean only 2% interest. He pays 20% capital gains tax on his gain on the sale ($120,000 minus his $60,000 basis), and ordinary income tax on the interest payments Jean will make—taxed at

Joe's top 28% income tax rate. Joe comes out ahead on the deal by getting a higher sales price for the property and charging less interest.

Unfortunately for sellers, the IRS is well aware of this scheme. If an installment sale contract does not provide for adequate interest, part of the sales price must be treated as interest for tax purposes. This amount is called "unstated interest" or "original issue discount," depending upon the circumstances. The seller must reduce the stated sales price, and increase his or her annual interest income, by this interest amount. For the buyer, the property's basis is the stated purchase price, less the amount considered to be unstated interest.

How much interest is too little? Generally, an interest rate is inadequate if it is less than the applicable federal rate of interest (AFR). The AFR is set by the IRS each month. You can find it on the IRS website at www.irs.gov (look for the Index of Applicable Federal Rates).

Calculating how much additional interest must be paid is very complicated. Refer to IRS Publication 537, *Installment Sales*, for more information; or, better yet, see an accountant.

Loans on Rental Property Used for Nonrental Purposes

You can take out a loan secured by your rental property and use the proceeds for nonrental purposes. If you do this, you can't deduct interest you pay on the loan as a rental expense. Whether it is deductible at all, and to what extent, depends on what you use the money for:

- **Personal purposes.** You get no deduction if you use the loan proceeds to buy something for your personal use—for example, you take a vacation or buy new appliances for your residence. Personal interest is not deductible, except for interest paid for a mortgage for a personal residence or second home (and some interest on student loans). You'd be much better off using a home equity loan for such expenses because then you can deduct the interest (up to a $100,000 loan) as an itemized personal deduction.

- **Investment purposes.** You may get a deduction if you use the loan for investment purposes—for example, to purchase stocks or bonds or some other investment. You can deduct investment interest as an itemized personal deduction. However, you can deduct investment interest only from investment income. Thus, if you have no investment income, you get no deduction. If your interest expense exceeds your investment income, you cannot deduct the overage. You must carry it forward to deduct in a future year when you have enough investment income.

- **Business purposes.** You can deduct the interest if you use the loan proceeds for a business other than renting residential property— for example, a landlord borrows money on his rental property to purchase equipment for his construction business. You can fully deduct business interest as a business expense in the year in which it is paid (or incurred in the case of accrual basis taxpayers; see Chapter 17). Sole proprietors (people who individually own their businesses) deduct interest expenses on IRS Schedule C, *Profit or Loss From Business (Sole Proprietorship)*.

Keeping Track of Borrowed Money

Here's a simple rule you should follow whenever you borrow money for your rental activity: NEVER, NEVER commingle borrowed funds with money that is not for, or from, your rental activity. Instead, deposit the money in a separate rental bank account.

If you don't follow this rule, you could be in for trouble: If you deposit borrowed money in a bank account that you use to pay bills for both landlord and other purposes, it could be difficult to determine what you spent the money on.

EXAMPLE: Linda borrows $10,000 from the bank to remodel her rental house. She deposits the money in her personal checking account. The account already contains $5,000. Over the next several months, she writes checks to pay for food, her home mortgage, personal clothing, and an architect to remodel her rental. How does Linda know whether the money she borrowed was used for her rental house or personal expenses?

She could have avoided this problem had she deposited the money in a separate rental account.

If you do commingle borrowed funds, you'll have to deal with the following IRS rules on tracing loan proceeds:

30-Day Rule

If you buy something for your rental activity within 30 days of borrowing money, the IRS presumes that the payment was made from those loan proceeds (up to the amount of the loan). This is true regardless of the method or bank account you use to pay the rental expense. If you receive the loan proceeds in cash, you can treat the payment as made on the date you receive the cash instead of the date you actually make the payment.

> EXAMPLE: Frank gets a loan of $1,000 on August 4 and receives the proceeds in cash. Frank deposits $1,500 in his bank account on August 18 and on August 28 writes a check on the account for a landlord expense. Also, Frank deposits his paycheck and other loan proceeds into the account, and pays his personal bills from the account during the same period. Regardless of these other transactions, Frank can treat $1,000 of the deposit he made on August 18 as being paid on August 4 from the loan proceeds. In addition, Frank can treat the landlord expense he paid on August 28 as made from the $1,000 loan proceeds deposited in the account.

Allocation Rules

If you don't satisfy the 30-day rule, special allocation rules determine how loan proceeds deposited in a bank account were spent for tax purposes. Generally, the IRS will assume that loan proceeds were used (spent) before:

- any unborrowed amounts held in the same account, and
- any amounts deposited after the loan proceeds.

EXAMPLE: On January 9, Edith opened a checking account, depositing a $5,000 bank loan and $1,000 in unborrowed money. On February 13, Edith takes $1,000 from the account for personal purposes. On February 15, she takes out $5,000 to pay for a repair to the roof of her rental property. Edith must treat the $1,000 used for personal purposes as made from the loan proceeds, leaving only $4,000 of the loan in the account for tax purposes. As a result, she may deduct as a landlord expense the interest she pays on only $4,000 of the $5,000 she used to pay for the repair.

Start-Up Expenses

What Are Start-Up Expenses?...220

Determining Your Business Start Date 222

    Rental Business Begins When You Offer Property for Rent............................222

    Expanding an Existing Rental Business..224

Avoiding the Start-Up Rule's Bite 225

How to Deduct Start-Up Expenses..226

    Expenses You Can Deduct..228

    Costs That Are Not Start-Up Expenses...228

If Your Business Doesn't Last 15 Years..231

If Your Business Never Begins 232

L andlords often need to spend money to get their rental business started. Costs you incur before you are actually in business are called start-up expenses. Special tax rules govern the deduction of these costs. If you are a landlord who is already actively engaged in the residential rental business, you may not need to read this chapter. But if you aren't yet in business or are considering expanding your residential rental business into new geographic areas, this material explains what type of expenditures are start-up expenses and how you can deduct these costs.

What Are Start-Up Expenses?

Start-up expenses are the costs you incur to get your rental business up and running. Any expense that would be deductible as an operating expense by an ongoing business is a start-up expense when it's incurred before a business begins. Common start-up expenses for landlords include:

- minor or incidental repairs to get a rental property ready to rent
- outside office expenses paid for before a rental business begins, such as office rent, telephone service, utilities, office supplies, and office equipment rental
- home office expenses
- the cost of investigating what it will take to create a successful residential rental business, including research on potential real estate markets
- insurance premiums (but not title insurance)
- maintenance costs for a rental property paid for before the property is offered for rent—for example, landscaping and utilities (but not the cost of connecting utilities)
- costs for recruiting and training employees before the business opens—for example, hiring and training an apartment manager
- costs to create and set up a website
- fees paid to a market research firm to analyze the demographics, traffic patterns, and general economic conditions of a neighborhood

- business licenses, permits, and other fees, and
- fees paid to lawyers, accountants, consultants, and others for professional services; however, legal and other fees paid to purchase a rental property are not start-up expenses.

Unlike operating expenses, start-up expenses cannot automatically be deducted in a single year. This is because the money you spend to start a rental (or any other) business is a capital expense—a cost that will benefit you for more than one year. Normally, you can't deduct these types of capital expenses until you sell or otherwise dispose of the business. However, a special tax rule allows you to deduct up to $5,000 in start-up expenses the first year you are in business, and then deduct the remainder, if any, in equal amounts over the next 15 years.

> **EXAMPLE:** During 2015, Ed, a Los Angeles resident, is thinking about purchasing a rental house in Las Vegas. He has never been a landlord before, but he thinks it might be a good investment. He starts looking for a house to buy. However, he discovers that it is not so easy to find a suitable property. He makes six trips to Las Vegas over the next year. He incurs substantial travel expense but finds no property he likes. Then, on the seventh trip, he discovers his dream rental house. He quickly buys it and takes title on September 1. The house is vacant but requires some repairs. Ed hires a handyman to do the work and arranges for a gardener to take care of the lawn and landscaping on a weekly basis. On November 1, he lists the property for rent by taking out an ad in the local newspaper. He finds a tenant who moves in on December 1.
>
> Before November 1 (the date he offered the house for rent) Ed paid the following expenses during 2015:
>
> | | |
> |---|---:|
> | Travel, lodging, and food for six unsuccessful trips to Las Vegas | $3,800 |
> | Travel, lodging, and food for one successful Las Vegas trip | 500 |
> | Gardener | 100 |
> | Utilities | 100 |
> | Repairs | 7,000 |
> | Total | $11,500 |

All of these expenses are start-up expenses except for the $500 travel costs to find the property Ed ended up buying. Those costs must be added to the property's tax basis and depreciated. This leaves $11,000 in deductible start-up expenses. Ed may deduct $5,000 of the $11,000 on his tax return for the current year. He can deduct the remaining $6,000 in equal installments over the first 180 months (15 years) he's in business, starting with the month his rental business began (November). He deducts $33.33 for every full year he's in business until he has completely deducted the $6,000 (assuming his rental business lasts that long).

Obviously, you want to spend no more than the first-year limit on start-up expenses so you don't have to wait 15 years to get all of your money back. There are ways you can avoid spending more than the limit. These are described in more detail below. But first, you need to understand when a rental business begins for tax purposes.

Determining Your Business Start Date

A crucial moment in your tax life as a landlord is when your rental business begins. Once your business is up and running, the start-up expense rule will not apply. Until then, you need to count every penny you spend to make sure you don't go over the limit for currently deductible start-up expenses.

Rental Business Begins When You Offer Property for Rent

The general rule is that a new business begins for tax purposes when it starts to function as a going concern and performs the activities for which it was organized. (*Richmond Television Corp. v. U.S.*, 345 F.2d 901 (4th Cir. 1965).) For a rental business, this is when you first offer property for rent. You don't have to actually rent out your property—that is, have it occupied by tenants—you only have to put it on the rental market. (*Francis v. Comm'r.*, T.C. Memo 1977-170.)

EXAMPLE: In 1993, Freddie and Sarah Charlton bought lakefront property in Texas that contained several vacant and run-down rental cabins. They began to rehabilitate the cabins in late 1994. They deducted $27,724 on their 1994 tax return for supplies, taxes, travel, utilities, legal and professional expenses, and car and truck expenses for the cabin rental activity. However, the cabins weren't offered for rent or actually rented out until 1998. Both the IRS and tax court denied the deductions. The court held that the Charltons' rental activity didn't become a business until 1998 when the cabins were offered for rent. Thus, the $27,724 was not a business operating expense and could not all be deducted in one year. Instead, it had to be deducted as a start-up expense after the Charltons' rental business began. (*Charlton v. Comm'r.*, 114 T.C. 333.)

Obviously, you must actually own a rental property before you can rent it out. Thus, your rental business doesn't begin until you take ownership of the property, make the building available for immediate occupancy, and offer it for rent. In other words, a rental business does not begin when you make an offer to buy, put a deposit on, or sign a sales contract for a property you plan to rent.

The date you offer your property for rent is an important one that you should plan for and make careful note of. You should also be prepared to prove you offered your property for rent on the date you claim.

Have Proof of When Your Rental Business Began

Being able to show the IRS a copy of an advertisement to rent your property is a great way to prove your property was available for rent. You don't need to buy an expensive ad—a free ad in the local penny saver will do. Or a copy of a free rental listing with an apartment rental service or local college or university will also establish that your property was available. Another way to show property was offered for rent is to place a For Rent sign on the property and take a picture of it. The picture must be date stamped. If you purchase a property that is already occupied by a tenant, you can use a copy of your first rent check to establish when you were in business.

Expanding an Existing Rental Business

If you've never owned a rental property, it's easy to tell when your rental business begins—the date you offer your first property for rent. But what if you already own rental property and decide to purchase additional rental property? The cost of expanding an existing business is a business operating expense, not a start-up expense. As long as business expansion costs are ordinary and necessary, they are currently deductible.

> EXAMPLE: Alex owns an apartment building that he has rented out for over two years. This rental (which qualifies as a business) has been so successful that he decides to purchase another apartment building. He spends $4,000 in travel expenses looking for properties to buy. Because Alex is already in business, these costs are currently deductible as business operating expenses—they are not start-up expenses.

However, your expenses will be currently deductible only if the expansion involves an activity that is "within the compass" of your existing rental business. In other words, it must be part of "the normal expansion" of your business. (*Malmstedt v. Comm'r.*, 578 F.2d 520 (4th Cir. 1978).) The costs of expanding into a *new* business are start-up expenses, not operating expenses.

The IRS and tax court have taken a very narrow view of what constitutes a rental business. They have held that a landlord's rental business only exists in the geographic area where the property is located. Thus, a landlord who buys (or seeks to buy) property in a different area is starting a new rental business. This means the expenses for expanding in the new location are start-up expenses.

> EXAMPLE: Patrick O'Donnell was a Chicago resident who owned two apartments in Las Vegas. He took a two-day trip to Miami to investigate buying a rental property there. However, he decided not to go through with the deal. Both the IRS and tax court denied him a deduction for his travel expenses. The court found that, even though O'Donnell was in the rental business in Las Vegas, his business did not extend to Miami, so he couldn't deduct the trip as an operating expense. (*O'Donnell v. Comm'r.*, 62 T.C. 781.) Had O'Donnell purchased the property, his travel expenses would have been neither operating expenses nor start-up costs; instead, he would

have had to add them to the basis of the property and depreciate them over 27.5 years. (See Chapter 5.)

In another case, the tax court held that a husband and wife who owned several rental properties in North Carolina started a new rental business (as opposed to expanded their existing rental business) when they purchased a rental house in Richmond, Virginia. This was so, even though they lived in Richmond. (*Odom v. Comm'r.*, T.C. Memo 1982-531.)

Forming New Business Entities

Another situation where a landlord could be viewed as starting a new rental business, not expanding an existing one, is where a new business entity such as a limited liability company or partnership is formed to own the new property. This is often done in an attempt to limit a landlord's legal liability. (See Chapter 1.)

EXAMPLE: Harriet and her husband own an LLC that, in turn, owns an apartment building. They decide to purchase a new apartment building. They form a second LLC, unrelated to the first, to own this property, hoping separate ownership entities will insulate each property from debts or lawsuits arising from the other property. The second LLC could be viewed by the IRS as an entirely new rental business. Any costs the second LLC incurs before the new apartment building is offered for rent would be start-up expenses.

Avoiding the Start-Up Rule's Bite

The start-up tax rule will adversely affect you only if you spend more than the $5,000 first-year limit before your rental business begins. Amounts over the limit will have to be deducted over 15 years. So, if possible, you want to stay under the limit. To do this, you will need to keep careful track of how much you spend. If you go near or over the limit, cut back on your spending until your rental business begins.

As a landlord, there are many expenses you can put off paying until after you are in business. For example, you can hold off on expensive repairs you don't absolutely have to do before you list the property for rent. Repairs you pay for after the property is available for rent will be currently deductible operating expenses, not start-up expenses.

If you must spend more than the first-year limit on start-up expenses, go ahead and do it. But at least try to keep your total start-up expenses below $50,000. This is because your first-year deduction limit will be reduced by any amount you spend over these amounts on start-up expenses.

> ⚠ CAUTION
> **Don't wait on repairs that significantly affect your tenants.** If you hold off on major repair work, your tenant may reasonably object to living in a construction zone, and may request alternate housing or a rent reduction. Consider taking care of major work that needs to be done before you offer your property for rent—the tax advantages of waiting may begin to appear less attractive once you have to deal with unhappy tenants. A better approach may be to plan to do work at turnover time, when the unit is vacant. At turnover, you are still in business because you've previously rented or offered the property for rent.

If you've already spent more than the first-year limit on start-up items, but you have to buy something more before you start your rental business, try to postpone paying for it until after your business begins. That way, you can currently deduct the expense, if it qualifies as a business operating expense. (This assumes you're a cash basis taxpayer—someone who reports income and expenses on the date they are actually paid, not on the date when an agreement to pay is made. The vast majority of landlords use cash basis accounting; see Chapter 17.) If you can get your rental business started quickly, your creditors should not have to wait long to be paid.

How to Deduct Start-Up Expenses

There is a limit on the amount of start-up expenses you are allowed to deduct the first year you are in business. For the past several years, the limit has been $5,000. You'll have to deduct any expenses in excess of the first-year limit in equal amounts over the first 180 months (15 years) you're in business. This process is called amortization. The 180 months is the minimum amortization period; you can choose a longer period if you wish (almost no one does).

However, you won't be entitled to the full $5,000 first-year deduction if you have more than $50,000 in start-up expenses. Your first-year deduction is reduced by the amount by which such start-up expenditures exceed the $50,000 limit. For example, if you have $53,000 in start-up expenses, you may only deduct $2,000 the first year, instead of $5,000. If you have $60,000 or more in start-up expenses, you get no current deduction. The whole amount must be deducted over 180 months.

CAUTION

Investors can't deduct start-up expenses. Only people engaged in a business can deduct start-up expenses. Investors in real estate are not considered to be "in business" for tax purposes. (*Sorrell v. Comm'r.,* 882 F.2d 484 (11th Cir. 1989).) (See Chapter 2 for a detailed discussion of investors versus landlords for tax purposes.)

You used to have to attach a separate written statement to your tax return electing to claim start-up expenses as a current deduction. This is no longer required. Instead, you are automatically deemed to have made the election for the year in which your business began. All you must do is list your start-up costs as "Other expenses" on your Schedule E (or other appropriate return). You don't have to specifically identify the deducted amounts as start-up expenditures for the election to be effective.

One reason for this change is that you can't include a separate written statement with an electronically filed return and the IRS is trying to encourage electronic filing.

If you don't want to currently deduct your start-up expenses, you can forgo the deemed election by clearly capitalizing your start-up expenses instead. You must do this on your federal income tax return for the tax year in which your business began. Your return must be filed on time (including any extensions) and this election is irrevocable. If you do this your start-up costs become part of the tax basis of your business.

Expenses You Can Deduct

You can deduct as start-up expenses any costs that would be currently deductible as operating expenses after your rental business begins. This means the expenses must be ordinary, necessary, directly related to the business, and reasonable in amount. (See Chapter 3 for a discussion of operating expenses.) For example, you can't deduct the cost of pleasure travel or entertainment unrelated to your rental business. These expenses would not be deductible as operating expenses by an ongoing rental business, so you can't deduct them as start-up expenses either. See "What Are Start-Up Expenses?" above, for common examples of deductible start-up expenses for landlords.

Costs That Are Not Start-Up Expenses

Some costs related to opening a rental business are not considered start-up expenses. Many of these costs are still deductible, but different rules apply to them.

Real Property and Other Long-Term Assets

Real property and other long-term assets you purchase for your rental business that will last for more than one year are not considered part of your start-up costs. This includes the property you buy to rent and any long-term personal property you purchase for your rental property, such as appliances, carpeting, furniture, or lawn mowers. It also includes any long-term property you buy to run your business, such as computers, office furniture and equipment, and cars and other vehicles. These items are capital assets and their costs are capital expenses.

You must depreciate the cost of this property over its useful life—27.5 years for residential real property and five or seven years for most personal property. (In the case of some personal property, you have the option of deducting the cost in one year under Section 179—see Chapter 5 for more on Section 179.) Chapter 5 explains how to depreciate long-term assets. However, you can't take depreciation deductions until your property is placed in service—for example, you can't begin to depreciate a rental building until you make it available for rent.

Ordinarily, the largest single expense you will have that you cannot deduct as a start-up expense is the cost of your rental property—for example, the house or apartment building that you purchase to rent. For tax purposes, the cost of the rental property includes not just the purchase price, but expenses related to the purchase, including:

- bidding costs, application fees, and similar expenses
- costs to appraise or otherwise determine the property's value
- architectural, engineering, environmental, geological, or inspection services for the property—for example, termite inspection fees
- expenses for preparing or reviewing the property's acquisition documents, such as bids, offers, sales agreements, or purchase contracts
- costs to negotiate the purchase terms or structure, including tax advice
- expenses for evaluating and examining the property's title—for example, abstract fees and attorneys' fees
- costs to obtain regulatory approval or secure permits
- property conveyance costs, including sales and transfer taxes and title registration costs—for example, recording fees and title insurance fees
- finders' fees and brokers' commissions including amounts contingent on successful closing of the purchase, and
- the cost of services provided by a qualified intermediary in a like-kind exchange. (IRS Reg. § 1.263(a)-2.)

You cannot deduct any of these expenses as start-up expenses. Instead, you add these costs to the rental property's basis (the property's value for tax purposes) and then depreciate the property's cost (including these amounts) over 27.5 years.

TIP

Some costs associated with purchasing property might be start-up expenses. There are certain expenses related to buying real property that you can deduct as start-up expenses if you meet all the requirements. These expenses include casualty insurance premiums (for example, fire insurance), and charges for utilities or other services for the property before closing.

Real Property Improvements

The cost of improvements you make to rental property are not start-up or operating expenses. Instead, these are capital expenses that you must depreciate. The cost of any repairs you make to rental property, on the other hand, are start-up expenses before your rental business begins and operating expenses after you are in business. (*Gordon v. Comm'r. and Jarrett v. Comm'r.*, T.C. Summ. Op. 2013-91.) The difference between an improvement and a repair is that a repair merely keeps property in good operating condition, while an improvement makes it more valuable, useful, or long-lived. For example, fixing a crack in an existing foundation is a repair; but adding a new foundation to a building is an improvement. Telling the difference between a repair and an improvement can be difficult. (See Chapter 4.)

Travel Expenses

Travel expenses to get your rental business going are deductible start-up expenses with one important exception: Travel costs to buy a particular rental property are not start-up expenses. Instead, they are capital expenses that must be added to the cost of the property and depreciated. (See Chapter 11.)

Interest and Taxes

You cannot deduct interest on a rental property mortgage (or any other interest) or real estate taxes as start-up expenses. Points you pay to obtain a mortgage are considered interest. You can deduct these costs as you pay them, once your real estate business begins. (See Chapter 7.)

Organizational Costs

Costs you pay to form a partnership, limited liability company, or corporation are not part of your start-up costs. However, under a different rule, you can deduct $5,000 of these costs the first year you are in business and any amount remaining over the first 180 months you are in business. (I.R.C. § 248.)

CAUTION
If you form a single-member LLC, don't spend more than $5,000 in organizational expenses. Because single-member LLCs are considered "disregarded entities" for tax purposes, the IRS doesn't allow these entities to deduct organizational expenses over $5,000. Instead any expenses over that amount must be capitalized, which means they would not be deductible until the LLC is dissolved. (Treasury Regs. §§ 1.263(a)-5(d)(1) and (3).) So, if you're forming a single-member LLC, it's best to avoid spending over $5,000 in organizational expenses, which generally should not pose a problem.

If Your Business Doesn't Last 15 Years

Many rental businesses don't last for 180 months. If you had more than the first-year limit in start-up expenses and are in the process of deducting the excess amount, you don't lose the value of your deductions if you sell or close your rental business before you have had a chance to deduct all of your start-up expenses. You can deduct any leftover start-up expenses as ordinary business losses. (I.R.C. § 195(b)(2).) This means that you may be able to deduct them from any income you have that year, deduct them in future years, or deduct them from previous years' taxes. However, there are rules that limit deductions for losses from a real estate activity. (See Chapter 16.)

Keep Good Expense Records

You should keep careful track of every expense you pay before your rental business begins. Obviously, you should keep receipts and canceled checks. You should also keep evidence that will help show that the money went to investigate your new business—for example, correspondence and emails with real estate brokers, lenders, accountants, and attorneys, and copies of advertisements. You will need these records to calculate your deductions and prove your expenses to the IRS if you face an audit.

If Your Business Never Begins

Many people investigate starting a rental business, but the venture never gets off the ground. General start-up costs are expenses you pay before you decide to start a new business or acquire a specific existing business. They include all of the costs of doing a general search for, or preliminary investigation of, a business—for example, costs to analyze potential markets. If you never start the business, these costs are personal (and not deductible). In other words, they are a dead loss.

One intended effect of this rule is that you can't deduct travel, entertainment, or other "fun" expenses by claiming that you incurred them to investigate a rental business unless you actually start the business. Otherwise, it would be pretty tough for the IRS to figure out whether you were really considering a new venture or just having a good time.

> **EXAMPLE:** Kim spends $5,000 on a two-week Hawaii vacation. While there, she spends two days looking at rental properties for sale, but doesn't buy anything. She has never been a landlord, thus owning rental property would be a new business. The cost of her trip is not a start-up expense.

To obtain a deduction for a rental business that never begins, you must enter into a transaction for profit and later abandon the transaction. To do this, you must go beyond a general investigatory search and focus on acquisition of a specific rental property. For example, you'd be able to take a deduction if you entered into a contract to purchase a rental property, but the sale fell through. You could deduct the acquisition costs you incurred in the failed purchase on IRS Form 4797, *Sales of Business Property.* These are the costs that would have been added to the property's basis, and not deducted, had the acquisition been successful. These could include, for example, the cost of inspection and termite reports, earnest money or deposits that were lost, and the cost of traveling to the property.

The Home Office Deduction

Qualifying for the Home Office Deduction..234

    Threshold Requirements..235

    Additional Requirements 237

Calculating the Home Office Deduction 240

    How Much of Your Home Is Used for Your Rental Business? 241

    What Expenses Can You Deduct?..242

Simplified Home Office Deduction Method 248

    How the Simple Method Works..248

    Is the Simplified Method a Good Deal?..250

IRS Reporting Requirements 250

Audit-Proofing Your Home Office Deduction...251

    Prove That You Are Following the Rules..251

    Keep Good Expense Records...251

Deducting an Outside Office 252

    Renting an Office...252

    Using an Office in Your Rental Building 252

    Buying a Separate Office Building...253

he federal government helps out business owners by letting them deduct their home office expenses from their taxable income. This is true whether you own your home or apartment or are a renter. If you own the home where your home office is located (as most landlords do), the home office deduction isn't as valuable as it is for those who are renters. This is because your mortgage interest is deductible whether or not you have a home office, while rent is not deductible without a home office. Still, homeowners who qualify for the deduction will be able to recoup some of their business-related costs by understanding and using this deduction.

Qualifying for the Home Office Deduction

In the past, the IRS took the position that landlords couldn't take the home office deduction. However, the tax court has held that landlords who meet the requirements may take the deduction, and landlords have successfully done so.

> **EXAMPLE:** Edwin Curphey, a dermatologist, owned six rental properties in Hawaii that he managed by himself. He converted a bedroom in his home into an office that he used exclusively for bookkeeping and other activities related to management of his rental properties. The room was furnished with a desk, bookcase, filing cabinet, calculators, and answering machine. The closet of the room was used only to store items used for the rental properties, such as lamps, carpets, and other furnishings, For Rent signs, and a toolbox. Because Curphey met the requirements for the deduction, the tax court held he could deduct his home office expenses. (*Curphey v. Comm'r*, 73 T.C. 766 (1980).)

Moreover, changes in the tax law that took effect in 1999 make it easier than it has ever been for landlords (and other business owners) to take the home office deduction, and harder for the IRS to successfully object. Still, the IRS doesn't go out of its way to encourage landlords to take the deduction. Indeed, you won't find a single word about it in any IRS publication or form.

There are strict requirements you must meet to qualify for the home office deduction. You are entitled to the home office deduction if:

- your rental activities qualify as a business
- you use your home office exclusively for your rental business, and
- you use your home office for rental business on a regular basis.

After you meet these three threshold requirements, you must also satisfy *any one* of the following four requirements:

- you regularly and exclusively use your home office for administrative or management activities for your rental business and have no other fixed location where you regularly perform such activities
- you perform your most important rental activities at your home office
- you meet business-related visitors, such as tenants, at your home office, or
- you use a separate structure on your property exclusively for rental business purposes.

Will Taking the Deduction Increase Your Audit Chances?

Some people believe that taking the home office deduction invites an IRS audit. The IRS denies this. But even if taking the deduction increases your audit chances, the risk of an audit is still low (see Chapter 1). Moreover, you have nothing to fear from an audit if you're entitled to take the deduction and you keep good records to prove it.

Threshold Requirements

To take the home office deduction, you must have a home office—that is, an office or other workplace in your home that you use regularly and exclusively for your rental business. Your home may be a house, apartment, condominium, mobile home, or even a boat. Your home can even be a part of your rental property—for example, an apartment in a multiunit apartment building you own, or one-half of a duplex—but, you must actually live in it.

Your office may be all or part of a bedroom, den, or other space in your home that is physically and functionally part of your residence. You can also take the deduction for separate structures on your property that you use for business, such as an unattached garage or workshop. Any space that is not part of your residence is not subject to these rules—for example, space inside your rental building that you use for office work, maintenance, storage, or other landlord purposes.

Your Rental Activities Must Be a Business

Your rental activities must qualify as a business for tax purposes if you want to take the home office deduction. The deduction is not available if your rental activity qualifies only as an investment. Whether your rental activity is a business depends on how much time and effort you put into it. To be a business, you must be actively involved in managing your property on a regular, systematic, and continuous basis. You don't have to work full time as a landlord—in fact, you can have only a single rental unit and still be a business for tax purposes. You just must be able to show that you are actively involved in managing the rental. (See Chapter 2 for more on when a rental activity constitutes a business for tax purposes.)

You Must Use Your Home Office Exclusively for Business

You can't take the home office deduction unless you use part of your home exclusively for your rental business. In other words, you must use your home office *only for your rental business.* The more space you devote exclusively to your business, the more your home office deduction will be worth.

If you use part of your home—such as a bedroom—as your rental business office, and you use that same space for personal purposes, you won't qualify for the home office deduction.

If you use the same room (or rooms) for your office and for other purposes, you'll have to arrange your furniture and belongings so that a portion of the room is devoted exclusively to your business. Place only your business furniture and other business items in the office portion of the room. Business furniture includes anything that you use for your business, such as standard office furniture like a desk and chair, and tools and other items you use in your rental business.

The IRS does not require you to physically separate the space you use for business from the rest of the room. However, doing so will help you satisfy the exclusive-use test. For example, if you use part of your living room as an office, you could separate it from the rest of the room with folding screens or bookcases.

Although you must use your home office exclusively for your rental business, you and other family members or visitors may walk through it to get to other rooms in your residence.

As a practical matter, the IRS doesn't have spies checking to see whether you're using your home office just for business. However, complying with the rules from the beginning means you won't have to worry if you are audited.

You Must Use Your Home Office Regularly

It's not enough to use a part of your home exclusively for business; you must also use it regularly. For example, you can't place a desk in a corner of a room and claim the home office deduction if you almost never use the desk for your business.

Unfortunately, the IRS doesn't offer a clear definition of regular use. The agency has stated only that you must use a portion of your home for business on a continuing basis—not just for occasional or incidental business. One court has held that 12 hours of use a week is sufficient. (*Green v. Comm'r.*, 79 T.C. 428 (1982).)

Many landlords probably spend less than 12 hours per week working in their home offices. As long as they work regularly, they probably pass muster with the IRS. Thus, for example, even in the case of Edwin Curphey (see example at the beginning of "Qualifying for the Home Office Deduction," above), who owned only six rental units but had clearly defined home office space, the IRS didn't raise the issue of how much time he spent in his home office (it couldn't have been much).

Additional Requirements

Using a home office exclusively and regularly for your rental business is not enough to qualify for the home office deduction: You must also satisfy at least one of the additional three tests described below.

You Perform Administrative and Management Work at Your Home Office

You qualify for the home office deduction if:

- you regularly and exclusively use your home office for administrative or management activities for your rental business, and
- there is no other fixed location where you regularly conduct these activities.

Home offices that meet these requirements are deemed to qualify as the principal place of business for your rental activity. Administrative or management activities include, but are not limited to: keeping books and records, ordering supplies, scheduling appointments, talking to tenants or a resident manager on the phone, arranging for repairs, or writing a rental advertisement. Provided you have no other fixed location where you regularly do these things—for example, an outside office—you'll get the deduction. This makes it easy for almost any landlord to qualify for the deduction. All you have to do is set up a home office that you regularly and exclusively use to manage or administer your rental business.

Under these rules, you can even have an outside office or workplace and still qualify for the home office deduction, as long as you use your home office to perform management tasks and you don't perform substantial management tasks at your outside office.

> **EXAMPLE:** Bill owns a six-unit apartment building. He has a small workshop in the building's basement that he uses to perform repairs and other maintenance work. He also has a home office where he takes care of all the management tasks for his rental business, such as record keeping. Bill may take the home office deduction.

You may also perform some management tasks in a place other than a fixed location, such as your car.

You Perform Your Most Important Rental Activities at Home

If you can't satisfy the requirements discussed above, you can still qualify for the home office deduction if you perform your most important rental business activities—those activities that most directly generate your rental income—at home.

If you do, your home office qualifies as your principal place of business. This leads to the question: How do landlords decide where they do their most important work? The IRS might argue that they do their most important work at their rental properties, not in their home offices. After all, this is where their tenants live, where they show their properties, perform maintenance, and so forth. On the other hand, a landlord could argue that the bookkeeping and management activities he or she performs from home are most important. This is an unanswered question.

> EXAMPLE: Charles is a lawyer who owns a large apartment building. He performs some bookkeeping work for his rental business from his law office. Thus, he doesn't satisfy the rules discussed above. However, Charles concludes that his home office still qualifies as his principal place of business because it is the place where he performs his most important rental business-related work. Charles employs a resident manager to take care of his building, so he rarely goes there. He deals with his manager and performs the bulk of his bookkeeping from his home office, so he reasonably claims that it is the location from which he earns most of his rental income. The IRS is unlikely to challenge this.

If the work landlords do at their home offices and at their rental properties is of equal importance, then their principal place of business is where they spend more than half of their time. If you can show that you spend more time at your home office than at your rental properties, your home should qualify as your principal place of business.

You Meet Business Visitors at Home

Even if your home office is not your principal place of business, you may deduct your expenses for any part of your home that you use exclusively to meet with tenants, maintenance workers, vendors, or others involved with your rental business. You must physically meet with others in this home location—phoning them from there is not sufficient. And the meetings must be a regular part of your rental business; occasional meetings don't qualify.

It's not entirely clear how often you must meet these people at home for those meetings to be considered regular. However, the IRS has indicated that meeting people one or two days a week is sufficient. Exclusive use means you use the space where you meet tenants and others only for your rental business. You are free to use the space for business purposes other than meeting tenants—for example, doing your rental business bookkeeping or other paperwork. But you cannot use the space for personal purposes, such as watching television.

If you want to qualify under this part of the rule, keep a log or appointment book showing all the visits by your tenants and others.

You Use a Separate Structure for Rental Business

You can also deduct expenses for a separate freestanding structure, such as a garage or shed, if you use it exclusively and regularly for your rental business. The structure does not have to be your principal place of business, and you do not have to meet tenants there.

Exclusive use means that you use the structure only for your rental business.

> EXAMPLE: Gina uses a storage shed in the rear of her house exclusively to store tools and supplies she uses for her rental business. She may take the home office deduction for the shed.

Calculating the Home Office Deduction

This is the fun part—figuring out how much the home office deduction will save you in taxes. You can always use the actual expense method discussed below. However, you have the option of using a new simplified method of calculating your deduction. (See "Simplified Home Office Deduction Method," below.)

How Much of Your Home Is Used for Your Rental Business?

To calculate your home office deduction, you need to determine what percentage of your home you use for your rental business. The law says you can use "any reasonable method" to do this. Obviously, you want to use the method that will give you the largest home office deduction. To do this, you want to maximize the percentage of your home that you claim as your office. There is no single way to do this for every home office. Try both methods described below and use the one that gives you the larger deduction.

Square Footage Method

The most precise method of measuring your office space is to divide the square footage of your home office by the total square footage of your home. For example, if your home is 1,600 square feet and you use 400 square feet for your home office, 25% of the total area is used for business. Of course, you must know the square footage of your entire home and your office to make this calculation. Your home's total square footage may be listed on real estate documents or plans; you'll have to measure your office space yourself. You don't need to use a tape measure; you can just pace off the measurements.

You are allowed to subtract the square footage of common areas such as hallways, entries, stairs, and landings from the total area that you are measuring. You can also exclude attics and garages from your total space if you don't use them for business purposes. You aren't required to deduct the common area footage, but doing so will give you a larger deduction because your overall percentage of business use will be higher.

Room Method

Another way to measure is the room method. You can use this method only if all of the rooms in your home are about the same size. Using this method, you divide the number of rooms used for business by the total number of rooms in the home. Don't include bathrooms, closets, or other storage areas. You may also leave out garages and attics if you don't use them for business. For example, if you use one room in a five-room house for your rental business, your office takes up 20% of your home.

> **TIP**
> **The room method often yields a larger deduction.** Even though IRS Form 8829, *Expenses for Business Use of Your Home* (the form you must file to claim the home office deduction), seems to require you to use the square footage method, this isn't the case. As long as all of the rooms in your home are about the same size, you can use the room method. Using the room method will often result in a larger deduction.

What Expenses Can You Deduct?

The home office deduction is not one deduction, but many. Most costs associated with maintaining and running your home office are deductible. However, because your office is in your home, some of the money you spend also benefits you personally. For example, your utility bill pays to heat your home office, but it also keeps the rest of your living space warm. The IRS deals with this issue by dividing home office expenses into two categories: direct expenses, which benefit only your home office, and indirect expenses, which benefit both your office and the rest of your home.

Direct Expenses

You have a direct home office expense when you pay for something just for the home office portion of your home. This includes, for example, the cost of painting your home office, carpeting it, or hiring someone to clean it. The entire amount of a direct home office expense is deductible.

Virtually anything you buy for your office is deductible. However, you may have to depreciate permanent improvements to your home over 39 years, rather than deduct them in the year when you pay for them. Permanent improvements are changes that go beyond simple repairs, such as adding a new room to your home to serve as your office. (See Chapter 4 for more information on improvements versus repairs.)

You Can Deduct Business Expenses Even If You Don't Qualify for the Home Office Deduction

Many business owners believe that they can't deduct any expenses they incur while working at home unless they qualify for the home office deduction. This is a myth that has cost many taxpayers valuable deductions. Even if you don't qualify for or take the home office deduction, you can still take tax deductions for expenses you incur while working at your rental business at home. These are expenses that arise from the fact that you are doing business as a landlord, not from your use of the home itself.

These include:

- **Telephone expenses.** You can't deduct the basic cost of a single telephone line into your home, but you can deduct the cost of long-distance rental business calls and special phone services that you use for your business (such as call waiting or message center). You can also deduct the entire cost of a second phone line that you use just for your rental business.

- **Business equipment and furniture.** The cost of office furniture, copiers, fax machines, and other personal property you use for your rental business and keep at home is deductible, whether or not you qualify for the home office deduction. If you purchase these items specifically for your rental business, you can deduct them using the de minimis safe harbor if they cost less than $500, expense them (deduct them in one year) under Section 179, or depreciate them over several years. If you convert personal property you already own to business use, you may depreciate the fair market value. If you use the property for both business and personal reasons, you can only deduct the business use percentage of the item. The IRS requires you to keep records showing when the item was used for business or personal reasons—for example, a diary or log with the dates, times, and reasons the item was used. See Chapter 5 for a detailed discussion of these rules.

You Can Deduct Business Expenses Even If You Don't Qualify for the Home Office Deduction (continued)

- **Computer equipment.** Computers and peripheral equipment (such as printers) you use for your rental business are deductible whether or not you qualify for the home office deduction. However, if you don't qualify for the home office deduction, you must prove that you use your computer more than half of the time for business by keeping a log of your usage. If you qualify for the home office deduction, you don't need to keep track of how much time you spend using your computer for business.
- **Supplies.** Supplies for your rental business are currently deductible as an operating expense if you elect to use the de minimis safe harbor or the materials and supplies deduction (see Chapter 3). Otherwise, you must depreciate them or expense them under Section 179, as explained in Chapter 5.

Indirect Expenses

An indirect expense is a payment for something that benefits your *entire home*, including both the home office portion and your personal space. You may deduct only a portion of this expense—the home office percentage of the total.

Most of your home office expenses will be indirect expenses, including:

- **Rent.** If you rent your home or apartment, you can use the home office deduction to deduct part of your rent—a substantial expense that is ordinarily not deductible. Your tax savings will be particularly great if you live in a high-rent area.
- **Mortgage interest and property taxes.** Whether or not you have a home office, you can deduct your monthly mortgage interest and property tax payments as a personal itemized income tax deduction on your Schedule A, *Itemized Deductions* (the tax form where you list your personal income tax deductions). But if you have a home office, you have the option of deducting the home office percentage of your mortgage interest and property tax payments on Schedule E as part

of your home office deduction. If you do this, you may not deduct this amount on your Schedule A (you can't deduct the same item twice). There is no great tax advantage for a landlord to do this; it just switches the deduction from one tax form to another.

- **Depreciation.** If you own your home, you're also entitled to a depreciation deduction for the office portion of your home. See Chapter 5 for a detailed discussion of depreciation.
- **Utilities.** You may deduct your home office percentage of your utility bills for your entire home, including electricity, gas, water, heating oil, and trash removal.
- **Insurance.** Both homeowners' and renter's insurance are partly deductible as indirect home office expenses. However, special insurance coverage you buy just for your home office—for example, insurance for your computer or other rental business equipment—is fully deductible as a direct expense.
- **Home maintenance.** You can deduct the home office percentage of home maintenance expenses that benefit your entire home, such as housecleaning of your entire house, roof and furnace repairs, and exterior painting. These costs are deductible whether you hire someone or do them yourself. If you do the work yourself, however, you can deduct only the cost of materials, not the cost of your own labor. Termite inspection, pest extermination fees, and snow removal costs are also deductible. Home maintenance costs that don't benefit your home office—for example, painting your kitchen—are not deductible at all.
- **Casualty losses.** Casualty losses are damage to your home caused by such things as fire, floods, or theft. Casualty losses that affect your entire house—for example, a leak that floods your entire home—are deductible in the amount of your home office percentage. Casualty losses that affect only your home office, for example a leak that floods only the home office area of the house, are fully deductible direct expenses. Casualty losses that don't affect your home office—for example, if only your kitchen floods—are not deductible as business expenses. However, they may be deductible as itemized personal deductions. (See Chapter 13 for a detailed discussion of casualty losses.)

- **Condominium association fees.** These fees (often substantial) are partly deductible as an indirect expense if you have a home office.
- **Security system costs.** Security system costs are partly deductible as an indirect expense if your security system protects your entire home. If you have a security system that protects only your home office, the cost is a fully deductible direct expense.
- **Local travel expenses.** If your home office is your principal place of business, you can deduct the cost of traveling from your home to other work locations for your rental business. For example, you can deduct the cost of driving from home to perform maintenance at your rental property. If you don't have a home office, these costs are not deductible. See Chapter 10 for a detailed discussion of the business mileage deduction.

Profit Limit on Deductions

The tax code significantly limits the size of any home office deduction: You cannot deduct more than the net profit you earn from a business you run from your home office. If your rental business earns a substantial profit, this won't pose a problem. But if your business earns very little or loses money, the limitation could prevent you from deducting part or even all of your home office expenses in the current year.

If your deductions exceed your profits, you can deduct the excess in the following year and in each succeeding year until you deduct the entire amount, assuming you earn profits in these years. There is no limit on how far into the future you can deduct these expenses; you can claim them even if you are no longer living in the home where they were incurred.

So, whether or not your business is making money, you should keep track of your home office expenses and claim the deduction on your tax return. The profit limitation applies only to the home office deduction. It does not apply to rental business expenses that you can deduct under other provisions of the tax code.

For these purposes, your profit is the gross income you earn from your rental business minus your rental business deductions other than your home office deduction. You must also subtract the home office portion of your mortgage interest, real estate taxes, and casualty losses.

Special Concerns for Homeowners

Until recently, homeowners who took the home office deduction were subject to a special tax trap: If they took a home office deduction for more than three of the five years before they sold their house, they had to pay capital gains taxes on the profit from the home office portion of their home. For example, if you made a $50,000 profit on the sale of your house, but your home office took up 20% of the space, you would have had to pay a tax on $10,000 of your profit (20% × $50,000 = $10,000).

Fortunately, IRS rules no longer require this. As long as you live in your home for at least two out of the five years before you sell it, the profit you make on the sale—up to $250,000 for single taxpayers and $500,000 for married taxpayers filing jointly—is not taxable. (See IRS Publication 523, *Selling Your Home*.) If you sold your house after May 6, 1997 and paid capital gains tax on the home office portion, you may be entitled to amend your return for the year you sold the house and receive a tax refund from the IRS.

However, you will have to pay a capital gains tax on the depreciation deductions you took after May 6, 1997 for your home office. This is the deduction you are allowed for the yearly decline in value due to wear and tear of the portion of the building that contains your home office. (See Chapter 5 for more information on depreciation deductions.) These recaptured deductions are taxed at a 25% rate (unless your income tax bracket is lower than 25%).

> EXAMPLE: Sally bought a $200,000 home in 2009 and used one of her bedrooms as her home office for her rental business. She sold her home in 2015 for $300,000, realizing a $100,000 gain (profit). Her depreciation deductions for her home office from 2009 through 2015 totaled $2,000. She must pay a tax of 25% of $2,000, or $500.

Having to pay a 25% tax on the depreciation deductions you took in the years before you sold your house is actually not a bad deal. This is probably no more—and is often less—tax than you would have had to pay if you hadn't taken the deductions in the first place and instead paid tax on your additional taxable income at ordinary income tax rates.

You can avoid such depreciation recapture if you use the new simplified method of calculating the home office deduction (see "Simplified Home Office Deduction Method," below). When you use this method, you deduct $5 per square foot of your home office and your depreciation deduction for the home office is deemed to be zero for the year. Thus, you have no depreciation recapture when you sell your home. Also, the adjusted basis of your home does not change.

Simplified Home Office Deduction Method

Lots of people who qualify for the home office deduction don't take it because they don't think it's worth the trouble or they are afraid it will result in an IRS audit. In a rare move to simplify life for taxpayers, the IRS has created a new simplified optional home office deduction calculation method. The simplified method went into effect for the 2013 tax year. You can't use the simplified deduction method for years earlier than 2013.

It's important to understand that all the regular rules for qualifying for the home office deduction still apply if you use the optional simplified method—that is, you must use a portion of your home regularly and exclusively for your rental business.

How the Simple Method Works

The simple method really is simple: You deduct $5 for every square foot of your home office. Thus, all you need to do is measure the square footage of your home office. For example, if your home office is 200 square feet, you'll get a $1,000 home office deduction. That's all there is to it.

You don't need to figure out what percentage of your home your office occupies. You also don't need to keep records of your direct or indirect home office expenses such as utilities, rent, mortgage payments, real estate taxes, or casualty losses. These expenses aren't deductible when you use the simplified method.

Another big plus: You don't have to complete Form 8829.

Homeowners using the new option cannot claim a depreciation deduction for their home office. However, they can claim allowable mortgage interest, real estate taxes, and casualty losses on the home as itemized deductions on Schedule A. These deductions need not be allocated between personal and business use, as is required under the regular method. Business expenses unrelated to the home, such as advertising, supplies, and wages paid to employees are still fully deductible.

When you use the simplified method, your home office deduction is capped at $1,500 per year. You'll reach the cap if your home office is 300 square feet. Thus, for example, if your home office is 400 square feet, you'll still be limited to a $1,500 home office deduction if you use the simplified method. You can't carry over any part of the deduction to future years.

As with the regular home office deduction, your total annual deduction using the simplified method is limited to the gross income you earned from the business use of your home during the year. Moreover, if you use the simplified method, you can't carry over any excess to a future tax year—something you can do when you use the regular method. Nor can you deduct amounts carried over from past years that you couldn't deduct using the regular method. For this reason, you should never use the simplified method if the profit from your business for the year is less than the amount of your simplified home office deduction.

You may choose either the simplified method or the regular method for any year (2013 or later). You choose your method by using it on your timely filed, original federal income tax return for the year. Once you have chosen a method for a tax year, you cannot later change to the other method for that same year. If you use the simplified method for one year and use the regular method for any subsequent year, you must calculate the depreciation deduction for the subsequent year using the appropriate optional depreciation table. This is true regardless of whether you used an optional depreciation table for the first year the property was used in business.

Is the Simplified Method a Good Deal?

Is it a good idea to use the new simplified home office deduction? Only if the deduction you could obtain using the regular method isn't much more than $1,500. The simplified method may work out well for homeowners whose home office deductions are often small because they have no rent. Moreover, using the simplified method eliminates having to pay tax on recaptured depreciation deductions for your home office when you sell your home. If you don't plan to live in your home for very long, this can be a substantial benefit.

If you're thinking about using the simplified method, you should figure your deduction using both methods and use the one that gives you the larger deduction. The regular method does require more record keeping than the optional method, but you probably keep these types of records anyway. Doing the required calculations and filling out the form can be challenging, but will be much easier if you use tax preparation software.

IRS Reporting Requirements

Reporting your home office deduction is simple. First, you figure out the amount of your deduction. You can do this by using the IRS worksheet contained in Publication 587, *Business Use of Your Home.* If you have enough rental income to take a home office deduction this year (Line 32 of the worksheet), report the amount (up to the profit limit) on Line 19 of your Schedule E. Write "Business Use of Home" on the dotted line beside the entry. If you don't have enough rental income to take a home office deduction this year, write nothing in your Schedule E. Keep your record of your home office expenses to use in a future year when you have more rental income.

You need not file IRS Form 8829, *Expenses for Business Use of Your Home.* This form is only filed by taxpayers who file IRS Schedule C, *Profit or Loss From Business (Sole Proprietorship).* Landlords do not file Schedule C (see Chapter 1).

Audit-Proofing Your Home Office Deduction

If the IRS audits you and questions your home office deduction, you want to be able to prove that you:

- qualify for the deduction, and
- have correctly reported the amount of your home office expenses.

If you can do both of those things, you should be home free.

Prove That You Are Following the Rules

Here are some ways to convince the IRS that you qualify for the home office deduction.

- Take a picture of your home office and draw up a diagram showing your home office as a portion of your home. Do not send the photo or diagram to the IRS. Just keep it in your files to use in case you're audited.
- Have all of your rental business mail sent to your home office.
- Use your home office address on all of your rental business cards, stationery, and advertising.
- Get a separate phone line for your rental business and keep that phone in your home office.
- Keep a log of the time you spend working in your home office. This doesn't have to be fancy; notes on your calendar will do.

Keep Good Expense Records

Be sure to keep copies of your bills and receipts for home office expenses, including:

- IRS Form 1098, *Mortgage Interest Statement* (sent by whomever holds your mortgage), showing the interest you paid on your mortgage for the year
- property tax bills and your canceled checks as proof of payment
- utility bills, insurance bills, and receipts for payments for repairs to your office area, along with your canceled checks paying for these items, and
- if you're a renter, a copy of your lease and rent receipts or your canceled rent checks.

Deducting an Outside Office

If you have an outside office for your rental activities, your tax life is simpler than if you use a home office. In addition, landlords who are investors, as well as business owners, can deduct expenses for an outside office.

Renting an Office

The rent and other expenses you pay for an outside office or other work space you use for your rental activity may be deducted the year they are paid as ordinary and necessary business expenses. None of the home office deduction rules apply to outside offices. You may deduct the rent you pay your landlord to use the property during the year. You may also deduct other expenses you pay the landlord, such as a portion of the landlord's property taxes or utility bills. Of course, you can deduct your own utility bills. You may deduct the cost of repairs you pay for, but permanent improvements to the property must be depreciated over several years. For example, you can currently deduct the cost of fixing the furnace, but you'd have to depreciate the cost of buying a new furnace. (See Chapter 5.)

Rental expenses for an outside office are reported on your Schedule E, the same as any other rental operating expense. List them on Line 18.

Using an Office in Your Rental Building

Many landlords use space inside their rental buildings as an office, workshop, or for storage. You may deduct the utilities you pay for the space, but you get no deduction for the rent you lose by not renting the space to tenants. You may depreciate the space along with the rest of your building. Use the 27.5-year depreciation period for residential property, if 80% of your total rentals from the building come from the dwelling units. Otherwise, you must use the 39-year term for nonresidential property. When you use a space in your building as an office, you use the fair rental value of the space to calculate this percentage.

EXAMPLE: Sam owns several rental properties, including a duplex with two small one-bedroom units of equal size. He rents one side of the duplex to a tenant to live in and uses the other side as his office for his rental activities. He charges his tenant $800 per month rent, which is also the fair rental value of his office. Less than 80% of the gross rental income from the duplex comes from dwelling units—$800 is 50% of $1,600. As a result, Sam must depreciate the entire duplex using the 39-year term for nonresidential property. He may deduct the full amount he spends for utilities for his office and for repairs.

See Chapter 5 for a detailed discussion of depreciation.

Buying a Separate Office Building

If you buy a separate building that is not a residential rental to use as your office, you may currently deduct as ordinary and necessary business expenses your mortgage interest and real estate taxes and expenses associated with the sale. In addition, you may depreciate the value of the real estate (not including the land) over 39 years. The cost of repairs may be currently deducted, but permanent improvements to the property must be depreciated. (See Chapter 4 for more on repairs versus improvements.)

Car and Local Transportation Expenses

Deductible Local Transportation Expenses 256

    Travel Must Be for Rental Activities...257

    Driving From and to Home 258

The Standard Mileage Rate...261

    How the Standard Mileage Rate Works 261

    Requirements to Use the Standard Mileage Rate 262

The Actual Expense Method...263

    How the Actual Expense Method Works...264

    Record-Keeping Requirements..265

    Vehicle Depreciation Deductions...265

    Leasing a Car...273

Other Local Transportation Expenses..273

Reporting Transportation Expenses on Your Tax Return..274

This chapter shows you how to deduct expenses for local transportation—that is, trips that don't require you to stay away from home overnight. These rules apply to local trips using any means of transportation, but this chapter focuses primarily on car expenses, the most common type of deduction for local travel. Overnight trips (whether by car or other means) are covered in Chapter 11.

> ## CAUTION
> **Transportation expenses are a red flag for the IRS.** Car and other local transportation expenses are always a key item for IRS auditors. It is easy to overstate them, so, if you're audited, the IRS will probably look carefully to make sure that you're not bending the rules. Your first line of defense against an audit is to keep good records to back up your deductions. This is something no tax preparation program or accountant can do for you—you must develop good record-keeping habits and follow them faithfully to stay out of trouble with the IRS.

Deductible Local Transportation Expenses

Local transportation costs are deductible in the year in which they are incurred as operating expenses if they are ordinary and necessary for your rental activity—meaning common, helpful, and appropriate for your activity. (See Chapter 3 for a detailed discussion of the ordinary and necessary requirement.) It makes no difference what type of transportation you use to make the local trips—car, van, pickup, truck, motorcycle, taxi, bus, or train—or whether the vehicle you use is owned or leased. You can deduct these costs as long as they are ordinary and necessary and meet the other requirements discussed below.

You can deduct local transportation expenses if your rental activity qualifies as a business or an investment for tax purposes. (*Horowitz v. Comm'r.*, T.C. Memo 1979-27.) If you do a lot of driving for your rental activity, however, there's a good chance you are engaged in a business, not an investment. Investors usually don't do much driving to or from their rental properties or for other business purposes because (by definition) they are not actively involved in the management of their rental properties. (See Chapter 2 for a detailed discussion of whether you qualify as a business or investor for tax purposes.)

Travel Must Be for Rental Activities

You can deduct only local trips that are for your rental activities—for example, to collect rental income or to manage, conserve, or maintain your rental property. Personal trips—for example, to the supermarket or the gym—are not deductible as transportation expenses. You can deduct the cost of driving to:

- your rental property
- where you have your principal place of business for your rental activity, including a home office
- places where you meet with tenants, suppliers, vendors, repair-people, attorneys, accountants, real estate brokers, real estate managers, and other people who help in your rental activity
- the bank where you do banking for your real estate activity
- the garbage dump where you haul refuse from your rental property
- a local college where you take landlord-related classes (educational expenses are deductible only if your rental activities qualify as a business; see Chapter 14), or
- a store where you buy supplies or materials for your real estate activity.

Moreover, you don't have to do all the driving yourself to get a car expense deduction. Any use of your car by another person qualifies as a deductible business expense if it is directly connected with your business. Thus, for example, you can count as business mileage a car trip your employee, spouse, or child takes to deliver an item for your rental business or for any other business purpose.

Travel Costs Before You Become a Landlord

The cost of local travel you do before you become a landlord, such as travel to investigate purchasing a rental property, is not a currently deductible operating expense. If your rental activity becomes a business, such travel is a start-up expense. Up to $5,000 in start-up expenses may be deducted the first year your rental business is in operation. Any amount over $5,000 must be deducted in equal installments over the first 180 months you're in business. Landlords who are only investors may not deduct such start-up expenses. (See Chapter 2.)

Driving From and to Home

Most local trips that landlords make for their rental activities start and end at home. Whether driving from home is deductible as an operating expense depends on whether you have a home office for your rental activity, and where you drive to.

You Have a Home Office

If you have a home office that qualifies as your principal place of business, you can deduct the cost of any trips you make from home to another location for your rental activity. You can get a lot of travel deductions this way. For example, you can deduct the cost of driving from home to your rental property or to the bank.

To deduct the cost of driving to and from your home office, it must qualify as your principal place of business. The rules for the home office deduction are used to determine whether a home office is a person's principal place of business. Under these rules, a home office qualifies if it is the place where you perform management or administrative tasks. Practically any landlord can set up a home office to perform such tasks—but you may not use the office for any other purpose.

> EXAMPLE: Kim owns five rental houses scattered throughout Southern California. She maintains a home office where she does bookkeeping and other administrative and management work for her rental business. She can deduct all of her rental-business–related trips from her home office, including trips she makes from home to any of her rental properties. Thanks to her home office, she can usually deduct 200 miles per month as a business trip expense.

You might think that landlords whose rental activities qualify as an investment (not a business) have no principal place of business since they are not in business. This is not the case, however. Landlords who are investors get the same transportation deductions as landlords who are in business, as long as their home office meets the requirements for the home office deduction. If it does, then their home office is treated as their principal place of business for the transportation deduction. This is so, even though the home office deduction itself is limited to landlords who are in business. (See Chapter 9 for more on the home office deduction.)

You Don't Have a Home Office

If you don't have a home office that qualifies as your principal place of business, your transportation deductions will be limited by the commuting rule. Commuting expenses are nondeductible personal expenses. Commuting means driving from where you live to your main or regular place of work for your rental activity. For landlords, this means driving from home to their rental properties or to their outside office (if they have one).

> **EXAMPLE:** Sue, an accountant, lives in a Chicago suburb and owns a five-unit apartment building in downtown Chicago, about ten miles away. Sue does no work for her rental activity from home. Instead, she does all of her rental-related bookkeeping and other management tasks from her accounting office. Because of the commuting rule, Sue may not deduct the cost of driving from her home to her rental properties, or to her accounting office to perform rental-related work.

Even if a trip from home has a business purpose—for example, to haul tools or supplies from home to your rental property—it is still considered commuting and is not deductible. (You may, however, deduct the cost of renting a trailer or any other extraordinary expenses you incur to haul the tools or supplies from your home.)

Once you arrive at your rental office or rental property, you may deduct trips to other rental-related locations. But not trips back home.

> **EXAMPLE:** Sue drives directly from home to her rental property to supervise a repair. She then drives directly to her office, and drives back home later that day. She may deduct the trip from her rental property to her rental office, but none of her other trips.

Travel to a Temporary Work Location

Even if you don't have a home office, some trips from home may be deductible. Remember, commuting occurs when you go from home to a permanent work location—either:

- your office or other principal place of business for your rental activity, or
- your rental property, or any other place where you have worked or expect to work for more than one year.

Travel between your home and a temporary work location is not considered commuting and is therefore deductible. A temporary work location is any place where you realistically expect to work less than one year. This may include the bank, post office, building supply store, local college where you take real estate courses, and similar places.

> EXAMPLE: Sue travels from her home to a building supply store to pick up a part for a repair to her rental property. This is not commuting and is deductible.

However, a place will cease to be a temporary work location if you continue to go there for more than one year.

> EXAMPLE: Sue goes from her house to the building supply store almost every week for over a year. The store is no longer a temporary work location, and her trips there from home are nondeductible commuting expenses.

You can convert a nondeductible commute into a deductible local business trip by making a stop at a temporary work location on your way to your office. Stopping at a temporary work location converts the entire trip into a deductible travel expense.

> EXAMPLE: One morning, Sue leaves home, stops off at the local newspaper office to place a rental advertisement, and then goes to her office. The entire trip is deductible because she stopped at a temporary work location on her way to her office.

Keep in mind, though, that making such stops is necessary only if you *don't* have a home office. If Sue had a home office, the commuting rule wouldn't apply and the trip would be deductible with or without the stop.

The Standard Mileage Rate

If you drive a car, SUV, van, pickup, or panel truck for your rental activity (as most landlords do), you have two options for deducting your vehicle expenses: You can use the standard mileage rate or you can deduct your actual expenses. Let's start with the easy one—the standard mileage rate.

How the Standard Mileage Rate Works

To use the standard mileage rate, you deduct a specified number of cents for every mile you drive for your rental activity. The IRS sets the standard mileage rate each year. For 2015, the rate is 57.5 cents per mile. To figure out your deduction, simply multiply your business miles by the applicable standard mileage rate.

> **EXAMPLE:** Ed drove his car 10,000 miles for his business in 2015. To determine his car expense deduction, he simply multiplies his business miles by the standard mileage rate. This gives him a total deduction for the year of $5,750 (57.5 cents × 10,000 = $5,750).

The big advantage of the standard mileage rate is that it requires very little record keeping. You only need to keep track of how many rental activity miles you drive, not the actual expenses for your car, such as gas, maintenance, or repairs. However, unless you drive a very inexpensive car that qualifies for very little depreciation, the standard mileage rate will usually give you a smaller deduction than the actual expense method.

If you choose the standard mileage rate, you cannot deduct actual car operating expenses—for example, maintenance and repairs, gasoline and its taxes, oil, insurance, and vehicle registration fees. All of these items are factored into the rate set by the IRS. And you can't deduct the cost of the car through depreciation or Section 179 expensing, because the car's depreciation is also factored into the standard mileage rate (as are lease payments for a leased car).

The only actual expenses you can deduct (because these costs aren't included in the standard mileage rate) are:

- parking fees and tolls for rental-related trips (but you can't deduct parking ticket fines or the cost of parking your car at your place of work)
- interest on a car loan, and
- personal property tax you paid when you bought the vehicle, based on its value—this is often included as part of your auto registration fee.

If, like most landlords, you use your car for both rental-related and personal trips, you can deduct only the rental use percentage of the above-mentioned interest and taxes.

> EXAMPLE: Ralph uses his car 50% for his rental activity and 50% for personal trips. He uses the standard mileage rate to deduct his car expenses. He pays $3,000 a year in interest on his car loan. He may deduct 50% of this amount, or $1,500, as an operating expense in addition to his rental activity mileage deduction.

Requirements to Use the Standard Mileage Rate

Not everyone can use the standard mileage rate. You won't be able to use it (and will have to use the actual expense method instead) if you can't meet the following two requirements.

First-Year Rule

You must use the standard mileage rate in the first year you use a car for your rental activity or you are forever foreclosed from using that method for that car. If you use the standard mileage rate the first year, you can switch to the actual expense method in a later year, and then switch back and forth between the two methods after that, provided the requirements listed below are met. For this reason, if you're not sure which method you want to use, it's a good idea to use the standard mileage rate the first year you use the car for business. This leaves all your options open for later years. However, this rule does not apply to leased cars.

There are some restrictions on switching back to the standard mileage rate after you have used the actual expense method. You can switch back to the standard mileage rate only if you used the straight-line method of depreciation during the years you used the actual expense method. This depreciation method gives you equal depreciation deductions every year, rather than the larger deductions you get in the early years using accelerated depreciation methods. You can't switch back to the standard mileage rate after using the actual expense method if you took accelerated depreciation, a Section 179 deduction, or bonus depreciation.

Five-Car Rule

You can't use the standard mileage rate if you have five or more cars that you use for your rental activity simultaneously.

The Actual Expense Method

Instead of using the standard mileage rate, you can deduct the actual cost of using your car for your rental activity. Although it requires more record keeping, you'll often get a larger deduction if you use the actual expense method instead of the standard mileage rate. The American Automobile Association estimated that the average cost of owning a car in 2015 was 59 cents per mile. This is more than the IRS allowed to be deducted under the standard mileage rate.

Nevertheless, many taxpayers choose the standard mileage rate because it's easier. You only need to keep track of how many miles you drive for your rental activity, instead of keeping track of how much you spend for gas, oil, repairs, and all your other car expenses. Moreover, if you don't drive many miles each year for your rental activity, the extra deduction you get from the actual expense method may not be worth the record keeping required.

How the Actual Expense Method Works

As the name implies, under the actual expense method, you deduct the actual costs you incur each year to operate your car, plus depreciation. If you use this method, you must keep careful track of all of your car expenses during the year, including:

- gas and oil
- repairs and maintenance
- depreciation of your original vehicle and improvements
- car repair tools
- license fees
- parking fees for rental activity trips
- registration fees
- tires
- insurance
- garage rent
- tolls for rental activity trips
- car washing
- lease payments
- interest on car loans
- towing charges, and
- auto club dues.

Watch Those Tickets

You may not deduct the cost of driving violations or parking tickets, even if you were on rental-related business when you got the ticket. Government fines and penalties are never deductible as a matter of public policy.

When you do your taxes, add up the cost of all these items. For everything but parking fees and tolls, multiply the total cost of each item by your car's business use percentage. You determine your business use percentage by keeping track of all the miles you drive for your rental activity during the year and the total mileage driven. You divide the business mileage by your total mileage to figure your business use percentage. For parking fees and tolls that are rental-activity related, include (and deduct) the full cost. The total is your deductible transportation expense for the year.

> **EXAMPLE:** Laura owns several rental houses in the Miami area. In one recent year, she drove her car 1,000 miles for her rental activity and 10,000 miles total. Her business use percentage is 10% (10,000 ÷ 1,000 = 10%). She can deduct 10% of the actual costs of operating her car, plus the full cost of any rental-related tolls and parking fees. Her expenses amount to $10,000 for the year, so she gets a $1,000 deduction, plus $50 in tolls and parking.

If you have a car that you use only for your rental activity, you may deduct 100% of your actual car costs. Be careful here. If you own just one car, it's hard to successfully claim that you use it only for your rental activity. The IRS is not likely to believe that you walk or take public transportation everywhere, except when you drive for your rental activity. (The IRS will know whether you have more than one vehicle available for personal use; people who claim transportation expenses must provide this information on their tax returns.)

Record-Keeping Requirements

When you deduct actual car expenses, you must keep records of all the costs of owning and operating your car. This includes not only the number of rental activity miles and total miles you drive, but also gas, repair, parking, insurance, tolls, and any other car expenses. (You'll find more information on record-keeping requirements in Chapter 17.)

Vehicle Depreciation Deductions

Using the actual expense method, you can deduct the cost of your vehicle. However, you can't deduct the entire cost in the year when you purchase your car. Instead, you must deduct the cost a portion at a time over several years, using a process called depreciation. (For more on depreciation generally, see Chapter 5.) Although the general concept of depreciation is the same for every type of property, special rules apply to depreciation deductions for cars. These rules give you a lower annual deduction for cars than you'd be entitled to using the normal depreciation rules.

This section focuses on the depreciation rules for passenger automobiles, as defined by the IRS. This category of vehicles includes almost all automobiles and other passenger vehicles—cars, trucks, pickups, vans, and SUVs. To understand the depreciation rules discussed in this section, you will need to be familiar with the general depreciation rules covered in Chapter 5.

Is Your Vehicle a Passenger Automobile?

First, you must figure out whether your vehicle is a passenger automobile as defined by the IRS. A passenger automobile is any four-wheeled vehicle made primarily for use on public streets and highways that has an unloaded gross weight of 6,000 pounds or less. This definition includes virtually all automobiles.

However, if your vehicle is classified as a truck or van by the manufacturer, it is a passenger automobile only if it has a gross loaded vehicle weight of 6,000 pounds or less. The gross loaded weight is based on how much the manufacturer says the vehicle can carry and is different from unloaded weight—that is, the vehicle's weight without any passengers or cargo. The truck or van classification can apply not only to traditional trucks or vans, but to other vehicles such as SUVs, minivans, and crossover vehicles. This is based on Department of Transportation rules that all car manufacturers must follow.

You can find out your vehicle's gross loaded and unloaded weight by looking at the metal plate in the driver's-side doorjamb, looking at your owner's manual, checking the manufacturer's website or sales brochure, or asking an auto dealer. The gross loaded weight is usually called the Gross Vehicle Weight Rating (GVWR for short). The gross unloaded weight is often called the curb weight.

Trucks that weigh 14,000 pounds or less when fully loaded are subject to the same rules as passenger automobiles, unless the vehicle is not likely to be used for personal purposes (as is true of moving vans, construction vehicles, tractors, and utility repair trucks). In that case, the vehicles are not considered passenger automobiles, and the limitations on depreciation discussed in this section don't apply. Instead, such vehicles are depreciated like any other personal property as described in Chapter 5.

Passenger Automobiles Are Listed Property

The IRS classifies all passenger automobiles as listed property—property that is often used for personal purposes. As explained in Chapter 5, the IRS imposes more stringent requirements on deductions for listed property to discourage fraudulent deduction claims. Because passenger automobiles are listed property, you must keep mileage records showing how much you use your car for rental activity and personal purposes. You must also file IRS Form 4562, *Depreciation and Amortization*, with your annual tax return.

How Much You Can Depreciate

Your depreciation deductions are based on your total investment in your car or other vehicle (also called your basis). You multiply the basis amount by the percentage of business use of the car to determine the total amount you may depreciate. For example, if you use a car 100% for business, you may depreciate its entire basis. If you use it 50% for business, you may depreciate only 50% of its basis. How you determine your car's basis depends on how you acquired it. If you buy a passenger automobile and use it for your rental activity that same year, your basis is its cost. You may include the entire cost, even if you financed part of the purchase with a car loan. The cost also includes sales taxes, destination charges, and other fees the seller charges. It does not, however, include auto license and registration fees.

If you trade in your old car to a dealer to purchase a new car, your basis in the car you purchase is the adjusted basis of the trade-in car, plus the cash you pay (whether out of your own pocket or financed with a car loan).

> EXAMPLE: Brenda buys a new pickup that she uses part of the time for her rental business. The pickup has a $20,000 sticker price. She trades in her old pickup and pays the dealer $15,000, all of which she finances with a car loan from her bank. Her trade-in has a $3,000 basis. Her basis in the new pickup is $18,000 ($3,000 + $15,000), even though the sticker price on the new pickup was $20,000.

If you convert a car that you previously owned for just personal use to use in your rental activity, your basis is the lower of what you originally paid for it (when you purchased it for personal use) or its fair market value at the time you convert it to rental activity use. Your basis will usually be its fair market value, as this is usually the lower number.

You can determine the fair market value of your car on the date of conversion by checking used car value guides, such as the *Kelley Blue Book*. These guides often give more than one value—for example, the *Kelley Blue Book* gives a private party value and a retail value. Using the higher value will give you a larger deduction. The best-known used car price guides (available free on the Internet) are:

- *Kelley Blue Book*: www.kbb.com
- Edmunds: www.edmunds.com, and
- NADA guides: www.nadaguides.com.

Look at more than one guide, because the prices can vary.

Depreciation Methods for Passenger Automobiles

Most landlords who own a small number of rental units don't use a single car 100% of the time for their rental activity. Instead, they use their car both for personal and rental activity purposes. If you use a passenger automobile for your rental activity less than 50% of the time, you must depreciate it using the straight-line method. This method gives you equal deductions each year except for the first and last year.

If you use your car more than 50% of the time for your rental activity, you may use accelerated depreciation, which gives you larger deductions the first few years you own your car. But, if you start out using a car more than 50% for your rental activity and your rental use falls below 50% in a later year, you must give back any extra depreciation you received using accelerated depreciation in the prior years. In other words, you must recalculate all of your deductions for the car using the straight-line method, and repay any difference between this amount and the deductions you actually took using another method.

The following table shows how much of the cost of an automobile may be depreciated each year using the three different depreciation methods and applying the half-year convention. (If more than 40% of all the depreciable property you placed in service during the year was placed in service during the last quarter of the year, you'll have to use the mid-quarter convention; see Chapter 5.)

Automobile Depreciation Table			
Year	200% Declining Balance Method (midyear convention)	150% Declining Balance Method (midyear convention)	Straight-Line Method (midyear convention)
1	20%	15%	10%
2	32%	25.5%	20%
3	19.2%	17.85%	20%
4	11.5%	16.66%	20%
5	11.5%	16.66%	20%
6	5.76%	8.33%	10%

Depreciation Limits for Passenger Automobiles

Passenger automobiles have a five-year class life (but it takes six calendar years to depreciate a car; see "Deducting Personal Property" in Chapter 5). As a result, you'd think it would take at most six years to fully depreciate a car. Unfortunately, this is usually not the case. Depreciating a passenger automobile is unique in one very important way: The annual depreciation deduction for automobiles is limited to a set dollar amount each year. The annual limit applies to all passenger vehicles, no matter how much they cost. Because the limits are so low, it can take many years to fully depreciate a car, far longer than the six years it takes to depreciate other assets with a five-year class life.

In 2003, the IRS established two different sets of deduction limits for passenger automobiles: one for passenger automobiles other than trucks and vans, and one for trucks and vans that qualify as passenger automobiles (based on their weight) and are built on a truck chassis. This includes minivans and many sport utility vehicles (as long as they meet the weight limit).

The charts below show the maximum annual depreciation deduction allowed for passenger automobiles and trucks and vans placed in service in 2015. Both charts assume 100% rental activity use of the vehicle. You can find the current deduction limits in IRS Publication 946, *How to Depreciate Property*, and Publication 463, *Travel, Entertainment, Gift, and Car Expenses*.

These figures are the maximum amount you can deduct each year, regardless of what depreciation method you use. The depreciation limits are not reduced if a car is in service for less than a full year. This means that the limit is not reduced when the automobile is either placed in service or disposed of during the year.

Depreciation Limits for Passenger Automobiles				
(must be reduced by percentage of personal use)				
Year Placed in Service	1st tax year	2nd tax year	3rd tax year	4th and later years
2015	$3,160 (plus $8,000 if bonus depreciation extended to 2015)	$5,100	$3,050	$1,875

Depreciation Limits for Trucks and Vans				
(must be reduced by percentage of personal use)				
Year Placed in Service	1st tax year	2nd tax year	3rd tax year	4th and later years
2015	$3,460 (plus $8,000 if bonus depreciation extended to 2015)	$5,600	$3,350	$1,975

For the past several years, businesses that purchase new personal property have been able to benefit from 50% first-year bonus depreciation. This allows them to deduct 50% of the cost of qualifying property the first year it is purchased. Bonus depreciation expired at the end of 2014, but it is expected to be extended through 2015, and likely beyond. However, as this book went to press, Congress had not yet acted on the extension—it may not do so until late 2015 or even early 2016. If bonus depreciation is extended through 2015, it will apply to business vehicles. If so, it is likely that you'll be able to add $8,000 to your depreciation limit for 2015—that is, you'll be able to depreciate $11,160 for a passenger vehicle instead of $3,160. However, you may use bonus depreciation only for new vehicles you use more than 50% of the time for business purposes.

The deduction limits above are based on 100% rental activity use of the vehicle. If, like most landlords, you don't use your car solely for your rental activity, the limits are reduced based on your percentage of personal use.

In addition, if, like most landlords, you use your car less than 51% for your rental business, you'll have to use the slowest method of depreciation—the straight-line method. You must continue to use this method even if your business use rises over 50% in later years.

Section 179

If you use your passenger vehicle more than 50% of the time for your rental activity, you could be entitled to use Section 179 expensing. Section 179 permits you to deduct the full cost of personal property you use at least 51% of the time for your rental activity. Your rental activity must qualify as a business for you to use Section 179. This deduction is discussed in detail in Chapter 5. If you qualify, you may combine Section 179 expensing with bonus and regular depreciation, in that order. However, your total deduction cannot exceed the annual limits listed in the charts above. There is usually no point in using Section 179 for a vehicle, because you'll likely reach the annual limit the first year using bonus depreciation and/or accelerated depreciation. It's best to avoid using Section 179 because it is subject to an annual income limit.

Depreciation Beyond the Five-Year Limit

Because of the annual limits on depreciation deductions for passenger automobiles, you usually won't be able to deduct the entire cost of a car over the five-year depreciation period. Don't worry—as long as you continue to use your car for business, you can keep taking annual deductions after the five-year depreciation period ends, until you recover your full basis in the car.

Auto Repairs and Improvements

Auto repairs and maintenance costs are fully deductible in the year you pay them. Add these costs to your other annual expenses when you use the actual expense method. (You get no extra deduction for repairs when you use the standard mileage rate.) If you fix your car yourself, you may deduct the cost of parts and depreciate or deduct tools, but you can't take a deduction for your time or labor.

Special Rule for Heavy Vehicles

The annual dollar limits in the charts above don't apply if you use Section 179 to deduct the cost of a vehicle that is not a passenger vehicle. They don't apply to trucks, pickups, RVs, vans, SUVs, and other vehicles that don't come within the passenger automobile definition—that is, vehicles with a gross loaded weight of more than 6,000 pounds (see "Is Your Vehicle a Passenger Automobile?" above). This means that you could buy an SUV (or van, truck, pickup, or RV) weighing more than 6,000 pounds for your rental business and deduct the cost in the first year, up to the Section 179 limit.

A law enacted at the end of 2004 limits the Section 179 deduction for SUVs to a maximum of $25,000.

For example, suppose Terry pays $100,000 for a 7,000-pound SUV that she uses 100% of the time for her rental business. Terry may deduct $25,000 of the SUV's cost in 2014 using Section 179. Her remaining $80,000 basis is depreciated in 2015 and later under the normal rules. In 2014, she gets an $11,160 depreciation deduction (assuming bonus depreciation is extended through 2014) so her total deduction for that year is $36,160.

Unlike repairs, improvements to your car must be depreciated over several years, not deducted all in the year when you pay for them.

Improvements must be depreciated separately from the vehicle itself— that is, they are treated as a separate item of depreciable property. The same rules, however, apply to depreciating improvements as regular auto depreciation. Combine the cost of the original vehicle and the improvements for purposes of the annual automobile depreciation limit. The recovery period begins when the improvement is placed in service.

Leasing a Car

If you lease a car that you use in your rental activity, you can use the actual expense method to deduct the portion of each lease payment that reflects the rental activity percentage use of the car. You cannot deduct any part of a lease payment that is for commuting or personal use of the car.

> **EXAMPLE:** John pays $400 a month to lease a Lexus. He uses it 10% for his rental activity and 90% for personal purposes. He may deduct 10% of his lease payments ($40 a month) as a local transportation expense for his sales business.

Leasing companies typically require you to make an advance or down payment to lease a car. You can deduct this cost as well, but you must spread the deduction out equally over the entire lease period.

You may use either the actual expense method or the standard mileage rate when you lease a car for business. However, if you want to use the standard mileage rate, you must use it the first year you lease the car and continue to use it for the entire lease term. If you use the standard mileage method, you can't deduct any portion of your lease payments. Instead, this cost is covered by the standard mileage rate set by the IRS.

Other Local Transportation Expenses

You don't have to drive a car or other vehicle to get a tax deduction for local trips. You can deduct the cost of travel by bus or other public transit, taxi, train, ferry, motorcycle, bicycle, or any other means. However, all the rules limiting deductions for travel by car also apply to other transportation methods. The same record-keeping requirements apply as well.

Reporting Transportation Expenses on Your Tax Return

Report your local transportation deduction on Line 6 of IRS Schedule E. Combine it with your travel expenses (see Chapter 18). You must also complete and file Part V of IRS Form 4562, *Depreciation and Amortization*. This form requires that you answer the following questions about your vehicle use:

- total business/investment miles driven during the year
- total commuting miles driven during the year
- total other personal (noncommuting) miles driven during the year, and
- whether you had another vehicle available for personal use.

As you can see, by looking at your answers to these questions, the IRS can determine what percentage of the time you claim to use your car for your rental activity and for personal use. The IRS will likely think something is wrong if you claim to use your car 100% of the time for your rental activity, but say you have no other car available for personal use.

11

Travel Expenses

What Are Travel Expenses? 276

Where Is Your Tax Home? 277

Your Trip Must Be for Rental Business 277

Deductible Travel Expenses 281

Traveling First Class or Steerage 282

Taking People With You 282

How Much You Can Deduct 283

Calculating Time Spent on Rental Activities 284

50% Limit on Meal Expenses 285

Maximizing Your Travel Deductions 288

Plan Ahead 288

Make a Paper Trail 288

Maximize Your Rental Activity Days 289

Take Advantage of the Sandwich Day Rule 290

f you travel overnight for your rental activity, you can deduct your airfare, hotel bills, meals, and other expenses. If you plan your trip carefully, you can even mix landlord business with pleasure and still take a deduction. However, IRS auditors closely scrutinize deductions for overnight travel and many taxpayers get caught claiming these deductions without proper records to back them up. To stay within the law (and avoid unwanted attention from the IRS), you need to know how this deduction works and how to properly document your travel expenses.

What Are Travel Expenses?

For tax purposes, travel expenses are the amounts you spend when you travel away from your tax home overnight for your business (rental) activity. You don't have to travel any set distance to take a travel expense deduction. However, you can't take this deduction if you just spend the night in a motel across town. You must travel outside your city limits. If you don't live in a city, you must go outside the general area where your tax home is located.

You must stay away overnight or at least long enough to require a stop for sleep or rest. You cannot satisfy the rest requirement by merely napping in your car.

> **EXAMPLE:** Phyllis lives in Los Angeles. She flies to San Francisco to deal with a repair problem in a rental house she owns there. She spends the night in a hotel, and returns home the following day. Her trip is a deductible travel expense.

If you don't stay overnight, your trip will not qualify as travel. However, this does not necessarily mean that you can't take a tax deduction. Local trips for your rental activity are also deductible (see Chapter 10), but you are entitled to deduct only your transportation expenses—the cost of driving or using some other means of transportation. You may not deduct meals or other expenses like you can when you travel and stay overnight.

EXAMPLE: Philip drives from his home in Los Angeles to San Diego to show his rental property to prospective tenants and returns home that same day. His 200-mile round-trip is a deductible local trip. He may deduct his expenses for the 200 miles he drove, but he can't deduct the breakfast he bought on the way to San Diego.

RELATED TOPIC

How to deduct local travel. For a detailed discussion of tax deductions for local travel, see Chapter 10.

Where Is Your Tax Home?

Your tax home is the entire city or general area where your principal place of business for your rental activity is located. If you run your rental activity out of your residence, your tax home is the city or area where you live.

The IRS doesn't care how far you travel for business. You'll get a deduction as long as you travel outside your tax home's city limits and stay overnight. Thus, even if you're just traveling across town, you'll qualify for a deduction if you manage to stay outside your city limits.

EXAMPLE: Pete's tax home is in San Francisco. He drives to Oakland to check up on an apartment building he owns. He decides to spend the night in an Oakland hotel rather than brave the traffic back to San Francisco. Pete's stay qualifies as a deductible travel expense even though the distance between San Francisco and Oakland is only eight miles. Pete can deduct his hotel and meal expenses.

If you don't live in a city, your tax home covers the general area where you typically reside—the area within about 40 miles of your home.

Your Trip Must Be for Rental Business

In order to deduct the cost of your trip, it must be primarily for your rental activity. This means that you must have a rental purpose in mind before starting out, and you must actually do something for your rental activity while you're away. Examples of rental business purposes include:

- traveling to your rental property to deal with tenants, maintenance, or repairs
- traveling to building supply stores or other places to obtain materials and supplies for your rental activity
- traveling to your rental property to show it to prospective tenants
- learning new skills to help in your rental activity, by attending landlord-related classes, seminars, conventions, or trade shows, and
- traveling to see people who can help you operate your rental activity, such as attorneys, accountants, or real estate brokers.

On the other hand, rental-related activities do not include:

- sightseeing
- recreational activities that you attend by yourself or with family or friends, or
- attending personal investment seminars or political events.

Use common sense when deciding whether to claim that a trip is for your rental activity. If you're audited, the IRS is likely to question any trip that doesn't have some logical connection to your rental activity.

> CAUTION
>
> **Travel for building improvements is not deductible.** You cannot deduct the cost of traveling away from home if the primary purpose of the trip is to improve your rental property. The cost of travel for improvements must be added to the cost of the improvement and recovered by taking depreciation over many years. In contrast, travel costs for repairs are currently deductible operating expenses. See Chapter 4 for a detailed discussion of how to tell the difference between repairs and improvements for tax purposes.

Travel Must Be Ordinary and Necessary

To be deductible, your travel expenses must be ordinary and necessary. This means that the trip and the expenses you incur must be helpful and appropriate for your rental activity, not necessarily indispensable. Traveling to a rental property is not always ordinary and necessary.

EXAMPLE: Rayford Strickland owned two parcels of real estate about 500 miles from his tax home in Texas. During a two-year period, he made 80 trips to the property at a claimed cost of $11,000. The properties generated a total of $1,653 in income during this time. The IRS and tax court disallowed Strickland's travel expense deductions. The court found that the 80 trips were not an ordinary and necessary expense because Strickland was unable to provide any explanation of why it was necessary to make so many trips to the two properties. (*Strickland v. Comm'r.*, 43 T.C. Memo 1061.)

Travel Before You Become a Landlord

You must be involved in an ongoing rental activity to deduct your business trips. Trips you take to investigate acquiring your first rental property are not currently deductible business travel expenses.

EXAMPLE: Michelle, a San Francisco resident, has never owned any rental property, but would like to buy some. She has heard that there are good buys in Reno, Nevada, so she takes several trips there to search for income properties. She can't currently deduct her travel expenses because she is not yet in business.

Travel to View Rental Properties for Sale

There are several hurdles to deducting travel expenses you incur while looking at rental properties to purchase. You may not deduct expenses you incur to find new properties to buy if your rental activity is an investment, instead of a business, for tax purposes. Investors may not deduct expenses incurred to find new investments. Most landlords are in business. (*Frank v. Comm'r.*, 20 T.C. 511.) (See Chapter 2 for a detailed discussion of whether a rental activity qualifies as a business or investment.)

If your rental activity is a business, travel costs to look for properties to purchase fall into two categories:

- expenses incurred to look at properties you purchase, and
- expenses incurred to look at properties you don't purchase.

Expenses you incur to look at a property you end up buying must be added to the basis of your property and depreciated over 27.5 years along with the rest of the property. (Rev. Rul. 77-254.) This means it will take a long time to fully deduct your travel expenses for a property you buy.

If you look at rental property on a trip, but don't buy it, your travel expenses can be currently deductible as an operating expense, but only if you are already engaged in a rental business in the geographic area where the property is located. Unfortunately for landlords who like to travel, the IRS and courts have taken a restrictive view of the geographic area in which a small landlord is in business, holding that it extends only to the area where the landlord already owns property.

> **EXAMPLE:** Patrick O'Donnell, a Chicago resident who owned two apartments in Las Vegas, took a two-day trip to Miami to investigate buying a rental property there. However, he decided not to go through with the deal. Both the IRS and tax court denied him a deduction for his travel expenses. The court found that, even though O'Donnell was in the rental business in Las Vegas, his business did not extend to Miami. Because he was not in business in Miami, he couldn't deduct as a business operating expense his costs to travel there to look at properties. If he had actually bought a rental property in Miami, his travel expenses to purchase it would still not currently be deductible. Instead, he would have to add the cost to the property's basis and depreciate it over 27.5 years. However, if he had also incurred expenses to look at properties he didn't buy before finding the property he did buy, those expenses could be deducted as business start-up expenses. (See Chapter 8.) (*O'Donnell v. Comm'r*, 62 T.C. 781.)

It's unclear exactly how large an area the IRS and tax court would say a small landlord does business in. For example, would O'Donnell in the above example have been able to deduct the expenses of looking for rental properties in Reno, Nevada, or Los Angeles? No one knows. It is clear, however, that your best case for being able to deduct travel expenses is where you look for property in or near an area where you already own rental real estate. Once you start traveling outside of the area where you already own rental property, you'll have a tougher time claiming the deduction with the IRS, especially if you travel to a vacation destination like Miami or Hawaii.

If you travel outside your area of business to look at new rental properties and decide to take your chances with the IRS and claim the deduction, be sure to properly document your expenses and the time you spend looking for rental properties on your trip. You'll have a problem only if you're audited. But, claiming large travel deductions as a landlord will definitely increase your chance of getting audited.

Deductible Travel Expenses

Subject to the limits covered in "How Much You Can Deduct," below, virtually all of your travel expenses are deductible. These costs fall into two broad categories: your transportation expenses and the expenses you incur at your destination.

Transportation expenses are the costs of getting to and from your destination—for example:

- fares for airplanes, trains, or buses
- driving expenses, including car rentals
- shipping costs for your personal luggage or other things you need for your rental activity, and
- 50% meal and beverage expenses, and 100% lodging expenses you incur while en route to your final destination.

If you drive your own car to your destination, you may deduct your costs using the standard mileage rate, or you can deduct your actual expenses. You may also deduct your mileage while at your destination. (See Chapter 10 for more on mileage deductions.)

You may also deduct your food and lodging expenses while at your destination. Destination expenses include:

- hotel or other lodging expenses for days you work at your rental activity
- 50% of meal and beverage expenses
- taxi, public transportation, and car rental expenses at your destination
- telephone, Internet, and fax expenses
- computer rental fees

- laundry and dry cleaning expenses, and
- tips you pay on any of the other costs.

You may deduct 50% of your entertainment expenses if you incur them for your rental activity. You can't deduct entertainment expenses for activities that you attend alone; this solo entertainment obviously wouldn't be for business purposes. (See Chapter 14 for a detailed discussion of the special rules that apply to deductions for entertainment expenses.)

Traveling First Class or Steerage

You may not deduct lavish or extravagant expenses, but the IRS gives you a great deal of leeway here. You may, if you wish, travel first class, stay at four-star hotels, and eat at expensive restaurants. On the other hand, you're also entitled to be a cheapskate—for example, you could stay with a friend or relative at your destination to save on hotel charges and still deduct your meals and other expenses.

Taking People With You

You may deduct the expenses you pay for a person who travels with you only if he or she:

- is your employee
- has a genuine business reason for going on the trip with you, and
- would otherwise be allowed to deduct the travel expenses.

These rules apply to your family as well. This means you can deduct the expense of taking your spouse, child, or other relative only if the person is your employee and his or her presence is essential to your rental activity.

> EXAMPLE: Jason lives in Dallas and owns an apartment building in Tulsa, Oklahoma. He hires his son Dave to assist him in doing repairs for his property. He may deduct the cost of traveling to Tulsa with Dave to do repairs.

In addition, you may deduct the travel costs of your spouse or any other relative who is a co-owner of the rental property you travel to visit, provided that he or she spends sufficient time on rental activities.

If you bring your family along simply to enjoy the trip, you may still deduct your own business expenses as if you were traveling alone—and you don't have to reduce your deductions, even if others get a free ride with you. For example, if you drive to your destination, you can deduct the entire cost of the drive, even if your family rides along with you. Similarly, you can deduct the full cost of a single hotel room even if you obtain a larger, more expensive room for your whole family.

How Much You Can Deduct

If you spend all of your time at your destination on rental business, you may deduct 100% of your expenses (except meal expenses, which are only 50% deductible—see below). However, things get more complicated if you mix business and pleasure. Different rules apply to your transportation expenses and the expenses you incur while at your destination (destination expenses).

Travel within the United States is subject to an all-or-nothing rule: You may deduct 100% of your transportation expenses only if you spend *more than half of your time* on rental activities while at your destination. In other words, your rental activity days must outnumber your personal days. If you spend more time on personal activities than on rental activities, you get no transportation deduction.

You may also deduct the destination expenses you incur on days when you do rental-related tasks. Expenses incurred on personal days at your destination are nondeductible personal expenses. (The rules used to determine what constitutes a rental activity day are discussed below.)

> EXAMPLE: Tom's tax home is in Atlanta, but he owns an apartment building in New Orleans. He takes the train to New Orleans to supervise extensive remodeling of his property. He spends six days in New Orleans, where he spends all of his time on rental business, and spends $900 for his hotel, meals, and other living expenses. On the way home, he stops in Mobile for three days to visit his parents and spends $100 for lodging and meals there. His round-trip train fare is $250. Tom's trip consisted of six rental activity days and three personal days, so he spent more than half

of the trip on rental activities. He can deduct 100% of his train fare and the entire $900 he spent while on business in New Orleans. He may not, however, deduct the $100 he spent while visiting his parents.

If your trip is primarily a vacation—that is, you spend more than half of your time on personal activities—the entire cost of the trip is a nondeductible personal expense. However, you may deduct destination expenses that are directly related to your rental activity. This includes things like phone calls or faxes. It doesn't include transportation, lodging, or food.

As long as your trip is primarily for your rental activity, you can add a vacation to the end of the trip, make a side trip purely for fun, or enjoy evenings at the theater or ballet, and still deduct your entire airfare. What you spend while having fun is not deductible, but you can deduct all of your rental activity and transportation expenses.

> **EXAMPLE:** Bill flies to Miami where he spends four days working on his rental property. He spends three extra days in Miami swimming and enjoying the sights. Because he spent over half his time on rental business—four days out of seven—the cost of his flight is entirely deductible, as are his hotel and meal costs while he worked on his rental property. He may not deduct his hotel, meal, or other expenses during his vacation days.

Calculating Time Spent on Rental Activities

To calculate how much time you spend on rental activities while on a trip, compare the number of days you spend on rental-related work to the number of days you spend on personal activities. You spend a day on rental activities if you:

- spend more than four hours doing rental-related work
- are not at a particular place for your rental activity—for example, to show a vacant rental unit even if you spend most of the day on personal activities
- spend more than four hours on travel for your rental activity (travel time begins when you leave home and ends when you reach your hotel, or vice versa)

- drive at least 300 miles for your rental activity. You can average your mileage. For example, if you drive 600 miles to your destination in two days, you may claim two 300-mile days, even if you drove 500 miles on one day and 100 miles on the other.
- spend more than four hours on some combination of travel and your rental activities
- are prevented from working rental activities because of circumstances beyond your control, such as a transit strike or terrorist act, and
- stay at your destination between days you work on rental activities, if it would have cost more to go home and return than to remain where you are. This sandwich rule allows you to count weekends as rental activity days, if you work at your travel destination during the previous and following week.

EXAMPLE: Mike lives in New Orleans and owns several rental properties in Denver. Mike drives from his home to Denver, making the 1,100-mile drive in three days. He arrives in Denver on Saturday night. Mike rests and attends church on Sunday. On Monday, he deals with repairs for one of his rental houses. Mike works on this for five hours on Monday and three hours on Tuesday, spending the rest of his time resting and sightseeing. On Wednesday, he spends about two hours working at his rental property and spends the rest of the day sightseeing. He spends Thursday and Friday sightseeing. He then drives straight home on Saturday, taking another three days. Mike's trip consisted of eight rental activity days: six travel days, one sandwiched day (the Sunday before the Monday he worked on his rental property), and the one day he worked more than four hours. He had four personal days—the two days he worked less than four hours and the two days he spent sightseeing.

Be sure to keep track of your time while you're away. You can do this by taking notes on your calendar or travel diary. (See Chapter 17 for a detailed discussion of record keeping while traveling.)

50% Limit on Meal Expenses

You may deduct the cost of meals you eat on traveling days and days you spend working on your rental activity, as defined in the previous section.

However, the IRS figures that you have to eat, whether you're at home or away on a trip for your rental activity. Because meals you eat at home ordinarily aren't deductible, the IRS won't let you deduct all of your food expenses while traveling. Instead, you can deduct only 50% of your meal expenses while on a trip. There are two ways to calculate your meal expense deduction: You can keep track of your actual expenses or use a daily rate set by the federal government.

Deducting Actual Meal Expenses

If you use the actual expense method, you must keep track of what you spend on meals (including tips and tax) while traveling and at your destination. When you do your taxes, you add these amounts together and deduct half of the total.

> **EXAMPLE:** Frank travels from his home in Santa Fe, New Mexico, to Reno, Nevada, to deal with a vacant rental unit. He gets there by car. While on the road, he spends $200 for meals. In Reno, he spends another $200 on the days he spends more than four hours dealing with his rental. His total meal expense for the trip is $400. He may deduct half of this amount, or $200.

Meals that constitute entertainment (for example, if you take a rental-business partner to a business lunch) are subject to the rules on entertainment expenses covered in Chapter 14.

You do not necessarily have to keep every receipt for your meals, but you need to keep careful track of what you spend, and you should be able to prove that the meal was for business. (See Chapter 14 for a detailed discussion of record keeping for meal expenses.)

Using the Standard Meal Allowance

When you use the actual expense method, you must keep track of what you spend for each meal. This can be a lot of work, so the IRS provides an alternative method of deducting meals: Instead of deducting your actual expenses, you can deduct a set amount for each day of your trip. This amount is called the standard meal allowance. It covers your expenses for meals, beverages, tax, and tips. The amount of the allowance depends on where and when you travel.

The advantage of using the standard meal allowance is that you don't have to keep track of how much you spend on meals and tips. However, you have to keep records to prove the time, place, and rental purpose of your travel. (See Chapter 17 for more on record keeping.)

The disadvantage is that the standard meal allowance is one-half of what federal workers are allowed to charge for meals while traveling, and is therefore relatively modest. In 2015, the full rate federal workers could charge for domestic travel ranged from $46 per day for travel in the least expensive areas to up to $71 for high-cost areas, which includes most major cities. And because you can generally deduct only half of your meal and entertainment expenses, your deduction is limited to one-half of the federal meal allowance. If you use the standard meal allowance and spend more than the allowance, you get no deduction for the overage.

The standard meal allowance includes $5 per day for incidental expenses—tips you pay to porters, bellhops, maids, and transportation workers. If you wish, you can use the actual expense method for your meal costs and the $5 incidental expense rate for your tips. However, you'd have to be a pretty stingy tipper for this amount to be adequate.

The standard meal allowance is revised each year. You can find the current rates for travel within the United States on the Internet at the U.S. General Services Administration website at www.gsa.gov or in IRS Publication 1542, *Per Diem Rates (for Travel Within the Continental United States)*.

You can claim the standard meal allowance only for days you work on rental activities. If you travel to more than one location in one day, use the rate in effect for the area where you spend the night. Remember, you are allowed to deduct only 50% of the federal worker rate as a business expense.

> EXAMPLE: Art travels from Los Angeles to Chicago, where he spends five days showing a vacant rental unit to prospective tenants. Chicago is a high-cost locality, so the daily meal and incidental expense (M&IE) rate is $71. Art figures his deduction by multiplying the daily rate by five and dividing this in half: 5 days × $71 = $355; $355 × 50% = $172.50.

If you use the standard meal allowance, you must use it for *all of the rental-related trips you take during the year.* You can't use it for some trips and use the actual expense method for others. For example, you can't use the standard allowance when you go to an inexpensive destination and the actual expense method when you go to a pricey one.

Because the standard meal allowance is relatively small, it's better to use it only if you travel exclusively to low-cost areas, or if you are simply unable or unwilling to keep track of what you actually spend for meals.

Maximizing Your Travel Deductions

Here are some simple strategies you can use to maximize your business travel deductions:

Plan Ahead

Plan your itinerary carefully before you leave to make sure your trip qualifies as a tax-deductible trip. This means you must spend more than half of your days on rental activities for your transportation to be deductible. If you know you're going to spend three days on rental activities, arrange to spend no more than two days on personal activities so that your trip meets the requirements. If you're traveling overseas for more than 14 days, you'll have to spend at least 75% of your days on rental activities to deduct your transportation—you may be able to do this by using strategies to maximize your rental activity days.

Make a Paper Trail

If the IRS audits you, they will probably question you about travel deductions. Of course, you'll need to have records showing what you spent for your trips. However, you'll also need documents proving that your trip was for your existing rental activity. You can do this by:

- making a note in your calendar or daily planner of all rental-related work you do—be sure to note the time you spend on each rental activity

- obtaining and saving business cards from anyone you meet while dealing with rental problems—for example, contractors or repair people
- noting in your calendar or daily planner the names of all the people you meet for your rental activity on your trip
- keeping the programs or agendas from any conventions or training seminars you attend, as well as any notes you made, and
- keeping copies of rental-related correspondence or emails you sent or received before the trip.

Maximize Your Rental Activity Days

If you mix business with pleasure on your trip, you have to make sure that you have enough rental activity days to deduct your transportation costs. You'll need to spend more than 50% of your days on your rental activity.

You don't have to work all day for that day to count as a rental activity day: Any day in which you work at least four hours on rental matters is a rental activity day, even if you goof off the rest of time. The day will count as a rental activity day for purposes of determining whether your transportation expenses are deductible, and you can deduct your lodging, meal, and other expenses during the day, even though you only worked four hours.

You can easily maximize your rental activity days by taking advantage of this rule. For example, you can:

- work no more than four hours on rental activities in any one day whenever possible
- spread your work over several days—for example, if you need to do a repair that takes 12 hours, spread the work over three days instead of one or two, and
- avoid using the fastest form of transportation to your destination—travel days count as rental activity days, so you'll add rental activity days to your trip if you drive instead of fly. Remember, there's no law that says you have to take the quickest means of transportation to your destination.

However, you can't work super slowly just to be able to claim you spent more than four hours a day on rental activities. Your work schedule must be believable and reasonable.

> **EXAMPLE:** Otto Harris lived in St. Louis, Missouri, and owned investment real property in Charlotte, North Carolina, where he also had relatives. Over the course of a year, he made three trips to Charlotte. He claimed that during the first two trips he worked on the property seven to nine hours a day, six days a week, clearing underbrush, cutting down thick foliage, chopping dead wood, raking leaves, and cleaning up trash. During his last trip of the year, which occurred over Christmas and lasted 11 days, he claimed he spent his time neatly stacking the wood he had cut on his previous trips into neat one-foot piles as required by a local ordinance. The tax court permitted Harris to deduct the travel costs for his first two trips, but not the third. It found that it was credible that Harris worked six to nine hours a day on the first two trips to clear his property. However, the court simply could not believe that it could take him 11 days to stack some wood. The court concluded that it was likely that Harris had actually spent the majority of his time celebrating Christmas with his relatives. (*Harris v. Comm'r.*, T.C. Memo 1978-332.)

Take Advantage of the Sandwich Day Rule

Days when you do no rental-related work still count as rental activity days if they are sandwiched between rental activity days, as long as it was cheaper to spend that day away than to go back home for the off days. If you work on Friday and Monday, this rule allows you to count Saturday and Sunday as rental activity days, even if you don't do any work.

> **EXAMPLE:** Kim lives in Boston and owns a rental condominium in Miami. She flies to Miami to deal with repairs and show her unit to prospective renters. She arrives on Wednesday and returns the following Wednesday. She does not engage in any rental activities over the weekend and goes to the beach instead. Nevertheless, because it was cheaper for her to stay in Miami than to fly back to Boston for the weekend and return to Miami, she may count Saturday and Sunday as rental activity days. This means she can deduct her lodging and meal expenses for those days.

Hiring Help

Deducting Payments to Workers...292

   Operating Expenses...292

   Start-Up Expenses 293

   Depreciation Expenses..294

Employees Versus Independent Contractors...294

   Tests to Determine Workers' Tax Status..296

   Common Classifications for Workers 297

Tax Rules When Hiring Independent Contractors..298

   Threshold for IC Income Reporting...300

   Obtaining Taxpayer Identification Numbers...301

   Filing IRS Form 1099-MISC..302

   Reporting Requirements Don't Apply to Corporations......................................305

   New Hire Reporting Requirements for ICs..305

   Paying Independent Contractors' Expenses...306

Tax Rules for Employees..306

   Employer's FICA Contributions..307

   FUTA..308

   FITW 308

   State Payroll Taxes...309

Hiring Your Family..311

   Employing Your Children 311

   Employing Your Spouse...313

   Rules to Follow When Employing Your Family..314

Hiring a Resident Manager 318

   No Payroll Taxes for Free Lodging...319

   Minimum Wage Requirements...320

W henever you hire a worker to help you with your rental business, you will be faced with a number of tax-related questions:

- Are your payments to the worker deductible?
- Is the worker an employee or independent contractor?
- If the worker is an independent contractor, what tax-reporting requirements do you have?
- If the worker is an employee, what payroll tax rules must you comply with?
- Are there special rules that apply when you hire a family member?

This chapter goes over the host of tax rules that apply to landlords who hire people to help them with their rental business and explains how you can comply with those rules.

Deducting Payments to Workers

You may deduct all or most of what you pay a person who performs services for your rental activity. It doesn't matter how you measure or make the payments. You can pay a salary or a set fee for a job, or you can pay by the hour. You can even provide free rent in exchange for services.

The money you pay a worker will fall into one of the following three categories of deductible rental expenses:

- operating expenses
- start-up expenses, or
- depreciation.

The general rules for each of these types of expenses are discussed in earlier chapters; this section explains how workers' pay falls into all of these categories.

Operating Expenses

Most of the time, amounts you pay workers will be operating expenses. These expenses are currently deductible as long as they are:

- ordinary and necessary
- reasonable in amount

- paid for services actually performed, and
- actually paid or incurred in the year the deduction is claimed (as shown by your payroll records).

A worker's services are ordinary and necessary if they are common, accepted, helpful, and appropriate for your rental activity—they don't have to be indispensable. A worker's pay is reasonable if the amount is within the range that other landlords pay for similar services. These requirements usually won't pose a problem when you hire a worker to perform any legitimate function for your rental activity.

> EXAMPLE: Ken hires Karen, a gardener, to perform gardening work on his three rental houses. He pays her $200 per month—what similar workers are typically paid in the area. Ken can deduct his monthly payments to Karen as an operating expense. If Karen works a full year, Ken will get a $2,400 deduction.

Payments to workers for personal services are not deductible as business expenses.

> EXAMPLE: Ken also hires Karen to perform gardening services for his personal residence. These services are personal, not related to Ken's rental activity. Thus, Ken may not deduct her pay as an operating expense. Indeed, such payments are not deductible at all.

Special rules (described below) apply if you hire family members to work in your rental activity. See Chapter 3 for more on operating expenses.

Start-Up Expenses

Amounts you pay workers for services performed during the start-up phase of your rental activity are start-up expenses. Up to $5,000 in start-up expenses may be deducted in the first year in which your rental activity is in operation. Any amount over the limit must be deducted in equal installments over the first 180 months you're in business. (See Chapter 8 for more on deducting start-up costs.)

EXAMPLE: Michelle purchases her first rental property—a small house in need of a new paint job. She hires Al, a professional painter, to paint the house. After Al completes his work, Michelle lists the house for rent. Michelle paid Al $2,000 to paint her house. His fee is a start-up expense because it was incurred before Michelle's rental activity had begun—that is, before she offered the property for rent. Michelle may deduct the $2,000 the first year she is in business.

Depreciation Expenses

Amounts you pay workers to help purchase, transport, install, or improve long-term assets, are not business operating expenses. Instead, these costs are added to the basis (cost) of the asset and get depreciated over time with the asset. In certain situations, you may be able to currently deduct these costs under Section 179.

EXAMPLE: John buys a dilapidated apartment building for $250,000. He pays Jackie, a licensed contractor, $50,000 to refurbish the building. John paid Jackie the money to improve a long-term asset—a building. Thus, he may not currently deduct the $50,000. Instead, once the building is offered for rent, he may depreciate the cost over 27.5 years. He gets to deduct $1,818 per year, except for the first and last years.

Employees Versus Independent Contractors

As far as the IRS is concerned, there are only two types of people you can hire to help in your rental activity: employees and independent contractors (ICs). It's very important to understand the difference between these two categories because the tax rules for each are very different. If you hire an employee, you become subject to a wide array of state and federal tax requirements. You may have to withhold taxes from your employees' earnings and pay other taxes for them out of your own pocket. You must also comply with complex and burdensome bookkeeping and reporting requirements. If you hire an independent contractor, none of these requirements apply.

Initially, it's up to you to determine whether any person you hire to help in your rental activity is an employee or an IC. However, your decision about how to classify a worker is subject to review by various government agencies, including:

- the IRS
- your state's tax department
- your state's unemployment compensation insurance agency, and
- your state's workers' compensation insurance agency.

These agencies are mostly interested in whether you have classified workers as independent contractors when you should have classified them as employees. The reason is that you must pay money to each of these agencies for employees, but not for independent contractors. As more workers are classified as employees, the more money flows into the agencies' coffers. In the case of taxing agencies, employers must withhold tax from employees' paychecks and hand it over to the government; ICs pay their own taxes, which means the government must wait longer to get its money and faces the possibility that ICs won't declare their income or will otherwise cheat on their taxes. If an agency determines that you misclassified an employee as an IC, you may have to pay back taxes, fines, and penalties.

Independent Contractors Are Not the Same as Construction Contractors

The terms independent contractor and construction contractor are often confused. The two are not the same. A construction contractor (often simply called a contractor) is a self-employed person who performs construction work or building remodeling work for customers. An independent contractor is any person who performs services for others without being classified as an employee for legal purposes. Most construction contractors are independent contractors, but many people besides construction contractors are independent contractors.

Tests to Determine Workers' Tax Status

Scrutinizing agencies use various tests to determine whether a worker is an IC or an employee. The determining factor is usually whether you have the right to control the worker. If you have the right to *direct and control* the way a worker performs—both the final results of the job and the details of when, where, and how the work is done—then the worker is your employee. On the other hand, if you have only the right to accept or reject the final results the worker achieves, then that person is an IC.

An employer may not always exercise its right of control. For example, if an employee is experienced and well trained, the employer may not feel the need to closely supervise him or her. But the employer still has the right to step in at any time, which distinguishes an employment relationship from an IC arrangement.

> EXAMPLE: Anne hires John to serve as resident manager for her triplex. John works ten hours per week. Anne has full control over the work John does. She must approve any repair he makes and provide any tools or supplies he needs to perform his maintenance duties. Anne has the right to fire John at any time if she is unhappy with his performance.
>
> If John proves to be an able and conscientious worker, Anne may choose not to supervise him very closely. But Anne has the right to do so at any time. John is Anne's employee.

In contrast, a worker is an independent contractor if the landlord does not have the right to control the person on the job. Because the worker is an independent businessperson not solely dependent on you (the hiring party) for a living, your control is limited to accepting or rejecting the final results the IC achieves.

> EXAMPLE: Anne hires Mary, a real estate manager, to keep track of her rental income and expenses and to help with her taxes. Anne is only one of Mary's many clients. Anne doesn't tell Mary how to do her accounting tasks; Mary is a professional who already knows how to do her work. Mary sets her own hours, provides her own equipment, and works from her own home office. Mary is an independent contractor.

Because Mary is clearly running her own business, it's virtually certain that Anne does not have the right to control the way Mary performs her accounting services. Anne's control is limited to accepting or rejecting the final result. If Anne doesn't like the work Mary has done, she can refuse to pay her.

There's no clear-cut way for auditors to figure out whether you have the right to control a worker you hire. After all, they can't look into your mind to see whether you are controlling a worker (or whether you believe that you have the right to do so). They rely instead on indirect or circumstantial evidence indicating control or lack of it—for example, whether you provide a worker with tools and equipment, where the work is performed, how the worker is paid, and whether you can fire the worker.

CAUTION
Part-time workers and temps can be employees. Don't assume that a person you hire to work part time or for a short period automatically qualifies as an IC. People who work for you only temporarily or part time are your employees if you have the right to control the way they work.

Common Classifications for Workers

Let's apply the IRS rules for worker status to the type of people landlords commonly hire.

People Who Offer Services to the Public

People who offer their services to the general public are almost always independent contractors. This includes most of the people landlords hire—for example:

- repairmen
- construction contractors
- gardeners
- plumbers
- electricians
- carpet layers
- painters

- roofers, and
- people who provide professional services to the public, such as real estate brokers, real estate appraisers, architects, real estate management companies, lawyers, accountants, and bookkeepers.

Virtually all the factors considered by the IRS will ordinarily point to IC status whenever a person provides services such as these to the public at large.

People Who Work Solely for You

Any person who works just for you will likely be your employee. These will often be family members, but not always.

> **RESOURCE**
> **Need more information about independent contractors?** For a detailed discussion of the practical and legal issues business owners face when hiring ICs, see *Working With Independent Contractors*, by Stephen Fishman (Nolo).

Tax Rules When Hiring Independent Contractors

As far as taxes are concerned, hiring independent contractors is very simple. When you hire an independent contractor, you don't have to withhold or pay any state or federal payroll taxes on the IC's behalf. In contrast, when you hire an employee you must withhold federal and state taxes and pay one-half of the worker's Social Security and Medicare taxes out of your own pocket. (See "Tax Rules for Employees," below.) This is one of the great benefits of hiring ICs.

However, if your rental activity is a business for tax purposes, there is one tax detail you will have to take care of when you hire an IC: If you pay an unincorporated IC $600 or more during the year for business-related services, you must:

- file IRS Form 1099-MISC telling the IRS how much you paid the worker, and
- obtain the IC's taxpayer identification number.

The IRS imposes these requirements because it is very concerned that to avoid paying taxes, many ICs don't report all the income they earn. To help prevent this, the IRS wants to find out how much you pay ICs you hire and make sure it has their correct tax ID numbers.

This requirement applies only to landlords whose rental activities qualify as a business for tax purposes. Landlords who are merely investors need not comply. However, most landlords qualify as business owners and it is to your advantage to do so. See Chapter 2 for a detailed discussion.

The IRS can impose monetary penalties on landlords who fail to comply with the reporting requirements. The penalty is $500 for each 1099-MISC you intentionally fail to file. The penalty is less if the failure is not intentional, ranging from $50 to $250, depending on how quickly you fix the error by filing the 1099-MISC.

Complying with this requirement may help you avoid future problems with the IRS. Here's why: the IRS has an Automated Underreporter program in which IRS computers match information that landlords report on Schedule E about expenses paid with the Form 1099-MISCs the landlords file reporting payments to independent contractors. If you claim a deductible expense for a payment to an independent contractor, but have not filed the required Form 1099-MISC, the IRS may send you a notice asking you to explain the discrepancy or pay additional taxes. Your return could also be flagged for an audit.

Rental Agents Must Report IC Payments

If a rental agent manages your rental property, the agent must comply with the reporting requirements explained in this section. The agent must also report to the IRS the amount of rent he or she pays you each year. (IRS Reg. § 1.6041-1.)

For example, suppose Gale is a rental agent who manages rental property for Howard. Gale finds tenants, arranges leases, collects rent, deals with tenant complaints, and hires and makes payments to repairmen. Gale subtracts her commission and any maintenance payments from the rental payments and remits the remainder to Howard. Gale must comply with the IC reporting requirements when she hires repairmen and others to perform services for Howard's property. In addition, she must file a 1099-MISC form with the IRS each year reporting the amount of rent payments she remits to Howard.

Threshold for IC Income Reporting

You need to obtain an unincorporated IC's taxpayer ID number and file a 1099-MISC form with the IRS only if you pay the IC $600 or more during a year for rental-related services. It makes no difference whether the sum was one payment for a single job or the total of many small payments for multiple jobs.

> **EXAMPLE:** Andre hires Leslie to paint a rental house and pays her $1,000. Because Andre paid Leslie more than $600 for rental-related services, Andre must file Form 1099-MISC with the IRS reporting the payment, and obtain Leslie's taxpayer ID number.

In calculating whether the payments made to an IC total $600 or more during a year, you must include payments you make for parts or materials the IC used in performing the services. For example, if you hire an electrician to rewire a rental building and he charges you separately for the electrical wiring and other materials he installs, the cost must be included in the tally. However, not all payments you make to ICs are counted toward the $600 threshold.

Payments for Merchandise

Under current law, you don't need to include in the $600 threshold payments you make solely for merchandise.

> **EXAMPLE:** Betty hires Al, an IC electrician, to rewire her apartment building. She pays him $1,000 for new lighting fixtures. The payment need not be counted toward the $600 threshold because the fixtures are merchandise.

Payments for Personal Services

You need only count payments you make to ICs for services they perform in the course of your rental activity. You don't count payments for services you make to ICs for personal or household services or repairs—for example, payments to babysitters or gardeners and housekeepers for your personal residence. Running your home is not a rental activity.

EXAMPLE: Landlord Joe pays Mary a total of $1,000 during the year for gardening services for his residence. None of the payments count toward the $600 threshold because they don't relate to Joe's rental activity. Joe need not obtain Mary's taxpayer ID number or file a 1099-MISC form reporting the payments to the IRS.

Obtaining Taxpayer Identification Numbers

Some ICs work in the underground economy—that is, they're paid in cash and never pay any taxes or file tax returns. The IRS may not even know they exist. The IRS wants you to help it find these people by supplying the taxpayer ID numbers from all ICs who meet the requirements explained above.

If an IC won't give you his or her number or the IRS informs you that the number the IC gave you is incorrect, the IRS assumes the person isn't going to voluntarily pay taxes. So it requires you to withhold taxes from the compensation you pay the IC and remit them to the IRS. This is called backup withholding. If you fail to backup withhold, the IRS will impose an assessment against you equal to 28% of what you paid the IC.

How to Avoid Backup Withholding

Backup withholding can be a bookkeeping burden for you. Fortunately, it's very easy to avoid it. Have the IC fill out and sign IRS Form W-9, *Request for Taxpayer Identification Number and Certification*, and retain it in your files. (You can download it from the IRS website at www.irs.gov.)

You don't have to file the W-9 with the IRS. This simple form merely requires the IC to list his or her name and address and taxpayer ID number. Partnerships and sole proprietors with employees must have a federal employer identification number (EIN), which they obtain from the IRS. In the case of sole proprietors without employees, the taxpayer ID number is the IC's Social Security number.

If the IC doesn't already have an EIN, but promises to obtain one, you don't have to backup withhold for 60 days after he or she applies for one. Have the IC fill out and sign the W-9 form, stating "Applied For" in the space where the ID number is supposed to be listed. If you don't receive the IC's ID number within 60 days, start backup withholding.

Backup Withholding Procedure

If you are unable to obtain an IC's taxpayer ID number or the IRS informs you that the number the IC gave you is incorrect, you'll have to do backup withholding. You must begin doing so after you pay an IC $600 or more during the year. You need not backup withhold on payments totaling less than $600.

To backup withhold, deposit with your bank 28% of the IC's compensation every quarter. You must make these deposits separately from any payroll tax deposits you make for employees. Report the amounts withheld on IRS Form 945, *Annual Return of Withheld Federal Income Tax*. This is an annual return you must file by January 31 of the following year. See the instructions to Form 945 for details. You can download it from the IRS website at www.irs.gov.

Filing IRS Form 1099-MISC

The IRS wants to know how much ICs earn each year so it can make sure they are reporting all their income. This is accomplished by requiring people and companies that hire ICs to report the amount of their payments to the IRS on IRS Form 1099-MISC. You must file a 1099-MISC form for each IC you paid $600 or more during the year. You must obtain official 1099-MISC forms from the IRS for filing. You cannot photocopy the form. Each 1099-MISC form contains three parts and can be used for three different workers. All your 1099-MISC forms must be submitted together along with one copy of Form 1096, which is a transmittal form—the IRS equivalent of a cover letter. To order the official IRS forms (which are scannable), go to Order Information Returns and Employer Returns Online (www.irs.gov/Businesses/Online-Ordering-for-Information-Returns-and-Employer-Returns) and the IRS will mail them to you. Alternatively, you can obtain usable 1099-MISC forms from stationery stores and office supply companies. You can also generate 1099-MISC forms by using property management software or accounting and tax software.

Filling out Form 1099-MISC is easy. Follow this step-by-step approach:

- List your name and address in the first box titled PAYER'S name.
- Enter your taxpayer identification number in the box entitled PAYER'S federal identification number.
- The IC you have paid is called the "RECIPIENT" on this form, meaning the person who received the money. Provide the IC's taxpayer identification number, name, and address in the boxes indicated. For sole proprietors, you list the individual's name first, and then you may list a different business name, though this is not required. You may not enter only a business name for a sole proprietor.
- Enter the amount of your payments to the IC in Box 7, entitled NONEMPLOYEE COMPENSATION. Be sure to fill in the right box or the IRS will consider the Form 1099-MISC invalid.
- Finally, if you've done backup withholding for an IC who has not provided you with a taxpayer ID number, enter the amount withheld in Box 4.

The Form 1099-MISC contains five copies. These must be filed as follows:

- Copy A, the top copy, must be filed with the IRS no later than February 28 of the year after payment was made to the IC. If you don't use the remaining two spaces for other ICs, leave those spaces blank. Don't cut the page.
- Copy 1 must be filed with your state taxing authority if your state has a state income tax. The filing deadline is probably February 28, but check with your state tax department to make sure. Your state may also have a specific transmittal form or cover letter you must obtain.

TIP

Getting more time to file 1099-MISCs. You can obtain a 30-day extension of the time to file a 1099-MISC form by filing IRS Form 8809, *Application for Extension of Time to File Information Returns.* The form must be filed with the IRS by February 28 (or March 31 if filing electronically). The extension is not granted automatically: You must explain why you need it. The IRS will send you a letter of explanation approving or denying your request. See the instructions for Form 8809 for more information.

- Copy B and Copy 2 must be given to the worker no later than January 31 of the year after payment was made.
- Copy C is for you to retain for your files.

File all the IRS copies of each 1099-MISC form together with Form 1096, the simple transmittal form. Add up all the payments reported on all the 1099-MISC forms and list the total in the box indicated on Form 1096. File the forms with the IRS Service Center listed on the reverse of Form 1096.

Filing 1099-MISCs Electronically

You have the option of filing your 1099-MISCs with the IRS electronically instead of by postal mail. If you file electronically, the deadline to provide your 1099s to the IRS is extended to March 31. Also, you don't have to file IRS Form 1096.

Unfortunately, you can't simply go on the IRS website, fill out a 1099 online, and file it electronically. You must use software that meets IRS requirements. You can use accounting software such as *QuickBooks* or *Xero*, or online 1099 filing services such as tax1099.com, and many others.

You can electronically file 1099s directly with the IRS by using its FIRE Production System. To do so, you must get permission from the IRS by filing IRS Form 4419, *Application for Filing Information Returns Magnetically/Electronically*. This form need only be filed one time, and can be filed online. You must obtain a Transmitter Control Code (TCC) from the IRS; and create a user ID, password, and ten-digit PIN for your account. For more details, visit the IRS Filing Information Returns Electronically (FIRE) Web page at www.irs.gov/Tax-Professionals/e-File-Providers-&-Partners/Filing-Information-Returns-Electronically-(FIRE).

You can also send 1099-MISCs to independent contractors electronically—that is, by email. However, you may do this only if the contractor agrees. If the contractor doesn't agree, you must deliver a printed copy of the 1099-MISC by mail or in person.

Reporting Requirements Don't Apply to Corporations

Under current law, the filing and ID requirements discussed above don't apply to corporations. This has long been one of the advantages of hiring incorporated ICs—there is no need to file anything with the IRS.

> EXAMPLE: Landlord Bob pays $5,000 to Yvonne, a CPA, to perform accounting services. Yvonne has formed her own one-person corporation called Yvonne's Accounting Services, Inc. Bob pays the corporation, not Yvonne personally. Because Bob is paying a corporation, he doesn't need to report the payment on Form 1099-MISC or obtain Yvonne's personal tax ID number.

There are two exceptions to the rule that you don't have to file 1099-MISC forms for payments to corporations. You must report all payments of $600 or more you make to a doctor or lawyer who is incorporated. This is necessary only where the payments are for your landlord activity—for example, you hire an incorporated attorney to handle a tenant eviction. You don't need to report payments you make to incorporated doctors or lawyers for personal services.

New Hire Reporting Requirements for ICs

Several states require that businesses that hire independent contractors file a report with a state agency providing the contractor's contact information and how much you pay the worker. The purpose of these requirements is to aid in the enforcement of child support orders issued against independent contractors.

The following states impose reporting requirements for those hiring independent contractors: Alaska, California, (if paid over $600 per year), Connecticut (if paid over $5,000 per year), Delaware, Iowa, Massachusetts (if paid over $600 per year), Nebraska, New Hampshire, New Jersey, New York, Ohio (if paid over $2,500 per year), and West Virginia. Find the state agency to contact at the U.S. Department of Health & Human Services website, "State New Hire Reporting Contacts and Program Information," at www.acf.hhs.gov/programs/css/resource/state-new-hire-reporting-contacts-and-program-information.

Paying Independent Contractors' Expenses

Independent contractors often incur expenses while performing services for their clients or customers—for example, for travel or materials. Although many ICs want their clients to separately reimburse them for such expenses, it's better for you not to do so. ICs who pay their own expenses are less likely to be viewed as your employees by the IRS or other government agencies. Instead of reimbursing expenses, pay ICs enough so they can cover their own expenses.

However, it's customary in some businesses and professions for the client to reimburse the IC for expenses. For example, a lawyer who handles an eviction or other legal matter for your rental business will usually seek reimbursement for expenses such as photocopying, court reporters, and travel. If this is the case, you may pay these reimbursements without concern about misclassification problems.

When you reimburse an IC for a business-related expense, you get the deduction for the expense, not the IC. You should not include the amount of the reimbursement on the 1099-MISC form you file with the IRS reporting how much you paid the IC, because the reimbursement is not considered income for the IC.

Tax Rules for Employees

Whenever you hire an employee other than your spouse or child, you become an unpaid tax collector for the government. You are required to withhold and pay both federal and state taxes for the worker. These taxes are called payroll taxes or employment taxes. Federal payroll taxes consist of:

- Social Security and Medicare taxes—also known as FICA
- unemployment taxes—also known as FUTA, and
- federal income taxes—also known as FITW.

You must periodically pay FICA, FUTA, and FITW to the IRS, electronically. You are entitled to deduct as a business expense payroll taxes that you pay yourself. You get no deductions for taxes you withhold from employees' pay.

Every year, employers must file IRS Form W-2, *Wage and Tax Statement*, for each of their workers. The form shows the IRS how much the worker was paid and how much tax was withheld.

However, if you hire your spouse or child to work in your rental activity, you may not have to pay some or all of the payroll taxes you must pay when you hire nonrelatives.

RESOURCE

Find out more about payroll taxes. IRS Publication 15, Circular E, *Employer's Tax Guide*, provides detailed information on payroll tax requirements. You can get a free copy by calling the IRS at 800-TAX-FORM, by calling or visiting your local IRS office, or by downloading it from the IRS website at www.irs.gov.

Employer's FICA Contributions

FICA is an acronym for Federal Income Contributions Act, the law requiring employers and employees to pay Social Security and Medicare taxes. FICA taxes consist of a 12.4% Social Security tax on income up to an annual ceiling. In 2015, the annual Social Security ceiling was $118,500. Medicare taxes are not subject to any income ceiling and are levied at a 2.9% rate up to an annual ceiling—$200,000 for single taxpayers and $250,000 for married couples filing jointly. Income above the ceiling is taxed at a 3.8% rate. This combines to a total 15.3% tax on employment income up to the Social Security tax ceiling.

Ordinarily, employers and employees split the cost of FICA taxes—the employer pays half and withholds the other half from the employee's pay. This means that each pays a 7.65% tax up to the Social Security tax ceiling.

You are entitled to deduct (as an operating expense) the portion of the tax that you pay yourself.

The ceiling for the Social Security tax changes annually. You can find out what the Social Security tax ceiling is for the current year from IRS Publication 15, Circular E, *Employer's Tax Guide*; the amount is printed right on the first page.

FUTA

FUTA is an acronym for the Federal Unemployment Tax Act, the law that establishes federal unemployment taxes. Most employers must pay both state and federal unemployment taxes. Even if you're exempt from the state tax, you may still have to pay the federal tax. Employers alone are responsible for FUTA—you may not collect or deduct it from employees' wages.

You must pay FUTA taxes if:

- you pay $1,500 or more to employees during any calendar quarter—that is, any three-month period beginning with January, April, July, or October, or
- you had one or more employees for at least some part of a day in any 20 or more different weeks during the year. The weeks don't have to be consecutive, nor does it have to be the same employee each week.

The FUTA tax rate is usually 6%, although in practice you rarely pay this much. You are given a credit of 5.4% if you pay the applicable state unemployment tax in full and on time. This means that the actual FUTA tax rate is usually 0.6%. In 2015, the FUTA tax was assessed on only the first $7,000 of an employee's annual wages. Therefore, the full amount of the tax is $42 per year per employee. However, employers in several states must pay more than $42 in FUTA tax because their states failed to repay unemployment insurance loans from the federal government.

FITW

FITW is an acronym for federal income tax withholding. You must calculate and withhold federal income tax from your employees' paychecks. Employees are solely responsible for paying federal income tax. Your only responsibility is to withhold the funds and remit them to the government. If you fail to do this, you'll get into big trouble with the IRS. You get no deductions for FITW; it wasn't your money to begin with.

State Payroll Taxes

Employers in every state are required to pay and withhold state payroll taxes. These taxes include:

- state unemployment compensation taxes in all states
- state income tax withholding in most states, and
- state disability taxes in a few states.

Unemployment Compensation

Employers in every state are required to contribute to a state unemployment insurance fund. Employees make no contributions, except in Alaska, New Jersey, Pennsylvania, and Rhode Island, where employers must withhold small employee contributions from employees' paychecks. The employer contributions are a deductible expense.

If your payroll is very small—less than $1,500 per calendar quarter— you probably won't have to pay unemployment compensation taxes. In most states, you must pay state unemployment taxes for employees if you're paying federal unemployment taxes. However, some states have stricter requirements. Contact your state labor department for the exact rules and payroll amounts.

Income Taxes

All states except Alaska, Florida, Nevada, South Dakota, Texas, Washington, and Wyoming have income taxation. If your state has income taxes, you must withhold the applicable amount from your employees' paychecks and pay it to the state taxing authority. Each state has its own income tax withholding forms and procedures. Contact your state tax department for information. Of course, employers get no deductions for withholding their employees' state income taxes.

Disability Insurance

California, Hawaii, New Jersey, New York, and Rhode Island have state disability insurance programs that provide employees with coverage for injuries or illnesses that are not related to work. Employers in these states must withhold their employees' disability insurance contributions from their pay. Employers must also make their own contributions in Hawaii, New Jersey, and New York—these employer contributions are deductible.

Workers' Compensation Insurance

Employers in all states (subject to some important exceptions) must provide their employees with workers' compensation insurance to cover work-related injuries. Workers' compensation is not a payroll tax. Employers purchase a workers' compensation policy from a private insurer or the state workers' compensation fund. Your workers' compensation insurance premiums are deductible as an insurance expense (see Chapter 14).

> **CAUTION**
>
> **Employers in California must withhold for parental leave.** California recently became the first state to require paid family leave. Employers in California must withhold money from their employees' paychecks (as part of the state's disability insurance program) to fund this leave program. For more information on the program, go to www.edd.ca.gov/disability/paid_family_leave.htm.

> **TIP**
>
> **Bookkeeping expenses are deductible.** Figuring out how much to withhold, doing the necessary record keeping, and filling out the required forms can be complicated. If you have a computer, software programs such as *QuickBooks* can help with all the calculations and print out your employees' checks and IRS forms. The cost of such software is deductible—you can deduct the full cost in one year under Section 179 or depreciate the cost over three years (see Chapter 5). You can also hire a bookkeeper or payroll tax service to do the work. Amounts you pay a bookkeeper or payroll tax service are deductible operating expenses. You can find these listed in the phone book or on the Internet under "payroll tax services." You can also find a list of payroll service providers on the IRS website. Be aware, however, that even if you hire a payroll service, you remain personally liable if your payroll taxes are not paid on time. The IRS recommends that employers: (1) keep their company address on file with the IRS, rather than the address of the payroll service provider, so that the company will be contacted by the IRS if there are any problems; (2) require the payroll service provider to post a fiduciary bond in case it defaults on its

obligation to pay any penalties and interest due to IRS deficiency notices; and (3) ask the service provider to enroll in and use the Electronic Federal Tax Payment System (EFTPS) so the employer can confirm payments made on its behalf.

Hiring Your Family

Whoever said, "Never hire your relatives" must never have read the tax code. The tax law promotes family togetherness by making it highly advantageous for landlords to hire family members.

Employing Your Children

Believe it or not, your children can be a great tax savings device. If you hire your children as employees to do legitimate work in your rental activity, you may deduct their salaries from your rental income as an operating expense. Your child will have to pay tax on his or her salary only to the extent it exceeds the standard deduction amount for the year—$6,300 in 2015. Moreover, if your child is under the age of 18, you won't have to withhold or pay any FICA (Social Security or Medicare) tax on the salary (subject to a couple of exceptions).

These rules allow you to shift part of your income from your own tax bracket to your child's bracket, which should be much lower than yours (unless you earn little or no income). This can result in substantial tax savings.

EXAMPLE: Carol hires Mark, her 18-year-old son, to perform gardening, repair, and maintenance services for her four-unit apartment building. He works ten hours per week and she pays him $15 per hour (the going rate for such work in her area). Over the course of a year, she pays him a total of $9,000. She need not pay FICA tax for Mark because he's not yet 18. When she does her taxes for the year, she may deduct his $9,000 salary from her rental income as an operating expense. Mark pays tax only on the portion of his income that exceeds the $6,300 standard deduction—so he pays federal income tax only on $2,700 of his $9,000 salary. With such a small amount of income, he is in the lowest federal income tax bracket—10%. He pays $270 in federal income tax for the year. Had Carol not hired Mark and done the work herself, she would have lost her $9,000 deduction and had to pay income tax on this amount—a 25% tax in her tax bracket. Thus, she would have had to pay an additional $2,250 in federal taxes. Depending on the state where Carol lives, she likely would have had to pay a state income tax as well.

What About Child Labor Laws?

You're probably aware that certain types of child labor are illegal under federal and state law. However, these laws generally don't apply to children under the age of 16 who are employed by their parents, unless the child is employed in a hazardous occupation. Hazardous occupations include driving a motor vehicle, being an outside helper on a motor vehicle, and operating various power-driven machines, including machines for woodworking and metal forming, sawing, roofing, wrecking, excavation, and demolition operations.

A child who is at least 16 may be employed in any nonhazardous occupation. Children at least 17 years of age may spend up to 20% of their time driving cars and trucks weighing less than 6,000 pounds as part of their job if they have licenses and no tickets, drive only in daylight hours, and go no more than 30 miles from home. They may not perform dangerous driving maneuvers (such as towing). Also, many states have laws specifying when, and for how long, children may work, limiting the hours and days of the week (and imposing more stringent limits during the school year). For detailed information, see the Department of Labor website, www.dol.gov.

No Payroll Taxes

One of the advantages of hiring your child is that you need not pay FICA taxes for your child under the age of 18 who works in your trade or business, or your partnership, if it's owned solely by you and your spouse.

Moreover, you need not pay federal unemployment (FUTA) taxes for services performed by your child who is under 21 years old.

However, these rules do not apply—and you must pay both FICA and FUTA—if you hire your child to work for:

- your partnership, unless all the partners are parents of the child, or
- your corporation (few small landlords are incorporated).

No Withholding

In addition, if your child has no unearned income (for example, interest or dividend income), you must withhold income taxes from your child's pay only if it exceeds the standard deduction for the year. The standard deduction was $6,300 in 2015 and is adjusted every year for inflation. Children who are paid less than this amount need not pay any income taxes on their earnings. However, you must withhold income taxes if your child has more than $300 in unearned income for the year and his or her total income exceeds $1,050 (in 2015).

Employing Your Spouse

You don't get the benefits of income shifting when you employ your spouse in your business, because your income is combined when you file a joint tax return. You'll also have to pay FICA taxes on your spouse's wages, so you get no savings there either.

The real advantage of hiring your spouse is in the realm of employee benefits. You can provide your spouse with employee benefits such as health and accident insurance. You can take a tax deduction for the cost of the benefit and your spouse doesn't have to declare the benefit as income, provided the IRS requirements are satisfied. This is a particularly valuable tool for health insurance—you can give your spouse health insurance coverage as an employee benefit.

Another benefit of hiring your spouse is that you can take rental-related trips together and deduct the cost as a travel expense, as long as your spouse's presence was necessary (for your rental activity, not for you personally).

Rules to Follow When Employing Your Family

The IRS is well aware of the tax benefits of hiring a child or spouse, so it's on the lookout for taxpayers who claim the benefit without meeting the requirements. If the IRS concludes that your children or spouse aren't really employees, you'll lose your tax deductions for their salary and benefits—and they'll have to pay tax on their benefits. To avoid this, you should follow these simple rules:

Rule 1: Your Child or Spouse Must Be a Real Employee

First of all, your child or spouse must be a bona fide employee. Their work must be ordinary and necessary for your rental activity, and their pay must be compensation for services actually performed. Their services don't have to be indispensable, but they must be common, accepted, helpful, and appropriate for your business. Any real work for your rental can qualify—for example, you could employ your child or spouse to perform yard work or routine maintenance for your rental properties; or they could clean your office, answer the phone, and help with book-keeping. You get no business deductions when you pay your child for personal services, such as babysitting or mowing your lawn at home.

The IRS won't believe that an extremely young child is a legitimate employee. How young is too young? The IRS has accepted that a seven-year-old child may be an employee (see "Hardworking Seven-Year-Old Was Parents' Employee," below), but probably won't believe that children younger than seven are performing any useful work for your rental activity.

You should keep track of the work and hours your children or spouse perform by having them fill out time sheets or time cards. You can find these in stationery stores or you can create a time sheet yourself. It should list the date, the services performed, and the time spent performing the services. Although not legally required, it's also a good idea to have your spouse or child sign a written employment agreement specifying his or her job duties and hours. These duties should only be related to your business.

Hardworking Seven-Year-Old Was Parents' Employee

Walt and Dorothy Eller owned three trailer parks and a small strip mall in Northern California. They hired their three children, ages seven, 11, and 12, to perform various services for their businesses including pool maintenance, landscaping, reading gas and electric meters, delivering leaflets and messages to tenants, answering phones, doing minor repairs, and sweeping and cleaning trailer pads and parking lots. The children worked after school, on weekends, and during their summer vacations.

The Ellers paid their children a total of $17,800 over a three-year period and deducted the amounts as business expenses. The IRS tried to disallow the deductions, claiming that the children's pay was excessive. The court allowed most of the deductions, noting that these hardworking children performed essential services for their parents' businesses. The court found that the seven-year-old was a bona fide employee, but ruled that he should earn somewhat less than his older brother and sister because 11- and 12-year-old children can generally handle greater responsibility and do more work than seven-year-old children. Thus, while the older siblings could be paid $5,700 for their services over the three years in question, the seven-year-old could reasonably be paid only $4,000. (*Eller v. Comm'r.*, 77 T.C. 934 (1981).)

Rule 2: Compensation Must Be Reasonable

When you hire your children, it is advantageous (taxwise) to pay them as much as possible. That way, you can shift more of your income to your children, who are probably in a much lower income tax bracket. Conversely, you want to pay your spouse as little as possible, because you get no benefits from income shifting; you and your spouse are in the same income tax bracket (assuming you file a joint return, as the vast majority of married people do). Moreover, your spouse will have to pay Social Security tax on his or her salary—an amount that is not tax deductible. (As your spouse's employer, you'll have to pay employment taxes on your spouse's salary as well, but these taxes are deductible business expenses.)

However, you can't just pay whatever amount will result in the lowest tax bill: Your spouse's and/or your child's total compensation must be reasonably related to the value of the work performed. Total compensation means the sum of the salary plus all the fringe benefits you provide, including health insurance and medical expense reimbursements, if any. You shouldn't have a problem as long as you don't pay more than you'd pay a stranger for the same work. In other words, don't try paying your child $100 per hour for yard work just to get a big tax deduction. Find out what workers who perform similar services in your area are being paid.

To prove how much you paid (and that you actually paid it), you should pay your child or spouse by check, not cash. Do this once or twice a month, just as you would for any other employee. The funds should be deposited in a bank account in your child's or spouse's name. Your child's bank account may be a trust account.

Rule 3: Comply With Legal Requirements for Employers

You must comply with most of the same legal requirements when you hire a child or spouse as you do when you hire a stranger.

At the time you hire: When you first hire your child or spouse, you must fill out IRS Form W-4. You (the employer) use it to determine how much tax you must withhold from the employee's salary. A child who is exempt from withholding should write "exempt" in the space provided and complete and sign the rest of the form. You must also complete U.S. Citizenship and Immigration Services Form I-9, *Employment Eligibility Verification*, verifying that the employee is a U.S. citizen or is otherwise eligible to work in the United States. Keep both forms. You must also record your employee's Social Security number. If your child doesn't have a number, you must apply for one. In addition, you must have an employer identification number (EIN). If you don't have one, you may obtain it by filing IRS Form SS-4.

Every payday: You'll need to withhold income tax from your child's pay only if it exceeds a specified amount. You don't have to withhold FICA taxes for children younger than 18. You must withhold income tax and FICA for your spouse, but not FUTA tax. If the amounts withheld, plus the employer's share of payroll taxes, exceed $2,500 during a calendar quarter, you must deposit the amounts monthly by electronically depositing them with the IRS.

Every calendar quarter: If you withhold tax from your child's or spouse's pay, you must deposit it with the IRS. You can make these deposits yourself using the IRS's free Electronic Federal Tax Payment System ("EFTPS"); see www.eftps.gov. If you do not want to use EFTPS, you can arrange for your tax professional, financial institution, payroll service, or other trusted third party to make electronic deposits on your behalf. If you deposit more than $1,000 a year, you must file Form 941, *Employer's Quarterly Federal Tax Return*, with the IRS showing how much the employee was paid during the quarter and how much tax you withheld and deposited. If you need to deposit less than $2,500 during a calendar quarter, you can make your payment along with the Form 941, instead of paying monthly. Employers with total employment tax liability of $1,000 or less may file employment tax returns once a year instead of quarterly. Use new IRS Form 944, *Employer's Annual Federal Tax Return*. You must receive written notice from the IRS to file Form 944 instead of Form 941. If you haven't been notified, visit www.irs.gov and enter "file employment taxes annually" in the search box.

Each year: By January 31 of each year, you must complete and give your employee a copy of IRS Form W-2, *Wage and Tax Statement*, showing how much you paid the employee and how much tax was withheld. You must also file copies with the IRS and Social Security Administration by February 28. You must include IRS Form W-3, *Transmittal of Wage and Tax Statements*, with the copy you file with the Social Security Administration. If your child is exempt from withholding, a new W-4 form must be completed each year.

You must also file Form 940, *Employer's Annual Federal Unemployment (FUTA) Tax Return*. The due date is January 31; however, if you deposited all of the FUTA tax when due, you have ten additional days to file. You must file a Form 940 for your child even though you are not required to withhold any unemployment taxes from his or her pay. If your child is your only employee, enter his or her wages as "exempt" from unemployment tax.

RESOURCE

Need more information on employing family members? IRS Publication 15, Circular E, *Employer's Tax Guide*, and Publication 929, *Tax Rules for Children and Dependents*, provide detailed information on these requirements. You can get free copies by calling the IRS at 800-TAX-FORM, by calling or visiting your local IRS office, or by downloading them from the IRS website at www.irs.gov.

Hiring a Resident Manager

Landlords who don't want to do all the work themselves often hire a resident manager (also called an apartment manager) to handle the day-to-day details of running an apartment building, such as dealing with repairs, showing and renting vacant units, and collecting rent. As the name implies, a resident manager lives at the rental property. In some states and cities—California, for example—resident managers are required if an apartment building exceeds a certain size (16 or more units in California; nine or more units in New York City).

You should have a resident manager sign an employment agreement spelling out his or her duties and pay. Detailed guidance on how to hire a resident manager, including a sample employment agreement, can be found in *Every Landlord's Legal Guide*, by Marcia Stewart, Ralph Warner, and Janet Portman (Nolo).

Resident or apartment managers are employees of the landlords who hire them. This is so, whether they are paid a regular salary or are compensated wholly or partly with reduced rent. Not a single court decision or IRS ruling has ever held otherwise. (PLR 8128117.) All of the tax rules for hiring employees discussed in "Tax Rules for Employees," above, apply to resident managers, but there are a couple of special rules you need to know about.

Management Companies Are Not Employees

Instead of, or in addition to, hiring a resident manager, some landlords hire property management companies to manage their rentals. Such companies are often used by owners of large apartment complexes or absentee landlords who live far away from their rental property. Typically, you sign a contract spelling out the management company's duties and fees. Such companies normally charge a fixed percentage—typically 5% to 10%—of the rent collected. Such fees are a deductible rental expense. Schedule E contains a line where they are deducted.

A management company is an independent contractor, not your employee. The people who work for the company are its employees or independent contractors—you are not responsible for their payroll taxes. The rules for independent contractors covered above apply to management companies.

No Payroll Taxes for Free Lodging

If you pay a resident manager a regular salary, you must pay and with-hold federal payroll taxes, which consist of Social Security and Medicare taxes, unemployment taxes, and federal income taxes. However, you need not pay or withhold any federal payroll taxes on the value of free lodging you provide a resident manager for a rental property if:

- the lodging is at your rental property—that is, the manager lives in a unit at your rental building
- the lodging is furnished for your convenience, and
- you require the manager to live there as a condition of employment—in other words, the manager has no choice in the matter. (I.R.C. § 119.)

It is not difficult for any landlord who hires a resident manager to satisfy these requirements.

Under the rules, you furnish lodging for your convenience if you do it for a substantial business reason, other than providing the employee with additional pay. Obviously, landlords have a substantial business reason to have someone living at their rental property—they need a person there 24 hours a day to take care of tenants, maintenance, and security. Moreover, as mentioned above, resident managers are required by law in some states.

The condition of employment test is met if you require the employee to accept the lodging because he or she needs to live at your rental property to properly perform his or her duties. The very nature of resident managers' duties require that they live at the rental property. It's a good idea to have a written employment agreement with a resident manager, including a clause requiring the manager to live at your rental property. This clause can simply say: "In order to properly accomplish the duties of Resident Manager, Employee is required to live at Employer's rental property at [address] as a condition of employment."

> **EXAMPLE:** Anne owns a triplex. She rents two of the units to regular tenants, but she gives John, the tenant of the third unit, an $800 per month reduction in rent in return for his working as her resident manager. John takes care of repairs, maintenance, and gardening for the building. Although John is Anne's employee, she need not withhold or pay any payroll taxes on the $800 in free monthly rent she pays John.

Minimum Wage Requirements

Whether you pay your manager a salary or with a rent reduction, you need to comply with federal and state minimum wage requirements. The federal minimum wage was $7.25 per hour as of July 24, 2009. If your state's minimum wage is higher than the federal minimum wage, you must pay the higher rate. Twenty-nine states have minimum wages that are higher than the federal minimum—for example, as of 2015, the minimum wage in California is $9 per hour while in Washington State it is $9.47 per hour. Moreover, several cities have their own minimum wage laws. For information on the minimum wages of all states, see www.dol.gov/whd/minwage/america.htm.

If the total number of hours a manager works, multiplied by the applicable minimum hourly wage, exceeds the rent reduction or other fixed rate of pay, you are in violation of the minimum wage laws. Depending on the state, you may not be able to count the full amount of the rent reduction when making this calculation. For example, in California you can only count two-thirds of the fair market value of the rental you provide a manager for purposes of complying with the minimum wage laws.

Federal wage and hour laws also require employers to pay time-and-a-half if an employee works more than 40 hours per week (with a few exceptions). Some states, most notably California, require overtime to be paid if an employee works more than eight hours in a day, even if the employee works less than 40 hours in a week.

For information on your minimum wage laws, overtime rules, and record-keeping requirements, see the U.S. Department of Labor website at www.dol.gov. You can also contact the nearest office of the U.S. Labor Department's Wage and Hour Division, or a local office of your state's department of labor or employment.

Casualty and Theft Losses

What Is a Casualty? 324

    External Force Required 325

    Theft or Vandalism 326

Calculating a Casualty Loss Deduction 326

    Insurance 327

    Property a Total Loss 328

    Property a Partial Loss 328

    Deducting Separate Components 329

    Damage to Your Home Office 331

    Effect of Casualty Losses on Basis 331

Disaster Area Losses 332

Repair and Replacement Costs for Casualty Losses 332

Casualty Gains 333

Tax Reporting and Record Keeping for Casualty Losses 335

B ad things can happen to good rental property. If your rental property is damaged or destroyed by a sudden event like a fire or flood, or if you have a loss due to vandalism or theft, you may be able to obtain a tax deduction for all or part of your loss. These types of losses are called casualty losses.

What Is a Casualty?

A casualty is damage, destruction, or loss of property due to an event that is sudden, unexpected, or unusual. Deductible casualty losses can result from many different causes, including, but not limited to:

- earthquakes
- fires
- floods
- government-ordered demolition or relocation of a building that is unsafe to use because of a disaster
- landslides
- oil spills
- sonic booms
- storms, including hurricanes and tornadoes
- terrorist attacks
- theft
- vandalism, including vandalism to rental property by tenants, and
- volcanic eruptions.

One thing all the events in the list above have in common is that they are sudden—they happen quickly. Suddenness is the hallmark of a casualty loss. Thus, loss of property due to slow, progressive deterioration is not deductible as a casualty loss. For example, the steady weakening or deterioration of a rental building due to normal wind and weather conditions is not a deductible casualty loss.

Many legal disputes have occurred over whether an event was sufficiently sudden to cause a deductible casualty loss. Some of these are summarized in the following chart:

Casualty Loss	Not a Casualty Loss
Damage to shoreline buildings due to sudden erosion caused by wave or wind action during a storm (Rev. Rul. 76-134)	Damage to buildings due to gradual soil erosion or subsidence (Rev. Rul. 76-134)
Termite damage occurring in a single year (*Rosenberg v. Comm'r.*, 198 F.2d 46)	Termite damage occurring over three-year period (*Dodge v. Comm'r.*, 25 T.C. 1022)
Death of trees over 10-day period due to massive insect attack (Rev. Rul. 79-174)	Destruction of trees caused by Dutch elm disease (*Burns v. United States*, 174 F.Supp. 203 (D. Ohio 1959))
Damage and destruction of plants and trees over four-month period caused by a sudden and unusual drought (*Ruecker v. Comm'r.*, T.C. Memo 1981-257)	Death of trees caused by a three-year-long drought (*Kemper v. Comm'r.*, 30 T.C. 546)
Destruction of barn caused by high winds during a storm (*Stein v. Comm'r.*, T.C. Memo 1955-57)	Collapse of patio roof caused by dry rot, rather than wind (*Chipman v. Comm'r.*, T.C. Memo 1981-194)

Although damage to property due to routine wear and tear over time is not a deductible casualty loss, routine wear and tear can result in a sudden event that causes a casualty loss.

> EXAMPLE: Phil owns a rental home with an aged water heater that has deteriorated over time due to routine wear and tear. One day the water heater suddenly bursts, causing rust and water damage to rugs and drapes in Phil's property. The damage to the water heater itself is not a casualty loss since it was due to routine wear and tear. But the damage to the rugs and drapes is a deductible casualty loss because it was caused by a sudden, unexpected, and unusual event—a burst water heater.

External Force Required

There must be some external force involved in a casualty loss. Thus, you get no deduction if you simply lose property or it is damaged or destroyed due to your own negligence. However, a deductible casualty loss can be caused by another person's carelessness or negligence. For example, you can deduct as a casualty loss sudden damage caused by a negligent contractor or workman.

> EXAMPLE: Richard and Ruth Marx noticed that the roof to their house was leaking and hired a building contractor to repair it. Not long afterward, the roof leaked again during a storm, but this time the leak was much worse: It caused the drywall ceiling of the home to fall in, resulting in substantial damage to the interior. The tax court permitted the Marxes to claim a casualty loss for the damage, finding that the massive leaks were sudden and unexpected, were caused by the contractor's negligence, and were independent of the preexisting minor leak. (*Marx v. Comm'r.*, T.C. Memo 1991-598.)

Theft or Vandalism

You may also obtain a casualty loss deduction if anything on or in your rental property is stolen or vandalized. The taking of property must be illegal under the laws of the state where it occurred and it must have been done with criminal intent. You should file a police report when a theft occurs or if your property is vandalized. You must deduct losses from a theft or vandalism in the tax year in which the loss is discovered.

> EXAMPLE: Lorraine, the owner of a four-unit apartment building, is forced to evict one of her tenants for nonpayment of rent. After the tenant moves out, she discovers that he has completely trashed the apartment— among other things, stopping the toilet with diapers, breaking mirrors, staining carpets, and punching holes in the walls. Lorraine can deduct the uninsured portion of the cost of the vandalism as a casualty loss.

Calculating a Casualty Loss Deduction

You usually won't be able to deduct the entire cost of property damaged or destroyed by a casualty. How much you may deduct depends on whether the property involved was stolen, completely destroyed, or partially destroyed, and whether the loss was covered by insurance. You must always reduce your casualty losses by the amount of any insurance proceeds you receive, or reasonably expect to receive in the future. If more than one item is stolen, damaged, or destroyed, you must figure your deduction separately for each.

One good thing about casualty losses is that they are not subject to the restrictions on deducting passive losses discussed in Chapter 16. You can simply ignore the complex passive loss rules when determining how much you may deduct.

Insurance

You may take a deduction for casualty losses to your rental property only to the extent that the loss is not covered by insurance. If the loss is fully covered, you get no deduction. You can't avoid this rule by not filing an insurance claim. If you have insurance coverage, you must timely file a claim, even if it will result in cancellation of your policy or an increase in your premiums. If you have insurance and don't file an insurance claim, you cannot obtain a casualty loss deduction. (I.R.C. § 165(h)(4)(E).)

You must reduce the amount of your claimed casualty loss by any insurance recovery you receive or reasonably expect to receive, even if it hasn't yet been paid. If it later turns out that you receive less insurance than you expected, you can deduct the amount the following year. If you receive more than you expected and claimed as a casualty loss, the extra amount is included as income for the year it is received.

You must also reduce your claimed loss by the amount of any of the following payments or services you receive or expect to receive:

- the cost of any repairs made by a tenant that you don't pay for
- payments to you by the tenant to cover the cost of repairs
- any part of a federal disaster loan that is forgiven
- court awards for damage or theft loss, minus any attorneys' fees or other expenses incurred to obtain the award, and
- the value of repairs, restoration, or cleanup services provided for free by a relief agency such as the Red Cross.

Property a Total Loss

If the property is completely destroyed or stolen, your deduction is calculated as follows:

Adjusted basis
− Salvage value
− Insurance proceeds
= Deductible loss

Your adjusted basis is the property's original cost, plus the value of any improvements, minus any deductions you took for depreciation or Section 179 expensing—see Chapter 5. You determine the basis for your building, land improvements, and landscaping separately.

Salvage value is the value of whatever remains after the property is destroyed. This usually won't amount to much. For example, if a rental house burns down completely, there may be some leftover bricks, building materials, personal property, and other items with some scrap value. Obviously, if a personal property item is stolen, there will be no salvage value at all.

> EXAMPLE: Sean's rental house burns down and is completely destroyed. The house had an adjusted basis of $100,000. Sean only had $50,000 of fire insurance coverage. The house's salvage value is $2,000. Sean's deductible casualty loss is $48,000, calculated as follows:
>
> | | | |
> |---|---|---|
> | Adjusted basis | $ | 100,000 |
> | Salvage value of building | − | 2,000 |
> | Insurance recovery | − | 50,000 |
> | Deductible loss | $ | 48,000 |

Property a Partial Loss

If the property is only partly destroyed, your casualty loss deduction is the *lesser* of:

- the decrease in the property's fair market value, or
- its adjusted basis.

You must reduce both amounts by any insurance you receive or expect to receive. Unless you've owned the property for many years, the fair market value measure is usually less and is the one you must use.

If you've experienced a casualty loss, you can use an appraiser to determine the reduction in fair market value of your partly damaged property. However, this is often too expensive or impractical. Instead, most people use the cost of repairing the property to determine the fair market value reduction. You can use the cost of cleaning up or of making repairs after a casualty as a measure of the decrease in fair market value if:

- the repairs are actually made
- the repairs are necessary to bring the property back to its condition before the casualty
- the amount spent for repairs is not excessive
- the repairs take care of the damage only, and
- the value of the property after the repairs is not, due to the repairs, greater than its value before the casualty. (IRS Reg. § 1.165-7(a)(2)(ii).)

EXAMPLE: The chimney in Sally's rental duplex collapses during an earthquake. She has no earthquake insurance coverage. She pays $5,000 to a building contractor to repair the chimney back to the condition it was in before the earthquake. She figures her casualty loss deduction as follows:

1. Adjusted basis of duplex before earthquake	$ 96,000
2. Fair market value before earthquake	125,000
3. Fair market value after earthquake	− 120,000
4. Decrease in fair market value (based on cost of repair)	5,000
5. Amount of loss (line 1 or line 4, whichever is less)	5,000
6. Insurance reimbursement	− 0
7. Deductible loss	$ 5,000

Deducting Separate Components

You must calculate casualty loss to rental property separately for each item that is damaged or destroyed. (IRS Reg. § 1.165-7(a)(2)(ii).) This may include a building, land improvements under the building, landscaping, and other land improvements apart from the building. However, you don't need to separately deduct personal property items inside a rental property, such as stoves and refrigerators.

> EXAMPLE: Tim's rental house is damaged by a tornado. The twister not only damaged the building, but tore up his landscaping—trees and shrubs—as well. Tim must separately calculate his casualty loss for the building and the landscaping. The adjusted basis of the building is $166,000. The trees and shrubs have an adjusted basis of $4,500. Tim hires an appraiser who determines that the fair market value of the building immediately before the tornado was $200,000, and was $152,000 immediately afterwards. The fair market value of the trees and shrubs immediately before the casualty was $4,000 and afterwards was $400. Tim received $40,000 in insurance to cover the loss to the building.

Tim calculates his casualty loss for the building as follows:

1. Adjusted basis of house before tornado	$ 166,000
2. Fair market value before tornado	200,000
3. Fair market value after tornado	− 152,000
4. Decrease in fair market value	48,000
5. Amount of loss (line 1 or line 4, whichever is less)	48,000
6. Insurance reimbursement	− 40,000
7. Deductible loss	$ 8,000

Tim separately calculates his loss for the landscaping as follows:

1. Adjusted basis of landscaping before tornado	$ 4,500
2. Fair market value before tornado	4,000
3. Fair market value after tornado	− 400
4. Decrease in fair market value	3,600
5. Amount of loss (line 1 or line 4, whichever is less)	3,600
6. Insurance reimbursement	− 0
7. Deductible casualty loss	$ 3,600

Damage to Your Home Office

If you qualify for the home office deduction, you may deduct losses due to damage to, or destruction of, your home office as part of your home office deduction.

You can deduct casualty losses that affect your entire house as an indirect home office expense. The amount of your deduction is based on your home office use percentage.

> **EXAMPLE:** Dana's home, valued at $500,000, is completely destroyed by a fire. Her fire insurance covered only 80% of her loss, or $400,000, leaving her with a $100,000 loss. Her home office took up 20% of her home. She can deduct 20% of her $100,000 loss, or $20,000, as an indirect home office deduction.

You can fully deduct casualty losses that affect only your home office—for example, if only your home office is burned in a fire—as direct home office expenses. However, you can't take a business expense deduction for casualty losses that don't affect your home office at all—for example, if your kitchen is destroyed by fire. (See Chapter 9 for a detailed discussion of the home office deduction.)

If the loss involves property you use for your rental activity that is in your home office but is not part of your home—for example, a burglar steals your home office computer—you can deduct the entire value of that loss directly, rather than as part of the home office deduction.

Effect of Casualty Losses on Basis

Any casualty loss you claim on your taxes reduces the basis of the property. Insurance or other reimbursements you receive also reduce your basis. This will increase your gain when you sell the property (see Chapter 5).

> **EXAMPLE:** Paula owns an apartment building with a $500,000 adjusted basis. It suffers a $50,000 uninsured casualty loss from a storm. Paula deducts the $50,000 casualty loss and reduces the basis in the apartment building to $450,000. If Paula had insurance covering the loss, she would have gotten no casualty loss deductions and still would have had to reduce the basis of her building by $50,000.

Disaster Area Losses

If you suffer a deductible casualty loss in an area that is declared a federal disaster by the president, you may elect to deduct the loss for your taxes for the previous year. This will provide you with a quick tax refund since you'll get back part of the tax you paid for the prior year. If you have already filed your return for the prior year, you can claim a disaster loss against that year's income by filing an amended return (see Chapter 19).

> EXAMPLE: Tom's apartment building is damaged by a flood in August of 2015. Tom suffers a deductible casualty loss of $10,000. The area in which his building is located is declared a federal disaster area. Tom may deduct his $10,000 casualty loss on his 2014 taxes, even though he has already paid them, by filing an amended return for the year. As a result, he gets a $2,500 tax refund for that year.

You can determine if an area has been declared a disaster area by checking the Federal Emergency Management Administration (FEMA) website at www.fema.gov/disasters.

Repair and Replacement Costs for Casualty Losses

The cost of repairing or replacing business property damaged or destroyed in a casualty event is not part of a casualty loss; neither are cleanup costs. The cost of replacing or repairing property destroyed or damaged due to a casualty event ordinarily must be depreciated as an improvement—a restoration. (IRS Reg. § 1.263(a)-3(k)(1)(iii).)

> EXAMPLE: Landlord Jason owns an apartment building with an adjusted basis of $500,000. He spends $50,000 to repair storm damage, including repairs to the roof and cleanup expenses. He reduces the basis of his building by this amount. The $50,000 spent to fix the building must be depreciated.

However, under the IRS repair regulations that took effect in 2014, a building owner is only required to depreciate restoration costs to the extent of the property's adjusted basis immediately before the casualty event that damaged or destroyed the building. Any costs over this amount may be currently deducted if they constitute repairs under the IRS repair regulations discussed in Chapter 4. (IRS Reg. § 1.263(a)-3(k) (4)(ii).) Most of the time, such deductible expenses will be cleanup costs following the casualty event.

> **EXAMPLE:** Assume that Landlord Jason from the above example spent $550,000 to fix his building, instead of $50,000. This included $525,000 to replace substantial portions of the building—a restoration expense that must be depreciated, and an additional $25,000 for cleanup costs. He must depreciate $500,000 of the costs—the amount of his building's adjusted basis. Any portion of the remaining $50,000 that constitutes a repair under the IRS repair regulations may be currently deducted. The $25,000 cleanup costs are currently deductible because they qualify as a repair expense.

If, unlike the above example, the restoration expenses do not exceed the building's adjusted basis, but the restoration and repair expenses added together exceed the adjusted basis, the repair expenses not used to offset the adjusted basis may be deducted.

> **EXAMPLE:** Martha rents out a small home with an adjusted basis of $30,000. A storm destroys her roof and floods her basement. She spends $25,000 to replace her roof—a restoration expense that must be depreciated. She also has $10,000 in cleanup costs—a repair expense: $35,000 in total expenses minus $30,000 adjusted basis = $5,000. Thus Martha can deduct $5,000 of her cleanup expenses.

Casualty Gains

In some cases, the insurance reimbursement you receive will exceed the value of the property that is damaged or destroyed. In this event, you have a casualty gain, not a deductible loss.

> EXAMPLE: In 1970, Rick bought a rental house for $18,000. He made no further improvements or additions to the property. Thirty years later, when the house was worth $250,000, it was destroyed in a storm. Rick received $146,000 from the insurance company. He had a gain of $128,000 ($146,000 − $18,000).

If you have a gain, you might have to pay tax on that gain. If you owned the property one year or more, the gain is a capital gain taxed at capital gains rates. Gains on property owned less than one year are taxed at ordinary income tax rates. (Ordinary rates are higher than capital gains rates for everyone except taxpayers in the lowest tax brackets; see Chapter 1.)

However, if you have a gain on damaged property, you can postpone paying tax on it if you replace or restore the property. You must replace the property with new property that is similar or related in service or use to the property it replaces. For example, you can replace a rental house with another rental house or apartment building; but you can't replace it with a home you live in.

You do not have to use the same funds you receive as reimbursement for your old property to acquire the replacement property. If you spend the money you receive from the insurance company for other purposes, and borrow money to buy replacement property, you can still postpone reporting the gain if you meet the other requirements.

The cost of restoring or replacing the property must be at least as much as the reimbursement you receive. If the cost is less than the reimbursement, you must include the gain in your income up to the amount of the unspent reimbursement.

> EXAMPLE: Rick (from the above example) spent $144,000 to rebuild his rental house. Because this is $2,000 less than the insurance proceeds he received ($146,000), he must include $2,000 in his taxable income for the year.

To postpone reporting your gain, you must restore or replace the damaged or destroyed property within two years after the close of the first tax year in which any part of your gain is realized. If the property is in a federal disaster area, this period is increased to four years. If it is located in the Hurricane Katrina disaster area, the replacement period is increased to five years.

Tax Reporting and Record Keeping for Casualty Losses

Casualty losses are a hot ticket item for the IRS. Claiming them will increase your chances of being audited. Make sure you can document your losses. You'll need to have:

- documents showing that you owned each asset you claimed was damaged, stolen, or destroyed—for example, a deed or receipt
- contracts or purchase receipts showing the original cost of the item, plus any improvements you made to it
- copies of your old tax returns showing all your depreciation and Section 179 deductions for the property, and
- evidence of the property's fair market value, such as insurance records, an appraisal, or receipts for the cost of repairing it.

You report casualty losses to rental property on part B of IRS Form 4684, *Casualties and Thefts*, and then transfer the deductible casualty loss to Form 4797, *Sales of Business Property*, and the first page of your Form 1040. The amount of your deductible casualty loss is subtracted from your adjusted gross income for the year. These reporting requirements differ from those for other deductions covered in this book, which are reported on IRS Schedule E, Form 1040.

Additional Deductions

Dues and Subscriptions 338

Education Expenses 338

Before You Are in Business 339

Traveling for Education 340

Gifts 341

Insurance for Your Rental Activity 342

Homeowners' Insurance for Your Home Office 342

Car Insurance 342

Prepaying Your Insurance Premiums 343

Legal and Professional Services 344

Buying Long-Term Property 344

Management Fees 344

Starting a Business 345

Accounting Fees 345

Meals and Entertainment 345

Whom Can You Entertain? 346

You Must Discuss Your Rental Activity 346

Calculating Your Deduction 347

Taxes 347

Real Property Taxes 347

Employment Taxes 349

Tax Break for Accessibility Changes 349

Energy Efficiency Deduction 350

Unpaid Rent 351

This chapter looks at some common deductible operating expenses that you are likely to incur in the course of your rental activity, such as real estate taxes, insurance, and legal fees. You can deduct these costs as operating expenses as long as they are ordinary, necessary, and reasonable in amount—and meet the additional requirements discussed below.

Dues and Subscriptions

Dues you pay to professional, business, and civic organizations are deductible expenses, as long as the organization's main purpose is not to provide entertainment facilities to members. You can deduct dues paid to:

- apartment owner associations
- real estate boards
- local chambers of commerce and business leagues, and
- civic or public service organizations, such as a Rotary or Lions club.

You get no deduction for dues you pay to belong to other types of social, business, or recreational clubs—for example, country clubs or athletic clubs. For this reason, it's best not to use the word dues on your tax return because the IRS may question the expense. Use other words to describe the deduction—for example, if you're deducting membership dues for an apartment owners' organization, list the expense as apartment owners' association membership fees.

You may also deduct the cost of publications you read for your rental activity—magazines or journals on real estate, taxation, law, or finance. Subscription websites dealing with real estate are also deductible. (Don't forget to deduct the cost of this book!)

Education Expenses

You may deduct your expenses for landlord-related education—for example, a seminar or course on buying or operating rental property. You may also deduct the cost of attending a real-estate–related convention or meeting as an education expense. To qualify for an education deduction, you must be able to show the education:

- maintains or improves skills required to be a successful landlord, or
- is required by law or regulation to maintain your professional status.

EXAMPLE 1: Jerry owns three rental houses. He attends a one-day seminar on how to make more money from rental property offered by The Learning Annex, a company that produces educational seminars on various subjects. The cost is deductible as an education expense.

EXAMPLE 2: Herb is a landlord and licensed real estate broker. Every year, he is required by his state real estate licensing board to take 30 hours of continuing education to maintain his status as a licensed broker. He may deduct the cost as an education expense.

Deductible education expenses include tuition, fees, books, and other learning materials. They also include transportation and travel (see below). You may also deduct expenses you pay to educate or train your employees.

Before You Are in Business

You cannot currently deduct education expenses you incur before your rental activity begins. For example, if you have never owned rental property and attend a course on how to be a successful landlord, you may not deduct the expense as an education expense. However, if you do end up buying rental property, you may deduct the expense as a start-up expense. You can deduct up to $5,000 in start-up expenses the first year your rental activity is in operation. You must deduct any amount over the applicable limit in equal installments over the first 180 months you're in business. (See Chapter 8.)

Likewise, if you're not already involved in the real estate field, you may not deduct the cost of attending courses to become a licensed real estate broker. (IRS Reg. § 1.162-5(a).)

Lifetime Learning Credit

Instead of taking a tax deduction for your rental-business–related education expenses, you may qualify for the lifetime learning credit. A tax credit is a dollar-for-dollar reduction in your tax liability, so it's even better than a tax deduction.

The lifetime learning credit can be used to help pay for any undergraduate or graduate-level education, including nondegree education to acquire or improve job skills (for example a continuing education course). If you qualify, your credit equals 20% of the first $10,000 of postsecondary tuition and fees you pay during the year, for a maximum credit of $2,000 per tax return. However, the credit is phased out and then eliminated at certain income levels: It begins to go down if your modified adjusted gross income is over $55,000 ($110,000 for a joint return) and you cannot claim the credit at all if your MAGI is over $65,000 ($130,000 for a joint return). The limits are adjusted for inflation each year. These are the limits for 2015.

You can take this credit not only for yourself, but for a dependent child (or children) for whom you claim a tax exemption, or your spouse as well (if you file jointly). And it can be taken any number of times. However, you can't take the credit if you've already deducted the education cost as a business expense.

EXAMPLE: Bill, a self-employed real estate broker with a $40,000 AGI, spends $2,000 on continuing real estate education courses. He may take a $400 lifetime learning credit (20% × $2,000 = $400).

Traveling for Education

Transportation expenses you pay to travel to and from a deductible educational activity are deductible. This includes transportation between your home and the educational activity. Going to or from home to an educational activity does not constitute nondeductible commuting. If you drive, you may deduct your actual expenses or use the standard mileage rate. (See Chapter 10 for more on deducting car expenses.)

There's no law that says you must take your education courses as close to home as possible. You can travel outside your geographic area for education, even if the same or a similar educational activity is available near your home or place of business. Companies and groups that sponsor educational events are well aware of this rule and take advantage of it by offering courses and seminars at resorts and other enjoyable vacation spots such as Hawaii and California. Deductible travel expenses can include airfare or other transportation, lodging, and meals. (See Chapter 11 for more on deducting travel expenses.)

Gifts

You may deduct the cost of gifts you make in the course of your rental business—for example, to thank or maintain goodwill with a vendor, tenant, or employee. This includes holiday gifts to tenants. However, the gift expense deduction is limited to $25 per person per year. Any amount over the $25 limit is not deductible. If this amount seems low, that's because it was established in 1954! In addition, there are special record-keeping requirements for gifts. (See Chapter 17.)

> **EXAMPLE:** Landlord Lisa gives a $60 Christmas gift to the gardener who takes care of her rental properties. She may deduct $25 of the cost.

The $25 limit applies only to gifts to individuals. It doesn't apply if you give a gift to an entire company. Such companywide gifts are deductible in any amount, as long as they are reasonable. However, the $25 limit does apply if the gift is intended for a particular person or group of people within the company.

If you give a gift to a family member of a tenant, the gift is considered to be an indirect gift to the tenant and is subject to the $25 limit. Thus, you are limited to a single $25 gift deduction for each tenant and his or her entire family.

Insurance for Your Rental Activity

You can deduct the premiums you pay for almost any insurance related to your rental activity. This includes fire, theft, and flood insurance for rental property, as well as landlord liability insurance. If you have employees, you may deduct the cost of their health and workers' compensation insurance. Unemployment insurance contributions you make for your employees are deducted either as insurance costs or as taxes, depending on how they are characterized by your state's laws.

The one type of insurance that may not be deducted as an operating expense is title insurance you obtain when you purchase rental property. Its cost is added to the basis of the property and depreciated over 27.5 years. The same rule applies to insurance premiums you pay on property under construction. (See Chapter 5.)

Homeowners' Insurance for Your Home Office

If you have a home office and qualify for the home office deduction, you may deduct the home office percentage of your homeowners' or renters' insurance premiums. For example, if your home office takes up 20% of your home, you may deduct 20% of the premiums. You can deduct 100% of any coverage that you add to your homeowners' policy specifically for your home office and/or rental property. For example, if you add an endorsement to your policy to cover business property, you can deduct 100% of the cost.

Car Insurance

If you use the actual expense method to deduct your car expenses, you can deduct the cost of insurance that covers liability, damages, and other losses for vehicles used in your rental activity as an operating expense. If you use a vehicle only for your rental activity, you can deduct 100% of your insurance costs. If you operate a vehicle for both your rental activity and for personal use, you can deduct only the part of the insurance premiums that applies to the rental use of your vehicle. For example, if you use a car 10% for your rental activity and 90% for personal reasons, you can deduct 10% of your insurance costs.

If you use the standard mileage rate to deduct your car expenses, you can't take a separate deduction for insurance. The standard rate is intended to cover all your automobile costs, including insurance. (See Chapter 10 for more on vehicle deductions.)

Prepaying Your Insurance Premiums

Many landlords make a single payment for an entire year of insurance coverage. This type of prepayment is fully deductible in the year it was made, provided it complies with the 12-month rule. Under this rule, cash basis taxpayers (which includes most small landlords) may deduct a prepaid expense such as insurance in the current year, if the term of the insurance coverage extends no longer than the earlier of: 12 months, or the end of the tax year after the tax year in which the payment was made.

> EXAMPLE: On July 1, 2015, Irving pays $2,000 for a new insurance policy for his rental building. The policy covers the period from July 1, 2015 through the end of 2016. Irving can deduct the entire $2,000 payment in 2015 because the coverage ends at the end of 2016—the year after he paid for the policy.

There is one small catch: If you previously followed the old rule under which expenses prepaid beyond the calendar year were not currently deductible, you must get IRS approval to use the 12-month rule. Approval is granted automatically by the IRS upon filing of IRS Form 3115, *Application for Change in Accounting Method.* You should attach one copy of the form to the return for the year of the change and send another copy to the IRS national office (not the service center where you file your return). The address is on the instructions for the form.

It is a good idea to get a tax pro to help you with this form because it may require some adjustment of the deductions you've taken for prepaid expenses in previous years under the old rule.

Legal and Professional Services

You can deduct fees that you pay to attorneys, accountants, property management companies, real estate investment advisors, and other professionals as operating expenses if the fees are for work related to your rental activity.

> **EXAMPLE:** Landlord Ira hires attorney Jake to evict a deadbeat tenant. The legal fees Ira pays Jake are a deductible operating expense.

Legal and professional fees that you pay for personal purposes generally are not deductible. For example, you can't deduct the legal fees you incur if you get divorced or you sue someone for a traffic accident injury. Nor are the fees that you pay to write your will deductible, even if the will covers rental property that you own.

Buying Long-Term Property

If you pay legal or other fees in the course of buying real estate or other long-term property, you must add the amount of the fee to the tax basis (cost) of the property. You deduct this cost over several years, through depreciation. This rule also applies to attorney fees incurred in legal disputes over who holds title to real estate, or in boundary disputes or condemnation proceedings.

Management Fees

The fees you pay a real estate management company to manage your property are deductible operating expenses. But be careful if you hire your child, spouse, or other relatives to serve as your manager. If you pay a relative more than the going market rate and you are audited, the IRS can deny your deduction for the excess amount. (IRS Reg. § 1.162-1(a).)

Starting a Business

Legal and accounting fees that you pay to start a rental business are deductible only as business start-up expenses. You may deduct them over the first 60 months you are in business. The same holds true for incorporation fees or fees that you pay to form a partnership or LLC. You may not deduct such fees if your rental activity is an investment for tax purposes, not a business. (See Chapter 8 for more on deducting start-up costs.)

Accounting Fees

You may deduct any accounting fees that you pay for your rental activity as a deductible operating expense—for example, fees you pay an accountant to set up or keep your books, prepare your tax return, or give you tax advice for your rental activity.

You may also deduct the cost of having an accountant or other tax professional complete the rental portion of your tax return—Schedule E and other rental activity tax forms—but you cannot deduct the time the preparer spends on the personal part of your return. Make sure that you get an itemized bill showing the portion of the tax preparation fee allocated to preparing your Schedule E.

Meals and Entertainment

Meal and entertainment expenses are usually not a big deduction item for a person running a small rental business. However, if you do spend money to take people out to lunch or dinner for your rental business, or treat them to a ballgame or play, you can deduct part of your entertainment expense if you satisfy strict IRS requirements.

RESOURCE

Find out more about meal and entertainment expenses. For detailed guidance about deducting meal and entertainment expenses, refer to IRS Publication 463, *Travel, Entertainment, Gift, and Car Expenses.* You can download it from www.irs.gov or call 800-TAX-FORM.

Whom Can You Entertain?

The entertainment deduction is, understandably, a great temptation for landlords who want to mix work with pleasure—and enjoy as much of the latter as possible. To prevent abuses, the IRS has something to say about your guest list. To obtain a deduction when entertaining, you must be with at least one person who can benefit your rental activity in some way. This could include:

- prospective buyers of your rental property
- investors or prospective investors in your real estate activity
- tenants or prospective tenants (not very common for residential real estate)
- suppliers
- employees
- independent contractors, such as construction contractors, architects, and repairmen
- government officials
- real estate agents
- real estate managers
- partners, or
- professional advisers such as your attorney or accountant.

If people who can't benefit your rental activity are also present and you pay their expenses, you can't deduct the cost.

You Must Discuss Your Rental Activity

Rental business entertainment expenses, like all operating expenses, are deductible only if they are ordinary and necessary. This means that the expense must be common, helpful, and appropriate for your rental activity. Moreover, you must have a discussion relating to your rental activity either before, during, or after a social event if you want to claim an entertainment deduction.

The IRS doesn't have spies lurking in restaurants, theaters, or other places of entertainment, so it has no way of knowing whether you really talk about your rental activity. You're pretty much on the honor system here. However, be aware that if you're audited, the IRS closely scrutinizes this deduction because many taxpayers cheat when they take it. You'll also have to comply with stringent record-keeping requirements. (See Chapter 17.)

Calculating Your Deduction

Expenses that you incur for entertainment can include meals (with beverages, tax, and tips), your transportation expenses (including parking), tickets to entertainment or sporting events, catering costs for parties, cover charges for admission to nightclubs, and rent you pay for a room in which to hold a dinner or cocktail party. As long as they meet the requirements explained above, they are deductible—but not in full. The tax rules specify that you may deduct only 50% of your entertainment expenses. For example, if you spend $50 for a meal in a restaurant, you can deduct $25. (Even though you can deduct only half of the expense, you must keep track of everything you spend and report the entire amount on your tax return.) The only exception to the 50% rule is for transportation expenses, which are 100% deductible.

Ordinarily, you cannot deduct the cost of entertaining your spouse or the spouse of a rental business associate. However, if your spouse is co-owner of the rental property involved, you may deduct his or her expenses.

Taxes

Most taxes that you pay in the course of your rental activity are currently deductible operating expenses.

Real Property Taxes

You can fully deduct your current year state and local property taxes on rental real property as an operating expense. However, if you prepay the next year's property taxes, you may not deduct the prepaid amount until the following year.

When you buy your rental property, the property taxes due for the year must be divided between the buyer and seller according to how many days of the tax year each held ownership of the property. You'll usually find information on this in the settlement statement you receive at the property closing.

Local Benefit Taxes and Special Assessments

Water bills, sewer charges, and other service charges assessed against your rental property are not real estate taxes, but they are deductible as operating expenses. (If a tenant pays these expenses, as sometimes happens with single-family house rentals, the landlord gets no deduction unless he or she reimburses the tenant. The tenant gets no deduction because these are personal expenses for the tenant.)

However, real estate taxes imposed to fund specific local benefits for property, such as streets, sidewalks, sewer lines, and water mains, are not currently deductible as operating expenses where they are imposed only on the property owners who will benefit from them. Because these benefits increase the value of your property, you must add what you pay for them to the tax basis of your property and depreciate them. (I.R.C. § 164(c)(1).) Most of these improvements can be depreciated over 15 years as land improvements (see Chapter 5).

However, there is an exception to this rule: Any part of a special assessment you pay that is for maintenance, repairs, or an interest charge for a local benefit for your property is deductible as an operating expense. You may claim this deduction only if the taxing authority sends you an itemized tax bill separately listing the amounts you must pay for construction, interest, and maintenance. (IRS Reg. § 1.164-4(b)(1).)

> EXAMPLE: A city assessed a front-foot benefit charge against property that was benefited by construction of a water system. The city's tax bill itemized the charge, showing how much was assessed for construction of the water system, interest, and maintenance costs. Taxpayers were allowed to currently deduct the amounts for interest and maintenance. (Rev. Rul. 79-201.)

Real Estate Transfer Taxes

When you purchase rental property, you must ordinarily pay state and local real estate transfer taxes. You cannot deduct these taxes in the year in which you paid them. Instead, add them to the basis of your property and depreciate them over time, as explained in Chapter 5.

Employment Taxes

If you have employees, you must pay half of their Social Security and Medicare taxes from your own funds and withhold the other half from their pay. These taxes consist of a 12.4% Social Security tax, up to an annual salary cap ($118,500 in 2015); and a 2.9% Medicare tax up to an annual ceiling—$200,000 for single taxpayers and $250,000 for married couples filing jointly. Net self-employment or wage income above the ceiling is taxed at a 3.8% rate. You may deduct half of this amount as a business expense. You should treat the taxes you withhold from your employees' pay as wages paid to your employees on your tax return. However, you need not pay employment taxes when you hire your children. (See Chapter 12.)

Tax Break for Accessibility Changes

A special tax law provision allows businesses (including landlords) to currently deduct up to $15,000 of the cost of making their buildings or other facilities—such as roads, walks, and parking lots—accessible to the elderly or disabled. (I.R.C. § 190.) These changes would ordinarily constitute improvements for tax purposes that would have to be depreciated over many years. This tax break is intended to encourage landlords and other business owners to make their facilities more accessible to the disabled and elderly. You may take this deduction whether or not the improvements you make are required by law.

The most you can deduct as a cost of removing barriers to the disabled and the elderly for any tax year is $15,000. However, you can add any costs over this limit to the basis of the property and depreciate them.

To qualify for the deduction, your renovations must comply with applicable accessibility standards. Detailed standards are set forth in the ADA Accessibility Guidelines, which can be found on the Internet at www.access-board.gov (search "guidelines & standards"). IRS Publication 535, *Business Expenses*, also contains a summary of these standards.

You may claim the deduction on your income tax return for the tax year you paid for the work, or the year you incurred the expenses. Identify the deduction as a separate item. The choice applies to all of the qualifying costs you have during the year, up to the $15,000 limit. You must maintain adequate records to support your deduction—keep your receipts.

> EXAMPLE: Jason owns an 80-year-old apartment building that is not wheelchair accessible. He installs four wheelchair ramps at a cost of $5,000. Ordinarily, this would be an improvement that Jason would have to depreciate. But due to the special rule, he may deduct the entire $5,000 in one year.

Energy Efficiency Deduction

The Energy Tax Incentives Act, enacted by Congress in 2005, created a brand-new deduction for expenses to make commercial buildings more energy efficient. It's intended to encourage building owners to upgrade their existing buildings and to design more energy-efficient new structures. The deduction may be used for both used and new buildings, but not for any building placed in service after December 31, 2014.

This deduction is not available for single-family homes or multifamily structures of three stories or less. In other words, you must own an apartment building of four or more stories to qualify. For details on how this complex deduction works, see IRS Notice 2006-52 (you can download it from the IRS website at www.irs.gov).

In a nutshell, you may deduct in one year up to $1.80 per building square foot when, as part of a plan to reduce your total energy costs, you upgrade your building's:

- interior lighting system
- heating, cooling, ventilation, and hot water system, or
- building envelope. (I.R.C. § 179D.)

For example, the owner of a 10,000-square-foot apartment building who qualified for the deduction could deduct $18,000 ($1.80 × 10,000 = $18,000).

To obtain the full deduction, the upgrade must reduce the power costs for the system involved by at least 50% as compared with a hypothetical reference building that meets the minimum requirements of Standard 90.1-2001 of the American Society of Heating, Refrigerating and Air-Conditioning Engineers (ASHRAE) and the Illuminating Engineering Society of North America. Copies of these standards can be obtained from the ASHRAE website (see below). If the reduction is less than 50%, a partial tax deduction of 60 cents per square foot is available if a 16⅔% energy savings target is met. There is no dollar limit on the deduction. The tax basis of your building is reduced by the amount of the deduction allowed.

The energy savings must be calculated using software that satisfies IRS requirements. Moreover, your building must be inspected by a "qualified individual" who certifies to the IRS that you've complied with all the requirements. IRS Notice 2006-52 details how to comply with these rules.

You'll likely need to hire a heating and ventilating engineer, refrigerating engineer, illuminating engineer, or other similar expert to get this deduction. For more information about such professionals, visit the following websites:

- American Society of Heating, Refrigerating and Air-Conditioning Engineers: www.ashrae.org, and
- Illuminating Engineering Society of North America: www.iesna.org.

Unpaid Rent

If tenants fail to pay the rent owed you, can you deduct the loss? The short answer for the vast majority of small landlords is No. (Some bad debts are deductible, but unpaid rent is almost never one of them.) Here's why:

IRS regulations provide that a worthless debt arising from unpaid rent is deductible only if you report the amount of rent you were supposed to be paid as income for that year (or a prior year). (IRS Reg. § 1.166-1(e).)

Landlords who can report this kind of yet-uncollected rent are operating on an accrual accounting basis (if you are an accrual basis taxpayer, you report rent as income as it becomes due, not when it's actually paid). The great majority of small landlords operate on a cash basis, which means they report rent as income only when it is actually paid to them by their tenants. Since cash basis landlords do not report rent that has never been paid on their tax returns, it's not deductible. (See Chapter 17 for a detailed discussion of accounting methods.)

> **EXAMPLE:** John and Margaret Kopunek rented a house in Sarasota, Florida, to a new tenant who stopped paying rent after a few months and moved out. After they kept the tenant's security deposit, the Kopuneks were left with $750 in unpaid rent. Because they were cash basis taxpayers, they did not report the $750 of rent that they never received as income on their tax return for the year. When they deducted the $750 from their taxes for the year as a bad debt, they were audited by the IRS and the deduction was denied. The tax court held that the IRS had acted properly. Having never reported the unpaid rent as income, the hapless Kopuneks could not deduct it as a bad debt. (*Kopunek v. Comm'r.*, T.C. Memo 1987-417.)

So, in order to deduct unpaid rent, you must report unpaid rent as income on your tax return for the year the rent was due—in other words, you'd have to adopt an accrual method of accounting. However, the deduction merely offsets the income you've already reported. Thus, there is no point in switching to the accrual method of accounting just to be able to write off unpaid rent; you won't save an extra penny in taxes.

Nor can you deduct unpaid rent as a casualty loss (see Chapter 13). The Kopuneks, from the example above, tried this and failed. (*Kopunek v. Comm'r.*, T.C. Memo 1987-417.)

The moral for landlords is clear: If you have deadbeat tenants, evict them as soon as possible and find a new tenant who will pay the rent. The legal fees to evict a tenant are deductible (see "Legal and Professional Services," above). You can obtain a court judgment against a defaulting tenant for the amount of the unpaid rent (less any security deposit you've retained). However, unless the tenant has money, earns a salary, or has assets you can get your hands on, such a judgment will be worthless. Courts do not collect such judgments for you; you must do it yourself.

Vacation Homes

The Vacation Home Tax Morass..354

Regular Rental Property...356

Tax-Free Vacation Home..357

    No Tax Due on Rental Income 357

    Tax Deductions...357

Vacation Home Used as Rental Property 359

    Deducting Expenses...360

    The Hobby Loss and Passive Loss Rules 362

Vacation Home Used as Residence...363

    You Cannot Deduct Losses 364

    Calculating Your Deductions 364

Calculating Personal and Rental Use...367

    Calculating Personal Use..368

    Calculating Rental Use 371

    Putting Your Calculations Together 371

Converting Your Home to a Rental Property..372

Millions of Americans own, or think about owning, a vacation home. Oftentimes, people help pay for the cost of owning a second home by renting it out for part of the year. With the advent of online rental services like Airbnb, VRBO, and HomeAway, such rentals have become more popular than ever. While this can help defray some of the costs, there are significant tax consequences when you rent out a vacation home that you or your family also use. These rules are complicated and different rules apply depending on how much time you use the home and how much time you rent it out. If you bought your vacation home simply to have fun and don't want tax concerns to ruin your vacations, you can skip this chapter. On the other hand, if you want to save all the taxes you can—even when you're on vacation—you need to read it carefully.

The Vacation Home Tax Morass

You're entitled to deduct operating expenses and depreciation for a rental property, but not for a home, condominium, or other real property that you or your family use as a personal residence. So, what do you do if you use the same property as both a rental and a vacation home or second home during the year?

Unfortunately for vacation homeowners, Congress has decided that they should not be allowed to deduct operating expenses and depreciation costs for the time they use a second home as a personal residence. There are complicated tax rules homeowners must follow to ensure that they don't deduct too much for their second home. If a home is used as both a rental property and a residence, these rules require that you allocate expenses between the two types of uses. The rules differ depending on the amount of time the property is used as a rental and a residence.

The rules apply to any type of dwelling—this is defined quite broadly: It includes a house, condominium, mobile home, or even a boat. However, hotels, motels, and other short-term rentals are not dwellings for these purposes. Nor does the term apply if you rent a room in your home to a short-term paying guest, and never use the room yourself.

To figure out what deductions you can take for a vacation home, you must determine what tax category your home falls into. For tax purposes, a vacation or second home can be a:

- regular rental property
- tax-free vacation home
- vacation home used as rental property, or
- vacation home used as a residence.

You must determine which tax category your vacation home falls within each year. It's possible for the same home to be treated as a tax-free vacation home one year and then as a vacation home used as a residence the next year.

Some of these categories receive much more favorable tax treatment than others, so it's important to understand the differences among them. That way, you'll be able to plan your use of your vacation home to receive more favorable treatment.

Every vacation home or second home in America falls into one of the tax categories listed in the chart below. The further down you go in the chart, the worse tax treatment you receive.

Vacation Home Tax Categories		
Personal Use	Rental Use	Tax Category
0 days	Any number of days	Regular rental property
15 days or more	Less than 15 days	Tax-free vacation home
Less than 15 days *or* no more than 10% of the rental days	15 days or more	Vacation home used as rental property
More than 14 days *or* more than 10% of the rental days	15 days or more	Vacation home used as residence

Beware—State Sales Taxes

You might be surprised to learn that most states require people who rent out their vacation homes to charge and collect state sales and lodging taxes on the income they earn from short-term rentals. Depending on where your vacation home is located, rental periods of up to six months may be considered short-term and therefore subject to sales taxes. However, many states have "casual use" rules that excuse rentals of only one or two days per year from such taxes.

These taxes are completely separate from income tax and are not collected by the IRS. They are collected by your state and/or local government. Like all sales taxes, they are paid by the person who purchases the goods or service, not the person who provides them. Your role is limited to collecting the taxes and remitting them to the appropriate state and/or local agency. Depending on where your property is located, you may have to pay the sales tax you collect several times a year or only once each year. The taxes are calculated as a percentage of the rent you collect and are paid in addition to the rent. For example, if you rent out your vacation home for one month and earn $2,000 in total revenue and your sales tax rate is 10%, you'll have to charge your renters $200 in sales taxes. You must collect and remit the funds to the appropriate agencies. Sales tax rates and procedures vary from state to state. You'll have to register your home with your state sales tax agency and, possibly, with your city and/or county. Contact the sales tax authorities for the state, county, and city where your property is located to determine your sales and lodging tax requirements. A list of website links for all state sales tax agencies can be found at www.salesandusetax.com.

Regular Rental Property

If you have a second home that you rent out 100% of the time and never use yourself or permit family members to use, the home is treated like any other rental property described in this book. You can skip to "Calculating Personal and Rental Use," below. This type of rental property is not really a vacation home or second home because its owner does not live in it at all.

Tax-Free Vacation Home

At the other end of the spectrum from a 100% rental property, is a vacation home or second home that you use most of the time for your own personal use and you rent out for only a handful of days during the year. Such homes are treated as personal second homes, not rental properties, for tax purposes. Your vacation home falls within this category if, during the year:

- you rent out your home for less than 15 days, and
- the home is used personally for 15 days or more (see "Calculating Personal and Rental Use," below, for what constitutes personal use). (I.R.C. § 280A(g).)

> EXAMPLE: Claudia rents her Florida beachfront condominium for 14 days during the summer. She lives in the condo herself for two months during the year. Her condo qualifies as a tax-free vacation home.

No Tax Due on Rental Income

Here's the great thing about vacation homes in this category: All the rental income you receive from them is tax-free, no matter how much you earn. This tax exclusion also applies to the 3.8% Medicare tax on high-income taxpayers which went into effect in 2013 (see Chapter 1).

> EXAMPLE: Claudia earned $2,000 from renting out her Florida condo for two weeks. She doesn't have to pay any federal tax on this income.

This rule can provide you with a real windfall if, like Claudia, you own a vacation home in a desirable area where people are looking for short-term rentals.

Tax Deductions

The tax deduction rules applicable to any personal vacation home or second home apply to homes in this category. Under these rules, all your real estate taxes are deducted as a personal itemized deduction on your IRS Schedule A. There is no dollar limit on the deduction, or any limit on how many vacation homes you can claim the deduction for each year. You may also deduct your mortgage interest as an itemized deduction (for a mortgage up to $1 million). If you are lucky enough to have more than one vacation home, you must select the one to be treated as the second home for purposes of the mortgage interest deduction. This selection is made anew each year, so that one vacation home may be selected as the second home one year, and another selected the next year.

How to Report Tax-Free Rental Income on Your Tax Return

In theory, because income from annual rentals of 14 days or less is tax-free, you shouldn't have to list it as income on your tax return. However, if you rent your vacation home through an online rental service such as Airbnb, VRBO, or FlipKey, the service will report the income you receive to the IRS on Form 1099-MISC or 1099-K. IRS computers match the income shown on these forms with the income you report on your Form 1040. Thus, if you don't include the rental income on your return, the IRS may question you about it. This doesn't mean the income is taxable, it just means the IRS may ask you about it—likely through correspondence. You'd then have to explain to the IRS that the income was not taxable. The IRS has provided no guidance on how to deal with this dilemma. However, here are three alternatives:

- First, don't list the rental income as income on your return, and deal with the IRS if and when it asks you about it.
- Alternatively, you can not list the rental income and also attach a written statement to your return explaining that the rental income you received was not taxable. This may reduce the chances the IRS will question you about it.
- Or you can list the rental revenue as "other income" on your Form 1040 and then add an entry reducing this amount to zero. Again, you should attach an explanation. This alternative may satisfy IRS computers since the income shown on the 1099-MISC will be listed on your return.

Either way, you should keep records showing that your rental met the tax-free criteria, including a copy of your rental agreement, the dates the home was rented, and the amount of rent charged.

Because the home is treated as a personal residence for tax purposes, you may not deduct any operating expenses for the property or take any depreciation deduction. You don't file Schedule E, the tax form landlords file to report their income and expenses, because your home is not considered a rental property for tax purposes.

> EXAMPLE: Assume that Claudia paid $5,000 in mortgage interest and $2,000 in taxes for her condo. She also incurred $600 in operating expenses—this was the fee she paid to a real estate management company to rent and take care of her condo. She may deduct the taxes and interest as an itemized deduction on her Schedule A. She gets no deduction for the $600 in operating expenses, and no depreciation deduction.

TIP
Tax-free treatment also applies to personal residences. The tax-free income tax treatment discussed in this section applies to your main residence, as well as a vacation or second home. Thus, you can rent your house up to 14 days a year and pocket the proceeds free of tax.

Vacation Home Used as Rental Property

The next category of vacation homes are those that are rented out 15 days or more each year and not used very often by their owners. You fall into this category if you rent your property for at least 15 days each year and make personal use of the property:

- fewer than 15 days during the year, or
- no more than 10% of the number of days during the year the property is rented for a fair rental.

> EXAMPLE 1: Miranda owns a vacation home in Aspen, Colorado. She uses it for 14 days during the year for a ski vacation. She rents it out to other vacationers for a total of 210 days during the year. Because she used the home less than 15 days and rented it out more than 15 days, it falls into the category of vacation home used as rental property.

EXAMPLE 2: Assume that Miranda uses her home for 21 days during the year. The home is still in this category because her personal use does not equal more than 10% of the time she rented it out: 10% × 210 rental days = 21 days, so Miranda would have to use her home for more than 21 days not to qualify.

How Will the IRS Know That Your Home Is a Vacation Home Used as a Rental?

The IRS will know whether your vacation home falls within this category because you must tell it. Line 2 of Schedule E requires you to list the actual number of days each rental property you own was occupied by renters, and the number of days it was used by you or your family for personal purposes.

2 For each rental real estate property listed, report the number of days rented at fair rental value and days with personal use. See instructions.		Fair Rental Days	Personal Use Days
	A		
	B		
	C		

Taxpayers who make little personal use of their vacation homes receive relatively favorable tax treatment. The home is treated as a rental property for tax purposes. Unlike the case with tax-free vacation homes, you must report and pay tax on your rental income. But you may deduct your rental expenses. You file Schedule E, the tax form for landlords, to report your rental income and expenses.

Deducting Expenses

How you deduct your expenses depends on whether they are direct expenses or other expenses from your rental activity.

Direct Expenses

Direct rental expenses consist of the money you spend to rent the vacation home and run your rental activity. These include fees charged by a management company you hire to handle your rental, advertising, broker's fees, listing fees, credit checks, office supplies for your rental activity, and depreciation or Section 179 expensing for office equipment you use for your rental activity (such as a computer). You can deduct the full amount of these expenses from your rental income on your Schedule E.

All Other Expenses

All other expenses are other costs you have left. These apply to the entire home, and consist of:

- real estate taxes
- mortgage interest for the vacation home
- operating expenses for the home, including repairs, maintenance, cleaning, insurance, and utilities, and
- depreciation.

You must allocate these expenses according to the amount of time the property was rented and the time it was used personally. This is based on the total number of days the property was used during the year. Expenses allocated to the rental period may be deducted on IRS Schedule E, the same as any other rental expense. In addition, you may take an itemized personal deduction for real estate taxes paid during the period of personal use. However, you can't take an itemized personal deduction on IRS Schedule A for the prorated amount of mortgage interest you paid on the days you personally used the property instead of renting it out. Reason: The property does not qualify as your residence for tax purposes. This is nondeductible personal interest. (I.R.C. § 163(h)(4)(A)(i)(II).)

EXAMPLE: Miranda's vacation home was used a total of 231 days during the year: Miranda used it for 21 days and she rented it out for 210 days. The allocation would be 21/231 for personal use and 210/231 for rental use. Converted to percentages, this comes to 9% personal use and 91% rental use. These percentages must be used to allocate Miranda's deductions. Miranda may deduct the following amounts on her Schedule E:

Expense	Amount	Deduction Percentage	Deduction Amount
Direct expenses (advertising, broker's fee)	$ 500	100%	$ 500
Real estate taxes	3,000	91	2,730
Mortgage interest	12,000	91	10,920
Operating expenses (utilities, repairs, insurance)	2,000	91	1,820
Depreciation	5,000	91	4,550
Total	$ 22,500		$ 20,520

In addition, Miranda can deduct 9% of her real estate taxes as a personal itemized deduction on her Schedule A. This is a $270 deduction; $1,980 of her expenses for the year are not deductible because these are expenses other than taxes allocated to the time she personally used the vacation home.

The Hobby Loss and Passive Loss Rules

There are two sets of tax rules that may prevent you from deducting all or part of your expenses from a vacation home used as a rental: the passive loss rules and the hobby loss rules.

Passive Loss Rules

List the rental income you receive from a vacation home used as a rental property on your Schedule E. You may deduct your rental expenses against this income. If you have expenses left over, you've incurred a loss on the property—in other words, you've spent more on your rental property than you earned on rent during the year.

EXAMPLE: Miranda had deductible rental expenses of $20,520 for her vacation home used as a rental property. She earned $16,000 in rent from the vacation house during the year. This leaves her with a $4,520 annual loss.

Vacation home owners like Miranda would like to deduct their annual losses from the income they earn during the year from other sources, such as job or investments. That way, they can lower their tax bill for the year. However, losses from vacation rentals are subject to draconian rules limiting their deductibility—these rules are called the passive loss rules. Many small landlords can avoid the rules under exceptions provided for them in the tax law, but it can be particularly difficult for owners of vacation homes to do so. See Chapter 16 for a detailed discussion of the passive loss rules.

Hobby Loss Rules

The hobby loss rules are another set of rules that apply to vacation homes used as rentals. If the IRS determines that the primary motive you have for renting your vacation home is something other than to earn a profit, it will conclude that the home is a hobby. In this event, you'll only be able to deduct your income from the home from the expenses you pay for it. These rules have the same impact as the passive loss rules, but are even worse because there are no exceptions from them if they apply. To avoid being subject to these rules, you must behave so that the IRS will believe that you want to earn a profit from your vacation home, rather than owning it just for pleasure or some other purpose not motivated by the desire for profit. See Chapter 2 for a detailed discussion on profit motive.

Vacation Home Used as Residence

The final category is for vacation home owners who rent their property 15 days or more during the year, but use it primarily as a residence. These homeowners get hammered by special vacation home tax rules. Your vacation home falls within this category if you rent it at least 15 days and it is used personally:

- more than 14 days during the year, or
- more than 10% of the number of days during the year the property is rented for a fair rental.

EXAMPLE 1: Paul owns a vacation home at Lake Tahoe. He rents it during the summer for 30 days and uses it himself for 90 days during the rest of the year. He used the property more than 14 days and more than 10% of the number of days it was rented out (10% × 30 rental days = 3 days).

EXAMPLE 2: Assume that Paul used the vacation home for 30 days, but rented it out for 330 days. He would avoid the vacation home used as residence category because his use equaled less than 10% of the number of days the property was rented (10% × 330 = 33 days).

If at all possible, you want to avoid flunking the 14-day/10% test. Keep careful track of how much time you spend at your vacation home. If you must spend more than 14 days at the home, you must rent it out enough so you can come within the 10% threshold.

You Cannot Deduct Losses

First of all, your deductions for the vacation home are limited to your rental income from the home. If your expenses exceed your income, you may not deduct the loss from other income you earn that year. The tax law says that such a loss can be carried forward to future years and deducted from your rental income from the property, if you have enough. In real life, however, this rarely happens because the property does not generate enough income. The passive loss rules and the exception to them (discussed in Chapter 16) do not apply to homes in this category.

Calculating Your Deductions

You are allowed to deduct your expenses from your rental income, but there are strict limitations designed to ensure that you don't deduct personal expenses as rental expenses. To begin with, you must deduct your expenses from your rental income in the following order:

- first, deduct your mortgage interest and real estate taxes
- next, deduct direct rental expenses—expenses that apply only to renting, such as management fees, advertising, rental fees or commissions, and credit checks
- then, you deduct your operating expenses, such as repairs, utilities, insurance, maintenance, and cleaning, and
- finally, if you have any rental income left, you deduct depreciation, as described in Chapter 5.

In addition, you must allocate all of your expenses—other than direct expenses from your rental activity—only to the extent that the property served as a rental, compared to the total time it was used during the year.

EXAMPLE: Paul uses his vacation home for 30 days during the year and rents it out for 90 days. Thus it was used a total of 120 days. Since 90 ÷ 120 = 75%, he can deduct 75% of his general expenses up to the amount of rental income he earned from the house, which was $10,000. He deducts his expenses in the following order and amounts:

| Expense | Amount | Allocation to Rental Use | | Amount Deducted This Year | Remaining Rental Income ($10,000 total) | Unused Deduction Carried Forward to Future Years |
		%	Amount			
Property tax	$ 2,000	75%	$ 1,500	$ 1,500	$ 8,500	$ 0
Mortgage interest	10,000	75	7,500	7,500	1,000	0
Direct expenses	1,000	100	1,000	1,000	0	0
Operating expenses	6,000	75	4,500	0	0	4,500
Depreciation	6,000	75	4,500	0	0	4,500
Total	$ 25,000		$19,000	$ 10,000	$ 0	$ 9,000

Paul deducts his rental income and expenses on Schedule E. Paul may also deduct 25% of his property tax and mortgage interest as a personal itemized deduction on his Schedule A. This is the amount of taxes and rent allocated to the time he personally used the vacation home. This amounts to a $3,000 deduction.

All in all, this is not a good result for Paul. He had $25,000 in expenses, but can deduct only $10,000. He has $9,000 in unused deductions he must carry forward to the next year.

One way to improve this outcome is to increase the amount of property tax and mortgage interest deducted as a personal itemized deduction on Schedule A. This way, more of your operating expenses and depreciation can be deducted from rental income. You can do this by using a different allocation formula for property taxes and interest. Instead of using the number of days the property was used during the year to figure your rental percentage, you use 365 days. This is not the way the IRS would like you to allocate these expenses, but courts have permitted it, reasoning that interest and taxes are paid for an entire year, not just when a vacation home is used. (*Bolton v. Comm'r.*, 694 F.2d 556 (9th Cir. 1982).)

EXAMPLE: If Paul used this alternate method, his allocation percentage for his tax and interest would be 25% instead of 75% (90 ÷ 365 = 25%). Thus, Paul would deduct only $500 of his property tax and $2,500 of his interest from his $10,000 in rental income. This would let him deduct an additional $5,000 in operating expenses and depreciation. He could deduct the other 75% of his taxes and interest as a $9,000 itemized deduction on his Schedule A. His Schedule E deductions would look like this:

Expense	Amount	Allocation to Rental Use %	Allocation to Rental Use Amount	Amount Deducted This Year	Remaining Rental Income ($10,000 total)	Unused Deduction Carried Forward to Future Years
Property tax	$ 2,000	25%	$ 500	$ 500	$ 9,500	$ 0
Mortgage interest	10,000	25	2,500	2,500	7,000	0
Direct expenses	1,000	100	1,000	1,000	6,000	0
Operating expenses	6,000	75	4,500	4,500	1,500	0
Depreciation	6,000	75	4,500	1,500	0	3,000
Total	$ 25,000		$13,000	$ 10,000	$ 0	$ 3,000

Another way to increase your deduction is to reduce your mortgage interest expense. Take out a home equity loan on your main home to purchase your vacation home. You can borrow up to $100,000 on your home and deduct the interest as an itemized deduction on your Schedule A. This interest expense won't count when you figure your deduction for your vacation home because the loan is on your main home, not your vacation home. This allows you to deduct more of your operating expenses and depreciation against your vacation rental income.

EXAMPLE: If Paul had taken out a $100,000 home equity loan on his main home to purchase his $160,000 vacation home, he would have reduced the annual mortgage interest on his vacation home from $10,000 to $3,500. His deductions would look like this:

Expense	Amount	Allocation to Rental Use %	Allocation to Rental Use Amount	Amount Deducted This Year	Remaining Rental Income ($10,000 total)	Unused Deduction Carried Forward to Future Years
Property tax	$ 2,000	25%	$ 500	$ 500	$ 9,500	$ 0
Mortgage interest	3,500	25	2,500	875	8,625	0
Direct expenses	1,000	100	1,000	1,000	7,625	0
Operating expenses	6,000	75	4,500	4,500	3,125	0
Depreciation	6,000	75	4,500	3,125	0	1,375
Total	$ 18,500		$13,000	$ 10,000	$ 0	$ 1,375

Calculating Personal and Rental Use

The tax category that a vacation home falls into depends on how many days during the year it is used for personal use by the owner and how many days it's rented. As you might expect, there are tax rules for determining this.

TIP

Keep track of guest stays at your vacation home. A good way to prove to the IRS how long your guests—paying and otherwise—stayed in your vacation home is to have them all sign and date a visitors' book. You can create one yourself or buy one from a stationery store.

Calculating Personal Use

A day of personal use of a vacation home is any day that it is used by:

- you or any co-owner of the property
- a member of your family or a member of the family of any co-owner (unless the family member uses the home as his or her main home and pays a fair rental price)
- anyone under an arrangement that lets you use some other home, or
- anyone at less than a fair rental price.

For these purposes, family members include your brothers and sisters, half-brothers and half-sisters, spouse, ancestors (parents, grandparents, and so on), and lineal descendants (children, grandchildren, and so on). However, renting your vacation home to your aunts, uncles, nieces, nephews, cousins, or friends does not count as personal use. If you rent your vacation home to anyone in this group of people *for a fair market price*, it is considered rental use.

The following examples were created by the IRS to help show how to determine days of personal use. (IRS Publication 527, *Residential Rental Property*.)

EXAMPLE 1: You and your neighbor are co-owners of a condominium at the beach. You rent the unit to vacationers whenever possible. The unit is not used as a main home by anyone. Your neighbor uses the unit for two weeks every year. Because your neighbor is co-owner of the unit, both of you are considered to have used the unit for personal purposes during those two weeks.

EXAMPLE 2: You own a rental property that you rent to your son. Your son has no interest in this property. He uses it as his main home. He pays you a fair rental price for the property. Your son's use of the property is not personal use by you because your son is using it as his main home, he has no interest in the property, and he is paying you a fair rental price. This rental is treated like any other normal rental.

EXAMPLE 3: You rent your beach house to Rosa. Rosa rents her house in the mountains to you. You each pay a fair rental price. You are using your house for personal purposes on the days that Rosa uses it because your house is used by Rosa under an arrangement that allows you to use her house.

EXAMPLE 4: You rent an apartment to your mother at less than a fair rental price. You are using the apartment for personal purposes on the days that your mother rents it because you rent it for less than a fair rental price.

What Is a Fair Rental Price?

The IRS doesn't provide much guidance in determining what constitutes a fair rental price. It simply says that a rent is not fair if it is substantially less than rents charged for similar properties. You should ask the following questions when comparing properties to determine if they are similar:
* Are they used for the same purpose?
* Are they approximately the same size?
* Are they in approximately the same condition?
* Do they have similar furnishings?
* Are they in similar locations?

The IRS says that, if the answer to any one of these questions is no, the properties probably are not similar.

The best way to determine a fair rental price is to obtain a written opinion from a real estate professional familiar with the vacation home rental market in the area. If you can't do this, look at rental listings for similar properties. Be sure to keep records of how you determined the fair rental price.

Days Used for Repairs and Maintenance

Any day that you spend working substantially full time repairing and maintaining your property is not counted as a day of personal use. You don't have to count such a day as a day of personal use even if family members use the property for recreation on the same day. It's a good idea to maintain and keep documentation showing that you performed repairs or maintenance on your rental, rather than using it for personal use. This can include receipts, time logs, and work reports.

> EXAMPLE: You own a cabin in the mountains that you rent during the summer. You spend three days at the cabin each May, working full time to repair anything that was damaged over the winter and to get the cabin ready for the summer. You also spend three days each September, working full time to repair any damage done by renters and getting the cabin ready for the winter. These six days do not count as days of personal use even if your family uses the cabin while you are repairing it.

You also don't need to count days you spend seeking tenants or dealing with realtors as personal days.

Deduct Your Travel Expenses

You may deduct your travel expenses when you journey to your vacation home to do repairs, maintenance, or deal with tenants or realtors. These consist of car expenses, airfare, or other transportation expenses if you don't travel by car, and meals eaten along the way. (See Chapter 11 for a detailed discussion.)

Trouble With Time-Shares

A time-share property is a vacation home that several people own together and share the use of. Ordinarily, you can rent your time-share interest, but you can forget about obtaining the favorable tax treatment given to vacation homes used as rentals discussed above. This is because personal use by any owner of a time-share is considered personal use by all of the owners—for example, if you use your time-share zero days, but the other owners use it 300 days, you have 300 days of personal use. This makes it virtually impossible for you to satisfy the fewer-than-15-days or 10%

personal use tests. Thus, a time-share you rent out will almost certainly fall within the vacation home used as residence category—the least favorable of the vacation home categories.

Calculating Rental Use

Any day you rent your vacation home at a fair market rent is a day of rental use no matter whom you rent it to, unless it's a family member who doesn't live there full time. Any day you rent your vacation home to anyone for less than a fair rental price is considered a day of personal use.

A fair rental price for your property is the amount of rent that a person who is not related to you would be willing to pay. The rent you charge is not a fair rental price if it is substantially less than the rents charged for other properties that are similar to your property.

Putting Your Calculations Together

Let's look at a comprehensive example to see how these rules operate. Dick owns a vacation home that he used himself for 14 days and rented as follows:

- two days to his brother, who paid a fair rental price, but doesn't live in the home full time
- four days to his mother, who paid nothing
- 14 days to a stranger who paid a fair market rental, and
- two days to a friend from the office who paid a below-fair-market price.

Dick's own use is personal use. The two days he rented it to his brother are also personal days because his brother doesn't live there full time. The four days his mother used the house are also personal days. The 14 days he rented it to strangers for a fair market price are rental days. The two days he let a friend use it for a below-market rental are personal days. His totals for the year are:

- Rental days = 14
- Personal days = 22.

The vacation home qualifies as a tax-free vacation home because it was used personally more than 14 days and rented less than 15 days.

This means Dick need not pay any income tax on the rental income he received. Had Dick rented it to the strangers for one more day, the house would have come within the vacation home used as residence category with very different tax results.

Converting Your Home to a Rental Property

The vacation home tax rules do not apply when you convert your main home to a rental property—that is, it is used only by renters, not shared by you and renters. Instead, you treat the home like any other rental property as described in the other chapters of this book. This means that no proration of expenses is required for the rental period, and your deductible rental expenses are not limited to your gross rental income.

This is so if:

- you rented or tried to rent the property for 12 or more consecutive months, or
- you rented or tried to rent the property for less than 12 consecutive months and the period ended because you sold the property.

EXAMPLE 1: On February 28, 2015, Mark moved out of the house he had lived in for six years because he accepted a job in another town. He rented his house at a fair rental price on April 1, signing a one-year lease with his tenant. Mark need not treat the house as a vacation home on his taxes for the year, even though both he and renters lived in it. He may deduct his operating expenses, taxes, interest, and depreciation for the period it was rented during the year.

EXAMPLE 2: On January 31, Melissa moved out of the condominium where she had lived for three years. She offered it for rent at a fair rental price beginning on February 1. She was unable to rent it until April. On September 15, she sold the condominium. Melissa need not treat the condo as a vacation home. Instead, she treats the condo as a rental for tax purposes while she offered it for rent and actually rented it. Thus, she may deduct the operating expenses, taxes, interest, and depreciation she incurred from February 1 until September 15.

Deducting Rental Losses

What Are Rental Losses? 375

Overview of the Passive Loss Rules 376

What Are the PAL Rules For? 377

How the PAL Rules Work 377

The $25,000 Offset 380

Requirements 381

Determining Your Offset Deduction 385

The Real Estate Professional Exemption 386

Real Estate Professional Test 388

Materially Participate in Rental Activity 397

Applying the Test 399

What Happens If You Qualify for the Exemption? 401

The Real Estate Professional Exemption Is Not Optional 402

Record Keeping for the Real Estate Professional Exemption 403

Rental Activities Not Subject to PAL Real Property Rental Rules 406

Rentals for Seven Days or Less 407

Rentals for 30 Days or Less 407

Vacation Homes 408

Deducting Suspended Passive Losses 409

You Must Have Passive Income 409

The $25,000 Offset 410

The Real Estate Professional Exemption 410

Profits From Sale of Property 410

Tax Reporting for Passive Rental Losses 412

Strategies for Dealing With the Passive Loss Rules 413

    Lower Your Rental Expenses 413

    Use Home Equity Loans 414

    Generate More Passive Income 414

At-Risk Rules 415

How to Deduct Rental Losses 418

    Calculating Your Net Operating Loss 418

    Carrying a Loss Back 420

    Electing to Carry Forward an NOL Instead 420

f, like many landlords, your tax deductions from your rental properties exceed your rental income, this is the single most important chapter in this book. Complex IRS rules may prevent you from deducting all or part of your rental losses from the other income you earn during the year, which could end up costing you thousands of dollars in extra taxes. However, there are also important exceptions to the rules that were created to help small landlords and others in the real estate industry.

Even if you're fortunate enough to earn a profit each year from your rentals, you still need to know about these rules and how they affect you. This chapter explains the rules in detail.

What Are Rental Losses?

You have a rental loss if all the deductions from a rental property you own exceed the annual rent and other money you receive from the property. If you own multiple properties, the annual income or losses from each property are combined (netted) to determine if you have income or loss from all your rental activities for the year. You report your rental income and deductible expenses on IRS Schedule E.

EXAMPLE: Tanya owns two rental houses. She receives $24,000 annually in rent from each house. She reports her annual expenses for the properties on Schedule E as follows:

Expense	Amount—House A	Amount—House B
Advertising	$ 100	$ 0
Auto and travel	200	200
Cleaning and maintenance	1,500	500
Insurance	2,000	1,800
Mortgage interest	10,000	7,000
Other interest	700	0
Repairs	600	1,000
Supplies	2,000	1,500
Taxes	2,400	2,000
Utilities	2,500	2,000
Depreciation	8,000	7,000
Total Expenses	$ 30,000	$ 23,000
Rents Received	$ 24,000	$ 24,000
Total Expenses	− 30,000	− 23,000
Income or (Loss)	$ (6,000)	$ 1,000

Tanya's deductible expenses for House A exceeded the $24,000 in rent she received by $6,000. So, she had a $6,000 rental loss for the year for the property. She had $1,000 of income on House B—her expenses for that property were $23,000 and she received $24,000 rent. Tanya subtracts her rental losses (the $6,000 loss on House A) from her rental income (the $1,000 profit on House B), leaving her with a $5,000 loss for the year from all her rental activities.

It is extremely common for landlords to have rental losses, especially in the first few years. Indeed, IRS statistics show that in the year 2006, over half of the filed Schedule E forms reporting rental income and expenses showed a loss. This amounted to over 5.2 million taxpayers. If you have a rental loss, you have plenty of company.

Often, you have a loss for tax purposes even if your rental income exceeds your operating expenses. This is because your depreciation deduction is included as an expense for these purposes (even though depreciation is not an operating expense—see Chapter 3 for more on operating expenses). Without the depreciation deduction, Tanya (in the above example) would have had income of $2,000 from House A, instead of a $6,000 loss.

If you have a rental loss for the year, you become subject to two sets of tax rules:

- the passive loss rules, and
- the at-risk rules.

The passive loss rules are by far the most important for most landlords, so we will discuss those rules first.

Overview of the Passive Loss Rules

Fasten your seat belts: We are about to embark on one of the most complicated, confusing, and frightening journeys a rental property owner can take—into the realm of the passive activity loss rules (PAL rules, for short). These rules can make you or break you come tax time.

RESOURCE

Need more information? The IRS has created a very useful, highly detailed guide to passive activity losses for its auditors called the *Passive Activity Loss Audit Technique Guide*. If you want more information on the passive loss rules, this is a good place to look. It's available to the public at the IRS website at www.irs.gov.

What Are the PAL Rules For?

Thirty years ago, landlords could freely deduct their rental losses from all of the other income they or their spouses earned during the year (assuming they filed a joint return). However, the unfettered deductibility of real estate losses led to enormous abuses. In the 1980s, wealthy individuals invested in real estate limited partnerships and other tax shelters created solely to generate large losses through depreciation, interest, and other deductions. The investors in these tax shelters would use the losses to offset their other income. The tax benefits obtained could far exceed the amount of money invested in the tax shelter.

All this came to an abrupt end in 1986, when Congress enacted the passive activity loss rules. (I.R.C. § 469.) These rules were designed to limit a taxpayer's ability to use rental or business losses to offset other income. The PAL rules apply to all business activities, but are particularly strict for rental real estate because real estate was the primary tax shelter.

How the PAL Rules Work

Most landlords earn income and incur expenses from more than one source—in addition to income and expenses from their rental property, they may earn a salary from a job, or make money from a business they own. They may also have investments other than rental property, such as stocks and bonds.

For purposes of the PAL rules, all the income you earn, and losses you incur, are divided into three separate categories:

- **Active income or loss.** Income or loss from any business activity, other than real estate rentals, in which you materially participate (actively manage); see "The Real Estate Professional Exemption" below for a detailed discussion of material participation. This includes salary and other income from a job, a business you run, or the money you earn from selling your personal services. Social Security benefits are included as well.

- **Passive income or loss.** Income or loss from (1) businesses in which you don't materially participate, and (2) all rental properties you own. Under the rules, income and loss from rental activities are automatically passive, whether or not the landlord materially participates in the rental activity. (Casualty losses from rental property are not passive losses—see Chapter 13.)
- **Portfolio income or loss.** Income or loss from investments, such as interest earned on savings, or dividends earned on stocks; gains or losses when investments are sold; expenses paid for investments.

Imagine three buckets, one for each of the three kinds of income or loss. Every penny you earn during the year must go into one of these three buckets. In addition, all the money you spend on investments or business activities, such as a rental real estate business, any business you actively manage, or any self-employment activity, also goes into one of the buckets. Money you spend for personal purposes, such as food and clothing, is not counted.

Active income or loss. Income or loss from your job or business activities (other than real estate rentals) in which you materially participate.

Passive income or loss. Income or loss from rental properties or businesses in which you don't materially participate.

Portfolio income or loss. Income or loss from any investments.

Here's the key to the PAL rules: The contents of the passive bucket must always stay in that bucket. You cannot use passive losses to offset income in the other two buckets. Nor can you use passive income to offset losses from the other buckets.

> EXAMPLE: Sidney is a successful doctor. This year, he has $200,000 in income from his practice and also earns $50,000 in income from investments. Sidney invests $25,000 in a real estate limited partnership tax shelter. The partnership owns several rental properties that operate at a substantial loss. At the end of the year, the partnership informs Sidney that his share of the partnership's annual operating loss is $75,000. Sidney's three buckets look like this:

Active

$200,000 medical practice income

Passive

$75,000 rental loss

Portfolio

$50,000 investment income

Sidney invested in the limited partnership because he wanted to use his share of the losses it generated to reduce his taxable income from his medical practice. However, come tax time, he's in for a shock. Because passive income or loss must stay in the passive bucket, Sidney cannot deduct his $75,000 passive loss from his medical practice income or his investment income. Because he earned no passive income during the year, he can't use his passive loss at all this year. His real estate tax shelter turned out to be useless.

This is what the PAL rules are intended to do: prevent you from deducting your passive losses (such as from rental activities) from your active or portfolio income. Thus, there is no point in investing in real estate rentals just to incur tax losses because you won't be able to use these losses to offset your other non-real-estate income.

The PAL rules have accomplished their purpose of preventing wealthy people from investing in rental real estate solely to create tax losses. But the rules apply to all owners of rental property, even landlords who are in the business of renting properties to earn a living and have no interest in obtaining tax losses. To prevent undue economic hardship on these people, special rules were created that wholly or partly exempt many small landlords and people active in the real estate industry from the PAL rules. These are:

- the $25,000 offset, and
- the real estate professional exemption.

> **SKIP AHEAD**
> **Owners of vacation homes and other short-term rentals aren't subject to the PAL rental activity rules.** If you own only these types of properties, you can skip ahead to "Vacation Homes."

The $25,000 Offset

Congress felt it was unfair to prevent landlords with moderate incomes from deducting their rental losses from their nonrental income. Thus, a special exception—the $25,000 offset—was fashioned for them. It permits landlords to deduct up to $25,000 in rental losses from any other nonpassive income they earn during the year. The offset applies to all rental properties that a landlord owns—that is, you don't get a separate $25,000 for each property you own. (I.R.C. § 469(i).)

> **EXAMPLE:** Recall Tanya from the example at the beginning of the chapter. She owned two rental houses and had a $6,000 loss from one and $1,000 in income from the other. She also has a job that pays her an $80,000 salary. In addition, Tanya earned $10,000 in dividends from stocks and incurred $1,000 in investment expenses (stockbroker commissions), leaving her with $9,000 in investment income. Her three buckets look like this:

Active	**Passive**	**Portfolio**
$80,000 income from job	$5,000 loss from rentals	$9,000 investment income

If Tanya were not a landlord, the PAL rules would bar her from deducting her passive loss from her rentals from her active or portfolio income. However, if Tanya qualifies for the $25,000 offset, which is available only for landlords, she can deduct her $5,000 loss from her nonpassive income that includes her salary and investment income.

The $25,000 offset is particularly important to small landlords. If your income isn't much over $100,000 and your annual rental losses are less than $25,000, it can give you complete relief from the onerous PAL rules.

Requirements

To qualify for the $25,000 offset, you must:
- actively participate in your rental activity
- come within the income limits, and
- be at least a 10% owner of the rental activity.

Any individual who meets these requirements may use the $25,000 offset. This is so whether he or she owns rental property alone or with one or more co-owners. General partners in partnerships that own rental property may use the exemption, but not limited partners. Nor can it be used for property owned by a corporation or trust.

Active Participation

You qualify for the $25,000 offset only if you actively participate in the running of your rental real estate. This is very easy to do. You don't have to work any set number of hours to actively participate; you simply have to be the person who makes the final decisions about approving tenants, arranging for repairs, setting rents, and other management tasks. If you manage your rentals yourself, you'll satisfy this requirement without any problem. The IRS probably won't even raise the issue if you're audited. Management tasks performed by your spouse are also counted in determining if you actively participate. (I.R.C. § 469(i)(6)(D).)

The only time you could have trouble with this requirement is if you hire a resident or nonresident manager or management company to manage your property for you. You cannot simply let the manager do everything. To actively participate, you or your spouse must exercise independent judgment, and not simply okay the actions of a manager or management company. For example, you must be the one who makes such important decisions as what the rent will be and whether to do a major repair or improvement. The manager can make recommendations about such matters, but the final decision must be yours. (S. Rep. No. 313, 99th Cong., 2d Sess. 738 (1986).)

Some management firms automatically issue letters to their clients stating that the client is "actively involved in management of the rental" and approves tenants, arranges for repairs, sets rental fees, and so on. IRS training materials advise IRS auditors to ignore such letters. Instead, if an IRS auditor questions whether you actively participate, he or she is instructed to ask to see a copy of your contract with your management company—the contract should show who has the right to make the final decisions. (Market Segment Specialization Program, *Passive Activity Losses Reference Guide*, pp. 2–7.)

Read your management contract and make sure it provides that you make the final decisions on important rental matters. It should read something like this: "Client shall make all major management decisions for the property, including final approval of all new tenants, rental rates, and repairs over $_____."

Lottery Winners Lose Out in Tax Court

Edward and Yolanda Hamilton owned rental property in Los Angeles. They incurred rental losses of $22,000 on the property in 2000. That same year, they won $136,000 in the California state lottery. While they were undoubtedly thrilled to win this money, it had some unexpected tax consequences for them. Without their lottery winnings, their MAGI was under $150,000 and they were eligible for the full $25,000 offset for their rental losses for the year. But when the IRS insisted they add their $136,000 lottery winnings to their MAGI, they were way over the $150,000 limit and became ineligible for the offset. They appealed to the tax court, claiming they shouldn't have to include the lottery winnings in their MAGI because they were not professional gamblers. The court held that they were out of luck. (*Hamilton v. Comm'r*, T.C. Memo 2004-161.)

Although a well-drafted contract will help show that you actively participate, be sure to document and keep copies of any correspondence with the management company (including emails) that establish your involvement in decision making and the management of the property.

Income (MAGI) Limits

The $25,000 offset is intended for landlords who earn moderate incomes. If your modified adjusted gross income (MAGI) is less than $100,000, you're entitled to the full $25,000 offset. It goes down as your MAGI increases, and is eliminated completely once your modified adjusted gross income exceeds $150,000. (I.R.C. § 469(i)(3).)

Your MAGI consists of all your taxable income for the year, not including taxable Social Security benefits and passive activity income or loss, minus the following expenses:

- self-employed health insurance premiums paid during the year
- contributions to SIMPLE retirement plans and Keogh retirement plans
- alimony paid during the year
- deductible tuition, fees, and student loan interest, and
- penalties for early withdrawal of savings. (I.R.C. § 469(i)(3)(F).)

For most taxpayers, their MAGI is all of their income, not counting their passive income or loss. If you get Social Security, you also deduct this amount from your income. Not being able to deduct passive losses from your MAGI can make it more difficult to fall within the $100,000 to $150,000 MAGI range.

> EXAMPLE: Ronald, a self-employed person, earned $150,000 in net income from his engineering consulting business this year and $5,000 in investment income. He also owned an apartment building that had a $25,000 loss. He can't deduct the $25,000 passive loss from the apartment building from his business or investment income. Because his MAGI is $155,000, he is not eligible for any offset.

The offset amount is $25,000 for both single and married taxpayers filing joint returns. Married people who file separate tax returns and live separately for the entire year are each entitled to a $12,500 offset.

However, married people who file separate returns and live together *any time* during the year get no offset at all. (I.R.C. § 469(i)(5)(B).)

The phaseout of the $25,000 offset works as follows. For every dollar your MAGI exceeds $100,000, you reduce your $25,000 offset by 50 cents. For example, if your MAGI is $110,000, you reduce your offset by $5,000 (50 cents × $10,000 = $5,000). In that case, you could deduct only $20,000 in passive losses for the year ($25,000 – $5,000 = $20,000). Once your MAGI is $150,000 or more, your offset disappears entirely (50 cents × $50,000 = $25,000).

There are a few ways you might be able to reduce your MAGI if it exceeds $150,000, or if you want to increase the amount of offset you are eligible for. One way is to defer some of the compensation you're owed to the following year. Another way is to make contributions to a Keogh plan, which you can deduct from your MAGI.

$25,000 Limit Applies to Tax Credits

Some rental property owners can obtain tax credits by rehabilitating their rental property or from the low-income housing tax credit. A tax credit is subtracted from your tax liability after you calculate your taxes. (See Chapter 1.) Because these credits come from your rental property, they go into your passive income or loss bucket, and are subject to the same passive loss rules as the rental property deduction. However, they get particularly favorable treatment when it comes to the $25,000 offset. You don't need to satisfy the active participation requirement to deduct these credits as part of your offset. In addition, for these credits, the phaseout of the $25,000 offset starts when your modified adjusted gross income exceeds $200,000 ($100,000 if you are a married individual filing a separate return and living apart at all times during the year). There is no phaseout of the $25,000 offset for low-income housing credits for property placed in service after 1989. But there's a catch: You can deduct these credits only to the extent you have taxable passive income for the year—no income, no credit. The credits are suspended to a future year when you have net passive income you must pay income tax on. Use IRS Form 8582-CR, *Passive Activity Credit Limitations*, to figure your allowable annual credit. (I.R.C. § 469(j)(5).)

EXAMPLE: Ronald's MAGI for the year is $155,000—he has $150,000 in net income from his engineering consulting business and $5,000 in investment income. He also has a $25,000 loss from an apartment building that he owns. Ronald makes a $15,000 contribution to his Keogh plan and tells one of his clients not to pay the $40,000 the client owes him until the following year. Ronald thereby reduces his MAGI from $155,000 to $100,000 and can now deduct the full $25,000 offset amount.

Ownership Requirement

To qualify for the offset, you must own at least 10% of all interests in your real estate activity for the entire year. If you're married, your spouse's ownership interests can be counted too. The ownership percentage is determined by the value of the property. For example, if the rental property is worth $100,000, you must own at least $10,000. If you own more than one rental building, you must own 10% or more of each building. (I.R.C. § 469(i)(6)(A).)

This rule should not pose a problem for most small landlords. However, it eliminates most owners of vacation time-shares, because a person who buys a time-share usually obtains less than a 10% interest in the property. (*Toups v. Comm'r.*, 66 T.C. Memo 370.)

If you own a condominium, you need own only 10% of the value of your particular condominium unit, not 10% of the entire building that contains many separate condominium units.

Determining Your Offset Deduction

Here's how to determine your deduction from the offset:
- First, subtract your passive activity deductions from your passive income. You should have a net loss; otherwise, you won't need the offset. For example, suppose Tess has two apartment buildings. One earned a $5,000 profit, the other had a $15,000 loss. Tess has a $10,000 passive loss for the year.

- Next, determine the amount of the offset you're eligible for. This will be $25,000 if your MAGI is $100,000 or less. Your offset will be less than $25,000 if your MAGI is $100,000 to $150,000. You get no offset at all if your MAGI is $150,000 or more. Suppose Tess's MAGI is $75,000. She qualifies for the full $25,000 offset. However, she only has $10,000 in passive losses this year, so she can't use the remaining $15,000 of the offset.
- Then, deduct the applicable amount of your offset from your active or portfolio income. Tess deducts her $10,000 passive loss from her active income, reducing it to $65,000 in taxable income for the year.

The Real Estate Professional Exemption

People in the real estate industry moaned and groaned about the passive loss rules. Because the PAL rules were intended to curtail the use of real estate tax shelters by passive investors, those actively engaged in the real estate business felt it was unfair to have the rules apply to them. Congress agreed and created a special exemption from the passive loss rules for real estate professionals. This rule provides substantially more relief than the $25,000 offset because there is no maximum offset amount or income limit requirements.

Landlords who qualify for the real estate professional exemption get extraordinary tax benefits unavailable to other people who earn income from rental property:

- First, real estate professionals can treat all of their losses from rental properties as active losses. This means they can deduct any rental activity losses they have for the year from all of their other income for the year, including active income and portfolio income. (I.R.C. § 469(c)(7).)
- Second, real estate professionals are not subject to the 3.8% Medicare tax on rental income that went into effect in 2013. This tax is imposed on all landlords with adjusted gross income over $200,000 for singles and $250,000 for married taxpayers filing jointly. Real estate professionals are specifically exempted from

the new tax, provided that they materially participate in the rental activity and such activity qualifies as a business. (See Chapter 19 for a detailed discussion of this new tax.)

These tax benefits are particularly valuable for landlords with high incomes or large rental losses. They can give real estate professionals who invest in real property a substantial financial advantage over landlords who don't qualify for them.

You don't have to be a real estate broker or developer to qualify for the real estate professional exemption. Any person who can pass the test discussed below will qualify. This includes full-time landlords and many part-time landlords as well.

Make sure the exemption applies to your type of business entity. The real estate professional exemption can be used by landlords who are individuals (including joint tenants and tenants in common), general partnerships, limited liability companies taxed like partnerships (most are), and S corporations. C corporations qualify only if 51% or more of their gross receipts come from real property businesses in which they materially participate. The exemption does not apply to limited partnerships, estates, and most types of trusts.

SKIP AHEAD

Do you have to worry about this stuff? The real estate professional exemption involves some very complex tax rules. Not every landlord needs to learn these rules. If, like many small landlords, you (or your spouse if you're married and file a joint return) work less than 750 hours at being a landlord and any other real estate activities during the year, you can skip this section. The exemption won't apply to you. On the other hand, if the $25,000 offset doesn't provide you with the relief you need from the PAL rules, you may choose to read this material to see how you can qualify for the exemption in the future. Moreover, if you want to avoid the new 3.8% tax on net investment income of higher-income taxpayers that went into effect in 2013, read this material carefully. Qualifying for the real estate professional exemption enables you to avoid this new tax.

> **CAUTION**
>
> **If you're a real estate professional—including a real estate broker, salesperson, developer, contractor, or real property manager—be sure to read this section carefully.** You may very well qualify for the exemption, and, if you do, you must take it. Unlike the $25,000 offset discussed in the previous section, the real estate professional exemption is not optional. If you qualify for it, you must apply it to your income and loss for the year. Usually this is a very good thing, but in some cases it can be costly.

There are two separate and distinct requirements to obtain the real estate professional exemption—you must:

- qualify as a real estate professional, and
- materially participate in your rental activities.

Real Estate Professional Test

To qualify as a real estate professional, you must:

- participate in one or more real property businesses
- "materially participate" in one or more of such businesses
- spend at least 51% of your annual work time at your real property business or businesses in which you materially participate, and
- spend at least 751 hours per year working at your real property businesses in which you materially participate. (I.R.C. § 469(c)(7).)

Participate in Real Property Businesses

Logically enough, to qualify as a "real estate professional," you must work at one or more real property trades or businesses during the year. You don't have to work solely as a landlord; other real estate businesses can count as well. Indeed, the more such businesses you have, the easier it can be to qualify as a real estate pro.

A real property trade or business means any real property development, redevelopment, construction, reconstruction, acquisition, conversion, rental, operation, management, leasing, or brokerage business. (I.R.C. § 469(c)(7)(C).) This covers virtually any real estate business activity. Most people who qualify for the exemption are engaged in one of the following activities:

- real estate rentals
- construction (contractor or builder)
- real estate brokerage work, or
- real property management.

You must be directly involved in one or more of these real property businesses to qualify for the exemption. Thus, for example, an attorney or accountant is not in the real property business, even if he or she advises people who are in the business. Mortgage brokers, lenders, and bankers don't qualify either, because the IRS views them as involved in the financial services industry, not real estate. (IRS Chief Counsel Advice 2015-04010.) Real estate sales agents, on the other hand, can qualify for the exemption. This is because they are usually paid on a straight commission basis which makes them independent contractors, not employees, for tax purposes. As independent contractors, they are in business and, therefore, can qualify for the exemption.

You Don't Have to Be a Licensed Broker to Be in the Brokerage Business

You don't have to be licensed by your state as a real estate broker to be in the real estate brokerage business for tax purposes. Any person who engages in one or more of the following activities is in the real estate brokerage business:

- selling, exchanging, purchasing, renting, or leasing real property
- offering to do the activities mentioned above
- negotiating the terms of real estate contracts
- listing real property for sale, lease, or exchange, or
- procuring prospective sellers, purchasers, lessors, or lessees.

It makes no difference whether a person who engaged in these activities is licensed as a real estate broker, agent, or salesperson. In one case, the tax court held that a person licensed as a real estate salesperson in California was engaged in a brokerage business for tax purposes because she sold, exchanged, leased, and rented property, and solicited listings. It made no difference that under California law a person must be licensed as a broker to be in the brokerage business. (*Agarwall v. Comm'r*, T.C. Summ. Op. 2009-29.)

If you are an employee in someone else's real property business, you do not qualify for the real estate professional exemption. You must own your own real property business or be a part owner of a business with more than a 5% ownership interest. If you work as an employee for a corporation, you must own more than 5% of your employer's outstanding stock.

Material Participation Test

You must "materially participate" in any of the real property businesses described above for the time you spend at it to count toward qualifying as a real estate professional. For example, if you're a landlord and also work as a real estate broker, you can count the brokerage activity only if you materially participate in it.

You materially participate in a business only if you are involved with its day-to-day operations on a regular, continuous, and substantial basis. (I.R.C. § 469(h).) The IRS has created several tests to determine material participation, based on the amount of time you spend working in real estate activities. You only need to pass one of the tests to show material participation. Most people use one or more of the first three tests.

500-hour test. You participated in the activity for more than 500 hours during the year. This is the most commonly used test.

Substantially-all test. You did substantially all the work in the activity during the year. To qualify for this, you will probably need to show that you worked at least 71% of the total hours devoted to the activity by all of the people involved. This includes hours spent working on the property by co-owners, employees, and independent contractors, such as property managers. If employees, subcontractors, or others also work in the real estate activity along with you, you'll need to have records showing how much time each person worked in the activity.

101-hour test. You participated in the business for more than 100 hours during the year, and you participated at least as much as any other person (including employees and independent contractors, such as property managers).

Requirements for Material Participation

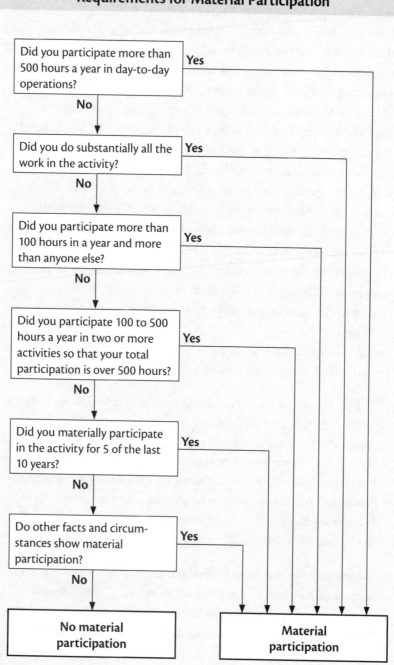

Significant participation activities test. You can use this test if you have two or more "significant participation activities" that you combine to equal 500 or more hours. A significant participation activity is real estate business activity in which (1) you spend more than 100 hours, and (2) such activity does not count as material participation under any of the other six tests—for example, you can't count an activity in which you work more than 500 hours since you materially participate in such an activity.

Past performance test. You satisfy any of the IRS tests for material participation for any five of the last ten years.

Facts and circumstances test. The facts and circumstances show that you materially participated. You can't use this test if (1) you didn't participate in the activity for at least 101 hours; (2) anyone worked more than you; or (3) anyone was paid to manage the activity. Few real estate pros have ever successfully used this test.

Any work you do for a business that you own, wholly or in part, counts as participation in the business, unless:

- the work is not customarily done by owners of that type of activity, and
- one of your main reasons for doing the work is to avoid application of the PAL rules. (IRS Reg. § 1.469-5(f)(2)(i).)

EXAMPLE: Martha has her own small real estate development company, which is co-owned by her husband, Bob. This year, business is slow. Martha figures that she'll end up spending only 500 hours working at the business for the year. To pass the 751-hour test, she hires her husband Bob to work 251 hours answering phones and doing clerical work for the development business. Unfortunately, Bob's time does not count as participation in the real estate activity because answering phones and doing clerical work is not work customarily done by the owner of a real estate development business.

In addition, you do not treat work you do in your capacity as an investor as participation in your real estate activity. This includes:

- studying and reviewing financial statements or reports on the activity's operations—including time spent reading this book!

- preparing or compiling summaries or analyses of the finances or operations of the activity for your own use, or
- monitoring the activity's finances or operations in a nonmanagerial capacity—for example, reviewing rental statements you receive from a rental management company that manages your property for you. (IRS Reg. § 1.469-5(f)(2)(ii).)

Courts have held that the time you spend organizing your personal records, preparing your taxes, paying bills, and reviewing monthly statements prepared by a real estate management company all constitute investor activities. (*Barniskis v. Comm'r.*, T.C. Memo 1999-258.) Time you spend doing these tasks cannot be counted to pass the material participation tests.

Absentee landlords who hire real property managers to do all of their work for them may have difficulty passing the material participation test. To materially participate, a landlord must be involved with the day-to-day operation of the rental property, something absentee landlords often don't do. If you live a substantial distance away from your rental property, the IRS will likely question whether you are really involved in day-to-day operations.

EXAMPLE: Josephine owns two five-unit apartment buildings in Las Vegas, but lives in Houston. She hires a real property management company to manage the properties. She is not involved with the day-to-day management of the buildings. Her involvement is limited to approving the management company's decisions. This year, she spent 50 hours dealing with her management company. She spent another 25 hours reading financial statements and otherwise dealing with her investment. Josephine has not materially participated in her rental activity. None of the time she spends reading financial statements counts as material participation. This leaves her with just 50 hours of work during the year, not enough to materially participate under any of the tests. She clearly doesn't satisfy the 500-hour or 101-hour tests. Nor does she meet the "you-did-all-the-work" test because the management company did most of the work.

If you're married, you combine the time your spouse spends materially participating in the business with your own time. This is so whether or not you and your spouse file a joint return. (IRS Reg. § 1.469-9(c)(4).) This can make it much easier to pass one of the material participation tests.

> EXAMPLE: Frank and Felicia are married and file a joint return. They own a four-unit apartment building they manage themselves. Felicia does most of the work, spending 400 hours a year dealing with tenants, showing vacant units, handling bookkeeping chores, and so forth. Frank does most of the repair work for the property, spending 120 hours a year on it. Together, Frank and Felicia spent 520 hours materially participating in their rental real estate activity—more than enough to pass the 500-hour test.

If you have multiple real estate businesses, you can group them together for purposes of the material participation tests. This way, you can combine the hours you work at them—for example, if you group two activities in which you work 300 hours per year, you'll end up with 600 hours (more than the 500 hours you need to materially participate).

IRS regulations provide that you can combine your activities for these purposes just about any way you want, so long as the result is reasonable under the circumstances. (IRS Reg. § 1.469-9(d).) One example provided by the IRS is that of an individual who owns two rental properties and a separate real property development business. He combines all three activities for purposes of the material participation rules and spends a total of 750 hours working at them during the year. Since this is more than 500 hours, he materially participated in them and qualifies as a real estate professional. (IRS Chief Counsel Memo. 201427016 (7/3/2014).)

If you own more than one rental property, you'll ordinarily want to group them all together so you can combine the hours you spend on each.

51% Test

Now that you've figured out which real property business or businesses you participated in during the year, you can apply the 51% test. This test requires that you spend more than half of your total working hours during the year working in all the real property businesses in which you materially participated. Again, be sure only to count the time at the real property business in which you materially participate. For example, if you materially participate in real estate management, but not at real estate brokerage, you can't use your brokerage hours to help pass the 51% test.

If you work full time at something other than one or more real property businesses, it will be next to impossible to pass the 51% test. For example, if you work 40 hours per week at a non-real-property business, you would have to work an average of 41 hours per week at one or more real estate activities in which you materially participate to pass the test. This would require you to put in an 81-hour week. The IRS is not likely to believe you do this unless you have extremely convincing documentation. IRS auditors are instructed to look carefully at W-2 forms when they audit taxpayers who claim the real estate professional exemption. If the W-2 shows that a taxpayer has a job not in real estate, the auditor will question whether the 51% test has been satisfied.

Fortunately, if you're married and file a joint return, it's sufficient for either spouse to pass the 51% test (and the 751-hour test discussed below). If one spouse passes both tests, both spouses are deemed to pass. Note that the same spouse must pass both tests. Thus, if you're married, you can work full time at a non-real-property business and still meet the test if your spouse spends all (or at least over half) of his or her work time managing your rental properties.

> **EXAMPLE:** Leo and Leona are married and file a joint return. Leo is a physician and doesn't spend any time working on real estate. Leona spends 100% of her annual work time managing apartment buildings the couple owns. The test is satisfied because Leona spends more than half of her time working in the real property business. If Leo spends 20% of his time managing their rental property and Leona spends 40% of her time on real property business, they will not satisfy the 51% test. To meet the 51% test, one spouse must spend at least 51% of his or her time working at a real property business—you can't combine time to reach the 51%.

If you or your spouse is involved in more than one real property business in which one of you materially participates, you can add the time you spend in each of the businesses to see if you pass the 51% test.

> EXAMPLE: John works 800 hours per year as a part-time bookkeeper. He owns rental property on which he works 100 hours per year. He also works 701 hours per year as a real estate broker. John passes the 51% test because he spent a combined 801 hours working in real estate businesses and 800 hours in other activities.

751-Hour Test

It's not enough that you (or your spouse) spend more than half of your work time in a real property business. After all, if you had no other work, you'd spend more than half your work time on real estate if you spent only one hour a year on it. To avoid this result, you or your spouse must spend at least 751 hours per year working at your real property business or businesses in which you materially participate. This amounts to only 14.5 hours a week. As with the 51% requirement, you can combine the time you spend working at multiple real estate activities in which you materially participate.

> EXAMPLE: John worked 200 hours per year on his rental properties (which was enough to materially participate in them) and 601 hours as a real estate broker. By combining both of these real estate business activities, John exceeds the 751-hour limit.

People like John, who work full or part time as a real estate broker, contractor, developer, or other real estate professional, will likely have little trouble meeting the 751-hour requirement. The people who have trouble passing this test are those whose sole real property business is managing their rentals. If you own only a few units, it's unlikely you will need to spend 751 hours per year dealing with them. (And, ironically, if you have stable, long-term tenants who place few demands on their landlord, you'll have less reason to spend time on that rental.) One real property management expert estimates that landlords who manage their rental properties themselves must spend four hours working on each unit per month. At that rate, you would need to own at least 16 rental units to work 751 hours per year.

Materially Participate in Rental Activity

If you passed the previous four tests, you qualify as a real estate professional. However, this doesn't mean you get to treat the income or loss from your real estate rentals as nonpassive. You're allowed to do so only for those rentals in which you materially participate during the year.

The material participation rules covered above apply here as well. However, the time you spend on real estate businesses other than rentals is not considered when you determine if you materially participated in your rental activity. Thus, for example, you'll materially participate in your rental activity if you (or you and your spouse together) spend more than 500 hours working at it during the year, or pass one of the other material participation tests.

Moreover, the rules for grouping your rental activities differ for this test. If you own more than one rental property, the default rule is that each one is a separate rental activity in which you must materially participate to treat it as nonpassive.

Fortunately, you don't have to stick with this default rule. You can file a statement (called an election) with your tax return stating that you want all of your rental activities grouped together as one single activity. This way, you can combine the time you spend working on each rental property to satisfy the material participation tests. If you fail to file the election, you'll have to show that you materially participated in each rental property you own to treat that property's income or loss as nonpassive. For most landlords, this is impossible to do, which makes filing a timely election very important.

> EXAMPLE: Donald Trask owned 33 rental properties in California. He combined all of his income and losses from all of the properties on one Schedule E and claimed a loss of over $27,000 for the year 2001. Trask established that he was a real estate professional—he worked full time in his rental business and spent more than 750 hours at it. However, Trask failed to file an election to treat all of his 33 rental activities as one activity. This meant he had to materially participate in each rental property. Trask admitted that he did not materially participate in any of his many rentals when viewed separately. Thus, he didn't qualify for the exemption for any of his properties. (*Trask v. Comm'r*, T.C. Memo 2010-78 (2010).)

To make an election to treat all your rental activities as one activity, you'll need to draft a statement like the one below and attach it to your tax return:

Tax Year: Taxpayer Name: _____

Taxpayer Identification Number: _____

In accordance with Regulation 1.469-9(g)(3), taxpayer states that he/she is a qualifying real estate professional, and elects under I.R.C. § 469(c)(7)(A) to treat all interests in rental real estate as a single rental real estate activity.

_____

Your Signature

Note that this election is an all or nothing proposition: You must group all of your rental properties together as a single activity, or group none of them. You can't pick or choose which properties to include. Of course, ordinarily, you'll want as many properties as possible included in your single rental activity so you can combine all the time you spend on them to pass the 500-hour or other material participation tests.

The election can be filed in any year in which you qualify for the real estate professional exemption. It only needs to be filed once—it applies automatically to all future years that you qualify for the exemption. It may be revoked only if you have a material change in circumstances. The fact that the election is less advantageous to you in a particular year is not a material change in circumstances. (IRS Reg. § 1.469-9(g).)

! CAUTION

Filing an election could cause problems if you have suspended losses. Suspended losses are unused passive losses from prior years. If you have substantial suspended losses from multiple rental properties, think carefully before filing an election to treat them as a single activity. The election could make it difficult for you to deduct your suspended losses when you sell your property.

You May Be Able to File Your Election Late

Unfortunately, many landlords, and many tax preparers, are unaware of the need to file an election to group their rental activities to qualify for the PAL exemption. Many have been treating all their rental properties as a single activity on their tax returns without filing the election. If they get audited by the IRS, their failure to file this simple piece of paper can cost them their PAL exemption and force them to give back all or part of the rental losses they claimed on their return.

Fortunately, the IRS allows real estate professionals in this situation to file a retroactive PAL election and keep their exemption. To do so, you must have filed returns consistent with a single-activity election for all the years to which the late election is to apply. You must also show the IRS that you had "reasonable cause" for the late election. Reasonable cause could be that you reasonably relied on a qualified tax professional and he or she failed to advise you to make the election. The election is made by filing Form 1040-X to amend your most recent return and attaching a statement with the required information. The amended return should show zero tax if you meet all the eligibility requirements because the return should have been filed consistently with having made a grouping election that enabled you to pass the material participation test. If you're currently under examination by the IRS, a copy of the amended return should also be filed with the examiner. For more details, see Rev. Proc. 2011-34, available at www.irs.gov/pub/irs-drop/rp-11-34.pdf.

Applying the Test

Let's take a look at a couple of examples applying the real estate professional exemption tests.

EXAMPLE 1: Max and Maxine are married and own two duplexes they rent out. They have filed an election with their tax return to treat both properties as a single rental activity for tax purposes. Max works full time (1,800 hours per year) as an accountant. Maxine is a licensed real estate agent. She spends

2,000 hours per year working in this real property business. Max and Maxine both work at managing their rental property. This doesn't take much time. Max spent 70 hours this year, and Maxine 80 hours.

- Do they participate in one or more real property businesses? Yes. Maxine works as an agent and they both work at being landlords.
- Do they "materially participate" in one or more of such businesses? Yes. Maxine spent 2,000 hours working at real estate brokerage—more than enough to materially participate under the more-than-500-hour test. Together, the couple spent 150 hours managing their rental property. This is far too little for the 500-hour material participation test; but they qualify under the 101-hour test because no one else worked on their rentals as much as they did.
- Did one person spend at least 51% of their annual work time at a real property business in which they materially participated? Yes. Max can't pass the test. He spent almost all his time working at accounting. But Maxine passes the test because she spent 100% of her time working on real property activities.
- Did one person spend at least 751 hours per year working at a real property business they materially participated in? Yes. Maxine easily passes—she put in a whopping 2,080 hours on real property activities. Since Maxine passes the 51% and 751-hour tests, both Max and Maxine are deemed to pass.
- Did they materially participate in their rental activities? Yes. Together the couple materially participated in their duplexes because they spent 150 hours managing them during the year.

Max and Maxine may treat as nonpassive any income or loss from their rental activity for the year. Thus, if they incur a loss, they may deduct it from other income they earn, such as Max's accountant income. If they earn a profit, it won't be subject to the Net Investment Income tax.

EXAMPLE 2: Bill is a retired teacher who owns a small apartment building. He spent 600 hours managing the building this year, and worked at no other activity. His wife does not work and is not involved with the rental.

- Do they participate in one or more real property businesses? Yes. Bill worked at being a landlord.

- Do they "materially participate" in one or more of such businesses? Yes. Bill spent 600 hours managing his rental—more than enough to materially participate under the 501-hour test.
- Did one person spend at least 51% of their annual work time at a real property business in which they materially participated?
  Yes. Bill easily satisfies this test because he worked at no non-real-estate activities.
- Did one person spend at least 751 hours per year working at a real property business they materially participated? No. Bill had to spend at least 751 hours working at real property activities to qualify for the exemption. He fails the test because he spent only 600 hours working at his rental.

Bill does not qualify for the exemption. Had he been able to spend an additional 151 hours working at his rental activity, he would have passed the 751 test. Alternatively, he (or his wife) could have worked at least 501 hours per year at some other real estate activity, such as selling real estate, and combined those hours with his rental activity hours to satisfy the 751-hour threshold. Had he done either, he could have treated his rental activity as nonpassive because he materially participated in it by working over 500 hours per year at it.

What Happens If You Qualify for the Exemption?

You must determine anew each year whether you qualify for the real estate professional exemption by applying the three tests discussed above. Any year you qualify, the income and loss from your rental property no longer goes into the passive bucket. It is now nonpassive income or loss. Any loss you have from the property may be deducted from your active or portfolio income, but not from any passive income. Likewise, any income from the property may be placed in the active or portfolio buckets and you can use it to offset any losses in those buckets. However, you may not use the exemption to reduce your income for the year to below zero—that is, to create a net operating loss for the year (see "Overview of the Passive Loss Rules," above).

Now, suppose you incurred passive losses from the property in previous years that you weren't able to deduct because you didn't qualify for the exemption or couldn't use the $25,000 offset. These unused passive losses are called suspended passive losses. They remain passive losses—they stay in your passive bucket. However, you may deduct them from income from your now-exempt rental property income. You can also deduct them from passive income in your passive bucket for the current year, or if you sell the exempt rental property (see "Deducting Suspended Passive Losses," below). Because they're in your passive bucket, you can't deduct these suspended losses from your active or portfolio income. (I.R.C. § 469(f)(1)(C).)

> **EXAMPLE:** Jill owns an apartment building. She has $20,000 of rental income in one year. For the first time, she qualifies for the real estate professional exemption. Jill has $10,000 in suspended rental losses from the property from prior years when she did not qualify for the exemption. She may deduct her $10,000 in suspended losses from her rental property income. This leaves her with $10,000 in rental income for the year.

The Real Estate Professional Exemption Is Not Optional

Usually, qualifying for the real estate professional exemption is highly beneficial taxwise. Indeed, real estate professionals who qualify can have a huge financial advantage over those who aren't so lucky, because they can deduct all their rental losses from any nonpassive income.

However, qualifying for the exemption will not benefit you if you have substantial passive income from non-real-estate rental businesses. This is because you can't use your rental losses to offset such passive income. It's left to sit and you can't deduct it until a future year, when you have enough passive losses. If you don't have enough losses, it could sit forever.

> **EXAMPLE:** This year, Felix earns $20,000 in passive income from two limited partnerships. His rental properties have a $20,000 loss. Unfortunately for Felix, he qualifies for the real estate broker exemption from the passive loss rules. This means he must treat the $20,000 in rental losses as nonpassive loss. As a result, he may not deduct it from his $20,000 in passive income.

Unfortunately for people like Felix, the real estate professional exemption is mandatory, not optional. If you qualify, you are not allowed to deduct your losses from your exempt rental real property from passive income. The only way to avoid this is to make sure you don't qualify for the exemption. This is not hard to do—for example, you can hire a management company to manage your rentals for you so you will not materially participate in them. Or, you could just make sure you work less than 751 hours per year in real estate activities.

> EXAMPLE: Assume that Felix makes sure he does not qualify for the real estate professional exemption by working less than 751 hours in real estate this year. Now, his $20,000 in rental losses is passive. He may deduct this amount from his $20,000 in passive income from limited partnerships, leaving him with zero passive income to pay tax on.

Record Keeping for the Real Estate Professional Exemption

To know whether you qualify for the real estate professional exemption, you must know how many hours you (and your spouse, if you're married) spent during the year working in (1) real estate businesses of all kinds, (2) rental real estate activities, and (3) all non-real-estate work activities.

If the IRS audits you, you'll need good records of your annual work hours to preserve your real estate professional exemption. Under IRS regulations, you may use any "reasonable means" to keep track of your work time, including daily time reports, logs, appointment books, calendars, or narrative summaries. (IRS Reg. § 1.469-5T(f)(4).) The regulations don't require you to keep contemporaneous records—that is, records made at or near the time you did the work involved—but it is a good practice to do so.

CAUTION

You're an IRS target. The real estate professional exemption has been receiving much attention from the IRS lately. Tax pros report that many of their real estate professional clients are being audited on this issue. This attention is likely to increase in future years because even more landlords seek to qualify for the real estate professional exemption in order to avoid the Net Investment Income tax (see Chapter 19). The best way to protect yourself from the IRS is to keep adequate records.

Many taxpayers keep few or no records of their time. When they get audited, they sit down and write a narrative summary of work they did during the year, with estimates of the time they spent; or they rely on their oral testimony. This is a good way to lose your exemption.

> **EXAMPLE:** Judy Bailey kept a daily calendar for 1997 that listed the number of visits she made to her many rental properties, but the calendar did not quantify the number of hours that she spent on her rental activities. When the IRS audited Judy, she wrote a summary report, in which she generally explained the activities she performed at the rental properties and estimated the number of hours she spent on each rental property. Both the IRS and tax court found this summary to be inadequate. The court noted that Bailey's estimates were uncorroborated by any other evidence. She assigned hours to activities years after the fact, based solely on her judgment and experience as to how much time the activities must have taken her. The court concluded, therefore, that the summary was an unreliable "ballpark guesstimate." Bailey lost her exemption. (*Bailey v. Comm'r.*, T.C. Memo 2001-296.)

You should learn from Judy Bailey's mistakes. Keep careful track of the actual number of hours you (and your spouse) spend working on each activity during the year. You can note your time on a calendar, appointment book, log, or timesheet. It doesn't matter, as long as your records are accurate and believable. Get in the habit of initialing and dating tenant files, financial records, contracts, applications, and other documents you review. This will help document your participation.

If you work a regular job, you should have no problem keeping track of those hours. If you work about the same number of hours each week, you can even dispense with a calendar or other record of this time. Make every effort, however, to keep close track of the time you spend on real estate business activities. Remember, to qualify for the exemption, you'll have to show that you spent at least 51% of your time on real estate activities, and that these activities amounted to at least 751 hours.

Get into the habit of writing down the time you perform *any task* related to a real estate activity. This includes, of course, all the time you spend working on your rental properties. For example, you should include the time you spend:

- showing the property for rental
- taking tenant applications
- screening tenants (including ordering credit reports and evaluating them, and calling references)
- preparing and negotiating leases and other rental agreements
- cleaning and preparing units for rent, including "initiation" time you spend welcoming the tenant to the property and explaining your policies
- doing repairs yourself
- doing improvements yourself or arranging for others to do them
- hiring and supervising a resident manager
- purchasing supplies and materials for your rental business
- inspecting the property
- responding to tenant complaints and inquiries
- collecting and depositing rents
- evicting tenants
- writing and placing advertisements
- creating and maintaining a website you use to promote your rentals
- attending seminars or other educational events on how to manage rental property, such as educational events sponsored by your local landlord's association
- time spent attending landlord association meetings, and
- traveling for any of the activities listed above.

According to the IRS, time you spend traveling to look for new rental properties to purchase cannot be included in your rental activity hours because it is an investment activity. Moreover, the IRS also claims that time spent with real property managers does not count either.

Landlord Claimed There Were More Than 24 Hours in a Day

Alexander Firsow owned a rental property in a Maryland fishing area. To prove he was entitled to the real estate professional exemption, he prepared a computer spreadsheet for the IRS examiner showing that he had worked on the rental 606 hours in 1999 and 494 hours in 2000. Even though Firsow used a computer to prepare the spreadsheet, the IRS auditor denied the exemption, and the case went to tax court. The court noted that Firsow spent no more than two weeks per year at the rental property, performing maintenance work, but also fishing off the pier. There are only 336 hours in 14 days, so Firsow couldn't have spent more than that much time on his rental even if he had worked 24 hours a day. In effect, Firsow claimed that there were far more than 24 hours in a day! Needless to say, the court held that Firsow was not entitled to the exemption. (*Firsow v. Comm'r.*, T.C. Summary Opinion 2004-112.)

If you buy or sell a rental property during the year, keep track of the time involved as well—for example, finding the property, negotiating the purchase, arranging for financing, dealing with escrow, and so forth.

If you have a real estate business other than rentals, keep track of that time as well. For example, if you're a real estate broker, track the time you spend showing properties, marketing your services, and dealing with buyers and sellers.

Rental Activities Not Subject to PAL Real Property Rental Rules

Under the PAL rules, all rental activities are automatically deemed passive activities. Thus, all the income or loss you receive from them is passive income or loss unless you qualify for the real estate professional exemption. However, some types of short-term rental activities do not meet the definition of a rental activity for purposes of the passive loss rules. The income or loss you receive from them is not automatically passive.

Instead, income or loss from these activities is subject to the same test as any other nonrental business income or loss to determine which bucket it falls into—passive or active. Under the rules described above, income or loss from a nonrental business is active only if the owner materially participates in the business. You apply the same material participation rules discussed in "The Real Estate Professional Exemption," above.

Because these short-term rentals are not rental activities for purposes of the PAL rules, you can't use the $25,000 offset or the real property professional exemption. There are no similar exemptions from the PAL rules for activities that don't constitute rental real estate activities.

Rentals for Seven Days or Less

The PAL real property rental rules don't apply if you rent your property for an average period of seven days or less during the year. (IRS Reg. § 1.469-1T(e)(3)(ii)(A).) The average period is figured by dividing the total number of days the property was rented during the year by the number of separate rentals. This exception ordinarily applies to hotels and motels. It can also apply to vacation homes (see below). Time spent managing such properties cannot be counted for the 751-hour test to be a real estate professional. (IRS Reg. § 1.469-1T(e)(3)(ii); *Bailey v. Comm'r.*, T.C. Sum. Op. 2011-22.)

Rentals for 30 Days or Less

The PAL real property rental rules also don't apply if the average period of customer use is 30 days or less and significant personal services are provided with the rentals. A hotel with maid service, for example, would not be treated as a rental activity as long as the average rental period does not exceed 30 days. (IRS Reg. § 1.469-1T(e)(3)(iv).)

Significant services do not include services commonly provided for high-grade residential rentals, such as repairs, cleaning, maintenance, trash removal, elevators, security, or cable television. (IRS Reg. § 1.469-1T(e)(3)(iv)(B)(3).)

Vacation Homes

Many people own second homes that they use as both vacation homes and rental property. How does the tax code treat a vacation home or second home for tax purposes? It depends on how much you and your family use the home and how much you rent it out. (See Chapter 15.) If you use it less than 15 days or no more than 10% of the time you rent it out, the home is treated as a rental property for tax purposes. If your average rental period is more than seven days, the rental property passive loss rules covered in this chapter apply. If your average rental is seven days or less, it won't come under the rental property PAL rules—thus, it won't automatically be a passive activity.

> **EXAMPLE:** Glenda rented her Santa Barbara vacation home for a total of 35 days in one year. She rented the property five separate times, so she rented her house for seven days or less (35 ÷ 5 = 7). The house does not fall within the rental property PAL rules.

If the rental activity PAL rules do not apply to your second home because you rent it out on average for seven days or less, you may be losing a valuable tax advantage. You won't be able to obtain the $25,000 passive loss offset or the real estate professional exemption. In addition, you are then subject to the passive loss rules for nonrental business activities (assuming your vacation home rental qualifies as a business). This means you'll only be able to treat the income you earn, or loss you incur, from the home as active income or loss if you materially participate in its operation. This can be hard to do for a vacation home, especially if a real property management company manages it for you.

> **EXAMPLE:** Charles Akers owned a cabin in California. He hired a real property management company to rent out and take care of the cabin in return for 35% of the rent it earned. During 2004, the cabin was rented three times for a total of nine days—thus the average rental period was three days. Akers visited the cabin with his family a total of 27 times that same year. Akers listed over $20,000 in rental losses on Schedule E that he attempted to deduct from his other income. The IRS disallowed the deduction and the tax court agreed. Because Akers rented the cabin for an average period of

less than seven days, it did not qualify as a rental activity and Akers could not use the $25,000 offset. This meant that Akers could deduct the loss from his other active income only if he materially participated in the rental activity. The tax court found that Akers had not materially participated in the rental activity. Akers could not show that he participated more than 100 hours in the activity during the year, nor could he show that his participation exceeded that of anyone else. Since Akers didn't materially participate, his loss from the cabin was passive and could not be deducted from his other active income. (*Akers v. Comm'r.*, T.C. Memo 2010-85.)

If you are unable to deduct losses from a vacation home because of the passive loss rules, it may be desirable, taxwise, to make additional use of the home so that it is treated as residential property. Such vacation homes are not subject to any passive loss rules. Instead, special vacation home tax rules apply. These permit you to treat much of your mortgage interest as a tax deductible personal interest expense. (See Chapter 15.)

Deducting Suspended Passive Losses

Rental property passive losses you aren't allowed to deduct the year they are incurred are called suspended passive losses. They are not lost. Rather, they are carried forward indefinitely until either of two things happen: you have rental income, or you sell the property.

You Must Have Passive Income

You can deduct your suspended losses in any year in which you earn enough passive income. Because they are passive losses, they can't be deducted from your active or portfolio income.

> EXAMPLE: Joe has $10,000 in suspended passive losses from prior years. This year, he had $25,000 in income from his rental properties, and only $20,000 in deductions. Thus, he has $5,000 in passive income for the year. He may deduct his prior suspended losses from this income, leaving him no rental income to pay tax on for the year. He also earned $80,000 in salary from his job, but he can't deduct his suspended losses from this active income. He must carry forward his remaining $5,000 in suspended losses to future years.

The $25,000 Offset

Suspended losses may also be deducted by using the $25,000 offset. You can do this for any suspended loss from a property in which you actively participated during the year the loss was incurred.

> EXAMPLE: Tom had a $10,000 loss from his rental activities this year. He has $15,000 in suspended losses from the last two years (in both years, he actively participated in his rental activity). Because he qualifies for the $25,000 offset this year, he may deduct his $10,000 passive loss from this year and his $15,000 suspended losses from prior years.

The Real Estate Professional Exemption

If you qualify for the real estate professional exemption to the PAL rules, you may deduct your suspended losses from income you earn from the property.

Profits From Sale of Property

Finally, you may deduct your suspended passive losses from the profit you earn when you sell your rental property. To deduct your suspended losses upon sale, you must:
- sell "substantially all" of your interest in the rental activity
- sell to an unrelated party—that is, a person other than your spouse, brothers, sisters, ancestors (parents, grandparents), lineal descendants (children, grandchildren), or a corporation or partnership in which you own more than 50% (100% of your ownership interest), and
- the sale must be a taxable event—that is, you must recognize income or loss for tax purposes; this means tax-deferred Section 1031 exchanges don't count, except to the extent you recognize any taxable income. (I.R.C. § 469(g).)

To deduct your suspended losses from your profit, you must sell substantially all of your rental activity. If you own only one rental property, that property is your entire rental activity. If you own two or more properties, each property will be a separate rental activity unless you elected to group them together. As discussed above, such grouping can help you satisfy the material participation requirement if you want to qualify for the real estate professional exemption from the PAL rules. But it can lead to problems when you sell only one of your grouped properties and try to deduct any suspended losses you have for the property.

> EXAMPLE: Connie buys three rental houses in 2000. By 2004, she has $20,000 in suspended losses for each house. She decides she's had enough of the PAL rules and qualifies for the real estate professional exemption by becoming a real estate sales agent. To meet the material participation requirements, she elects in 2004 to treat all three houses as one rental activity. In 2015, she sells one of the houses. She cannot deduct her $20,000 in suspended losses because she has not sold substantially all her rental activity—the activity consists of three houses, and she has sold only one. Had Connie not elected to group her three houses into one activity, each one would be its own rental activity and she could deduct her suspended losses when she sold each one.

It's not entirely clear how much of your activity you must sell to sell substantially all of it—for example, if you own three properties must you sell all three or will two do? If you're presented with this problem, consult a tax professional.

If you meet the requirements for deducting profits from a sale, deduct your suspended losses in the following order:

- first, against income the passive rental activity earned during the year and any gain from its sale
- then, against net income earned during the year from all other passive activities, and lastly
- from any other income—that is, income from nonpassive activities (active and portfolio income). (I.R.C. § 469(g)(1).)

> **EXAMPLE:** Jason owns a rental house from which he has $60,000 in suspended losses. This year, Jason received $5,000 in income from the house, which was passive income. He also earned $90,000 in salary for the year, and $5,000 in passive income from a limited partnership interest he owns. Jason sells his house for a $30,000 profit. He deducts his $60,000 in suspended losses as follows:
>
> First, against the $5,000 passive income he earned from the house and his $30,000 profit from its sale. This leaves $25,000 in suspended losses ($60,000 − $35,000 = $25,000); next, against the income from his other passive activities—this is the $5,000 income he had from his limited partnership interest. This leaves $20,000 in suspended losses; and finally, from his $90,000 salary income, reducing his taxable income to $70,000 for the year.

As you can see from the example, if you have enough suspended losses, you may be able to deduct them from nonpassive income, such as salary income, that you earned during the year you sold your rental property.

Tax Reporting for Passive Rental Losses

The IRS wants to know if you have rental losses. They designed Schedule E to show them. The form requires you to separately deduct your expenses from your income for each rental property you own. The form will show if you have net income or loss for each rental property.

You may also have to complete IRS Form 8582, *Passive Activity Loss Limitations*. This complex tax form requires you to list your current and suspended losses for each rental property, and any other passive activities you are engaged in. You then go through several calculations to figure your deductible passive loss for the year, and the amount of passive loss you must carry forward to future years.

If you qualify for the $25,000 offset, you may not have to file Form 8582. This permits you to deduct up to $25,000 in passive losses from rental property, but your adjusted gross income (modified by some special rules) must be below $150,000. If, like most small landlords, you qualify for the offset, you don't need to file Form 8582 so long as:

- your rental real estate activities were your only passive activities
- you have no suspended losses or tax credits from prior years for your rentals
- your total losses from your rentals were not more than $25,000
- your modified adjusted gross income was not more than $100,000, and
- you don't own any rental real estate as a limited partner.

Thus, before you go to the trouble of filling out Form 8582, determine if you qualify for the $25,000 offset and meet the above requirements.

Strategies for Dealing With the Passive Loss Rules

If you are unable to get full relief from the PAL rules through the $25,000 offset and/or real estate professional exemption, there are some things you can do to limit their impact.

Lower Your Rental Expenses

The PAL rules bar you from deducting your rental expenses from non-passive income—income from your rental properties or other passive activities. If you don't have enough passive income to deduct all your losses, you can reduce your losses by lowering your expenses. For example, you could:

- pay less mortgage interest on your rental properties by borrowing less money—make a larger down payment when you buy the property or pay down your mortgage. (If you have substantial investments that generate portfolio income, such as stocks and bonds, you could sell them and use the money for this purpose.)
- spend less on repairs and other operating expenses, or
- defer expenses to future years when you might have more passive income.

Use Home Equity Loans

You can borrow up to $100,000 in home equity loans on your main residence and deduct the interest as a personal interest expense on your Schedule A. This is not a rental expense, thus it does not go on your Schedule E. This means the interest is not subject to the PAL rules. You can use the home equity loan to purchase a rental property, pay down an existing mortgage on a rental, or to pay for improvements, repairs, or operating expenses.

Generate More Passive Income

Generate more passive income to soak up your passive losses. There are two ways to do this:

- invest in a rental property or other business that produces passive income (only businesses in which you don't materially participate produce passive income), or
- sell your rental property or another passive activity you own, such as a limited partnership interest.

> CAUTION
>
> **Passive income may be subject to Net Investment Income tax.** If you have passive losses, passive income is a great thing to have. However, passive income can be too much of a good thing. If your passive income exceeds your passive losses, you'll have to add it to your taxable income for the year. It will be subject not only to regular income tax, but to the new 3.8% Net Investment Income tax if your adjusted gross income exceeds $200,000 if you're single and $250,000 if you're married and filing jointly. (See Chapter 19.)

Some investments are especially designed to produce passive income to soak up passive losses—these are called passive income generators—PIGs for short. Limited partnerships that invest in real estate that generates substantial annual income, such as conference centers, golf courses, and ski resorts, often fall into this category. Such PIGs are syndicated—that is, they're offered to the public through public offerings—and are actively marketed by brokers. If you're interested in investing in a PIG, you'll have no trouble finding out about them from stockbrokers, financial planners, financial publications, or the Internet. Of course, you should be careful when making any investment.

One way you cannot generate more passive income to absorb your rental income is to rent to a business you own or materially participate in. Under the "self-rental rule," such income is recharacterized as nonpassive and can't be used to offset real estate rental losses. (*Beecher v. Comm'r.*, 481 F.3d 717 (9th Cir. 2007); Treas. Reg. 1.469-2(f)(6).)

> EXAMPLE: Gary and Dolores Beecher are a married couple who owned two corporations engaged in the business of repairing automobile interiors and exteriors. They also owned five rental properties that resulted in substantial annual losses. The Beechers had a great idea: because they worked out of their home, they would lease their home office to their corporation. They would use this lease income—ordinarily, passive income—to offset the losses from their rentals. As a result of this combination of income and losses, the Beechers paid no tax on the rental income paid to them by their corporations—this amounted to over $85,000 of tax-free income over three years. Unfortunately, the IRS audited the Beechers and recharacterized their rental income from their corporations as active, not passive, income. Thus, it could not be used to offset their rental losses. Under the self-rental rule, income from the rental of property for use in a trade or business in which the taxpayer materially participates is treated as nonpassive income. The courts upheld the IRS's ruling.

At-Risk Rules

There is yet another set of rules, in addition to the passive loss rules, that may limit your deductions for your rental real estate losses. These are the at-risk rules. Fortunately, these rules aren't nearly as complicated as the PAL rules and they don't apply to most landlords. You usually don't have to worry about the at-risk rules unless you obtain seller financing or a loan from a relative at unusually favorable terms. The rules don't apply at all to rental property placed in service before 1987.

To prevent abusive tax shelters, the at-risk rules limit your annual deductible losses to the amount of money that you have at risk. At risk has nothing to do with insurance, and having insurance will not render you not at risk. At risk means how much money you could lose if a business activity goes belly-up. You are at risk to the extent of your investment in the activity.

In the case of rental real estate activities, you are at risk for:

- the total amount of cash you invest—for example, your cash down payment to purchase a rental property
- the adjusted basis of property you contribute to the activity, and
- most loans you obtain to purchase or otherwise operate your rental activity. (I.R.C. § 465.)

Most landlords borrow money to purchase their rental properties, and it is these borrowed funds that make up the great bulk of their at-risk amounts. You may include in your at-risk amount the amount of any type of loan you use for your real estate activity, except for nonrecourse loans from:

- the seller of the property or a person related to the seller
- a person who is related to you and gives you a loan at below-market rates or with other unusually favorable terms, or
- a person who receives a fee due to your investment in the real property or a person related to that person—for example, a real estate broker.

A nonrecourse loan is a loan for which you are not personally liable. The lender's only recourse if you fail to pay is to foreclose on the property and take over ownership. The mortgage document for a nonrecourse loan will contain an exculpatory clause providing that the borrower is not personally liable for the loan. A loan is a recourse loan if you are personally liable if it is not repaid on time—that is, the lender can not only foreclose on the property, but also obtain a deficiency judgment against you for the difference between the property's value at foreclosure and the amount you owe. With this deficiency judgment in hand, the lender can then go after your personal assets, such as your personal bank accounts.

However, you may include in your at-risk amount nonrecourse loans you obtain from banks, savings and loans, and other companies in the business of making real estate loans, or loans obtained from or guaranteed by the government. What all this means is that you may include all your borrowed funds in your at-risk amount unless you obtain seller financing or get a below-market nonrecourse loan from a relative. A person is related to you for these purposes if he or she is your spouse, brother, sister, ancestor (parent, grandparents), or lineal descendant (child or grandchild).

EXAMPLE 1: Stuart buys a rental home by making a $20,000 down payment and borrowing $180,000 from a bank. He is at risk for $200,000. This year, he loses $10,000 on the property. This is far less than his at-risk amount, so it doesn't affect his ability to deduct the loss.

EXAMPLE 2: Assume that, instead of using conventional financing as in the example above, Stuart purchases his home using creative financing. He gives the seller $1,000 cash and a car with an adjusted basis of $4,000. He borrows the remaining $195,000 from the seller, agreeing to a nonrecourse loan. Now, Stuart is at risk for only $5,000, because the $195,000 loan is not included in his at-risk amount. If he loses $10,000 on his property this year, he may only deduct $5,000. The remaining $5,000 loss is suspended and must be carried over to a future year when he has a sufficient amount at risk.

The at-risk rules are applied before the passive loss rules. So, Stuart in the example above, would be left with a $5,000 passive loss. He would then determine if he could deduct this loss by applying the PAL rules and exceptions discussed above.

If the at-risk rules prevent you from deducting a loss, you'll have to fill out IRS Form 6198, *At-Risk Limitations*.

If you purchase a rental property with seller financing, you need to carefully consider the effect of the at-risk rules. You might consider avoiding or limiting their application by obtaining at least some conventional financing, or by borrowing less by making a larger down payment.

How to Deduct Rental Losses

If, after applying the PAL rules and at-risk rules discussed above, you have a deductible loss from your real estate rentals, transfer it from your Schedule E to the first page of your IRS Form 1040. Use the loss to reduce the taxable income you report on your Form 1040 for the year. If you have other losses, you can deduct those losses from your income for the year as well. Other losses could include:

- casualty losses (see Chapter 13)
- deductible losses from other businesses you're involved in other than real estate, and
- losses incurred when you sell or otherwise dispose of rental or business property.

Calculating Your Net Operating Loss

If your total losses for the year exceed all your annual income from whatever source, you have a net operating loss (NOL, for short). Figuring the amount of an NOL is not as simple as deducting your losses from your annual income. Instead, you start with your adjusted gross income on your tax return for the year reduced by your itemized deductions or standard deduction (but not your personal exemption). This must be a negative number, or you won't have any NOL for the year. Your adjusted gross income already includes all the deductions you have for your losses. You then add back to this amount any nonbusiness deductions you have that exceed your nonbusiness income. These include the standard deduction or itemized deductions, deduction for the personal exemption, nonbusiness capital losses, IRA contributions, and charitable contributions. If the result is still a negative number, you have an NOL for the year. Schedule A of IRS Form 1045, *Application for Tentative Refund,* may be used to calculate an NOL.

EXAMPLE: Glenn Johnson owns several rental properties. He is single and has the following income and deductions on his Form 1040 for the year:

Income:

Wages from part-time job	$ 12,000
Interest on savings	1,425
Total income	$ 13,425

Deductions:

Net loss from rental business (gross income of $67,000 minus expenses of $87,000)	$ 20,000
Standard deduction	5,000
Personal exemption	3,200
Total deductions	$ 28,200

Glenn's deductions exceed his income by $14,775 ($28,200 – $13,425 = $14,775). However, to figure whether he has an NOL, certain deductions are not allowed. He uses Schedule A (Form 1045) to figure his NOL. The following items are not allowed on Schedule A (Form 1045):

Nonbusiness deductions (standard deduction, $5,000) minus nonbusiness income (interest, $1,425)	$ 3,575
Deduction for personal exemption	+ 3,200
Total adjustments to net loss	$ 6,775

Glenn's NOL is figured as follows:

Glenn's NOL before adjustment	$ 14,775
Reduced by disallowed items	– 6,775
Glenn's NOL	$ 8,000

Although it may not be pleasant to lose money over an entire year, an NOL has some important tax benefits: You can use it to reduce your taxes for prior or future years. Let's see how that works.

Carrying a Loss Back

Under the IRS's default rules, you must first apply an NOL to reduce your tax liability for previous years. This is called carrying back an NOL. When you do this, the IRS gives you a refund for all or part of the taxes you paid in those years. Ordinarily, an NOL is carried back to the previous two tax years. However, NOLs due to casualty losses in presidentially declared disaster areas occurring in 2008, 2009, or 2010 may be carried back up to five years by landlords in business.

To carry back an NOL, you file an amended tax return deducting the NOL from the income you reported in the prior years, and the IRS will send you a refund of all or part of the taxes you paid for one or both of those years, depending on the size of the NOL and your income for those years. You must first carry the entire NOL to the earliest carryback year. If your NOL is not used up, you can carry the rest to the next closest carryback year.

If you still have part of your NOL left, you then use it to reduce your income in future years—this is called carrying forward an NOL. You can carry forward an NOL for up to 20 years after the NOL year. You start by carrying it to the first tax year after the NOL year. If you do not use it up, you carry the unused part to the next year. You continue to carry any unused part of the NOL forward until the NOL is used up or you complete the 20-year carryforward period.

There are two ways to claim a refund for prior years' taxes from an NOL. You can file IRS Form 1040-X, *Amended U.S. Individual Income Tax Return*, within three years, or you can seek a quicker refund by filing IRS Form 1045, *Application for Tentative Refund*. If you file Form 1045, the IRS must send your refund within 90 days. However, you must file Form 1045 within one year after the end of the year in which the NOL arose.

Electing to Carry Forward an NOL Instead

Instead of carrying back an NOL as described above, you can elect to carry it forward to future years. Some people do this because they are afraid they'll get audited if they carry an NOL back and receive a refund of taxes they've already paid. You may also want to carry an NOL forward if you expect your income to rise substantially in future years and want to use your NOL in the future, when you'll be subject to a higher tax rate.

To make this choice, you must attach a statement to your original return filed by the due date (including extensions) for the NOL year. This statement must show that you are choosing to waive the carryback period under Section 172(b)(3) of the Internal Revenue Code. Write "Filed pursuant to Section 301.9100-2" at the top of the statement. File the amended return at the same address you used for your original return.

Filed pursuant to Section 301.9100-2

Tax Year: _____ Taxpayer Name: _____

Taxpayer Identification Number: _____

Taxpayer elects to waive the carryback period under I.R.C. § 173(b)(3).

_____
Your Signature

If you filed your return on time but did not file the statement with it, you must file the statement with an amended return for the NOL year within six months of the due date of your original return (excluding extensions). If you do not file this statement on time, you cannot waive the carryback period.

RESOURCE

Need to know more about NOLs? Refer to IRS Publication 536, *Net Operating Losses (NOLs) for Individuals, Estates, and Trusts,* for more information. You can download it from the IRS website at www.irs.gov, or obtain a paper copy by calling the IRS at 800-TAX-FORM.

Record Keeping and Accounting

What Records Do You Need? 424

    Paper Versus Electronic Records 425

    Create Your Own Spreadsheet 425

    Software 425

A Simple Record-Keeping System 427

    An Easy Filing System 428

    Separate Checkbook and Credit Cards 428

    Dealing With Receipts, Canceled Checks, and
        Other Supporting Documents 430

    Expense Journal 435

    Rental Income Journal 439

    Asset Records 441

    Records Required for Local Travel 445

    Records Required for Long-Distance Travel, Meals,
        Entertainment, and Gifts 449

    How Long to Keep Records 452

    When You Don't Have Proper Tax Records 453

Accounting Methods 454

    Cash Method 455

    Accrual Method 457

Tax Years 459

Your deductions for your rental activities are only as good as the records you keep to back them up. Any deduction you forget to claim on your tax return, or lose after an IRS audit because you lack adequate records, costs you dearly. Every $100 in unclaimed deductions costs the average midlevel-income landlord (in a 25% tax bracket) $25 in additional federal income taxes. This chapter shows you how to document your expenditures and other deductions so you won't end up paying more tax than you have to.

What Records Do You Need?

If, like most small landlords, you haven't formed a separate business entity to own your property and have no employees, you need just two types of records for tax purposes:

- a record of your rental income and expenses, and
- supporting documents for your income and expenses.

You need records of your income and expenses to figure out whether your rental activity earned a taxable profit or incurred a deductible loss during the year. You'll also have to summarize your rental income and expenses for each rental property in your tax return (IRS Schedule E).

You need receipts and other supporting documents, such as credit card records and canceled checks, to serve as insurance in case you're audited by the IRS. These supporting documents enable you to prove to the IRS that your claimed expenses are genuine. Some expenses—travel and entertainment, for example—require particularly stringent documentation. Without this paper trail, you'll lose valuable deductions in the event of an audit. Remember, if you're audited, it's up to you to prove that your deductions are legitimate.

If you own more than one rental property, you must separately keep track of your income and expenses for each property—don't mix them together. One reason for this inconvenient rule is that the IRS requires that you separately list your income and expenses for each property on your Schedule E. Also, you'll never know how much money you're making or losing on each property unless you separately track your income and expenses.

Paper Versus Electronic Records

The first choice you need to make is whether to keep paper records you create by hand or to use computerized electronic record keeping. Either method is acceptable to the IRS.

Although it may seem old-fashioned, many small landlord owners keep their records by hand on paper, especially when they are first starting out. You can use a columnar pad, notebook paper, or blank ledger books. There are also "one-write systems" that allow you to write checks and keep track of expenses simultaneously. Go to your local stationery store and you'll find what you need.

Manual bookkeeping may take a bit more time than using a computer, but it has the advantage of simplicity. You'll always be better off using handwritten ledger sheets, which are easy to create and understand and simple to keep up to date, instead of a complicated computer program that you don't understand or use properly.

If you want to use electronic record keeping, there are many options to choose from. These range from simple checkbook programs to sophisticated property management software. We won't discuss how to use these programs in detail. You'll need to read the manual or tutorial that comes with the program you choose. However, if you're not prepared to invest the time to use a computer program correctly, don't use it!

Create Your Own Spreadsheet

You can create your own spreadsheet to keep track of your expenses and income with a program such as *Excel*. Use one spreadsheet per rental and then total them all at the end of the year. See the discussion on how to track business expenses to see what you should include in your spreadsheet.

Software

There are different software options you can use to help you track your finances. Before getting one, make sure you understand what it offers and how you would use it. You don't want to get something too advanced if a simpler program will do because the more advanced programs can be harder to use and understand. Try to find the one that best suits your needs.

Personal Finance Software

A personal finance program such as *Quicken* may be perfectly adequate for a landlord with just a few units. These programs are easy to use because they work off of a computerized checkbook. When you buy something for your rental, you write a check using the program. It automatically inputs the data into a computerized check register, and you print out the check using your computer (payments can also be made online). You'll have to input credit card and cash payments separately.

You create a list of expense categories just like you do when you create a ledger sheet or spreadsheet. Programs like *Quicken* come with preselected categories, but these are not adequate for landlords, so you'll probably have to create your own. The expense category is automatically noted in your register when you write a check.

The program can then take this information and automatically create income and expense reports—that is, it will show you the amounts you've spent or earned for each category. This serves the same purpose as the expense journal. It can also create profit and loss statements.

Small Business Accounting Software

Small business accounting programs such as *QuickBooks* by Intuit can do everything personal financial software can do and much more, including create bills, reconcile bank accounts, generate sophisticated reports, create budgets, track employee time, calculate payroll withholding, and generate and maintain fixed asset records.

These programs are more expensive than personal finance software and are harder to learn to use. If you don't need their advanced features, there is no reason to use one of them. A list and comparison of most available accounting software packages and online subscription services can be found at http://en.wikipedia.org/wiki/Comparison_of_accounting_software.

Property Management Software

There are many software applications designed specifically for rental property management including *Quicken Rental Property Manager, Buildium, Yardi*, and *VMS*. These can be particularly helpful if you own more than ten units. These applications have features designed specifically with landlords in mind. For example, they can:

- identify tax-deductible rental property expenses
- track income and expenses by property
- create a Schedule E report to save you time on taxes
- show which rents have been paid
- show how rental properties are doing, and
- store lease terms, rental rates, and security deposits for each tenant.

If you're interested, you should visit the websites for these applications, try a demo, and see if you need and like their advanced features.

Special Concerns When You Hire Employees

If you have employees—such as a resident manager—you must create and keep a number of records, including payroll tax records, withholding records, and employment tax returns. And you must keep these records for four years.

For detailed information, see IRS Publication 15, Circular E, *Employer's Tax Guide*. You can get a free copy by calling the IRS at 800-TAX-FORM, by calling or visiting your local IRS office, or by downloading it from the IRS website at www.irs.gov. Also, contact your state tax agency for your state's requirements. A list of all 50 state tax agency websites can be found at www.taxsites.com/state.html.

A Simple Record-Keeping System

Here's a simple record-keeping system you can use if you own only a few rental units. You can implement it entirely by hand, or combine it with software applications such as spreadsheets.

An Easy Filing System

You will need to establish a system to deal with all your receipts, canceled checks, credit card statements, income and expense journals, and other records. Here's one way to do this:

- Each year, get a separate accordion folder for each rental property you own and label it with the name of the property—for example, 123 Main Street. This folder will contain your records for all your rental units at a single address. (If you wish, you can use a filing cabinet instead of an accordion folder.)
- Place several manila folders in the accordion folder: one for each expense category you have and one folder for your asset records.
- Once a month, file your receipts in the proper manila folders in chronological order—do this at the same time you complete your expense journal. If a receipt applies to more than one property, make copies to file with your receipts for each property.
- Keep your canceled checks for your rental checking account and credit card statements for your rental credit card together in chronological order. Use a separate accordion folder for this with files for each month of the year.
- Keep your income and expense journals and depreciation worksheet in your accordion folder for the appropriate property.
- At the end of the calendar year, safely store your accordion folders to use when you (or your accountant) prepare your tax returns. Make sure it contains all your receipts, income and expense journals, depreciation worksheet, car mileage records, listed property journal, appointment book or calendar, and any other records you'll need to prepare your tax returns.
- Get a new accordion folder and create a new set of records for the new year. (The folders are a tax deductible supplies expense.)

Separate Checkbook and Credit Cards

One of the first things you should do (if you haven't done it already) is set up a separate checking account for your rental activity. Your rental checkbook will serve as your basic source of information for recording your rental expenses and income. Deposit all of your rental income into the account and make rental-related payments by check from the account. Don't use your rental account to pay for personal expenses or your personal account to pay for rental activity items.

Using a separate account will provide these important benefits:

- It will be much easier for you to keep track of your rental income and expenses if you pay them from a separate account.
- Your rental account will clearly separate your personal and rental activity finances; this will prove very helpful if the IRS audits you.
- Your rental account will help convince the IRS that your rental is a for-profit activity. People with not-for-profit activities don't generally have separate bank accounts to fund their pursuits. (See Chapter 2 for more on establishing your tax status.)

> **CAUTION**
> **Some states require landlords to use a separate account for tenants' security deposits.** Check your state's laws, available online at www.nolo.com and in *Every Landlord's Legal Guide*, by Marcia Stewart, Ralph Warner, and Janet Portman (Nolo). If your state requires a separate account, you may need to establish two accounts for your business—one for general rental activity, and one for security deposits.

Setting Up Your Bank Account

You don't have to open your rental checking account at the same bank where you have your personal checking account. Shop around and open your account with the bank that offers you the best services at the lowest price.

When You Write Checks

If you already keep an accurate, updated personal checkbook, do the same for your rental activity checkbook. If, however, you tend to be lax in keeping up your checkbook (as many of us are), you're going to have to change your habits. Now that you're a landlord, you can't afford this kind of carelessness. Unless you write large numbers of rental activity checks, maintaining your checkbook won't take much time.

When you write rental activity checks, you may have to make some extra notations besides the date, number, amount of the check, and the name of the person or company to which the check is written. If the purpose of the payment is not clear from the name of the payee, describe the rental reason for the check—for example, the equipment or service you purchased.

You can use the register that comes with your checkbook and write in all this information manually, or you can use a computerized register. Either way works fine as long as the information is complete and up to date.

Don't Write Checks for Cash

Avoid writing checks payable to cash, because this makes it hard to tell whether you spent the money for a rental purpose. Writing cash checks might lead to questions from the IRS if you're audited. If you must write a check for cash to pay a rental expense, be sure to include the receipt for the cash payment in your records.

Use a Separate Credit Card for Rental Activity Expenses

Use a separate credit card for rental activity expenses instead of putting both personal and rental items on one card. Credit card interest for rental activity purchases is 100% deductible, while interest for personal purchases is not deductible at all (see Chapter 7). Using a separate card for rental-related purchases will make it much easier for you to keep track of how much interest you've paid for such purchases. If you have more than one personal credit card, you can use one for your rental activity only—you don't need to get a special business credit card.

Dealing With Receipts, Canceled Checks, and Other Supporting Documents

The IRS lives by the maxim "Figures lie and liars figure." It knows very well that you can claim anything in your books and on your tax returns, because you create or complete them yourself. For this reason, the IRS requires that you have documents to support the deductions you claim on your tax return. In the absence of a supporting document, an IRS auditor may conclude that an item you claim as a rental activity expense is really a personal expense, or that you never bought the item at all. Either way, your deduction will be disallowed or reduced.

The supporting documents you need depend on the type of deduction. However, at a minimum, every deduction should be supported by documentation showing:

- what you purchased for your rental activity
- how much you paid for it, and
- whom (or what company) you bought it from.

Make Digital Copies of Your Receipts

According to an old Chinese proverb, the palest ink is more reliable than the most retentive memory. However, when it comes to receipts, ink is no longer so reliable. Receipts printed on thermal paper (as most are) fade over time. By the time the IRS audits your return, you may find that all or most of the paper receipts you've carefully retained in your files are unreadable.

Because of the fading problem, you should photocopy your receipts if you intend to rely on hard copies. Obviously, this is time consuming and annoying. But there is an easier alternative: Make digital copies of your receipts and throw away the hard copies.

Making a digital copy of a receipt used to require a scanner, which could be cumbersome and inconvenient. This is no longer necessary. If you have an iPhone or other smartphone with a camera, you can use that to take digital photographs of receipts. Because you are likely to have your phone with you anyway, this is easy and convenient. After a business dinner, simply make a digital copy of your receipt and then throw it away. You don't have to worry about losing it or storing it.

There are many inexpensive smartphone applications you can use to copy and keep track of receipts. Two of the most popular are Shoeboxed. com and Expensify.com. Using these and other similar apps, you can add notes and then upload the digital photos to an online account for permanent storage. These apps can even automatically categorize your expenses, and you can export your data to *QuickBooks, Quicken, Excel, Freshbooks,* and other accounting software.

You must meet additional record-keeping requirements for local transportation, travel, entertainment, meal, and gift deductions, as well as for certain long-term assets that you buy for your rental activity. (These rules are covered below.)

You can meet the basic requirements by keeping the following types of documentation:

- canceled checks
- sales receipts
- account statements
- credit card sales slips
- invoices, and
- petty cash slips for small cash payments (these are preprinted receipts that say you paid in cash; you can get them at any stationery store).

Canceled Check + Receipt = Proof of Deduction

We're about to disabuse you of a commonly held belief—that a canceled check will prove that you purchased the item it paid for, especially if you note on the check (or on your register) what the check was for. For example, suppose Manny owns three rental houses. He buys a $500 snowblower to use at his rental properties from the local home supply store. He writes a check for the amount and gets a receipt. How does he prove to the IRS that he has a $500 rental expense?

Manny assumes that if he saves his canceled check when it's returned from his bank, that's all the proof he needs. He's wrong. All a canceled check proves is that he spent money for something. It doesn't prove what he bought. Of course, Manny can write a note on his check describing what he purchased, but why should the IRS believe what he writes on his checks himself?

MANNY FARBER	2345
123 SHADY LANE	
ANYTOWN, IL 12345	Date Feb. 2, 20xx 12-34/5780

Pay to the order of The Acme Home Supply Store $ 500.00

Five hundred and no cents ———————————— Dollars

Piggy Bank
100 Main Street
Anytown, IL 12345

Memo Snowblower   Manny Farber

⑈ 578000358⑈ 5355‖05556‖05555 ‖⑈

Does Manny's sales receipt prove that he bought his snowblower for his rental activity? Again, no. A sales receipt proves only that somebody purchased the item listed in the receipt. It does not show who purchased it. You could write a note on the receipt stating that you bought the item, but you could easily lie. Indeed, for all the IRS knows, you could hang around stores and pick up receipts people throw away to give yourself tax deductions.

Acme Home Supply Store 4546 Main Street Anytown, IL 12345							**509257**	
CUSTOMER'S ORDER NO. 14601			DATE February 1, 20xx					
NAME								
ADDRESS								
CITY, STATE, ZIP								
SOLD BY SF	CASH	C.O.D.	CHARGE	ON ACCT.	MDSE. RETD.	PAID OUT		
QUAN.		DESCRIPTION			PRICE	AMOUNT		
1	1	Snow Blower 500			500	500		
2								
3								
4								
5								
6								
7								
8								
9								
10								
11					Total	500		
12								
RECEIVED BY								
		KEEP THIS SLIP FOR REFERENCE						

However, when you put a canceled check together with a sales receipt (or an invoice, a cash register tape, or a similar document), you have concrete proof that you purchased the item listed in the receipt. The check proves that you bought something, and the receipt proves what that something is.

This doesn't necessarily prove that you bought the item for your rental, but it's a good start. Often, the face of a receipt, sales slip, or the payee's name on your canceled check will strongly indicate that the item you purchased was for your rental activity. But if it's not clear, note the purpose of the purchase on the document. Such a note is not proof of how you used the item, but it will be helpful. For some types of items that you use for both rental and personal purposes—computers are one example—you might be required to keep careful records of your use. (See "Asset Records," below, for the stricter rules that apply to these types of expenses.)

Credit Cards

Using a credit card is a great way to pay rental expenses. The credit card slip will prove that you bought the item listed on the slip. You'll also have a monthly statement to back up your credit card slips.

Account Statements

Sometimes, you'll need to use an account statement to prove an expense. Some banks no longer return canceled checks, or you may pay for something with an ATM card or another electronic funds transfer method. Moreover, you may not always have a credit card slip when you pay by credit card—for example, when you buy an item over the Internet. In these situations, the IRS will accept an account statement as proof that you purchased the item. The chart below shows what type of information you need on an account statement.

Proving Payments With Bank Statements	
If payment is by:	**The statement must show:**
Check	Check number Amount Payee's name Date the check amount was posted to the account by the bank
Electronic funds transfer	Amount transferred Payee's name Date the amount transferred was posted to the account by the bank
Credit card	Amount charged Payee's name Transaction date

Filing Your Receipts

If you pay an expense with a check, note the check number on the receipt. If you pay by credit card, mark it with the code CC. If you own multiple rental properties, indicate which property the receipt is for by marking it with a code. Make up any code that makes sense to you—for example, "Main St." You don't need to note the unit number, even if a check was for an expense for a specific unit. If a receipt applies to all your properties, say so on it (and make duplicates to place in each property's folder). File your receipts by expense category.

Expense Journal

You need to keep track of what you spend on your rental properties. Track your expenses by creating an expense journal—a listing of all your expenses by category. This will show what you buy for your rental activity and how much you spent. It's very easy to do this. You can write your journal out on paper, or you can set up a computer spreadsheet program, such as *Excel*, to do it. Or, if you already have or would prefer to use a financial computer program such as *Quicken*, you can do that instead. You can also use programs especially designed for landlords, such as *Quicken Rental Property Manager* or *Buildium*.

Creating an Expense Journal

You can easily create an expense journal by using paper divided into columns, or by using a professional multicolumn book you can get from any stationery or office supply store. These multicolumn pages are also called ledger sheets. Get ledger sheets with at least 14 columns. Devote a separate column to each major category of expense you have. Alternatively, you can purchase accounting record books with the rental expense categories already printed on them.

Your rental expense categories in your expense journal should be keyed to the categories on IRS Schedule E, the tax form you file to report your rental expenses and income. This is how the IRS wants you to categorize your expenses when you report them on your taxes, so you should use these categories in your records. This way, you simply transfer the totals from your records to your Schedule E when you do your taxes.

Schedule E lists 13 expense categories:
- advertising
- auto and travel
- cleaning and maintenance
- commissions
- insurance
- legal and other professional fees
- management fees
- mortgage interest paid to banks
- other interest
- repairs
- supplies
- taxes, and
- utilities.

The ins and outs of Schedule E are discussed in Chapter 18. Refer to that chapter if you need more information about these categories. You may not need to use all of these categories—for example, if you manage your rentals by yourself, you probably don't need the management fees or commissions categories.

The Schedule E categories probably include most of your expenses, but you may have others that are not listed—for example:
- home office expenses
- gifts
- homeowners' association dues for rental condominiums and planned-unit developments
- start-up expenses
- entertainment expenses
- telephone or voice mail expenses
- employee expenses
- education expenses
- casualty losses, and
- equipment rental.

You should also have one final category called "miscellaneous" for occasional expenses that don't fit any existing category. However, don't use a miscellaneous category on your Schedule E—it's not allowed. You

Allocating Expenses Among Multiple Properties

If you own more than one rental property, some of the items you buy will benefit more than just one property. Good examples are tools and office supplies you use for all your properties, or legal, accounting, or other professional services that apply to all your properties. In this event, you'll have to allocate the expense among your properties. The IRS does not require that you use any particular method to do this. But whatever method you use must be reasonable and used consistently.

One allocation method is simply to divide the expense involved equally among your properties. This makes sense where the properties generate about the same rental income each year.

For example, suppose Stuart owns three rental houses. He pays $300 for a new lawn mower he will use for all three houses. He allocates $100 of the cost to each rental house.

If your rental properties vary greatly in size, a more reasonable way to allocate expenses is by the gross income they generate. For instance, suppose Marjorie owns a rental house, a duplex, and a four-unit apartment building. She allocates expenses for all the properties according to the monthly rental income she receives from each one, as follows:

House	$1,000
Duplex	2,000
Apartments	4,000
Total	$7,000

She determines an allocation percentage for each property by dividing its monthly rental by the total rental income she receives.

House	$1,000 ÷ $7,000	=	14%
Duplex	$2,000 ÷ $7,000	=	29%
Apartments	$4,000 ÷ $7,000	=	57%

She pays $300 for a lawn mower she will use for all the properties. She allocates the cost as follows:

House	14% × $300	=	$42
Duplex	29% × $300	=	$87
Apartments	57% × $300	=	$171

must have a descriptive category for each expense; you can't claim an expense as miscellaneous.

Don't list your depreciation expenses in your expense journal. These belong in your separate asset records.

You won't need a category for your car expenses unless you use the actual expense method to figure your deduction.

Now, sit down with your bills and receipts and sort them into categorized piles to determine which categories you need in your expense journal. In separate columns, list the check number, date, and name of the person or company paid for each transaction. If you pay by credit card or check, indicate it in the check number column.

Once a month, go through your check register, credit card slips, receipts, and other expense records and record the required information for each transaction. Also, total the amounts for each category when you come to the end of the page and keep a running total of what you've spent for each category for the year to date. After recording the expense, you should file the receipts, checks, and so on in the appropriate manila folder.

The following example shows a page from an expense journal for the month of May.

Rental Expense Journal—1000 Main St.

Date	Check No.	Transaction	Amount	Adver-tising	Cleaning and main-tenance	Insurance
5/1	123	Acme Mortgage Co.	1,000			
5/3	124	Empire Plumbing Co.	200			
5/7	125	Bill's Gardening Service	80		80	
5/10	VISA	Daily Eagle Newspaper	50	50		
5/15	VISA	Gardening World	75			
5/18	126	Gloria Gonzalez	50		50	
5/23	127	County Tax Assessor	400			
5/30	128	Acme Insurance Co.	500			500
		Total this page	2,355	50	130	500
		Total year to date	8,750	100	450	1,000

continued below

Legal and other professional fees	Mortgage interest paid to banks	Other interest	Repairs	Supplies	Taxes	Travel	Miscellaneous
	1,000						
			200				
				75			
					400		
0	1,000	0	200	75	400	0	0
500	5,000	100	900	300	400	500	0

Rental Income Journal

Of course, you must also keep track of how much money you earn from your rentals and report it to the IRS on your Schedule E. This will primarily consist of the rent you collect. But it could also include:

- fees you charge tenants for paying rent late
- garage or other parking charges
- interest you earn on tenant security deposits
- security deposits you retain to pay for repairs, unpaid rent, or other expenses
- laundry income
- the value of services tenants provide in lieu of rent, or
- payments tenants make to you for repairs or other expenses. (See Chapter 4.)

Any interest you earn on your tenants' security deposits is also rental income, unless state or local law requires you to repay it to your tenants on a yearly basis or when they move out.

Interest you earn on your rental checking account, if any, is not rental income. It is personal interest. Do not include it in your rental income on Schedule E.

As with your rental expenses, you can keep track of your rental income manually by using ledger sheets. You may also use computer spreadsheets, accounting programs like *Quicken*, or programs specially designed for landlords.

Whatever method you use, you must keep separate track of the income you earn for each rental property you own. Thus, you'll have separate ledger sheets, spreadsheets, or computer listings for each property.

Here is an example of an income journal for the month of May, created using ledger sheets. The rental property is a four-unit apartment building.

May Rental Income—123 Main St.

Unit #	Rent	Laundry	Garage	Late fees	Interest	Other	Total income
1	1,000		50			100	1,150
						(payment for broken window-pane)	
2	900		50				950
3	1,100			25			1,125
4	1,150						1,150
All Units		160			17		177
Total this page	4,150	160	100	25	17	100	4,552
Total year to date	20,750	800	500	65	72	250	22,437

Asset Records

You need a separate set of records for your long-term assets. These consist primarily of your rental building or buildings, but they also include property such as computers and office furniture, appliances you separately depreciate, and real property improvements. Such long-term property is ordinarily depreciated over several years, not deducted in a single year as are operating expenses. Depreciation is covered in detail in Chapter 5.

When you purchase any property with a useful life of more than one year, you must keep records to verify:

- when and how you acquired the asset
- the purchase price
- how you used the asset
- the cost of any improvements—for example, adding a new roof to a rental building
- Section 179 deductions taken (see Chapter 5)
- deductions taken for depreciation
- when and how you disposed of the asset
- the selling price, and
- expenses of the sale.

You should create a depreciation worksheet showing this information for all your long-term assets, and update it each year. The instructions to IRS Form 4562, *Depreciation and Amortization*, contain a blank worksheet. You can also use a spreadsheet or computer accounting program such as *QuickBooks*. You don't need to file the worksheet with your tax returns, but it will provide you with all the information you need to claim your depreciation deductions on your taxes. And you will need it if you are audited.

> EXAMPLE: Jack purchased a rental house for $145,000 in 2014. He elected to use segmented depreciation in which he separately depreciated the building, land improvements, and personal property in the house. (See Chapter 5 for a detailed discussion of depreciation.)
>
> In April 2015, he added a new roof to the house. Later that year, Jack purchased a lawn mower and computer for his rental business, which he elected to deduct in a single year using Section 179. The chart below shows his 2015 depreciation worksheet.

Depreciation Worksheet

Description of Property	Date Placed in Service	Cost or Other Basis	Business/Invest-ment Use %	Section 179 Deduction
House—building	1/14	$111,250	100%	0
House—land improvements	1/14	5,000	100%	0
House—personal property	1/14	6,000	100%	0
Subtotal—2014 Property				
House—new roof	4/15	10,000	100%	0
Subtotal—2015 Property				
Lawn mower	6/15	500	100%	500
Computer	8/15	2,000	100%	2,000
Subtotal—2015 Property				
Grand Total—2015				$2,500

continued below

continued from above

Depreciation Prior Years	Basis for Depreciation	Depreciation Method/Convention	Recovery Period	Rate or Table %	Depreciation Deduction
$7,922	$111,240	SL/MM	27.5	3.636%	$4,045
725	5,000	150DB/HY	15	8.550%	427
3,120	6,000	200DB/HY	5	19.200%	1,152
					5,624
257	10,000	SL/MM	27.5	3.636%	364
					364
0	0				0
0	0				0
					0
					$5,988

Abbreviations Used for Depreciation Methods and Conventions	
Straight-Line Depreciation	SL
150% Declining-Balance Depreciation	150DB
200% Declining-Balance Depreciation	200DB
Mid-Month Convention	MM
Half-Year Convention	HY
Mid-Quarter Convention	MQ

Listed Property

The IRS is especially interested in certain kinds of property that taxpayers can easily use personally—yet claim that they purchased for their business. To minimize the chances of abuse, the IRS separates these properties into a list—which is called listed property. Listed property gets extra scrutiny and has special documentation requirements. Listed property includes:

- cars, boats, airplanes, motorcycles, and other vehicles
- computers, and
- any other property generally used for entertainment, recreation, or amusement—for example, cameras and camcorders.

Keep an appointment book, logbook, rental diary, or calendar showing the dates, times, and reasons for which the property is used—both for rental and personal purchases. You also can purchase logbooks for this purpose at stationery or office supply stores.

EXAMPLE: Bill purchases a computer he uses 50% for rental business and 50% to play games. He must keep a log showing his rental use of the computer. Below is a sample from one week in his log.

Usage Log for Personal Computer

Date	Time of Rental Activity Use	Reason for Use	Time of Personal Use
5/1	2 hours	Rental bookkeeping	
5/2			1 hour
5/3	1 hour	Rental bookkeeping	
5/4			2 hours

You usually have to document your use of listed property even if you use it only for your rental activity. However, there is an exception to this rule for computers: If you use a computer or computer peripheral (such as a printer) only for your rental activity and keep it at your office, you need not comply with the record-keeping requirement. This includes computers that you keep at your home office if the office qualifies for the home office deduction.

> **EXAMPLE:** John owns four rental properties and uses his home office exclusively for his rental activities. The office qualifies for the home office deduction. He buys a $2,000 computer for his office and uses it exclusively for his rental activities. He does not have to keep records showing how he uses the computer.

This exception applies only to computers and computer peripheral equipment. It doesn't apply to other items such as calculators, copiers, fax machines, or typewriters.

Asset Files

You should establish an asset file where you keep all your records supporting your depreciation deductions. This doesn't have to be anything fancy. An accordion file will work fine. Make a separate file for each rental property you own.

Keep your real property closing statements and any documentation showing the cost of the land, such as appraisals and property tax statements.

File your receipts for each long-term asset you purchase, as well as canceled checks or credit card statements proving how much you paid. It's particularly important to keep receipts for real property improvements, because these will affect the tax basis of your real property. (See Chapter 5.)

You need not file any of these supporting documents with your tax returns, but you must have them available in case the IRS audits you and questions your depreciation deductions.

Records Required for Local Travel

If you use a car or other vehicle for rental business purposes, you're entitled to take a deduction for gas and other auto expenses. You can either deduct the actual cost of your gas and other expenses, or take the standard rate deduction based on the number of rental miles you drive.

Either way, you must keep a record of:

- your mileage
- the dates of your rental business trips
- the places you drove for rental business, and
- the rental business purpose for your trips.

The last three items are relatively easy to keep track of. You can record the information in your appointment book, calendar, or day planner. Or, you can record it in a mileage log.

Calculating your mileage takes more work. The IRS wants to know the total number of miles you drove during the year for rental business, commuting, and personal driving other than commuting. Commuting is travel between home and your office or other principal place where you conduct your rental activity. If you work from a home office, you'll have no commuting mileage. Personal miles include, for example, trips to the grocery store, personal vacations, or visits to friends or relatives.

To keep track of your business driving, you can use either a paper mileage logbook that you keep in your car or an electronic application. Logbooks are available in any stationery store; there are dozens of apps that you can use to record your mileage with an iPhone or similar device. Whichever you choose, there are several ways to keep track of your mileage; some are easy and some are a bit more complicated.

52-Week Mileage Book

The hardest way to track your mileage—and the way the IRS would like you to do it—is to keep track of every mile you drive every day, 52 weeks a year, using a mileage logbook or rental diary. This means you'll list every trip you take, whether for rental or personal reasons. If you enjoy record keeping, go ahead and use this method. But there are easier ways.

Tracking Rental Mileage

An easier way to keep track of your mileage is to record your mileage only when you use your car for your rental activity. If you record your mileage with an electronic app, check the manual to see how to implement this system. If you use a paper mileage logbook, here's what to do:

- obtain a mileage logbook and keep it in your car with a pen attached
- note your odometer reading in the logbook at the beginning and end of every year that you use the car for rental purposes. (If you don't know your January 1 odometer reading for this year, you might be able to estimate it by looking at auto repair receipts that note your mileage.)
- record your mileage and note the rental purpose for the trip every time you use your car for rental purposes, and
- add up your rental activity mileage when you get to the end of each page in the logbook. (This way, you'll only have to add the page totals at the end of the year instead of all the individual entries.)

Here's an example of a portion of a page from a mileage logbook.

Date	Destination	Rental Purpose	Mileage at Beginning of Trip	Mileage at End of Trip	Rental Miles	User's Name
5/1	Acme Hardware store, Fresno	Purchase supplies	50,000	50,020	20	Jack S.
5/10	123 Main St., Fresno	Inspect rental property	50,100	50,175	75	Jack S.
5/20	123 Main St., Fresno	Repair rental property	50,500	50,575	75	Jack S.
5/30	Lawyer's office, 666 1st St., Stockton	Consult with lawyer re: eviction	51,000	51,050	50	Jack S.

At the end of the year, your logbook will show the total rental activity miles you drove during the year. Calculate the total miles you drove during the year by subtracting your January 1 odometer reading from your December 31 reading.

If you use the actual expense method, you must also calculate your percentage of rental use of the car. Do this by dividing your rental miles by your total miles.

> EXAMPLE: Yolanda owns six rental properties over 100 miles apart. At the beginning of the year her odometer reading was 34,201 miles. On December 31, it was 58,907 miles. Her total mileage for the year was therefore 24,706. She recorded 31 rental trips in her mileage logbook for a total of 4,140 miles. Her rental use percentage of her car is 17% (4,140 ÷ 24,706 = 16.7%).

Sampling Method

The sampling method is the easiest way to track your mileage. Under this method, you keep track of your rental mileage for a sample portion of the year and use your figures for that period to extrapolate your rental mileage for the whole year.

This method assumes that you drive about the same amount for rental purposes throughout the year. To back up this assumption, you must scrupulously keep an appointment book showing your rental activity appointments all year long. If you don't want to keep an appointment book, don't use the sampling method.

Your sample period must be at least 90 days—for example, the first three months of the year. Alternatively, you may sample one week each month—for example, the first week of every month. You don't have to use the first three months of the year or the first week of every month; you could use any other three-month period or the second, third, or fourth week of every month. Use whatever works best for you—you want your sample period to be as representative as possible of the rental travel you do throughout the year.

You must keep track of the total miles you drove during the year by taking odometer readings on January 1 and December 31 and deduct any atypical mileage before applying your sample results.

EXAMPLE: Tom, the owner of three apartment buildings he manages himself, uses the sample method to compute his mileage by keeping track of his rental miles for the first three months of the year. He drove 7,000 miles during that time, and had 1,000 rental activity miles. His rental use percentage of his car was 14%. From his January 1 and December 31 odometer readings, Tom knows he drove a total of 27,000 miles during the year. However, Tom drove to the Grand Canyon for vacation, so he deducts this 1,000-mile trip from his total. This leaves him with 26,000 total miles for the year. To calculate his total rental miles, he multiplies the yearlong total by the rental use percentage of his car: 14% × 26,000 = 3,640. Tom claims 3,640 rental activity miles on his Schedule E.

Keeping Track of Actual Expenses

If you take the deduction for your actual auto expenses instead of using the standard rate (or if you are thinking about switching to this method), keep receipts for all of your auto-related expenses, including gasoline, oil, tires, repairs, and insurance. Create a category for auto expenses in your expense journal. Also, when you figure your depreciation deduction for the year, you'll need to include the amount you're entitled to deduct for depreciation of your auto. (See Chapter 10 for more on using the actual expense method, including vehicle depreciation.)

Allocating Your Rental Miles

You are required to list on Schedule E your car expenses for each rental property you own. This is no problem if you only own one property. But things can get more complicated if you own more than one, because you may make some trips that benefit more than one property at the same time—for example, a trip to the hardware store to purchase supplies you'll use for all your properties. In this event, you must allocate your mileage among your properties. You can split your mileage equally or use a percentage based on the income your properties earn.

Use a Credit Card for Gas

If you use the actual expense method for car expenses, you should use a credit card when you buy gas. It's best to designate a separate card for this purpose. The monthly statements you receive will serve as your gas receipts. If you pay cash for gas, you must either get a receipt or make a note of the amount in your mileage logbook.

Costs for rental-related parking (other than at your office) and for tolls are separately deductible whether you use the standard rate or the actual expense method. Get and keep receipts for these expenses.

Records Required for Long-Distance Travel, Meals, Entertainment, and Gifts

Deductions for travel, meals, entertainment, and gifts are hot-button items for the IRS because they have been greatly abused by many taxpayers. You need to have more records for these expenses than for almost any others, and they will be closely scrutinized if you're audited.

Whenever you incur an expense for rental-related travel, meals, gifts, or entertainment, you must document the following five facts:

- **The date.** The date you incurred the expense will usually be listed on a receipt or credit card slip; appointment books, day planners, and similar documents have the dates preprinted on each page, so entries on the appropriate page automatically date the expense.
- **The amount.** You'll need to be able to prove how much you spent, including tax and tip for meals.
- **The place.** Where you incurred the expense will usually be shown on a receipt, or you can record it in an appointment book.
- **The rental activity purpose.** You'll have to be able to show that the expense was incurred for your rental activity—for example, that you took an out-of-town trip to inspect or repair one of your rental properties.

- **The rental activity relationship.** If entertainment is involved, you should record how the people at the event relate to your rental activity—for example, list their names and occupations and any other information needed to establish their relation to you as a landlord.

The chart below shows the information your records must contain for travel, meal and entertainment, and gift expenses.

Receipts to Keep	
Type of Expense	**Receipts to Save**
Travel	Airplane, train, or bus ticket stubs; travel agency receipts; rental car; and so on.
Meals	Meal check, credit card slip.
Lodging	Statement or bill from hotel or other lodging provider; your own written records for cleaning, laundry, telephone charges, tips, and other charges not shown separately on hotel statement.
Entertainment	Bill from entertainment provider; ticket stubs for sporting event, theater, or other event; credit card slips.

The IRS does not require you to keep receipts, canceled checks, credit card slips, or any other supporting documents for travel, meal and entertainment, and gift expenses that cost less than $75. *However, you must still document the five facts listed above.* This exception does not apply to lodging—that is, hotel or similar costs—when you travel for your rental activity. You do need receipts for these expenses, even if they cost less than $75.

All this record keeping is not as hard as it sounds. You can record the five facts you have to document in a variety of ways, and the information doesn't have to be all in one place. Information that is shown on a receipt, canceled check, or other item need not be duplicated in a log, appointment book, calendar, or account book. Thus, for example, you can record the five facts with:

Proof Required for Travel, Entertainment, and Gift Deductions

Records must show:	Amount	Time	Place or Description	Business Purpose and Relationship
Travel	Cost of each separate expense for travel, lodging, meals. Incidental expenses may be totaled in categories such as taxis, daily meals, and so on.	Dates you left and returned for each trip, and the number of days spent on business.	Name of city, town, or other destination.	Business purpose for the expense, or the benefit gained or expected to be gained.
Entertainment (including meals)	Cost of each separate expense. Incidental expenses such as taxis, telephones, etc., may be totaled on a daily basis.	Date of entertainment.	Name and address or location of place of entertainment. Type of entertainment, if not otherwise apparent. For entertainment directly before or after business discussion: date, place, nature, and duration.	Nature of business discussion or activity. Identities of people who took part in discussion and entertainment. Occupations or other information (such as names or titles) about the recipients that shows their business relationship to you. Proof you or your employee were present at business meal.
Gifts	Cost of gift.	Date of gift.	Description of gift.	Same as for entertainment.

- a receipt, credit card slip, or similar document alone
- a receipt combined with an appointment book entry, or
- an appointment book entry alone (for expenses less than $75).

However you document your expense, you are supposed to do it in a timely manner. You don't need to record the details of every expense on the day you incur it. It is sufficient to record them on a weekly basis. However, if you're prone to forget details, it's best to get everything you need in writing within a day or two.

How Long to Keep Records

You need to have copies of your tax returns and supporting documents available in case the IRS or another taxing agency (such as your state income tax agency) audits you. You might also need them for other purposes—for example, to get a loan, mortgage, or insurance. Keep your records for as long as the IRS has to audit you after you file your returns for the year. These statutes of limitation range from three years to forever—they are listed in the table below.

To be on the safe side, keep your tax returns indefinitely. They usually don't take up much space, so this shouldn't be a big hardship. Your supporting documents probably take up more space. Hang on to these for at least six years after you file your return.

Keep your long-term asset records for as long as you own the property and for three years after you sell or otherwise dispose of it.

Scanning Your Records
If you don't want to keep paper copies of your tax records, you can make digital copies by scanning them and storing them on a computer or in the "cloud." The IRS has approved the use of electronic storage systems for this purpose. (Rev. Proc. 97-22, 1997-1 CB 652.)

IRS Statutes of Limitations	
If:	**The limitations period is:**
You failed to pay all the tax due	3 years
You underreported your gross income for the year by more than 25%	6 years
You filed a fraudulent return	No limit
You did not file a return	No limit

When You Don't Have Proper Tax Records

Because you're human, you may not have kept all the records required to back up your tax deductions. Don't despair, all is not lost—you may be able to fall back on the *Cohan* rule. This rule (named after the Broadway entertainer George M. Cohan, who was involved in a tax case in the 1930s) is the taxpayer's best friend. The *Cohan* rule recognizes that you must spend at least some money when you own rental property, and so you must have at least some deductible expenses, even if you don't have adequate records to back them up.

If you're audited and lack adequate records for a claimed deduction, the IRS can use the *Cohan* rule to make an estimate of how much you must have spent, and allow you to deduct that amount. However, you must provide at least some credible evidence on which to base this estimate, such as receipts, canceled checks, notes in your appointment book, or other records. Moreover, the IRS will allow you to deduct only the smallest amount you might have spent, based on the records you provide. In addition, the *Cohan* rule cannot be used for travel, meal, entertainment, or gift expenses, or for listed property.

If an auditor claims you lack sufficient records to back up a deduction, you should always bring up the *Cohan* rule and argue that you should still get the deduction based on the records you do have. At best, you'll probably get only part of your claimed deductions. If the IRS auditor disallows your deductions entirely or doesn't give you as much as you think you deserve, you can appeal in court and bring up the *Cohan* rule again there. You might have more success with a judge. However, you can't compel an IRS auditor or a court to apply the *Cohan* rule in your favor. They have discretion to decide whether to apply the rule and how large a deduction to give you.

Reconstructing Tax Records

If you can prove that you possessed adequate records at one time, but now lack them due to circumstances beyond your control, you can reconstruct your records for an IRS audit. Circumstances beyond your control include acts of nature such as floods, fires, earthquakes, or theft. (Treas. Reg. § 1.275.5(c)(5).) If you lose your tax records while moving, that doesn't constitute circumstances beyond your control. To reconstruct the needed records, you either create brand-new records just for your audit or obtain other evidence to corroborate your deductions—for example, statements from people or companies from whom you purchased items for your rental activity.

Accounting Methods

An accounting method is a set of rules that you will use to determine when and how to report your income and expenses. Accounting methods might sound like a rather dry subject, but your choice about how to account for your rental expenses and income will have a huge impact on your tax deductions. You don't have to become as expert as a CPA on this topic, but you should understand the basics.

You must choose an accounting method when you file your first tax return for your rental activity. If you later want to change your accounting method, you must get IRS approval. There are two basic methods of accounting: cash basis and accrual basis. Almost all small landlords use the cash method because it's, by far, the simpler of the two.

Cash Method

Most individuals use the cash method for their personal taxes. The cash method is based on this commonsense idea: You haven't earned income for tax purposes until you actually receive the money, and you haven't incurred an expense until you actually pay the money. Using the cash basis method, then, is like maintaining a checkbook. You record income only when the money is received and expenses only when you actually pay them. If you borrow money to pay rental activity expenses, you incur an expense under the cash method only when you make payments on the loan.

The Cash Method of Paying Expenses

Although it's called the cash method, this method for paying business expenses includes payments by check, credit card, or electronic funds transfer, as well as payments by cash. If you pay by check, the amount is deemed paid during the year in which the check is drawn and mailed—for example, a check dated December 31, 2015, is considered paid during 2015 only if it has a December 31, 2015, postmark. If you're using a check to pay a substantial expense, you may wish to mail it by certified mail so you'll have proof of when it was mailed.

EXAMPLE 1: Helen has a vacant rental unit. She signs a lease with a new tenant on December 20, but the tenant does not give her a check for the first month's rent until January 5 of the following year. Using the cash method, Helen records the payment as income in January—when she receives it.

EXAMPLE 2: On December 1, 2015, Helen goes to the Acme home care store and buys a snowblower for her rental business. She buys the item on credit from Acme—she's not required to make any payments until March 1, 2016. Helen does not record the expense until 2016, when she actually pays for the snowblower.

EXAMPLE 3: On December 15, 2015, Helen buys a washer and dryer for the rental property, and pays for them with a credit card. She receives her statement from the bank that issued the card in January. Helen records the expense in December 2015,.

Constructive Receipt

Under the cash method, payments are constructively received when an amount is credited to your account or otherwise made available to you without restrictions. Constructive receipt is as good as actual receipt. If you authorize someone to be your agent to receive income for you, you are considered to have received it when your agent receives it. For example, you constructively receive a rental check when your apartment manager receives it from a tenant.

EXAMPLE: Your tenant has his monthly rent checks directly deposited into your rental checking account. Your tenant's January 2016 rent check is credited to your account on December 30, 2015, but you do not withdraw it or enter it into your passbook until January 5, 2016. You must include the amount in gross rental income for 2015—not 2016.

No Postponing Income

You cannot hold checks or other payments from one tax year to another to avoid paying tax on the income. You must report the income in the year you receive the payment or when it's made available to you without restriction.

EXAMPLE: On December 1, 2015, Helen receives a $1,000 rent check from a tenant. She holds the check and doesn't cash it until January 10, 2016. She still has to report the $1,000 as income for 2015 because she constructively received it that year.

No Prepayment of Expenses

The general rule is that you can't prepay expenses when you use the cash method—you can't hurry up the payment of expenses by paying them in advance. An expense you pay in advance can be deducted only in the year to which it applies.

However, there is an important exception to the general rule called the 12-month rule. Under this rule, you may deduct a prepaid expense in the current year if the expense is for a right or benefit that extends no longer than the earlier of:

- 12 months, or
- until the end of the tax year after the tax year in which you made the payment.

EXAMPLE 1: You are a calendar-year taxpayer and you pay $10,000 on July 1, 2015, for a landlord insurance policy that is effective for one year beginning the date you pay for the policy. The 12-month rule applies because the benefit you've paid for—a landlord insurance policy—extends only 12 months into the future. Therefore, the full $10,000 is deductible in 2015.

EXAMPLE 2: You are a calendar-year taxpayer and you pay $3,000 in 2015 for a landlord insurance policy that is effective for three years, beginning July 1, 2015. This payment does not qualify for the 12-month rule because the benefit extends more than 12 months. Therefore, you must use the general rule: $500 is deductible in 2015, $1,000 is deductible in 2016, $1,000 is deductible in 2017, and $500 is deductible in 2018.

To use the 12-month rule, you must apply it when you first start using the cash method for your rental activity. You must get IRS approval if you haven't been using the rule and want to start doing so. Such approval is granted automatically upon filing IRS Form 3115.

Accrual Method

In accrual basis accounting, you report income or expenses as they are earned or incurred, rather than when they are actually collected or paid. You don't have to wait until you see the money or actually pay money out of your checking account. The accrual method can be difficult to use because complex rules determine when income or expenses accrue.

Expenses

Under the accrual method, you generally deduct a rental expense when:

- you are legally obligated to pay the expense
- the amount you owe can be determined with reasonable accuracy, and
- you have received or used the property or services involved.

> EXAMPLE: Bill, the owner of two apartment buildings, borrows $10,000 from his bank to help remodel his rentals. He signs a promissory note on December 15, 2015, and receives the money the same day, but doesn't start making payments to the bank until the following January. Bill can deduct the expense in 2015 because he became legally obligated to pay the expense upon signing the note, the amount of the expense can be determined from the note, and he received the money that day.

Thus, when you use the accrual method, you can take a deduction for an expense you incur, even if you don't actually pay for it until the following year. You can't do this under the cash basis method. There are obvious advantages to getting a tax deduction this year without actually having to shell out any money until a future year. But don't get too excited—the flip side (treatment of income) pretty much cancels out this advantage.

Income

When it comes to income, the accrual method has significant disadvantages compared to the cash method. Under the accrual method, you report an amount in your gross income on the earliest of the following dates:

- when you receive payment
- when the income amount is due to you, or
- when you earn the income.

Thus, you may have to report an amount as income even if you haven't received it. For example, you'd have to report as income rent due even if a tenant has failed to pay it. You could later deduct the amount as a bad debt if it proves uncollectible. (See Chapter 14.) This is one important reason few small landlords use the accrual method.

> ### Obtaining IRS Permission to Change Your Accounting Method
>
> You choose your accounting method by checking a box on your tax form when you file your tax return. Once you choose a method, you can't change it without getting permission from the IRS. Permission is granted automatically for many types of changes, including using the 12-month rule to deduct prepaid expenses. You must file IRS Form 3115, *Application for Change in Accounting Method*, with your tax return for the year you want to make the change (if the change is automatically granted).
>
> Automatic approval can also be obtained to change to the cash method if you've been using the accrual method and come within one of the exceptions discussed above. However, changing your accounting method can have serious consequences, so consult a tax professional before doing so.

Tax Years

You are required to pay taxes for a 12-month period, also known as the tax year. Almost all small landlords use the calendar year as their tax year—that is, January 1 through December 31. Indeed, sole proprietors, partnerships, limited liability companies, and S corporations are required to use the calendar year.

However, in some cases it is possible to use a tax year that does not end in December (also known as a fiscal year). You need to get the IRS's permission to use a fiscal year. The IRS might grant you permission if you can show a good reason for it. For example, you rent a condo in a winter resort in January and February, but you incur the bulk of your annual expenses in December of each year because you need to get the condo ready to rent. Using a tax year other than the calendar year will more accurately show your annual income and expenses. To get permission to use a fiscal year, you must file IRS Form 8716, *Election to Have a Tax Year Other Than a Required Tax Year.*

All About Schedule E

Who Must File Schedule E?..462

Filling Out Schedule E 464

    Filing IRS Forms 1099 (Lines A and B)...467

    Property Description (Line 1)...467

    Dual Use Properties (Line 2) 467

    Qualified Joint Venture (Line 2) 468

    Rental Income (Line 3) 468

    Royalties Received (Line 4)...469

    Expenses (Lines 5–20)..469

    Rental Summary (Lines 21–26)...472

This chapter shows how to fill out IRS Schedule E, the tax form landlords use to report their income and deductions to the IRS. Starting with the form for the 2011 tax year, the IRS made several changes to Schedule E that require landlords to provide more information than in past years. This was done to help the IRS identify questionable issues and select tax returns with real estate activity for examination.

Who Must File Schedule E?

You must file Schedule E if, like most small landlords, you receive rental income from property that you own as an individual. It doesn't matter whether you own the rental property alone, with your spouse, or with one or more co-owners.

However, if you own or use your rental property in one of the following manners, you do not use Schedule E to report rental income or deductions for the property:

- **Ownership through a business entity.** Partnerships, limited partnerships, multi-member LLCs, and S corporations file IRS Form 8825, *Rental Real Estate Income and Expenses of a Partnership or an S Corporation,* to report rental income and deductions. This form is very similar to Schedule E. The individual LLC or partnership members (or S corporation shareholders) are each given a Schedule K-1 by the entity reporting their individual shares of annual income or loss from the rental activity. The individuals then list this amount on Part II of Schedule E, on page 2.

  However, a single-member LLC is ordinarily not treated as a separate entity for federal income tax purposes. Thus, if you are the sole member of an LLC, you normally file Schedule E, Part I.

- **Ownership as a real estate dealer.** A real estate dealer buys and sells real property as a business. (See Chapter 2.) Dealers file IRS Schedule C, *Profit or Loss From Business*, the tax form used by individual business owners other than landlords. However, if a dealer owns rental property as a long-term investment, then he or she must file Schedule E to report the income and expenses for that property.

- **Not-for-profit real property owners.** If your rental activity constitutes a not-for-profit activity for tax purposes, you report any deductible expenses on Schedule A, *Itemized Deductions.* (See Chapter 2.)
- **Tax-free vacation homes.** If you own a vacation home that you rent out for less than 15 days a year and use personally for 15 days or more, you don't need to file a Schedule E. The income from the home is tax free. (See Chapter 15.)
- **Hotels and motels.** If you operate a hotel, motel, or similar property where significant personal services (such as maid services) are provided to guests, you do not file a Schedule E. An individual owner of such a property files Schedule C, *Profit or Loss From Business.*

Husband and Wife Landlords

Many residential rental properties are co-owned by spouses. The long-standing rule has been that married couples who file a joint tax return can report their rental income and expenses on a single Schedule E that they file with their joint Form 1040 tax return. (See "Co-Ownership by Spouses" in Chapter 1 and IRS Reg. § 301.7701-1(a)(2) ("mere co-ownership of property that is maintained, kept in repair, and rented or leased does not constitute a separate entity for federal tax purposes").)

Like other co-owners of rental property, landlord spouses are not considered partners in a partnership (and don't have to file a partnership tax return) unless they provide significant personal services with the rental, such as maid service or food service. However, if landlord spouses were to be considered partners because of the services they provide with their rental, they may have an option that is not available to other co-owners of property. Under a new IRS rule, a married couple may elect to be taxed as a "qualified joint venture." If they qualify for the election, they are treated as sole proprietors for tax purposes and each spouse files a separate Schedule C reporting his or her share of rental income and expenses. (See "Co-Ownership by Spouses" in Chapter 1.) This does not reduce their taxes, but it does result in a much simpler tax return.

Filling Out Schedule E

Completing Schedule E is a relatively straightforward process. You fill out only the first page, which is called Part I. (Part I is also used for royalties, which have nothing to do with rental property.) Parts II–V on the second page are only used by partnerships, S corporations, estates, trusts, and real estate mortgage investment conduits (REMICs, a type of real estate investment).

You separately list on the schedule your income and expenses for each rental property you own. A rental property comprises all the rental units you have at a single address. If you own a multiunit building, you must add together the income and expenses from all the units and list the totals on Schedule E.

Schedule E is designed to be used by up to three rental properties, labeled A, B, and C; there are separate columns for each property. If you have more than three rental properties, complete and attach as many Schedule Es as you need for them all. But fill in lines 23a through 26 on only one Schedule E. The figures there as reported on one of your Schedule Es should be the combined totals for all properties reported.

If you own only a part interest in a rental property, report only your share of the property's income and expenses.

> EXAMPLE: Betty and Bettina each own a 50% interest in a duplex they rent out. Betty reports 50% of the property's income and expenses on her Schedule E, and Bettina reports the other 50% on her Schedule E.

If you and your spouse elect qualified joint venture status, you must divide all income, expenses, losses, and credits between you according to your respective interests in the venture—for example, if you're equal co-owners, you each get 50% of these items. You only file one Schedule E, but each of you must report your interest as separate properties on line 1. On lines 3 through 22 for each separate property interest, you must enter your share of the applicable income, deduction, or loss. (See Chapter 1 for a detailed discussion of qualified joint ventures.)

SCHEDULE E (Form 1040) Department of the Treasury Internal Revenue Service (99)	**Supplemental Income and Loss** (From rental real estate, royalties, partnerships, S corporations, estates, trusts, REMICs, etc.) ▶ Attach to Form 1040, 1040NR, or Form 1041. ▶ Information about Schedule E and its separate instructions is at *www.irs.gov/schedulee*.	OMB No. 1545-0074 20**14** Attachment Sequence No. **13**

Name(s) shown on return | Your social security number

Part I **Income or Loss From Rental Real Estate and Royalties** Note. If you are in the business of renting personal property, use **Schedule C or C-EZ** (see instructions). If you are an individual, report farm rental income or loss from **Form 4835** on page 2, line 40.

A Did you make any payments in 2014 that would require you to file Form(s) 1099? (see instructions) ☐ Yes ☐ No
B If "Yes," did you or will you file required Forms 1099? ☐ Yes ☐ No

1a Physical address of each property (street, city, state, ZIP code)

A
B
C

1b	Type of Property (from list below)	2 For each rental real estate property listed above, report the number of fair rental and personal use days. Check the **QJV** box only if you meet the requirements to file as a qualified joint venture. See instructions.		Fair Rental Days	Personal Use Days	QJV
A			A			☐
B			B			☐
C			C			☐

Type of Property:
1 Single Family Residence   3 Vacation/Short-Term Rental 5 Land   7 Self-Rental
2 Multi-Family Residence   4 Commercial   6 Royalties   8 Other (describe)

Income:	Properties:		A	B	C
3 Rents received	3				
4 Royalties received	4				
Expenses:					
5 Advertising	5				
6 Auto and travel (see instructions)	6				
7 Cleaning and maintenance	7				
8 Commissions.	8				
9 Insurance	9				
10 Legal and other professional fees	10				
11 Management fees	11				
12 Mortgage interest paid to banks, etc. (see instructions)	12				
13 Other interest.	13				
14 Repairs.	14				
15 Supplies	15				
16 Taxes	16				
17 Utilities	17				
18 Depreciation expense or depletion	18				
19 Other (list) ▶	19				
20 Total expenses. Add lines 5 through 19	20				
21 Subtract line 20 from line 3 (rents) and/or 4 (royalties). If result is a (loss), see instructions to find out if you must file **Form 6198**	21				
22 Deductible rental real estate loss after limitation, if any, on **Form 8582** (see instructions)	22	(	)(	)(	)

23a	Total of all amounts reported on line 3 for all rental properties	23a	
b	Total of all amounts reported on line 4 for all royalty properties	23b	
c	Total of all amounts reported on line 12 for all properties	23c	
d	Total of all amounts reported on line 18 for all properties	23d	
e	Total of all amounts reported on line 20 for all properties	23e	
24	**Income.** Add positive amounts shown on line 21. **Do not** include any losses	24	
25	**Losses.** Add royalty losses from line 21 and rental real estate losses from line 22. Enter total losses here	25	( )
26	**Total rental real estate and royalty income or (loss).** Combine lines 24 and 25. Enter the result here. If Parts II, III, IV, and line 40 on page 2 do not apply to you, also enter this amount on Form 1040, line 17, or Form 1040NR, line 18. Otherwise, include this amount in the total on line 41 on page 2	26	

For Paperwork Reduction Act Notice, see the separate instructions.   Cat. No. 11344L   Schedule E (Form 1040) 2014

Schedule E (Form 1040) 2014   Attachment Sequence No. **13**   Page **2**

Name(s) shown on return. Do not enter name and social security number if shown on other side.	Your social security number

Caution. The IRS compares amounts reported on your tax return with amounts shown on Schedule(s) K-1.

Part II   **Income or Loss From Partnerships and S Corporations**   **Note.** If you report a loss from an at-risk activity for which **any** amount is **not** at risk, you **must** check the box in column **(e)** on line 28 and attach **Form 6198.** See instructions.

27   Are you reporting any loss not allowed in a prior year due to the at-risk, excess farm loss, or basis limitations, a prior year unallowed loss from a passive activity (if that loss was not reported on Form 8582), or unreimbursed partnership expenses? If you answered "Yes," see instructions before completing this section.   ☐ **Yes**   ☐ **No**

28	(a) Name	(b) Enter P for partnership; S for S corporation	(c) Check if foreign partnership	(d) Employer identification number	(e) Check if any amount is not at risk
A			☐		☐
B			☐		☐
C			☐		☐
D			☐		☐

	Passive Income and Loss		Nonpassive Income and Loss		
	(f) Passive loss allowed (attach Form 8582 if required)	(g) Passive income from Schedule K-1	(h) Nonpassive loss from Schedule K-1	(i) Section 179 expense deduction from Form 4562	(j) Nonpassive income from Schedule K-1
A					
B					
C					
D					
29a Totals					
b Totals					

30	Add columns (g) and (j) of line 29a	30	
31	Add columns (f), (h), and (i) of line 29b	31	( )
32	**Total partnership and S corporation income or (loss).** Combine lines 30 and 31. Enter the result here and include in the total on line 41 below	32	

Part III   **Income or Loss From Estates and Trusts**

33	(a) Name	(b) Employer identification number
A		
B		

	Passive Income and Loss		Nonpassive Income and Loss	
	(c) Passive deduction or loss allowed (attach Form 8582 if required)	(d) Passive income from Schedule K-1	(e) Deduction or loss from Schedule K-1	(f) Other income from Schedule K-1
A				
B				
34a Totals				
b Totals				

35	Add columns (d) and (f) of line 34a	35	
36	Add columns (c) and (e) of line 34b	36	( )
37	**Total estate and trust income or (loss).** Combine lines 35 and 36. Enter the result here and include in the total on line 41 below	37	

Part IV   **Income or Loss From Real Estate Mortgage Investment Conduits (REMICs)—Residual Holder**

38	(a) Name	(b) Employer identification number	(c) Excess inclusion from Schedules Q, line 2c (see instructions)	(d) Taxable income (net loss) from Schedules Q, line 1b	(e) Income from Schedules Q, line 3b

39	Combine columns (d) and (e) only. Enter the result here and include in the total on line 41 below	39	

Part V   **Summary**

40	Net farm rental income or (loss) from **Form 4835.** Also, complete line 42 below	40	
41	Total income or (loss). Combine lines 26, 32, 37, 39, and 40. Enter the result here and on Form 1040, line 17, or Form 1040NR, line 18 ▶	41	

42	**Reconciliation of farming and fishing income.** Enter your **gross** farming and fishing income reported on Form 4835, line 7; Schedule K-1 (Form 1065), box 14, code B; Schedule K-1 (Form 1120S), box 17, code V; and Schedule K-1 (Form 1041), box 14, code F (see instructions) . .	42	

43   **Reconciliation for real estate professionals.** If you were a real estate professional (see instructions), enter the net income or (loss) you reported anywhere on Form 1040 or Form 1040NR from all rental real estate activities

Filing IRS Forms 1099 (Lines A and B)

Line A asks whether you made any payments during the year that required you to file IRS Forms 1099. If you answer yes, you have to answer in Line B whether you have already filed, "or will you file," the forms. Obviously, you should answer "yes" on Line B if you answered "yes" on Line A. If you haven't filed the required 1099 forms, you should do so as soon as possible.

When does a landlord have to file Forms 1099? There are several types of 1099 forms. The one that usually has to be filed by landlords is Form 1099-MISC. You must file Form 1099-MISC if (1) your rental activity constitutes a business for tax purposes, and (2) you hire an independent contractor to perform services for your activity and pay him or her more than $600 during the year—for example, you hire a repairperson, rental agent, or gardener.

You need not file any 1099 forms if your rental activity is an investment, not a business for tax purposes. (See Chapter 2.) See Chapter 12 for a detailed discussion of the rules for filing IRS Form 1099-MISC.

These new questions are an attempt by the IRS to encourage landlords and others who file Schedule E to file all required 1099s. This is part of the IRS's ongoing effort to prevent businesses from failing to report all their income.

Property Description (Line 1)

In Line 1, list your rental property's street address, city or town, state, and ZIP code. In the next box, provide the applicable number code showing the type of property.

Dual Use Properties (Line 2)

Line 2 has to do with rentals that you also used for personal purposes during the year. These are primarily vacation home and second home rentals. You are required to show on Schedule E the actual number of days the rental property was occupied by renters, and the number of days it was used by you or your family for personal purposes. If you used the property for personal purposes more than 14 days during the year, your deductions will be limited. You must prorate your expenses based on the number of days the property was used as a rental versus the days it was used as a personal residence. You deduct the personal portion of interest, taxes, and casualty losses on Schedule A. Your rental deductions on Schedule E are limited to the remaining gross income from the property and are subject to special ordering rules. Note that personal use includes not just use by you or your relatives, but any day you let anyone use the property without paying a fair market rent. (See Chapter 15 for a detailed discussion of tax issues for vacation homes.) If you didn't use the rental property for personal purposes, enter zero in the "Personal Use Days" column and 365 in the "Fair Rental Days" column (assuming you rented the property the entire year).

Qualified Joint Venture (Line 2)

If you and your spouse want your rental activity to be characterized as a qualified joint venture (or it is already a QJV), place an x in the QJV column. See Chapter 1 for a detailed discussion of qualified joint venture status for rentals owned by spouses.

Rental Income (Line 3)

Enter your total annual rental income for each property in Line 3. This will primarily consist of the rent your tenants pay you. But it could also include:

- laundry income
- fees you charge tenants for paying rent late
- garage or other parking charges
- interest you earn on tenant security deposits
- security deposits you retain to pay for repairs, unpaid rent, or other expenses
- the value of services tenants provide in lieu of rent, or
- payments tenants make to you for repairs or other expenses. (See Chapter 4.)

A security deposit you receive from a tenant is not rental income if you plan to return it when the tenancy ends. But, if you keep all or part of a security deposit when a tenant leaves, the amount you keep is rental income. Any interest you earn on your tenants' security deposits is also rental income, unless you are required to repay it to your tenants when they move out. Some cities require this under their rent control laws.

Interest you earn on your rental checking account, if any, is not rental income. It is personal interest. Do not include it in your rental income on Schedule E.

Royalties Received (Line 4)

Leave this blank unless you have royalty income—for example, income from copyrights or patents you inherited or purchased, or mineral leases. If you are a self-employed writer, inventor, artist, and so on you report your royalty income and expenses on Schedule C, *Profit or Loss From Business.*

Expenses (Lines 5–20)

You list your expenses for each property in the Expenses section, Lines 5–18. Your expenses must be broken down into categories; Schedule E lists the following expense categories:

- **Advertising.** This includes signs, classified ads, and other advertising expenses to rent your property.
- **Auto and travel.** This category includes both local and long-distance travel expenses. (See Chapters 10 and 11.) If you have both types of expenses, you must add them together.
- **Cleaning and maintenance.** This includes janitorial services, gardening, cleaning carpets, drapes, and rugs. Do not include repairs here—repairs are done to fix property after it's broken; maintenance keeps your property in good working order so it won't break down.
- **Commissions.** This category will apply to you only if you hire a rental agency or property management company to help you with your rentals. Such agencies and companies are typically paid a commission—that is, a percentage of the rent they collect (for example, 5% or 10%). Some property managers deduct their commissions from the rent they collect before they send it to the property owner. In this event, be sure to list the total amount

of rent charged in the rental income line, not the amount the property manager sends you after deducting the commission.

- **Insurance.** This includes any type of insurance for your rental activity, except for private mortgage insurance and title insurance (see Chapter 14).

- **Legal and other professional fees.** This includes tax advice and preparing tax forms for your rental activity. Some legal fees incurred for buying property aren't deductible; they are added to the property's basis and depreciated. (See Chapter 5.)

- **Management fees.** These are fees charged by rental agencies and property management companies. If you pay such fees, list the total here.

- **Mortgage interest paid to banks.** If you have a mortgage on your rental property, list the amount of interest you paid during the year to banks or other financial institutions. If you paid $600 or more in interest on a mortgage during the year, the financial institution should send you a Form 1098 or similar statement by February showing the total interest received from you. Points, including loan origination fees, charged only for the use of money must be deducted over the life of the loan. (See Chapter 7.) Include the amount you can deduct this year in your mortgage interest total.

- **Other interest.** This is interest you paid to a lender other than a bank or other financial institution—for example, interest on a credit card you use for rental expenses, or interest you pay to the seller of rental property you purchased with creative financing. Also, if you and at least one other person (other than your spouse if you file a joint return) were liable for and paid interest on a mortgage, and the other person received Form 1098, report your share of the deductible interest on this line. Attach a statement to your return showing the name and address of the person who received Form 1098. In the left margin next to the Other interest line, write "See attached."

- **Repairs.** Repairs keep your property in good working order. They do not add significant value to your property or extend its life. Do not include the cost of improvements in this line; they must be depreciated over several years. (See Chapter 4.)

- **Supplies.** This includes office supplies and supplies you use for repairs and maintenance—for example, paint and brushes, or fertilizer. It does not include materials you purchase to undertake improvements—for example, it would not include the cost of the shingles used to install a new roof on your rental property. You must depreciate these materials. (See Chapter 5.)
- **Taxes.** This includes employment taxes you pay if you have employees—for example, a resident manager.
- **Utilities.** This includes charges for water, garbage pickup, gas, and electricity you pay for your rental property. You may also deduct the cost of telephone calls for your rental activities—for example, calls to your renter. However, the base rate (including taxes and other charges) for local telephone service for the first telephone line into your residence is a personal expense that you cannot deduct. Don't include utilities for a home office here.
- **Depreciation.** You list your total depreciation deduction for each property in the depreciation line and then include the total for all properties in the right-hand column. You must also complete and attach Form 4562, *Depreciation and Amortization*, if you are claiming:
  - depreciation on property first placed in service during the year
  - depreciation on listed property including a vehicle, regardless of the date it was placed in service, or
  - a Section 179 expense deduction or amortization of costs that began during the year.

  You should complete depreciation worksheets for each of your properties, but you don't have to attach them to your return. (See Chapter 5 for a detailed discussion of depreciation.)
- **Other Expenses.** The Schedule E categories probably include most of your expenses, but you may have others that are not listed—for example:
  - home office expenses (Chapter 9)
  - gifts (Chapter 14)
  - homeowners' association dues for rental condominiums and planned-unit developments

- start-up expenses (Chapter 8)
- entertainment expenses (Chapter 14)
- wages and salaries for employees
- education expenses (Chapter 14)
- dues and subscriptions (Chapter 14)
- inspection fees, changing locks, bank charges on business accounts, apartment association dues
- casualty losses (Chapter 13), and
- equipment rental.

If you have expenses for these or other items, list them by category in the Other line. You create your own categories here.

You add up all your expenses for each property and put the total in Line 20.

Rental Summary (Lines 21–26)

You use this portion of Schedule E to show the amount of income you earned or loss you incurred from your rental activity, and the deductible portion of any loss.

- **Line 21.** You complete this line only if you have rental losses all or part of which are not deductible because of the at-risk rules. If this is the case, you need to complete IRS Form 6198, *At-Risk Limitations*, and attach it to your return. Few landlords are subject to the at-risk limitations. (See Chapter 16 for a detailed discussion of the at-risk rules.)
- **Line 22.** If you have a net loss for the year, the amount you can deduct may be limited by the passive activity loss rules. Most small landlords can deduct all or part of their losses by using the $25,000 offset exception to the passive activity rules. If you are able to deduct all your losses by using the offset, you don't need to file Form 8582, *Passive Activity Loss Limitations*. If you can't deduct all your losses by using the offset, you'll have to complete Form 8582 to figure the amount of loss you can deduct, if any. Enter the deductible amount of your loss, if any, on Line 22. (See Chapter 16 for a detailed discussion of the passive loss rules.)

- **Line 23a.** List the total of all income you reported on Line 3a for all your rental properties.
- **Line 23b.** Put a zero here unless you earned income from royalty properties such as patents or copyrights in works you didn't create yourself.
- **Line 23c.** List the total of all income you reported on Line 4 for all your rental properties. This will be the same number as in Line 23a.
- **Line 23d.** Put a zero here unless you earned income from royalty properties such as patents or copyrights.
- **Line 23e.** List the total of all mortgage interest payments you reported on Line 12 for all your rental properties.
- **Line 23f.** List the total of all the depreciation you reported on Line 18 for all your properties.
- **Line 23g.** List the total of all expenses you reported on Line 20 for all your properties.
- **Line 24 (Income).** Add any positive amounts shown on Line 21. Do not include any losses.
- **Line 25 (Losses).** Add royalty losses from Line 21 (if any) and rental losses from Line 22. Most landlords have no royalty losses.
- **Line 26** (**Total income or loss**). Combine Lines 24 and 25. If there are no other entries on Schedule E, this amount is transferred to Line 17 of Form 1040. Otherwise, it is combined with other amounts on Line 41, Page 2, Schedule E.
- **Line 43 (Reconciliation for Real Estate Professionals).** If you're exempt from the passive activity loss rules because you are a real estate professional and materially participated in the rental activity (see Chapter 16), enter here the total profit or loss from all rental real estate rental activities.

The Net Investment Income Tax

How the NII Tax Works 476

    What Is the NII Tax? 476

    Who Is Subject to the NII Tax 477

    Amount of the Tax 479

Real Estate Professional Exemption From the NII Tax 480

    Real Estate Professional 481

    Material Participation in Rental Activity 481

    Rental Activity a Business 482

Planning to Avoid the NII Tax 483

f your rentals earn a profit, starting in 2013 you became subject to a brand-new tax: the Net Investment Income tax ("NII tax" for short; also called the Medicare Contribution tax). Enacted to help fund Obamacare, this tax impacts many higher-income landlords. However, some lucky landlords are able to avoid it completely, no matter how high their incomes.

How the NII Tax Works

To put it mildly, the Net Investment Income (NII) tax is complicated. Here is an overview of how it works.

What Is the NII Tax?

The NII tax is a separate 3.8% income tax on unearned income—that is, income other than from a job or business in which you actively participate. Those subject to it—primarily higher-income taxpayers— must pay it in addition to their regular income taxes. This includes many landlords. The tax is included on Form 1040. You report the amount you're required to pay by completing IRS Form 8960, *Net Investment Income Tax—Individuals, Estates, and Trusts*, and attaching it to your return.

The NII tax is not a tax on real estate transactions; thus, you need not calculate it or pay it when you buy or sell property. However, any gain you realize when you sell rental property may be subject to the tax—but it won't be due until you pay your income taxes for year.

The NII tax went into effect on January 1, 2013. For 2014 and later, the tax is due in the following calendar year when tax returns are filed. However, you may need to include NII tax in your estimated taxes you file during the year, or be subject to a penalty.

Who Is Subject to the NII Tax

The NII tax is designed to affect higher-income taxpayers, leaving out many landlords. You will be subject to the NII tax only if:

- your adjusted gross income (AGI) exceeds an annual threshold amount, and
- you have net investment income.

Rental Property Owned Through a Pass-Through Entity

If you own real estate rentals through a pass-through entity, such as a limited liability company, partnership, or S corporation, the NII tax rules still apply to you at the individual level. Your share of the profits from the entity will pass through to your individual tax return and must be included with your other net investment income for purposes of the NII tax.

Income Thresholds

You'll be subject to the NII tax only if your AGI for the year exceeds $200,000 if you're single, or $250,000 if you're married filing jointly (the threshold is $125,000 for married couples filing separately). If you add up all of your income from every source, and the total is less than the applicable $200,000/$250,000 threshold, you will not be subject to this tax.

Only a small minority of taxpayers have this much income—about the top 2%. However, even if you ordinarily have less income than the applicable threshold, you may become subject to the NII tax in any year in which you sell rental property (or other investment property) for a substantial gain. Such gain will increase your AGI and could raise it over the threshold.

Moreover, these thresholds are not automatically adjusted for inflation. Thus, over time more and more people will become subject to the NII tax, unless Congress acts in the future to increase the thresholds to account for inflation.

> ## What Is AGI?
>
> Your AGI is not the same as your taxable income. It is the number on the bottom of your IRS Form 1040. It consists of your income from almost all sources, including wages, interest income, dividend income, income from certain retirement accounts, capital gains, alimony received, rental income, royalty income, and unemployment compensation, reduced by certain "above the line" deductions such as IRA contributions and one-half of self-employment taxes. If you have any foreign earned income, you must include it in your AGI as well. (I.R.C. § 1411(a)(1)(B).)

Net Investment Income

Even if your AGI exceeds the $200,000/$250,000 threshold, you'll be subject to the NII tax only if you have "net investment income." Indeed, you could earn millions of dollars and, if none of it is net investment income, you won't have to pay the tax.

Net investment income consists of:

- income from investment assets, including interest, dividends, rents (less expenses), and annuities
- income from any business in which you don't materially participate (aren't active in running), including real estate limited partnerships and other real estate investment businesses, and
- net capital gains (gains less capital losses) you earn upon the sale of property that is not part of an active business, including rental property, stocks and bonds, and mutual funds.

Net investment income does not include:

- income from a business in which you materially participate (actively run), any self-employment income, or wages you earn from employment
- tax-exempt income such as income from tax-exempt bonds, the amount of profit excluded from tax when you sell your principal residence ($250,000 for singles, $500,000 for married couples filing jointly), or income earned from renting your home for no more than 14 days during the year (see Chapter 15).

- withdrawals from retirement plans such as traditional or Roth IRAs, 401(k)s, or payouts from traditional defined-benefit pension plans, or
- life insurance proceeds, veterans' benefits, Social Security benefits, alimony, or unemployment benefits.

Amount of the Tax

The NII tax is a flat 3.8% tax. However, it is not imposed on your total AGI or investment income. Instead, it is assessed only on the portion of your income determined by a formula: The tax must paid on the *lesser* of (1) the taxpayer's net investment income, or (2) the amount that the taxpayer's adjusted gross income (AGI) exceeds the applicable threshold: $200,000 for single taxpayers, and $250,000 for married filing jointly.

> EXAMPLE: Burt, a single taxpayer, has a job that pays him $300,000 in wages. He also earned $50,000 in net investment income during the year. His AGI is $350,000. Burt must pay the 3.8% NII tax on the lesser of (1) his $50,000 of net investment income, or (2) the amount his $350,000 AGI exceeds the $200,000 threshold for single taxpayers—$150,000. Since $50,000 is less than $150,000, he must pay the 3.8% tax on $50,000. His NII tax for the year is $1,900 (3.8% × $50,000 = $1,900).

You only have to pay the NII tax on income over the $200,000/$250,000 threshold. Thus, for those at the lower end of the AGI threshold, the NII tax is fairly small. For example, a single taxpayer with a $201,000 AGI, including $50,000 in rental income, would only pay the 3.8% tax on $1,000.

Your net rental income is included in your net investment income, and thus makes you subject to the NII tax if your AGI is over the applicable threshold. Your net rental income consists of your gross (total) rents minus all deductible expenses you incur in operating your rental property. Your deductible expenses for these purposes will generally be the same as shown on your Schedule E (see Chapter 18). If you have a net loss from your rental activities, you can use it to reduce your AGI subject to the passive loss rules discussed in Chapter 16. This makes the rental property deductions covered in the rest of this book more valuable than ever.

> **EXAMPLE:** Ludmilla, a single taxpayer, earns $200,000 in gross rents and has $100,000 in expenses, ending up with $100,000 in net rental income that must be included in her AGI. She also has $250,000 in employee income. Her AGI is $350,000—$150,000 over the $200,000 NII tax threshold. She must pay the 3.8% NII tax on the lesser of $150,000 or $100,000. Since $100,000 is less, she owes $3,800 in NII tax for the year that she must pay along with her regular income taxes.

If you sell your rental property for a gain, the amount must be included in your net investment income for that year. This can make you subject to the NII tax, even if your AGI is ordinarily less than the $200,000/$250,000 threshold

> **EXAMPLE:** Luther and Linda, are married taxpayers, whose AGI each year is ordinarily about $100,000, including $20,000 in rental income. Thus, they ordinarily are not subject to the NII tax. However, this year they decide to sell one of their rental properties and earn a $200,000 profit. Their AGI for the year is now $300,000—$50,000 over the threshold. $50,000 is less than $300,000, so they must pay the 3.8% NII tax on $50,000, resulting in a $1,900 tax. This is in addition to regular capital gains tax they owe on their capital gain.

Real Estate Professional Exemption From the NII Tax

What if you earn all or most of your income from real estate rentals? Will the NII tax vastly increase your income taxes? Probably not. Most people who earn their living from landlording will be exempt from the tax because they'll qualify for a special exemption from the tax for real estate professionals. If you qualify for this exemption, you need not include your rental income or gains in your net investment income, no matter how large. You must satisfy three tests to be eligible for this exemption:

- you must be a real estate professional
- you must materially participate in the rental activity, and
- your rental activity must qualify as a business for tax purposes.

Real Estate Professional

The rules for qualifying as a real estate professional are discussed in detail in Chapter 16. The same rules apply for purposes of the NII tax. To qualify, you (or your spouse if you file jointly) must spend (1) over 50% of your work time in a real estate business or businesses, and (2) over 750 hours working in real estate businesses during the year. As a rule, people with full-time jobs outside of real estate cannot qualify.

Material Participation in Rental Activity

In addition to being a real estate professional, you must materially participate in each rental activity to qualify for this exemption. "Material participation" is discussed in detail in Chapter 16. There are various methods to establish material participation. The two most common are working over 500 hours at the activity during the year, or working 100 hours and more than anyone else.

If you have more than one rental property, unless you group your rentals together for these purposes, you'll have to materially participate in each individual rental. For example, if you have ten rentals, you'd have to materially participate for each of the ten, which would likely prove impossible. Fortunately, you are allowed to group your rental activities together for these purposes. This way, you can combine the time you spend working on each rental property to satisfy the material participation tests. You must file an election with the IRS to group your rental activities. This is discussed in detail in Chapter 16.

Ordinarily, you are only allowed to group your activities one time, and are then stuck with it. However, the IRS has decided to give real estate professionals who have previous grouped their activities a "fresh start." They are permitted to redo their groupings starting with the first year after 2013 (2014 or later) that they have sufficient income to be subject to the NII tax ($250,000 AGI for marrieds, $200,000 for singles) and have net investment income. (IRS Reg. § 1.469-11(b)(3)(iv).).

Rental Activity a Business

Finally, your rental activity must qualify as a business for tax purposes. The IRS NII regulations establish a safe harbor rule for when a rental estate activity conducted by a real estate professional is a business: So long as a real estate professional devotes more than 500 hours per year to the rental activity, it will automatically qualify as a business for these purposes and the rental income will not be subject to the NII tax. Alternatively, if a real estate pro has participated in rental real estate activities for more than 500 hours per year in five of the last ten tax years, the rental activity will qualify as a business. (IRS Reg. § 1.1411-4(g)(7).)

As discussed above, if you have more than one rental property, you are allowed to group your rental activities together for these purposes. This way, you can combine the time you spend working on each rental property to satisfy the material participation and 500-hour tests.

The 500-hour rule is a safe harbor, not a minimum requirement. Thus, you don't absolutely have to work a minimum of 501 hours per year at your rental activity for it to qualify as a business. You can work fewer hours and still qualify as a business. But, in the event of an IRS audit, whether you qualify will require a judgment call by the IRS after looking at all the circumstances involved. However, the preamble to the new regulations provides that ownership of even a single rental unit can qualify as a business. But, again, this depends on the circumstances— for example, the type of property, number of units, and the day-to-day involvement of the owner or its agent.

CAUTION

Landlords who earn profits from their rental activities will want to qualify as real estate professionals. Landlords with profit-making rentals didn't used to care whether they qualified as real estate professionals. It didn't matter because this classification only benefited landlords who had losses they wanted to deduct from their nonrental income. This has now changed. Qualifying as a real estate professional benefits landlords who earn profits because they won't have to pay the NII tax on them. Thus, landlords need to pay attention to whether they qualify as a real estate professional and how they'll prove it. The key to proving it and avoiding the IRS's wrath is keeping accurate records of how many hours you (and your spouse) work at your real estate activities during the year. See Chapter 16 for more guidance on record keeping.

Planning to Avoid the NII Tax

Obviously, the way to avoid the NII tax is to keep your AGI for the year below the $200,000/$250,000 threshold or have no net investment income. There are many ways to do this:

- increase rental losses you can deduct from your rental income
- avoid a large single-year gain when you sell rental property by using installment agreements which spread your payment over many years
- avoid a large single-year gain when you sell rental property by using a like-kind exchange which can defer tax on your gain indefinitely
- don't sell your rental property—when you die your heirs can inherit it tax-free
- convert as much income as possible to tax-exempt income that doesn't increase your AGI or net investment income—for example, take as many tax-free employee fringe benefits from your employer as you can instead of salary
- take stock options in place of some of your salary—when you exercise an ISO, you don't have income for NII tax or income tax purposes (however, you do have income for alternative minimum tax purposes)
- increase above-the-line deductions on your Form 1040—for example, make tax-deductible contributions to your 401(k), traditional IRA, or other qualified retirement plan; if you're over 70.5 years of age, donate an IRA of up to $100,000 to charity, and
- harvest capital losses to deduct from your gains.

Index

A

Accelerated depreciation methods for personal property, 164, 165–166, 198

Accessibility change deductions, 104, 349–350

Accounting fees, 345

Accounting methods
overview, 454
accrual method, 351–352, 457–459
bookkeeping, 11, 239, 310–311, 425, 426
cash method, 351–352, 455–457
IRS permission for accounting method changes, 454, 459
for routine maintenance safe harbor rules, 88
and unclaimed depreciation, 119
See also Record keeping

Accrual accounting method, 351–352, 457–459

Active income or loss bucket, 377–380, 401–402, 408–409. *See also* Real estate professionals' passive loss exemption

Active participation requirement for $25,000 PAL offset, 381–383

Actual expense method for meal expenses while traveling, 286, 287

Actual expense method for vehicle expenses, 263–273

overview, 263–264
credit card for buying gas, 449
leased vehicles, 273
record keeping, 264–265, 448
repairs and improvements, 272–273
vehicle depreciation deductions, 265–273

ADA Accessibility Guidelines, 350

Adaptations aspect of UOP B-A-R, 94, 101

Additions to buildings, 125, 137–141, 172–173

Adjusted basis
of building components, 103–104, 107
and property converted to rental use, 132–133, 160
and rental property as a gift, 132, 161
of replaced building components, 140–141
and selling rental property, 172–175

Adjusted gross income. *See* AGI

ADS (Alternative Depreciation System), 87–88, 100, 164, 167–168

Advance rent payments, 10

Advertising, on Schedule E, 469

AGI (adjusted gross income)
and capital gains tax rate, 175
and lifetime learning credit, 340
and NII Tax, 477, 478–480, 483
and passive loss deductions, 50

See also MAGI

Alarm and fire-protection systems as unit of property, 91–92

Allocation rules for using loan proceeds for rental activity, 217–218

Amortization, 8–9, 13, 212–213, 226–228. *See also* Depreciation

Applicable financial statement, 150, 152

Appraisals, property, 190–191

Assets
class lives of, 87–88, 100, 161–162
class-wide application of bonus depreciation, 157
partial disposition election, 140–141
record keeping for, 441–445
See also Capital assets; Personal property

At-risk rules, 11, 415–417

Attorneys. *See* Professionals, consulting with

Audits. *See* IRS audits

Automated Underreporter program (IRS), 31–32, 299

Automobiles. *See* Vehicle expenses

B

Backup withholding for ICs, 301–302

Balloon payments and prepaid interest deductions, 213

Bank accounts
for exclusive business use, 428–430, 434
for loan proceeds, 216–218

B-A-R (Betterment, Adaptation, or Restoration). *See* Unit of property B-A-Rs

Basis. *See* Adjusted basis; Tax basis

Behavior test of profit motive, 52–57

Below-market rentals, 48, 55, 371, 417

Betterment, Adaptation, or Restoration (B-A-R). *See* Unit of property B-A-Rs

Betterments, 86, 94, 96–98

Bona fide employees, 314–315

Bonus depreciation
for land improvements, 143
and listed property, 167
opting out of, 158
for personal property, 145, 155–158, 167
for vehicles, 270–271, 272

Bookkeeping, 11, 239, 310–311, 425, 426. *See also* Accounting methods; Record keeping

Brokers and real estate brokerage businesses, 389

Buildings
overview, 126
additions to, 125, 137–141, 172–173
building systems as units of property, 91–92
components of, 200
depreciation (*See* Depreciation of buildings)
expenses and SHST limits, 81, 87
improvements (*See* Improvements)
and land (*See* Cost allocation between land and buildings)
personal property inside of, 145–146
personal property not inside of, 146
placed in service date, 126–127
refreshes, 97
removal costs, 103–104

repairs (*See* Repairs)

replacing structural parts, 99

routine maintenance of, 83–84

structure (*See* Structural components of buildings)

value and SHST limits, 79–81

See also Rental property

Business entities

corporations, 25, 28, 305

limited partnerships, 24, 28

organizational costs, 230–231

reasons for forming, 27–29

S corporations, 25, 26, 83, 462, 477

and SHST election, 82–83

sole proprietorships, 17, 18–20, 21–23, 63, 463

starting a new rental business, 224

See also Limited liability companies; Partnerships

Businesses

bank account and credit cards for business only, 210–211, 428–430, 434, 449

business plan, 54, 57

expanding an existing rental business, 224–225

expenses incurred at home with no home office deduction, 243–244

qualifying as a business, 39–44, 236, 388–389

and Section 179 expensing, 169

size limitations and SHST, 79–83

start date, 222–225

and travel expenses for finding new properties, 279–281

See also Ownership

Buyer-seller valuation for separating value of buildings from land, 193–194

C

Calculations

fair market value of personal property, 200–201

quarterly estimated tax payments, 7

tax basis, 127–134

vacation home personal and rental use, 367–372

See also Deduction calculations; Depreciation calculations

California parental leave taxes, 310

Capacity, material increase in, 98

Capital assets

overview, 13, 228

and depreciation, 119–120, 121

and real estate losses, 45–46

See also Buildings; Real estate; Rental property

Capital expenses

overview, 11, 13

current expenses vs., 69

improvements to real property as, 230

start-up expenses as, 221

travel costs to buy a particular rental property as, 230

Capital gains

and adjusted basis, 173–175

casualty gains as, 334

on depreciation for home office deduction, 247

and like-kind exchanges, 175–178

as net investment income, 478, 480

and sale of rental property, 5, 45–46, 174–175, 179, 214–215, 247

tax paid on sale of home after May 6, 1997, 247

Capital losses, 45, 173–175

Car expenses. *See* Vehicle expenses

Carrying an NOL back or forward, 420–421

Cash basis accounting method, 351–352, 455–457

Casualty gains, 333–335

Casualty losses, 323–333

   overview, 324–325

   deduction calculations, 326–331

   disaster area losses, 332

   external force requirement, 325–326

   and home office deduction, 245

   insurance coverage for, 327

   record keeping, 335

   repair and replacement costs, 332–333

   separate components of, 329–330

   and tax basis, 331, 332–333

   tax reporting, 335

   total loss vs. partial loss, 328–329

Cell phones, 166–167

Certified financial statements, 150

Certified public accountants (CPAs). *See* Professionals, consulting with

Child labor laws, 312

Children as employee of their parent, 311–313, 314–318

Class lives of assets, 87–88, 100, 161–162

Cleaning expenses on Schedule E, 469

Cohan rule, 453–454

Commission expenses on Schedule E, 469–470

Community property states, 17, 23

Commuting rule for local transportation deductions, 259

Comparable land sales for valuing buildings separate from land, 194–195

Computers, 167, 244. *See also* Listed property

Computer software, 2, 425–427, 441

Condominiums, 92, 131, 138, 246, 385

Construction contractors vs. independent contractors, 295

Construction loans, 213–214

Constructive receipt of payments with cash method of accounting, 456

Convention deductions, business owners vs. investors, 45

Co-ownership

   and $25,000 offset, 381

   community property states, 17, 23

   and material participation test, 390–394

   not married co-owners, 18–20

   and property-related travel costs, 282–283

   by spouses, 20–23, 394, 463

   and use of vacation homes, 368–369

Corporations, 25, 28, 305. *See also* S corporations

Cost allocation between land and buildings, 184–195

   overview, 184–185, 186–187

   buyer-seller valuation method, 193–194

comparable land sales method, 194–195

improvement ratio calculations, 187–194

property tax bill method, 188–189

replacement cost method, 189–193

tax basis separate from land, 129–131, 184

tax-related penalties for unreasonable valuations, 185, 186

Cost basis. *See* Tax basis

Cost segregation. *See* Segmented depreciation

Cotenancy, 18–20, 23, 387

Cotenancy agreements, 19

CPAs (certified public accountants). *See* Professionals, consulting with

Credit card interest, 210–211

Credit cards, 210–211, 428–430, 434, 449

Creditors, 27

Current expenses, 68–69

D

Deductions

for accessibility changes, 104, 349–350

for bookkeeping expenses, 310–311

casualty (*See* Casualty losses)

depreciation (*See* Depreciation)

dues for professional, business, and civil organizations, 338

education expenses, 338–341

employees (*See* Employees; Independent contractors)

for energy efficiency changes, 104, 350–351

for gifts, 341, 449–452

home office (*See* Home office deduction)

insurance for rental activity, 342–343

interest (*See* Interest)

legal services, 344–345

losses (*See* Rental losses)

for maintenance, 107–110

for materials and supplies, 153–154

meals and entertainment, 285–288, 345–347, 449–452

operating expenses (*See* Operating expenses)

outside office deduction, 252–253

for parking, 10, 449

personal, 49–50, 211–212, 215–216, 245, 361

personal property (*See* Personal property deductions)

prepaid insurance, 343

professional services, 344–345

real property taxes, 347–349

repairs (*See entries beginning with* "Repairs")

for repairs, 107–113

start-up expenses, 225–228, 231

start-ups (*See* Start-up expenses)

theft (*See* Casualty losses)

tolls, 449

transportation (*See* Transportation, local; Travel expenses)

for vacation homes, 357–359, 360–362, 364–367, 408–409

vehicles (*See* Vehicle depreciation deductions)

Deduction calculations

overview, 8–9

for $25,000 PAL offset, 385–386

casualty losses, 326–331

home office, 240–242

meals and entertainment, 347

net operating loss, 418–419

suspended passive losses, 409–412

vacation home used as residence,
362–367

See also Actual expense deduction
method for vehicle expenses;
Depreciation calculations

Deduction information, 3–35

overview, 1, 8–9

business owners vs. investors, 44–46

and IRS audits, 11

and net loss on rental property,
10–11, 418–421, 472–473

and not-for-profit rentals, 49–50

proof of purchases, 431–434

replacement vs. repair, 77, 84,
110–111

value determination, 14–16

See also Expenses; IRS safe harbor
rules; Passive loss rules; Property
ownership and taxes; Rental losses

De minimis safe harbor, 88–89, 130

for materials and supplies, 154

maximum amount, 150–151

and personal property, 148–153

procedures for utilizing, 152–153

qualifying for, 151–152

Depreciation, 115–182, 183–203

overview, 13, 117–119, 122–124, 184

80% rule, 135

amortization and, 8–9, 13, 212–213,
226–228

applicable property, 119–122

bonus depreciation (*See* Bonus
depreciation)

of buildings (*See* Depreciation of
buildings)

and home office deduction, 247–248

land improvements, 142–144

of listed property, 167–168

methods (*See* Depreciation methods)

of non-start-up expenses, 228–231

for personal property, 125, 145,
155–158, 161–166, 197–199

and property placed in service date,
122–123, 125, 228–229

recapture (*See* Depreciation
recapture)

record keeping, 180, 181–182,
441–443

recovery period (*See* Recovery period)

and renting out a room in your
home, 29–31

and restoration due to casualty losses,
332–333

Section 179 (*See* Section 179
expensing)

segmented (*See* Segmented
depreciation)

separate deductions over time,
124–125

structures other than buildings, 143

tax reporting, 181–182, 471

unclaimed depreciation, 119

and unit of property components,
92–93

and vacation home used as residence
deductions, 364–367

vehicle improvements, 272–273

See also Tax basis

Depreciation calculations
  overview, 124
  bonus depreciation amount, 157–158
  deduction amount, 124
  improvement ratio, 187–194
  segmented depreciation, 201–203
  tax basis, 127–134
Depreciation methods
  overview, 122, 124, 164, 443
  150% declining balance, 143, 165–166, 203, 269, 443
  200% declining balance, 203, 269, 443
  for building improvements, 139
  double declining balance, 165
  for land improvements, 143–144
  MACRS, 124, 164, 167
  MACRS ADS, 87, 100, 124, 164, 167–168
  for passenger automobiles, 268–269
  for personal property, 164–166, 197–199
  See also Straight-line depreciation method
Depreciation of buildings, 126–141
  overview, 120–121, 126
  additions and improvements, 127, 137–141
  and adjusted basis, 172
  amount per year using straight-line method, 135–137
  and building refreshes, 97
  condominium special assessments for building improvements, 138
  cost basis, 127–131
  cost not the basis, 132
  deduction amount calculation, 124

  of disrepair restorations, 99–100
  improvements or replacement of building structure or structural components, 99–101, 139–141
  IRS tables, 136
  mixed-use property, 133–134
  partial disposition election, 140–141
  property acquired in an exchange, 134
  property converted to rental use, 132–133
  prorating first year of service, 136
  recovery period, 124, 134–136, 139
  self-constructed buildings, 134
  tax basis calculations, 127–134
Depreciation recapture
  and home office deduction, 247–248, 250
  and Section 179 expensing, 171
  and segmented depreciation, 195–196
  selling rental property, 118, 173–175
Depreciation worksheet, 441–443
Developers. *See* Real estate professionals
Digital copies, 431, 452
Direct expenses
  home office, 242–244, 245
  vacation homes, 361, 362, 364–367
Disability insurance tax, 309–310
Disaster area losses, 332
Disrepair restorations, 99–100
Double declining balance depreciation method, 165
Dual use properties, 467–468
Dues for professional, business, and civil organizations, 338

E

Education expenses, 338–341
Efficiency, material increase in, 98
80% rule for depreciation, 135
Electrical systems as unit of property, 91–92
Electronic record keeping
 digital copies, 431, 452
 paper vs., 425
 software, 2, 425–427, 441
Electronic tax filing, 33–34, 304
Elevators as unit of property, 91–92
Employees, 291–321
 overview, 292, 294–295
 deductions for payments to, 292–294
 independent contractors vs., 294–298
 as operating expenses, 292–293
 ordinary and necessary requirement
  for deductions, 292–293, 314
 and record keeping, 427
 resident manager, 318–321
 as start-up expenses, 293–294
 tax status, 296–298
 See also Independent contractors;
  Payroll taxes
Employers
 FICA contributions, 307
 and FUTA, 308
 legal requirements for employing
  family members, 316–318
 and minimum wage requirements,
  320–321
 See also Employees; Independent
  contractors; Payroll taxes
Employment agreement with resident
 manager, 320

Energy efficiency deduction, 104,
 350–351
Energy Tax Incentives Act (2005),
 350–351
Entertainment deductions for
 rental-related business, 345–347
Equipment used at home, no home
 office deduction, 243
Escalators as unit of property, 91–92
Escrow accounts, 130
Estimated taxes for landlords, 7
Exclusive-use test for home office
 deduction, 236–237
Expense journal, 435–439
Expenses
 and accrual accounting method, 458
 allocating among multiple properties,
  437, 448–449
 capital expenses, 11, 13, 69, 221, 230
 direct expenses, 242–244, 245, 361,
  362, 364–367
 repairs made prior to property placed
  in service date, 95, 113, 129
 on Schedule E, 469–472
 for vacation home used as rental
  property, 360–362
 See also Not deductible expenses;
  Operating expenses; Penalties;
  Start-up expenses

F

Facilitative costs of purchasing rental
 property, 128
Facilities of real estate dealers, 60–61
Facts and circumstances test of
 material participation, 392–394

Fair market value
   inherited property, 132, 161
   personal property, 200–201
   property converted to rental use,
      132–133, 160
   vehicle to be placed in service, 268
Fair rental price, 369, 371
Family members
   children as employees, 311–313,
      314–318
   as employees, 311–318
   ordinary and necessary requirement
      for employment, 314
   renting to, as not-for-profit activity, 48
   rules for employing family members,
      314–318
   spouse as employee, 313, 314–318
   travel expenses for, 283
   See also Married couples
Federal government unemployment
      insurance loans to states, 308
Federal Income Contributions Act.
      See FICA
Federal income tax withholding
      (FITW), 308, 316–317
Federal laws
   Americans with Disabilities Act, 350
   Energy Tax Incentives Act, 350–351
   FUTA, 308, 312–313, 316, 317
   repairs for complying with, 104
   against tax shelters, 377–379, 416
   See also FICA; IRS rules
Fees
   for appraisals, 130
   for delivery and installation, 151
   education-related, 339, 340
   as facilitative costs, 128

   for home with a home office,
      245–246
   for legal and professional services,
      344, 345, 352, 470
   for LLC structure, 28
   membership fees, 338
   mortgage-related, 209, 212, 470
   not deductible fees, 73
   as operating expenses, 69, 138, 139,
      359
   as ordinary and necessary, 66, 68
   purchasing rental property, 202, 229,
      344
   of qualified intermediary of like-kind
      exchange, 177
   for rental activities, 319, 344, 361,
      365, 470
   as rental income, 10, 439–440, 468
   as start-up expenses, 13, 220–221,
      294, 345
   and tax basis for property, 123, 128,
      159
   vehicle-related, 10, 262, 264–265,
      267, 449
   See also Penalties
FICA (Federal Income Contributions
      Act)
   overview, 5–6, 307
   and hiring children under 18, 311,
      312–313, 316
   and real estate dealers, 63
   for spouse employees, 313, 316–317
   See also Payroll taxes
50% bonus depreciation, 155–158
51% test for real estate professionals,
      394–396

Financial statements
  applicable financial statement and de
    minimus limits, 150, 152
  reviewing, as time spent on rental
    activity, 392–393
Financing. *See* Loans
Fire insurance premiums, 130
Fire-protection and alarm systems as
    unit of property, 91–92
First-year rule for standard mileage
    rate, 262–263
FITW (federal income tax
    withholding), 308, 316–317
500-hour test of material participation,
    390, 482
Five-car rule for standard mileage rate,
    263
Flipping, 59
Furniture used at home, no home office
    deduction, 243

G

Garage or parking fees, 10
Gas distribution system as unit of
    property, 91–92
General Accounting Office report on
    landlords misreporting rental real
    estate activities, 35
Gifts
  deductions for giving, 341, 449–452
  property received as, 132, 161
Gross rental income, 135

H

Half-year convention for personal
    property depreciation, 163

Hazardous occupations and children,
    312
Historic property, 12, 104
Hobby loss rules, 362, 363
Home equity loans, 211–212, 414
Home office deduction, 233–253
  overview, 234
  activities in home office
    requirements, 237–240
  audit-proofing your deduction, 251
  business owners vs. investors, 45
  calculating, 240–242
  casualty losses to home office, 331
  depreciation of, 135
  direct expenses, 242–244, 245
  expenses, 240–248
  and homeowners' insurance, 342
  indirect expenses, 244–246
  IRS reporting requirements, 250
  and local transportation, 246,
    258–259
  mortgage interest as business
    expense, 211
  profit limit on deductions, 246
  qualifying for, 234–240
  record keeping, 251
  selling your home, 247–248
  simplified method, 248–250
  threshold requirements, 235–237
Homeowners' insurance for home
    office, 342
Home sale exclusion for rental units,
    178–180
HVAC system as unit of property,
    91–92

I

ICs. *See* Independent contractors

Improvements
  overview, 137–138
  depreciating land improvements, 142–144
  depreciation of, 125, 137–141
  interest on loan for, 208
  to personal property, 147
  plan of improvement, 102
  restorations, 86, 94, 98–101
  and SHST limits, 81
  and tax basis, 138–139, 172–173, 278
  travel for, as not deductible, 278
  to units of property, 92
  upgrades as, 111
  See also IRS rules on repairs vs. improvements; Restorations; Unit of property B-A-Rs

Improvement ratio for valuing buildings separate from land, 187–194
  overview, 187–188
  buyer-seller valuation method, 193–194
  comparable land sales method, 194–195
  property tax bill method, 188–189
  replacement cost method, 189–193

Income
  and accrual accounting method, 458
  gross receipts and SHST limits, 82
  and lifetime learning credit, 340
  MAGI, 340, 382, 383–385, 386
  and NII tax, 477–478
  royalty income, 469
  and Section 179 expensing, 171
  See also AGI; Net Investment Income tax; Profits; Rental income

Income taxes
  of employees, 308, 309, 316–317
  estimated tax payments, 7
  on profits from sale of rental property, 5
  on rental income, 4
  state income taxes, 309
  See also Net Investment Income tax

Independent contractors (ICs)
  backup withholding for, 301–302
  billing for repairs and improvements separately, 103
  corporations as, 305
  employees vs., 294–298
  expenses of, 306
  new hire reporting requirements, 305
  ordinary and necessary requirement for deductions, 292–293, 314
  personal services of, 300–301
  real estate sales agents as, 389
  state reporting requirements, 305

Independent contractor tax rules, 298–306
  overview, 298–299
  backup withholding, 301–302
  for IC corporations, 305
  IRS Form 1099-MISC requirement, 299, 300, 302–304, 305
  and taxpayer identification number, 301
  threshold for reporting IC income, 300–301

Indirect expenses for home office
    deduction, 244–246
Individual ownership, 17–23
    overview, 17, 27–29
    co-ownership by spouses, 20–23
    co-owners not married to each other,
        18–20
    one unit owners, 17, 41
    See also IRS Form Schedule E; Sole
        proprietorships
Inherited or gifted property, 132, 161
Installment sales, 62, 214–215
Insurance
    and casualty losses, 327
    deductions for, 342–343
    expenses on Schedule E, 470
    homeowners' insurance for home
        office, 342
    private mortgage insurance, 209
Intended ordinary use, 101
Interest, 205–218
    overview, 206–207
    balloon payments and prepaid
        interest deductions, 213
    car loans, 211
    construction loans, 213–214
    on credit cards and personal loans,
        210–211
    on home equity loans, 211–212
    loan on rental property used for
        nonrental purposes, 215–216
    low or no interest loans, 214–215
    mortgage interest, 207–210,
        361–362, 364–367, 470
    nondeductible interest, 206, 207
    points and prepaid interest, 212–213
    on Schedule E, 470

from security deposits, 9
    See also Loans
Internal Revenue Service. *See* IRS;
    entries beginning with "IRS"
Investigatory expenses, 130
Investments
    interest on loan for purchase of, 216
    investment income and NII tax,
        478–479
    loan proceeds in the bank as, 206
    passive income generators, 414–415
    portfolio income or loss bucket,
        377–380, 401–402
    See also Real estate dealers; Real
        estate professionals' passive loss
        exemption; Rental property as
        investment
IRS (Internal Revenue Service)
    overview, 31
    and accounting method changes,
        454, 459
    Automated Underreporter program,
        31–32, 299
    home office deduction reporting
        requirements, 250
    and low or no interest loans, 215
    revenue procedure on married
        couples' tax forms, 23
    statutes of limitations, 453
    See also IRS audits; IRS rules; IRS
        safe harbor rules
IRS audits
    avoidance tips, 32–35, 299
    Cohan rule/insufficient records,
        453–454
    *Cost Segregation Audit Techniques
        Guide,* 196

and deductions, 11

and home office deduction, 235, 251

and profit motivation, 51–52

and real estate professionals' passive loss exemption, 403–404

reconstructing tax records, 454

IRS Form 1099-MISC, *Miscellaneous Income,* 299, 300, 302–304, 305, 467

IRS Form Schedule E, *Supplemental Income and Loss,* 461–473

and Automated Underreporter program, 31–32, 299

dual use properties section, 467–468

expenses section, 274, 435–439, 469–472

filing requirement, 462–463

filling out the form, 464, 467–473

property description, 467

rental income section, 439–440, 468–469

rental loss to profit ratio, 376

rental summary section, 472–473

royalty income section, 469

sample, 465–466

for vacation home, 360–362

IRS Form W-9, *Request for Taxpayer Identification Number and Certification,* 301–302

IRS rules

at-risk rules, 11, 415–417

dealer vs. nondealer rulings, 58–61

on expansion of a rental business vs. forming a new business, 224–225

materials and supplies deduction, 153–154

passenger automobile defined, 266

personal vs. business expense rules, 70–71

and segmented depreciation, 197

for single unit ownership as business, 41

for using loan proceeds for rental activity, 217–218

See also Passive loss rules

IRS rules on repairs vs. improvements, 76–107

overview, 76–77, 89, 137–138

complying with government regulations, 104

deducting costs for replaced building components, 139–141

defining the unit of property, 89–93

new IRS regulations affect on prior years, 105–107

removal costs, 103–104

repairs combined with improvements, 101–103

See also IRS safe harbor rules; *entries beginning with* "Unit of property"

IRS safe harbor rules

overview, 77, 78

on rental activity by real estate professional, 41–42

routine maintenance, 83–88

SHST, 79–83, 84–85, 87

ten-year rule, 84–86

utilizing safe harbor rules, 82–83, 88, 89, 152–153

See also De minimis safe harbor

J

Joint tenancy, 18–23, 387

L

Labor. *See* Employees; Independent contractors

Land
changes to, 142–143
depreciating improvements to, 142–144
as not depreciable property, 120
tax basis separate from, 129–131
See also Cost allocation between land and buildings

Landlords
approval for tenants' repairs or improvements, 109–110
estimated taxes, 7
mini-landlords, 29–31
misreporting rental activities, 35
personal labor as not deductible, 71
and tenants paying for repairs, 108–110
and unpaid rent, 351–352
See also Tenants

Landlord tax categories, 37–63
overview, 14, 38
business owner vs. investor, 39–44
business owner vs. investor tax treatment, 44–46
real estate dealers, 57–63, 462
See also Profit motivation

Laundry room income, 10

Laws. *See* Federal laws; State laws

Lawsuits, liability for, 27–29

Lawyers. *See* Professionals, consulting with

Leases
lease cancellation payments, 10
lease with option to buy, 10
triple net leases, 43
for vehicles, 273

Ledger sheets, 435–439

Legal and other professional services fees, 344, 345, 352, 470

Liability and business entities, 27–29

Lifetime learning credit, 340

Like-kind exchanges, 134, 175–178

Limited liability companies (LLCs)
overview, 25
limited liability from, 28–29
SHST election, 83
tax treatment, 26, 462

Limited liability companies, single-member, 231, 462. *See also* IRS Schedule E

Limited partnerships (LPs), 24, 28. *See also* Partnerships

Listed property
depreciation of, 166–168
record keeping for, 443–444
straight-line depreciation method for, 167, 168, 268, 271
vehicles, 267, 273

Loans
construction loans, 213–214
credit cards and personal loans, 210–211
low or no interest loans, 214–215
mortgages, 207–210, 416–417
nonrecourse loans, 416–417
refinancing a mortgage, 209
for rental property used for nonrental purposes, 215–216
for repairs, 208
See also Interest

Lobbying expenses as not deductible, 73

Local benefit assessments, 348

Local taxes, 348

Lodging taxes on vacation home rentals, 356

Long-term assets. *See* Capital assets

Long-term property, 119–120

Losses
hobby loss rules, 362, 363
on vacation homes, 364, 408–409
See also Casualty losses; Passive loss rules; Rental losses

Low-income housing tax credit, 12, 384

LPs (limited partnerships), 24, 28. *See also* Partnerships

M

MACRS (Modified Accelerated Cost Recovery System), 124, 164, 167

MACRS ADS (Modified Accelerated Cost Recovery System Alternative Depreciation System), 87, 100, 124, 164, 167–168

MAGI (modified adjusted gross income)
overview, 383
and lifetime learning credit, 340
limits for $25,000 PAL offset, 383–385, 386, 413
and lottery winnings, 382

Maintenance
combined with improvements, 101–103
deductions for, 107–110
ordinary and necessary requirement for deductions, 84–88

preventive maintenance, 112
record keeping, 85, 88, 95, 107–108, 111–112
repairs vs., 95
routine maintenance safe harbor, 83–88
on Schedule E, 469
and SHST limits, 81, 87
of vacation homes, 369–370
See also Improvements; Repairs

Maintenance plan, 85

Management companies
and active participation requirement for $25,000 PAL offset, 381–383
and facts and circumstances test of material participation, 394
as independent contractors, 31–32, 299, 319
and material participation test, 393
as operating expenses, 344, 359
and Schedule E, 469–470

Management fees, 344, 470

Marginal tax bracket, 15

Married couples
community property states, 17, 23
co-ownership by spouses, 20–23, 387
and facts and circumstances test of material participation, 394
and 51% test for real estate professionals, 395–396
joint tax returns, 21
qualified joint venture status, 21–23, 463, 468
spouse as employee, 313, 316–317
tax reporting, 463

Material changes to units of property, 96, 98

Material conditions or defects, 96–97

Material participation
overview, 39–40, 42–43
and co-ownership by spouses, 22
real estate professionals, 390–394, 397–398
and real estate professionals' NII tax exemption, 481

Maximum de minimis amount, 150–151

Meal deductions for rental-related business, 285–288, 345–347, 449–452

Medicare payroll taxes, 5–6, 307. *See also* FICA

Mid-month convention for depreciation, 136

Mid-quarter convention for personal property depreciation, 163–164

Mileage book for tracking mileage, 446–447

Mini-landlords, 29–31

Minimum wage requirements, 320–321

Mixed-use property
depreciation of, 133–134, 161
and mortgage deduction, 210

Modified Accelerated Cost Recovery System (MACRS), 124, 164, 167

Modified Accelerated Cost Recovery System Alternative Depreciation System (MACRS ADS), 87, 100, 124, 164, 167–168

Modified adjusted gross income. *See* MAGI

Mortgage interest, 207–210, 361–362, 364–367, 470

Mortgages, 207–210, 416–417

Multiple properties, allocating expenses among, 437, 448–449

N

Net Investment Income (NII) tax, 475–483
overview, 6, 15, 63, 476–479
amount of the tax, 479–480
business owners vs. investors, 45
and gain from selling rental property, 175
and IRS safe harbor rule, 41–42
and passive income, 414
planning for avoidance, 483
real estate professionals' exemption, 386, 480–483

Net operating loss (NOL), 10–11, 418–421, 472–473

New or different use, 101

NII tax. *See* Net Investment Income tax

NOL (net operating loss), 418–421, 472–473

Nonpassive income for real estate professionals' passive loss exemption, 377–380, 401–402

Nonrecourse loans, 416–417

Not deductible expenses
casualty losses to personal home not related to home office, 245
construction loan interest during construction period, 213
entertainment for spouses of business associates, 347

expense overpayment by co-tenants, 19

expenses for a business that never materializes, 232

fees, 73

gifts over $25 (first $25 is deductible), 341

home maintenance not related to home office, 245

interest paid with funds borrowed from the original lender, 207

investors' attendance at seminars or conventions, 45

land, 13

landlord's personal labor, 71

loans on rental property used for nonrental purposes, 209, 215–216

local transportation without a home office, 259

losses from not-for-profit rental property, 48

mini-landlords' phone line, 29

operating expenses, 67, 73

payments for personal services, 293, 344

personal expenses, 69

points, 212

political contributions and lobbying, 73

rental property purchase expenses, 229

rent due but not paid, 352

repairs made before property is placed in service, 95

and at risk limitations, 472

seller's taxes paid in real estate transaction, 129

travel for finding new properties, 279–281

travel for improvements, 278

and vacation homes, 359, 362, 364

See also Improvements; Passive loss rules; Penalties

Not-for-profit rental activity, 14, 47–50, 463

O

Office other than home office, 60–61, 252–253. *See also* Home office deduction

150% declining balance depreciation method, 143, 165–166, 203, 269, 443

101-hour test of material participation, 390

Online resources
filing IRS Form 1099-MISC, 304
low-income housing tax credit, 12
rehabilitation tax credit, 12
state income tax rates, 16
well-qualified real estate appraisers, 191

Operating expenses, 65–73
overview, 11, 13, 66
bookkeeping as, 310–311
business-related requirement, 69–71
and business start date, 222–223
as current expense, 68–69
expenses incurred at home with no home office deduction, 243–244
FICA taxes as, 307
fire insurance premiums, 130
interest, 208, 214

management fees as, 344

ordinary and necessary requirement for deductions, 66–68, 73, 338

payment to employees as, 292–293

principal of loan for repairs, 208

reasonable amount requirement, 72

requirements for deduction, 66–72

service charges assessed against rental property, 348

and travel expenses for finding new properties, 280–281

and vacation home used as residence deductions, 364–367

Ordinary and necessary requirement overview, 44

business expansion costs, 224

entertainment expenses, 346–347

for family member workers, 314

and IRS safe harbor rules, 78

and maintenance, 84–88

and maximum de minimis amount, 150–151

and office rental or purchase expenses, 252–253

and operating expense deductions, 66–68, 73, 338

for repairs, 76

start-up expenses, 228

transportation or travel expenses, 256, 278–279

worker's services as, 292–293

Organizational costs, 230–231

Outside office deduction, 252–253

Ownership

in community property states, 17, 23

individual ownership, 17–23, 27–29

as requirement for $25,000 PAL offset, 385

See also Business entities; Co-ownership; Property ownership and taxes

P

PAL rules. *See* Passive loss rules

Paper vs. electronic record keeping, 425

Parental leave taxes, California, 310

Parking expenses, 10, 449

Partial disposition election, 140–141

Partnerships

overview, 24

limited partnerships, 24, 28

and NII tax, 477

SHST election, 83

tax reporting, 19, 20, 462

tax treatment, 19, 20, 25–26, 462

tenancy in common or joint tenancy vs., 19–20

See also Limited partnerships

Passive activity rules and home equity loans, 212, 414

Passive income

for deducting passive losses, 409

generating, 414–415

passive income generators, 414–415

passive income or loss bucket, 377–380, 384, 401–402

See also Real estate professionals' passive loss exemption

Passive losses

passive income or loss bucket, 377–380, 384, 401–402

suspended losses, 398, 409–412

tax reporting, 412–413

Passive loss rules (PAL rules), 373–421

overview, 11, 376–377

$25,000 offset, 380–386, 408, 410, 412–413

and at-risk rules, 417

calculating offset deductions, 385–386

income or loss buckets, 377–380, 384, 401–402

lowering rental expenses vs., 413

rental activities outside of, 406–407

requirements for $25,000 offset, 381–385

suspended passive loss deductions, 398, 409–412

tax shelters vs., 377

and vacation homes, 362–363, 408–409

See also Real estate professionals' passive loss exemption

Past performance test of material participation, 392

Payroll taxes, 306–311

overview, 5–6, 306–307, 349

California parental leave taxes, 310

children as employee of their parent, 312–313

FITW, 308, 316–317

free lodging exempt from, 319–320

FUTA, 308, 312–313, 316, 317

on Schedule E, 471

state, 309–311

See also FICA

Penalties

driving violations or parking tickets, 264

for early withdrawal of savings, 383

as nondeductible expense, 73, 264

See also Fees; Tax-related penalties

Personal deductions

casualty losses not related to your home office, 245

home equity loan interest, 211–212

interest on loans used for nonrental purposes, 215–216

and not-for-profit rentals, 49–50

real estate taxes paid during personal use of vacation homes, 361

Personal finance software, 426

Personal loans, 210–211

Personal property

overview, 145–146

allocating business use and personal use, 70

and de minimis safe harbor, 88–89, 130, 148–153

and routine maintenance safe harbor, 87–88

as unit of property, 93

See also Listed property

Personal property deductions, 144–171

overview, 144, 147

bonus depreciation, 145, 155–158, 167

and de minimis safe harbor, 88–89, 130, 148–153

depreciation, 125, 145, 155–158, 161–166, 197–200

listed property, 166–168

materials and supplies deduction, 153–154

maximum de minimis amount, 150–151

property placed in service date, 159

property with useful life of 12 months or less, 149

Section 179 expensing, 168–171

tangible personal property and its components, 148–149, 153–154, 168–171

tax basis for personal property, 159–161

PIGs (passive income generators), 414–415

Placed in service. *See* Property placed in service date

Plan of improvement, 102

Plan of rehabilitation doctrine, 102

Plumbing systems as unit of property, 91–92

PMI (private mortgage insurance), 209

Points and prepaid interest, 212–213

Political contributions as not deductible, 73

Portfolio income or loss bucket, 377–380, 401–402. *See also* Real estate professionals' passive loss exemption

PPIFG (Producer Price Index for Finished Goods) adjusted basis determination method, 141

Prepaid expenses, 343, 456–457

Preventive maintenance, 112

Private mortgage insurance (PMI), 209

Producer Price Index for Finished Goods (PPIFG) adjusted basis determination method, 141

Professional exchange companies for like-kind exchange, 177–178

Professionals, consulting with

overview, 2

for cost segregation study, 197

fees for, 344, 345, 352, 470

for IRS repairs vs. improvements rules, 77

for like-kind property exchanges, 176

for selling "substantially all" rental activity, 411

for unclaimed depreciation, 119

Profits

like-kind exchanges vs., 175–178

as limit on home office deduction, 246

from sale of rental property, 5, 132, 410–412

See also Income; Rental income

Profit motivation, 46–57

overview, 46–47, 50

behavior test, 52–57

not-for-profit activity vs., 14, 47–50

three-of-five test, 51–52

and time shares, 54–55

Property management software, 2, 427, 441

Property ownership and taxes, 16–31

overview, 16–17

business owner vs. investor, 39–46

business plan for proving profit motive, 54, 57

cotenancy, 18–20, 23, 387

joint tenancy, 18–23, 387

one unit owners, 17, 41

ownership through a business entity, 24–29

qualifying as a business, 39–44

real estate dealers, 57–63
See also Businesses; Landlord tax
    categories
Property placed in service date
    buildings, 126–127
    and depreciation, 122–123, 125,
        136, 228–229
    personal property, 159
    repairs made prior to, 95, 113, 129
Property sales. *See* Selling rental
    property
Property taxes
    deductions for, 347–349
    and vacation homes used as a
        residence deductions, 364–367
    and valuing buildings separate from
        land, 188–189
Purchase price of property, 127–128,
    228–229, 344. *See also* Tax basis

Q

Qualified joint venture status, 21–23,
    463, 468
Qualifying intermediary in like-kind
    exchange, 177–178
Quality, material increase in, 98

R

Real estate
    appraisals, 190–191
    conversion to rental use, 132–133,
        160, 372
    deductions for taxes on, 347–349
    purchase price of, 127–128,
        228–229, 344

taxes at time of property purchase,
    129, 349
unadjusted basis, 79–82
See also Buildings; Land; Rental
    property; Vacation homes
Real estate dealers
    overview, 57–58
    and profit motivation, 58–61
    tax reporting, 462
    tax treatment, 61–63
Real estate professionals
    overview, 386–388, 481
    and IRS safe harbor rules, 41–42
    NII tax exemption, 386, 480–483
    reasons for qualifying as, 482–483
Real estate professionals' passive loss
        exemption, 386–406
    overview, 386–387, 388
    51% test, 394–396
    751-hour test, 396
    disadvantage of, 402–403
    examples of applying real estate
        professional exemption tests,
        399–401
    filing an election for grouping rental
        activities together, 397–399, 411
    filing a retroactive PAL exemption,
        399
    intentional failure to qualify, 403
    material participation in ongoing
        activities, 397–398
    material participation test, 390–394
    participation in real property
        business requirement, 388–390
    qualifying as a real estate
        professional, 388–396

record keeping, 403–406

rental activities not subject to, 406–407

and suspended losses, 410

yearly renewal, 397, 401

Reasonable amount requirement for operating expenses, 72

Reasonable compensation for family-member employees, 315–316

Receipts and supporting documents, 431–435, 450–452

Record keeping, 424–453

overview, 11, 424–427

and bank accounts or credit cards, 210–211, 216–218, 428–430, 434

and behavior test for proving profit motive, 55–57

bookkeeping, 11, 239, 310–311, 425, 426

business start date, 222–225

for casualty losses, 335

for depreciation, 180, 181–182, 441–443

for employees, 427

for home office expenses, 251

improvements vs. repairs, 103, 105–106

for investment property of real estate dealers, 61

for listed property, 166–167, 443–444

for local transportation, 445–449

for maintenance, 85, 88, 95, 107–108, 111–112

for materials and supplies expenses, 153

for meal expenses, 286, 449–452

paper vs. electronic, 425

property is placed in service date, 127

and qualifying as a business owner, 43–44

for real estate professionals' passive loss exemption, 403–406

for repairs, 95, 103, 107–108, 111–112

for Section 179 expensing, 170

software for, 2, 425–427, 441

for start-up expenses, 231

for travel expenses, 281, 288–289, 449–452

for vehicle expenses, 256, 264–265, 446–449

See also Accounting methods

Record-keeping system, 427–454

overview, 427

account statements, 434

asset records, 441–445

checkbook and credit cards for business only, 428–430, 434, 449

duplicating and retaining receipts, canceled checks, and supporting documents, 430–435, 450–452

expense journal, 435–439

filing system, 428, 435, 444–445, 452–453

rental income journal, 439–440

tax reports and supporting documentation, 452–454

Recovery period

overview, 122, 123

buildings, 124, 134–136, 139

class lives of assets, 87–88, 100, 161–162

and IRS tables, 136

and segmented depreciation, 195, 198, 203

and tax basis, 172

Refinancing a mortgage, 209

Regular-use test for home office deduction, 237

Rehabilitation tax credit, 12, 384

Rental agents. *See* Management companies

Rental expenses

renting an office, 244

renting out a room in your home, 29–31

tenant payment of, 10

Rental income

overview, 9–10

advance rent payments, 10

and allocation of expenses among multiple properties, 437

below-market rentals, 48, 55, 371, 417

and depreciation period for buildings, 135

estimated tax payments, 7

fees as, 10, 439–440, 468

generating passive income, 414–415

income taxes on, 4

journal for, 439–440

lease cancellation payments, 10

lease with option to buy tenant payments, 10

net loss, 10–11

property or services from tenants in lieu of rent, 9

sales tax or lodging tax for vacation home rentals, 356

on Schedule E, 468–469

self-rental rule, 415

Social Security and Medicare taxes exemption, 6

tax-free income from a vacation home or personal residence, 357, 358–359, 371–372

tax reporting, 35, 468–469

Rental losses

overview, 375–376

business owners vs. investors, 45–46

carrying a loss back, 420

carrying an NOL forward, 420–421

deductible losses, 418–421

net loss on rental property, 10–11

net operating loss, 418–421

and proof of profit motivation, 52–57

See also Passive loss rules

Rental property

overview, 356

allocating expenses among multiple properties, 437

appreciation of value, 10, 52, 53, 56, 59

condominiums, 92, 131, 138, 246, 385

costs associated with purchase, 127–128, 228–229, 344

liability for debts and lawsuits, 27–29

and passive loss rules, 413

personal property inside of, 145–146

property description on Schedule E, 467

real estate conversion to rental use, 132–133, 160, 372

replacement vs. repair, 77, 84, 110–111

space used for rental office, 251–252

taxes for, 4–8

tenant pays expenses, 10

travel expenses while looking for, 221–222, 224–225, 405

vacant rental property, 43, 48–49, 136

See also Property placed in service date; Real estate; Selling rental property

Rental property as investment

overview, 14, 39, 42–43

business owner and investor compared, 39–43

for-profit and not-for-profit vs., 14

and hours devoted to rental activity, 41–42

and local transportation expenses, 256

of real estate dealers, 61

and travel expenses for finding new properties, 279

Repairs, 75–113

betterments vs., 96–98

and casualty losses, 332–333

current expenses vs., 69

deductions for, 107–113

deductions for replacement vs. repair, 77, 84, 110–111

and de minimis safe harbor, 154

maintenance vs., 95

ordinary and necessary requirement for deductions, 76

before property is placed in service, 95, 113, 129

on Schedule E, 470

and SHST limits, 81

upgrades vs., 111

of vacation homes, 369–370

See also Improvements; Maintenance

Replacement costs

for casualty losses, 332–333

deductions, replacement vs. repair, 77, 84, 110–111

valuing buildings separate from land, 189–193

Replacement with casualty gains, 334

Resident managers

and active participation requirement for $25,000 PAL offset, 381–383

as employees, 296, 318–321

See also Management companies

Restorations

with casualty gains, 334

for casualty losses, 332–333

disrepair restorations, 99–100

routine maintenance vs., 86

unit of property B-A-Rs, 94, 98–101

Room method for home office deduction calculation, 241–242

Rooms in your home, renting out, 29–31

Routine maintenance safe harbor, 83–88

Royalty income, 469

S

Safe harbor. *See* IRS safe harbor rules

Safe harbor for small taxpayers (SHST), 79–83, 84–85, 87

Sampling method for tracking mileage, 447–448

Sandwich day rule for travel expenses, 285, 290

Schedule E. *See* IRS Form Schedule E

S corporations
overview, 25
and NII tax, 477
SHST election, 83
tax treatment, 26, 462

Section 179 expensing
and 50% bonus depreciation, 158
business owners vs. investors, 45
deduction limit, 170
depreciation recapture, 171
for heavy vehicles, 272
not applicable for personal property, 148
for passenger vehicles, 271
personal property deductions, 168–171

Security deposits, 9, 429

Security system and home office deduction, 246

Security systems as unit of property, 91–92

Segmented depreciation, 195–203
overview, 195–197
calculations, 201–203
cost segregation study, 197
delayed implementation of, 196
and fair market value of personal property, 199–201
and personal property, 197–199
record keeping for, 182
and SHST, 80

Self-employment taxes, 6, 44, 62, 478

Self-rental rule, 415

Seller financing and at-risk rules, 415–417

Selling rental property
overview, 171
adjusted basis, 172–175
business owners vs. investors, 45–46
and capital gains, 5, 45–46, 174–175, 179, 214–215, 247
depreciation recapture, 118, 173–175
home sale exclusion for rental units, 178–180
income tax on profits, 5
like-kind exchanges, 175–178
and mid-month convention for depreciation, 136
profits from, 5, 132, 410–412
and suspended losses, 398, 410–412
See also Real estate dealers

Seminar deductions, business owners vs. investors, 45

Services offered to the public, 297–298, 407, 463

Services provided with rental, 6, 19–20, 21

751-hour test for real estate professionals, 396

Short-term property, 120–121

SHST (safe harbor for small taxpayers), 79–83, 84–85, 87

Significant participation activities test of material participation, 392

Simplified home office deduction method, 248–250

Small business accounting software, 426

Social Security number, 301–302

Social Security payroll taxes, 5, 6, 307. *See also* FICA

Software, 2, 425–427, 441

Sole proprietorships
  married couples as, 21–23, 463
  as property co-owners, 18–20
  as property owner, 17
  real estate dealers as, 63
Special assessments, 138, 348
Spouses. *See* Married couples
Spreadsheets, 425, 441
Square footage method for home office
    deduction calculation, 241
Standard improvement ratio, 188
Standard meal allowance for travel
    expenses, 286–288
Standard mileage rate for vehicle
    expenses, 261–263, 273, 441–442
Start-up expenses
  overview, 11, 13, 45, 220–221
  business fails to start, 232
  business fails within 15 years, 231
  and business start date, 222–225
  costs that are not start-up expenses,
    228–231
  deductions for, 225–228, 231
  and expanding an existing rental
    business, 224–225
  legal and accounting fees, 345
  ordinary and necessary requirement
    for deductions, 228
  payments to employees, 293–294
  property-related costs before property
    placed in service, 229, 230
  repairs as, 95
  spending no more than $5,000 on,
    221–222, 225–226
State laws
  minimum wage requirements,
    320–321

reporting requirements for new hire
    ICs, 305
State taxes
  California parental leave taxes, 310
  income taxes, 15–16
  payroll taxes, 309–311
  sales tax for vacation home rentals,
    356
  tax credit allocation agency, 12
Storage facility fees, 10
Straight-line depreciation method
  overview, 164
  for buildings, 135–137, 203
  for listed property used 50% or less
    for rental activity, 167, 168, 268,
    271
  for personal property, 164, 168
  segmented depreciation vs. all
    straight-line method, 195
  for vehicles, 263, 268–269, 271
Structural components of buildings
  overview, 126, 200
  building structure as unit of
    property, 90
  class life for, 100
  condominiums, 92
  improvements or replacement of,
    99–101, 137, 139–141
  and partial disposition elections, 107
  personal property vs., 145–146, 198
  restorations, 98–99
  as unit of property, 90
Substantially-all test of material
    participation, 390
Substitute basis, 134
Supplies on Schedule E, 471

Supplies used at home, no home office deduction, 244

Suspended losses, 398, 409–412

T

Tangible personal property and its components, 148–149, 153–154, 168–171

Tax assessor's valuations, 189

Tax basis
overview, 123
accessibility changes over $15,000, 349
adjusted basis (*See* Adjusted basis)
for buildings, 127–134 (*See also* Cost allocation between land and buildings)
of car or other vehicle, 267–268
and casualty losses, 331, 332–333
cost basis, 127–131, 132–133
costs associated with purchase of rental property, 228–229
and depreciation period, 134–141
and depreciation recapture at sale of property, 118, 173–175
and improvements, 138–139, 172–173, 278
inherited property, 132, 161
interest on construction loan included in, 213–214
mixed-use property, 133–134, 161
payments to employees included in, 294
for personal property, 159–161
property acquired in an exchange or trade-in, 134, 160

property converted to rental use, 132–133, 160
real estate transfer taxes, 349
and repairs made before property is placed in service, 95, 129
of replaced and disposed of building components, 103–104
self-constructed buildings, 134
substitute basis, 134
and travel expenses for finding new properties, 280
unadjusted basis and SHST, 79–82

Tax brackets, 14–15, 16

Taxes
backup withholding for ICs without a valid Social Security number, 301–302
and disaster area losses, 332
filing tips, 32–35
income taxes, 4, 5, 6, 7, 308, 309, 316–317
and independent contractors (*See* Independent contractor tax rules)
local taxes, 348
and ownership (*See* Property ownership and taxes)
state taxes, 12, 15–16, 309–311, 356
tax credits, 12, 340, 384
tax year, 459
vacation home tax categories, 355
and value of deductions, 14–16
See also Independent contractor tax rules; Landlord tax categories; Net Investment Income tax; Payroll taxes; *entries beginning with* "IRS"

Tax home location, 277

Taxpayer identification numbers, 301–302

Tax-related penalties
for employees misclassified as ICs, 295
for failure to include NII tax in estimated taxes, 476
for failure to submit payroll taxes, 310–311
for filing wrong type of return, 23
for incorrect tax classification, 38
interest on income tax, 207
for landlord's failure to comply with IC tax rules, 299
as nondeductible expense, 73
for underpayment of estimated taxes, 7
for unjustified deductions, 11
for unreasonable cost allocation between land and buildings, 185, 186
for unreasonable value of land vs. buildings, 185, 186

Tax reporting
overview, 462–463
casualty losses, 335
depreciation, 181–182, 471
home office deduction, 250
local transportation, 274
married couples, 463
misreporting by landlords, 35
partnerships, 19, 20, 462
passive losses, 412–413
real estate dealers, 462
reconstructing tax records, 454
record keeping, 452–453

rental income, 35, 468–469
tax-free rental income from a vacation home or personal residence, 358–359, 463
transportation expenses, 274
See also IRS Form Schedule E

Tax shelters, federal laws against, 377–379, 416

Tax status. *See* Landlord tax categories

Tax treatment
overview, 25
business owners vs. investors, 44–46
LLCs, 26, 462
not-for-profit rentals, 49–50
partnerships, 19, 20, 25–26, 462
real estate dealers, 61–63
S corporations, 26, 462

Tax year, 459

Telephone expenses at home, 243

Tenancy in common, 18–20, 23, 387

Tenants
landlord approval for repairs or improvements, 109–110
and major repair work, 226
paying for repairs, 108–110
payment of rental expenses by, 10
property or services in lieu of rent, 9

Ten-year rule for routine maintenance safe harbor, 84–86

Theft or vandalism, 326. *See also* Casualty losses

30-day rule for using loan proceeds for rental activity, 217

Three-of-five test of profit motive, 51–52

Threshold requirements for home office deduction, 235–237

Time shares
  as profit or not-for-profit, 54–55
  and vacation home deductions,
    370–371
Toll expenses, 449
Transportation, local, 255–274
  overview, 256
  cost of non-automobile
    transportation, 273
  for deductible educational activity,
    340–341
  to and from deductible educational
    activity, 340–341
  home office, 246, 258–259
  no home office, 259, 260–261
  qualifying for deduction, 256–261
  record keeping, 445–449
  rental activities restriction, 257
  tax reporting, 274
  See also Travel expenses; Vehicle
    expenses
Travel expenses, 275–290
  overview, 276–277
  deductibility, 281–283
  for deductible educational activity,
    340–341
  deduction amounts, 283–285
  destination expenses, 281–282
  looking for rental property, 221–222,
    224–225, 405
  meal expenses, 285–288
  ordinary and necessary requirement,
    278–279
  planning ahead, 288
  prior to qualifying as a business,
    279–281
  record keeping, 281, 288–289,
    449–452
  rental activity days, 284–285,
    289–290
  rental business requirement, 277–281
  sandwich day rule, 285, 290
  on Schedule E, 469
  as start-up expenses vs. capital
    expenses, 230
  taking someone with you, 282–283
  tax home location, 277
  and vacation homes, 370
  See also Transportation, local; Vehicle
    expenses
Triple net leases, 43
12-month rule for prepaying expenses,
  343, 457, 459
200% declining balance depreciation
  method, 203, 269, 443

U

Unemployment compensation taxes,
  308, 309
Unit of property (UOP) B-A-Rs,
  93–101
  overview, 93–95, 137–138
  adaptations aspect, 94, 101
  betterments aspect, 94, 96–98
  restorations aspect, 94, 98–101
Units of property (UOPs), 89–93,
  103–104
Upgrades and energy efficiency
  deduction, 104, 350–351
Utilities on Schedule E, 471

V

Vacant rental property
  and depreciation, 136
  and IRS ruling on investment vs.
    for-profit rentals, 43
  as not-for-profit rental, 48–49
Vacation homes, 353–372
  overview, 48, 354–355
  calculating personal and rental use,
    367–372
  converting to rental property, 372
  deductions for, 357–359, 360–362,
    364–367, 408–409
  hobby loss and passive loss tax rules,
    362–363
  losses on, 408–409
  as not-for-profit activity, 47
  regular rental property status, 355,
    356
  rental income sales and/or lodging
    tax, 356
  tax-free status, 355, 357–359,
    371–372, 463
  tax status chart, 355
  time shares, 54–55, 370–371
  travel expenses to and from, 370
  used as a residence status, 355,
    363–367
  used as rental property status, 355,
    359–363
Valuing land and buildings. *See* Cost
    allocation between land and
    buildings
Vandalism or theft, 326. *See also*
    Casualty losses
Vehicle depreciation deductions,
    265–273
  overview, 265–266
  auto repairs and improvements,
    272–273
  depreciation beyond five-year limit,
    271
  heavy vehicles, 272
  leasing a car, 273
  passenger automobiles, 266–267,
    268–271
  Section 179 expensing, 271
  tax basis for vehicle, 267–268
  trucks and vans, 270
Vehicle expenses, 255–274
  driving from and to home, 258–261
  insurance, 342–343
  interest on loan, 211
  parking and tolls, 10, 449
  record keeping, 256, 264–265,
    446–449
  repairs, 272
  on Schedule E, 469
  standard mileage rate, 261–263, 273,
    445–447
  traveling outside your city to look for
    rental property, 281, 283
  See also Actual expense method
    for vehicle expenses; Vehicle
    depreciation deductions

W

Wear and tear vs. casualty losses,
    324–325
Workers. *See* Employees; Independent
    contractors
Workers' compensation insurance tax,
    310–311

⚖ NOLO | *Online Legal Forms*

Nolo offers a large library of legal solutions and forms, created by Nolo's in-house legal staff. These reliable documents can be prepared in minutes.

Create a Document

- **Incorporation.** Incorporate your business in any state.
- **LLC Formations.** Gain asset protection and pass-through tax status in any state.
- **Wills.** Nolo has helped people make over 2 million wills. Is it time to make or revise yours?
- **Living Trust (avoid probate).** Plan now to save your family the cost, delays, and hassle of probate.
- **Trademark.** Protect the name of your business or product.
- **Provisional Patent.** Preserve your rights under patent law and claim "patent pending" status.

Download a Legal Form

Nolo.com has hundreds of top quality legal forms available for download—bills of sale, promissory notes, nondisclosure agreements, LLC operating agreements, corporate minutes, commercial lease and sublease, motor vehicle bill of sale, consignment agreements and many more.

Review Your Documents

Many lawyers in Nolo's consumer-friendly lawyer directory will review Nolo documents for a very reasonable fee. Check their detailed profiles at **Nolo.com/lawyers**.

⚖ NOLO   *Save 15%* *off your next order*

Register your Nolo purchase, and we'll send you a **coupon for 15% off** your next Nolo.com order!

Nolo.com/customer-support/productregistration

On Nolo.com you'll also find:

Books & Software

Nolo publishes hundreds of great books and software programs for consumers and business owners. Order a copy, or download an ebook version instantly, at Nolo.com.

Online Legal Documents

You can quickly and easily make a will or living trust, form an LLC or corporation, apply for a trademark or provisional patent, or make hundreds of other forms—online.

Free Legal Information

Thousands of articles answer common questions about everyday legal issues including wills, bankruptcy, small business formation, divorce, patents, employment, and much more.

Plain-English Legal Dictionary

Stumped by jargon? Look it up in America's most up-to-date source for definitions of legal terms, free at nolo.com.

Lawyer Directory

Nolo's consumer-friendly lawyer directory provides in-depth profiles of lawyers all over America. You'll find all the information you need to choose the right lawyer.

DELL12